By The Same Author

The Enemy in the Streets
The Erotic Muse
In Failing Health

Burden of Proof

In the Superior Court of the State of California
In and for the County of Sutter
The People of the State of California
    v.
Juan Vallejo Corona

PARTIAL TRANSCRIPT OF COURT PROCEEDINGS
TUESDAY, JULY 27, 1971

THE COURT: *I will read the first count. Then we can make sure that the defendant understands it. This is an indictment which was filed on July 12, 1971, accusing the defendant, Juan Vallejo Corona, of twenty-five counts of violation of Section 187 of the Penal Code. I will read the first one, the first count. "The Grand Jury of the County of Sutter hereby accuses Juan Vallejo Corona of a felony, to wit: Violation of Section 187 of the Penal Code*

in that between—on or about May 8, 1971—"
INTERPRETER: *I don't—I can't get this. I don't have the vocabulary to—*
MR. HAWK: *Your Honor, insofar as the plea itself is concerned, I am willing to waive, and Mr. Corona is also, an exact reading.*
THE COURT: *Have you understood the statements of your counsel in English, Mr. Corona?*
THE DEFENDANT: *Si.*
THE COURT: *Well, I will finish reading the first count, then we will go just by number thereafter.*
MR. TEJA: *Your Honor, I don't want to interrupt, but I don't believe you were reading the first count. You got down to the date. I believe you were reading, perhaps, the second count.*
THE COURT: *All right. "A violation of Section 187, in that on or about May 19, 1971, in the County of Sutter, State of California, he murdered Kenneth Whitacre." What is your plea to count one of the information?*
THE DEFENDANT: *I am not guilty.*
THE COURT: *The second count also alleges a violation of Section 187, involving a Charles Fleming. What is your plea to that count?*
THE DEFENDANT: *Not guilty.*
THE COURT: *The third count alleges a violation of Section 187, involving—*
THE DEFENDANT: *Not guilty.*
THE COURT: *—involving a Melford Sample.*

THE DEFENDANT: *Not guilty.*

THE COURT: *The fourth count, another alleged allegation of 187, John Doe E-2-4.*

THE DEFENDANT: *Not guilty, sir.*

THE COURT: *The next one, Donald Smith, that's count five.*

THE DEFENDANT: *Not guilty.*

THE COURT: *Count six, John J. Haluka.*

THE DEFENDANT: *Not guilty, sir.*

THE COURT: *All of these, as the Court has indicated are allegations of a violation of Section 187 of the Penal Code. John Doe— count seven—John Doe E-5-7.*

THE DEFENDANT: *Not guilty, sir.*

THE COURT: *Count eight, Warren Kelley.*

THE DEFENDANT: *Not guilty.*

THE COURT: *Count nine, Sigurd Beierman.*

THE DEFENDANT: *Not guilty.*

THE COURT: *Count ten, John Doe, E-8-10.*

THE DEFENDANT: *Not guilty.*

THE COURT: *Count eleven, William Emery Kamp, K-a-m-p.*

THE DEFENDANT: *Not guilty, sir.*

THE COURT: *Count twelve, John Doe, E-10-12.*

THE DEFENDANT: *Not guilty.*

THE COURT: *Count thirteen, Clarence Hocking.*

THE DEFENDANT: Not guilty.

THE COURT: *Count fourteen, James W. Howard.*

THE DEFENDANT: *Not guilty.*

Burden
THE CASE OF

THE COURT: *Count fifteen, Jonah R. Smallwood.*
THE DEFENDANT: *Not guilty.*
THE COURT: *Count sixteen, Elbert T. Riley.*
THE DEFENDANT: Not guilty.
THE COURT: *Count seventeen, Paul B. Allen.*
THE DEFENDANT: *Not guilty, sir.*
THE COURT: *Eighteen, Edward Martin Cupp.*
THE DEFENDANT: *Not guilty, sir.*
THE COURT: *Count nineteen, Albert Hayes.*
THE DEFENDANT: *I am not guilty, sir.*
THE COURT: *Twenty, Raymond Muchache.*
THE DEFENDANT: *Not guilty, sir.*
THE COURT: *Twenty-first count, John H. Jackson.*
THE DEFENDANT: *Not guilty, sir.*
THE COURT: *Count twenty-two, Lloyd Wallace Wenzel.*
THE DEFENDANT: *Not guilty, sir.*
THE COURT: *Twenty-three, Mark Beverly Shields.*
THE DEFENDANT: *Not guilty, sir.*
THE COURT: *Count twenty-four, Sam Bonafide, also known as Joe Carriveau.*
THE DEFENDANT: *Not guilty, sir.*
THE COURT: *And count twenty-five, Joseph Maczak, Ma-c-z-a-k.*
THE DEFENDANT: *Not guilty, sir.*
THE COURT: *Do you wish the matter set down for trial?*
MR. TEJA: *I suppose so, Your Honor.*
MR. HAWK: *Yes, Your Honor.*

# of Proof
JUAN CORONA

by ED CRAY

With an afterword by Richard Hawk
Attorney for the Defense

Macmillan Publishing Co., Inc.
NEW YORK

The courtroom sketches between pages 180
and 181 are by Don Juhlin and are
reproduced here by courtesy of CBS News.

Macmillan Publishing Co., Inc.
866 Third Avenue, New York, N.Y. 10022
Collier-Macmillan Canada Ltd., Toronto, Ontario
Library of Congress Catalog Card Number: 73-7141

First Printing 1973

Printed in the United States of America

Contents

Burden of Proof

1

The Man with Buck Teeth

May 19-24, 1971

Goro Kagehiro was puzzled. No one had his permission to dig in the orchard. It might have been the state agricultural service or the county agent taking a soil sample. Kagehiro had told them that some of his young peach trees were sick. But the hole seemed too large—three and one-half feet down to the hardpan, two and one-half feet wide, six or seven feet long—a lot bigger than soil samples taken before on his ranch.

Kagehiro shrugged, then followed the workers thinning the peach trees. Corona's crew had done a good job; in another few hours they would finish the last trees. Kagehiro had to get the beer and potato chips to serve the men when the job was done. The hole could wait, whatever it was.

It wasn't until six that Wednesday evening that the fifty-seven-year-old farmer could get back to the young orchard. It had been a busy day. The seven-man crew had finished thinning the last orchard near the house at noon; four and one-half days to do the job was good, as good as any time in the twenty-one years Kagehiro had owned the orchards on Larkin Road.

While Sam, the six-month-old German Shepherd, frolicked from side to side in the dirt track between orchards, Kagehiro walked back to the hole between the young trees. If he could figure out what was making them sick, they would be full-bearing next year. The ranch would then yield thirty tons easily, he estimated. In the meantime, he had to ridge and disc before irrigating. It had been dry this year; the spring rains late. He would need more water than usual.

The empty hole had been filled in. Kagehiro frowned. He could see its outline easily enough, a rectangle of moist earth halfway between the sixth and seventh trees in the first row, beside the dirt track. The fresh dirt that had been piled neatly around the sides of the hole was shoveled back. The puppy sniffed in the dirt, nuzzling the wet clods drying in the still-warm evening air. Kagehiro walked around the hole.

The more Kagehiro thought about it, the more concerned he was. It could be the county agricultural agent, but Kagehiro didn't think the man would dig in the orchard without telling him. Maybe it was someone burying garbage. That happened all the time, but the field workers or contractors who buried their garbage usually asked permission, and the hole seemed too big for that anyway.

Kagehiro thought about the hole in his orchard throughout dinner. At eight o'clock that night, he decided to call the Live Oak Police Department. Maybe it was nothing and he would seem foolish, but maybe there was something there. Kagehiro was unable to get through when he dialed.

Shortly after eight o'clock the next morning, Kagehiro drove the five miles into the small community of Live Oak and reported the hole in his orchard. The officer on duty told Kagehiro that although he had a Live Oak address, his ranch was actually beyond the city limits. Instead, the officer called the Sutter County Sheriff's Department. They would send a deputy to meet Kagehiro at his ranch.

Deputy Sheriff Steve Sizelove was already parked in Kagehiro's driveway when the rancher returned from Live Oak. Somebody had dug a hole in his orchard, Kagehiro told the deputy. He had not given anyone permission. Maybe Sizelove would take a look at it and help Kagehiro dig it out.

With the deputy following him in the patrol car, Kagehiro drove along the dirt track to the trees a half-mile east of his house. Kagehiro parked, took two shovels from the back of the pickup, and led the deputy a few feet into the orchard.

The small mound covering the hole was clearly visible and lighter colored now that the once-wet dirt had dried. Here and there was a sprinkling of the red-brown hardpan which lay beneath the softer soil of the orchard.

Apologetically, Kagehiro suggested that maybe it was garbage. "It's a pretty good guess," Sizelove conceded, but it wouldn't take long to find out. Together, the two men began digging in the soil of the young peach orchard.

Within five minutes of digging in the loose soil, Sizelove's shovel struck something that "sounded kind of hollow." Working the shovel around in the small hole he had dug in the mound, Sizelove uncovered a piece of fabric, Levi's it looked like. He reached into the hole, grabbed at the pants leg and felt something with a "rubbery feeling" underneath.

Waving the rancher back from the mound, Sizelove widened the hole, uncovering a shoe. He tugged at the shoe to free it from the dirt; the shoe came loose in Sizelove's hand.

The deputy stared at the bare right foot, looked at the shoe in his hand, then dropped it on the ground. He had found the first body in what was to become the greatest mass murder in American history.

Sizelove backed off from the grave, pulling the small rancher with him. It was approximately eight-forty on the morning of Thursday, May 20, 1971.

Over his car radio, Sizelove talked with Detective Sergeant John Purcell in a second patrol car. Purcell said it would take him ten minutes to find his way to the Kagehiro Ranch and asked Sizelove to have the rancher waiting for him where the dirt road intersected Larkin Road. Purcell also told Sizelove to leave the grave alone for fear of disturbing evidence.

Purcell and Detective Harold Cochran arrived shortly after Sutter County Sheriff Roy Whiteaker, Undersheriff Frank Cartoscelli, Live Oak Chief of Police Jerry Davis, and a Live Oak policeman. They too had heard Sizelove's radio call. Purcell directed the immediate investigation.

While waiting for the department's photographer, the deputies present canvassed the area around the grave. At Purcell's order, Cochran poured a plaster cast of a tire track that Sizelove pointed out to him in the dirt road a few feet from the grave. Together he and Purcell took samples of the dirt in the orchard.

Deputy Sheriff Roger Mason arrived at nine-thirty. Mason had been with the Sutter County Sheriff's Department thirty months, and for the last two years had acted as the department's photographer. He took a picture of the small hole dug by Sizelove, the shoe and the exposed toe, then longer shots of the grave neatly lined up between the sixth and seventh rows of five-year-old peach trees.

It took the deputies a half hour to completely uncover the body in the grave. Mason shot photos for ten minutes more before the body was lifted from the three-and-one-half-foot-deep grave to the surface. A gray overcoat lay across the bottom of the grave.

Sizelove recognized the body—a man he had stopped early Monday morning walking along Colusa Highway. His name was Whitacre—Kenneth Whitacre—Sizelove remembered, and he had said he was from Palo Alto. The deputy had dismissed him as just another of the fruit tramps who hung out in lower Marysville across the river and had not bothered to write a field interrogation report.

Whitacre had been stabbed in the left side of his chest; the front of his blue-gray work shirt was covered with blood. His right hand had been cut behind the little finger, what Purcell's report called "a chop type wound." Whitacre's left cheek had been slashed, and the back of his head cleaved open at least twice.

When Mason was finally satisfied he had taken enough pictures, Purcell waved to the two morticians from the Chapel of the Twin Cities in Yuba City. The body was theirs. Purcell, Cochran, and Mason followed in a patrol car, Purcell to take Whitacre's fingerprints and Mason more pictures.

At two o'clock that afternoon, Doctor Thomas P. Connolly, Jr., a local physician and surgeon, performed the autopsy at the Twin Cities Mortuary. Doctor Connolly, a specialist in internal medicine, had been performing autopsies for the county on and off over a ten-year period. Whitacre, he told Detective Purcell, had died from the stab wound in the chest. The knife blade had slipped between the ribs, pierced the lung, and severed the aorta. Doctor Connolly estimated that the murder weapon had a blade eight to ten inches long. There were five separate head wounds, the largest four inches long, the deepest one slamming through both layers of the skull into the cranial vault. Whitacre's right wrist had also been slashed to the bone. Despite the multiple head wounds, the knife thrust into his aorta had killed him; blood pumping directly from his heart into his chest, Whitacre was for all practical purposes dead before he hit the ground.

There are two kinds of murder investigations—those in which the killer is known and those in which law enforcement officers must find the killer. Whichever kind of murder police are confronted with, the degree of proof they must have in order to secure a conviction depends upon whether the murderer, once apprehended, will confess. The easiest case to solve—and by far the most common—is the murder in which the killer himself calls police and confesses. (Sixty-five percent of all murders in the United States are committed by people who kill someone in their family; another ten percent involve murders by friends and acquaintances. In three out of four cases, the murderer and his victim know each other.)

The most difficult case to solve is the murder in which the assailant is unknown. As common as this sort of crime might be in detective fiction, it is comparatively rare in police work. It is in this type of case—the unknown assailant who neither surrenders nor confesses when confronted with the evidence—that police detectives make their reputation as investigators. That reputation is usually built on patient, dogged interrogation, on running down leads and rumors, sifting through physical evidence and statements. It is grinding work with little glamour or excitement involved in sleepless nights, lukewarm coffee, and unending report-writing.

The Sutter County Sheriff's Department began that kind of investigation into the death of Kenneth Edward Whitacre—white male adult, date of birth April 4, 1931, Social Security number 555-38-5821—a transient whose body had been buried in a peach orchard a half-mile east of Larkin Road midway between the county seat of Yuba City and the small town of Live Oak.

For Sheriff Roy D. Whiteaker, the death of the itinerant farmworker was doubly difficult. Elected just five months before as sheriff of Sutter County, the thirty-one-year-old Whiteaker was the youngest sheriff-coroner in California. He had campaigned as "the sheriff Sutter County deserves," a progressive-minded professional who dressed, according to Associated Press writer Doug Willis, "like one of the big-city detectives you see in television dramas."

For all of his professional appearance and smooth manners, however, Whiteaker did not personally have the experience to handle the investigation. Whiteaker had spent three years in the military police before joining the Yuba City Police Department. He spent four years as a patrolman, then five more as juvenile and narcotics officer. According to a reporter, "The minute he became a detective, he became a P.R. man for the police department. By the time he was ready to run, he was well known throughout the county." He had campaigned hard for the $16,464 job as sheriff, spending $6,126. His campaign contributors included two of his closest friends, District Attorney Dave Teja and Mrs. Teja, each of whom gave $50; and Teja's father, who donated $100. He defeated a six-year incumbent, H. P. "Shug" Ollar, 8,263 votes to 5,340.

Whiteaker's campaign literature claimed he had more than 2,300 hours of police training. By May 1971, after just five months in office, Whiteaker had completely restructured the sheriff's department, expanded patrols in rural areas, and inaugurated on-the-job training programs. But graduation from the Federal Bureau of Narcotics school and an associate in arts degree from two-year Yuba College in no way could prepare him for what was to follow. His professional manner, his accessibility to reporters, his efforts to modernize a rural sheriff's department, his good intentions—none of these could make up for his lack of experience. The death of Kenneth Edward Whitacre, FBI Number 715 288B, was the first investigation for which he had direct responsibility.

Detective Sergeant John Purcell, an eight-year veteran who doubled as chief deputy coroner, would have to take command of it. He was the most experienced investigator in the forty-member department, and he was considered to be one of the best detectives in the northern part of the state.

Purcell knew little about the dead man. Sizelove and Cochran had seen him on State Highway 20, halfway to the Colusa County line. At the time, Whitacre had been wearing the calf-length gray overcoat found under his body in the grave, and the heavy coat in hot weather was enough to make him memorable.

The first thing Purcell had to do was to try and trace Whitacre's trail through the last two days of his life. Purcell, Cochran, and Mason quickly checked the roads leading to Goro Kagehiro's new peach orchard, looking for the spot where Whitacre might have been killed. There was no evidence around the gravesite, and the three found nothing on the roads or tracks in the immediate area of the Kagehiro orchards.

Captain John Littlejohn, Detective Jerry Gregory, and Steve Sizelove were assigned the job of interviewing Kagehiro's scattered neighbors along Larkin and Edgar Roads. From shortly before ten o'clock in the morning until eight-forty-five that night of the first day, Gregory made eighteen stops, including two bunkhouses on the Blazer and Sullivan ranches. He had no luck; no one had seen a man matching Whitacre's description.

Deputy Denver L. Duncan was more successful when he came on duty at seven o'clock that evening. In the community of Tierra Buena, halfway between Yuba City on the east and the town of Sutter on the west, Duncan found a woman and a girl who said they had seen Whitacre about one o'clock Tuesday afternoon, the day before Whitacre's body was buried. The eleven-year-old-girl remembered that Whitacre had been wearing the long gray overcoat.

The Wednesday afternoon's edition of the Marysville *Appeal-Democrat,* the major daily serving the area, carried a small story on page one about the discovery of the body. That story turned up a couple of leads. Two people called the police to say that they had seen a man in a long overcoat—no, they didn't know his name—on Colusa Highway, walking east, back to Yuba City, oh, between seven-thirty and eight-thirty on Tuesday night.

An hour later, Sizelove began talking to people living along Colusa Highway in the Sutter area. Four of them had seen Whitacre, recognizing him from the photo of the dead man. Mrs. Ruby Roark confirmed her earlier phone call to the sheriff's department. She had seen Whitacre as late as eight-thirty on Tuesday night; he had stopped to take a drink from the water hose in front of the service station where she worked. She had last seen him—yes, that was his picture all right—walking east on Colusa, back toward Yuba City.

Police work is part drudgery, part record-keeping, and part memory to put the two together. It was memory that Sergeant Olie Coleman of the Marysville Police Department was relying on when he called Detective Gregory at the Sutter County Sheriff's Department at one o'clock on the afternoon of May 21. As a result of Coleman's call, Detective Gregory wrote in his report that evening, "About one year ago a man had been beaten and cut up very bad at the Guadalajara Restaurant, 332 First Street in Marysville, which was owned by Nativida [*sic*] Corona. Officer Coleman advised that a suspect in this matter was Juan Corona, a brother to Nativida Corona."

Juan Corona was living some place in Sutter County, contracting Mexican farm workers, Coleman told Gregory. Coleman "had talked to a man who knows the Corona brothers and the family," Gregory's report continued. "This informant had advised that Juan Corona was known to have fits of temper that were so bad the family had to take ropes and tie him down until he became quiet again."

Sheriff Roy Whiteaker's investigators now had a suspect.

Forty minutes later, Detective Gregory had contacted Sergeant Coleman's informant. The man didn't want his name revealed, but he "repeated the information about how Juan Corona had fits of temper and that on the night of the beating at the Guadalajara Juan Corona had been seen in the building with a short-handled hoe like those used for weeding beans.

"This informant also advised," Gregory's report continued, "that Natividad Corona was a queer and if someone talking to Juan even brought up the subject, directed at his brother or not, Juan Corona would go into one of his fits of temper."

Twenty minutes after talking to the anonymous informant, Gregory was at the Sullivan ranch, five miles north of Yuba City. Parking in front of the ranch office, Gregory shouted for Ray Duron, the foreman.

Gregory had talked to Duron the day before while canvassing the area for someone who might have seen Whitacre before he was killed. At the time, he had asked Duron if any of "his boys" had been in a fight or were there "other peculiar goings on there at the ranch." Duron had said no.

This time Gregory showed Duron a copy of Whitacre's picture taken in the mortuary by Deputy Mason. Duron shrugged. It was a stranger.

Did Juan Corona contract the Mexican labor for the ranch, Gregory asked.

Not all of it, Duron replied. Duron hired the five or six men who worked on the ranch all year around. Corona provided the extra crews needed two or three times a year for pruning, thinning, and harvesting and sometimes for other work too. Yes, Corona was there now, at the mess hall across the wide dirt oval in the center of the ranch's headquarters. Gregory wondered if he could show the picture to Corona.

Speaking in Spanish, Duron showed the labor contractor the picture of the buck-toothed man and asked if he had ever seen the man before. Corona looked at the photo for as long as thirty seconds, then passed the mug shot over to Duron. "No, he has never seen that man anywhere," Duron translated Corona's reply for Gregory, handing him back the photo.

The three talked for a few minutes, Duron and Corona speaking in Spanish, Gregory in English. Then Corona asked to see the picture again. According to Duron's later statement, Corona told the foreman in Spanish, "This fellow looks like he is dead already." Duron shrugged, "He is."

The next morning, Deputy Sheriff Steve Sizelove talked to three people who had seen the man in the long gray overcoat, shortly before Goro Kagehiro discovered the open hole in his orchard. Carol Jean Bordsen was on her way to work Wednesday morning when she saw Whitacre in front of the Forderhase place between eight-thirty and eight-forty, she was sure. Bill Forderhase thought it was between eight-thirty and nine o'clock when he saw the man, not thirty feet away, in front of his home. Yeah, that was the man—couldn't miss those buck teeth. He had been walking eastbound on Colusa Highway, towards Yuba City.

Meanwhile, John Purcell was independently confirming the fact that Whitacre was alive on the morning of Wednesday, May 19. Jerry Davis, the brother of Live Oak's police chief, saw Whitacre walking west on Colusa a little after eight o'clock in the morning. As Davis had driven by in the school bus, Whitacre had smiled and waved.

Late that same day, Deputy Robert Wilcox talked with Fred McVey who had been hauling hay to the Yuba City Mill on North Township Road. McVey had seen Whitacre walking on the highway about two miles east of the Forderhase home Wednesday morning about nine-thirty.

And sometime after one-thirty that afternoon, young Gina Cross Chapman saw him near her home, walking down the highway.

Monday night, four days after Whitacre's body was found, Deputy Wilcox interviewed Goro Kagehiro once again. As reported by Detective Purcell—Wilcox failed to write a report on the interview or take a verbatim statement—the deputy "learned that Corona, Juan, had contracted the thinning of his [Kagehiro's] peaches. The day the body was discovered was the last day on the job. Background on subject Corona indicates that he becomes violent when the subject of homosexuality is brought up."

The next sentence of his report suggests that Sergeant Purcell, like Gregory, had settled upon a prime suspect. "Corona drives a 1971 Chev. panel Calif. Lic. No. 107 BVR. This vehicle reportedly has wide tires and span similar to the tracks left at the scene (to be verified by the reporting officer). The vehicle in question last seen parked at the Sullivan ranch."

It was ten o'clock when Purcell finished his entry, too late to check the tracks that night. He would do it the next day. It wasn't a lot to go on, but it was better than nothing.

Sergeant Purcell was never to get an opportunity to compare the plaster cast lifted from the dirt track separating the groves on the Kagehiro ranch. While discing the Ferrie block on the Sullivan ranch that afternoon, Ernesto Garcia had come across a large indentation in the ground.

2

The Riverbank Graveyard

May 24-26, 1971

It was almost quitting time. Ernesto Garcia realized he wouldn't be able to finish discing the Louise orchard on the extreme west end of the Sullivan ranch. But one more day's work with the tractor if it didn't rain and he would be done with the entire Ferrie block.

Pulling the disc plow behind the tractor, Garcia shuttled from row to row in the prune orchard. The ground had been ridged, then irrigated some time before, the eroded ridges—called irrigation checks—then flattened out before the spraying. Juan Sanchez had turned up new ridges; now Garcia's disc plow would hew ten parallel tracks to cultivate the soil between the ridges that cut the orchard into an undulating checkerboard of now arid paddies.

Garcia followed the temporary boundaries of the irrigation checks until he came to the seventh and eighth rows. Instead of following the old checks when he reridged the orchard, Sanchez had veered away between the next row of trees. Garcia now would have to disc through what looked like bumpy ground, over the worn-down ridge.

Garcia stopped the tractor. In the soft ground next to what been the old ridge, there was a shallow depression. Garcia frowned: two feet, maybe three, wide, the four-inch depression ran six feet before stopping as abruptly as it had begun. Garcia had not seen anything like that before on the ranch.

Maybe José Ramirez knew something about it. He had worked on the Sullivan ranch for fifteen or sixteen years and knew all the orchards. Garcia didn't want to say anything to the ranch foreman, Ray Duron, not yet. He didn't want the foreman to think he was seeing bodies everywhere just because they had found that man in Kagehiro's orchard last week.

Ramirez was at his house when Garcia came in from the orchard. Together the two men went back to the Louise orchard to look at the depression. Ramirez agreed it looked like a grave; they had better tell Ray about it.

By the time the two ranch workers returned to the Sullivan head-quarters, Duron was gone, somebody said to a movie. They decided to wait until the following morning to tell the foreman what Garcia had discovered in the Louise orchard.

At six o'clock on the morning of May 25, Ramirez told Duron about the rectangular depression in the orchard. Would Duron "come and take a look at it because it looked kind of suspicious?"

Ramirez led Duron to the shallow depression in the prune orchard. Duron was worried, but he told Ramirez not to bother about it. It was probably a hole dug by the agricultural consultants to measure the depth of the hardpan in the orchards. Ramirez could go to work; Duron would take care of it.

It was seven o'clock in the morning when Duron met J. L. Sullivan, the wealthy ranch owner, at the ranch headquarters. Sullivan also looked at the depression and ordered Duron to notify the Sheriff's Department.

Duron called Detective Sergeant Purcell, to tell him what Garcia had discovered the night before in the prune orchards. Purcell said he and Detective Gregory would be there by eight-thirty and asked the foreman to meet them at the ranch office. Duron, Sullivan, and a second ranch foreman, Buck Harris, were waiting in front of the office when the two officers arrived.

With Duron leading the way, the five men drove to the Louise orchard, north on Onstott Frontage Road to Sanders, then west seven-tenths of a mile before turning left onto a dirt road that marked the westernmost limit of the Sullivan property. Gregory counted the trees as they drove along the dirt track, their vehicles raising a plume of dust back to the paved street. At the fifty-third tree, Duron pulled up, the sheriff's deputies parking behind him.

Situated between the seventh and eighth rows of trees, the depression was cocked at an angle; the soil compacted between four and six inches below the surface of the orchard. Sergeant Purcell decided to excavate the rectangular outline.

Duron and Gregory began digging at about eight-fifty while Purcell radioed the sheriff's department in Yuba City for the photographer. Undersheriff Frank Cartoscelli said he would be right out. They would put in a call for Mason.

Duron and Gregory had been digging for ten minutes in the loosely compacted soil when they discovered the body. Duron climbed out of the hole, Cartoscelli replacing him, and the undersheriff and Gregory probed the grave beneath their feet. While Deputy Mason took photos, the two officers uncovered first a leg, then an arm.

An hour after Duron and Gregory had first begun digging, the body in the six-foot-long grave had been outlined. With Sheriff Whiteaker, Live Oak Police Chief Davis, and Yuba City Chief of Police George Garcia looking on, a backhoe operator dug out the area around the body. It took more than two hours before the body could be exhumed, then turned over to the two men from the Chapel of the Twin Cities.

According to the joint report signed by Purcell and Gregory, the body was that of a man approximately five feet ten inches tall, with black hair. The corpse was clothed in two pairs of dark pants, the outer pair of a dark blue plaid material; a red, white, and blue plaid shirt under both a gray cardigan sweater and a suit coat; underwear; and one shoe. The mismatched clothing more than anything else identified the body, now "badly decomposed," according to the police report, as that of a drifter, one of those men who hung out around Wino Park in Marysville.

At the mortuary, Purcell and Gregory emptied the pockets of the mud-caked clothing. There was a package of matches, two Safeway market cash register receipts dated May 8, a box of W. E. Garrett snuff, a bar of Ivory soap, a half-bar of soap wrapped in a piece of paper, and a safety razor. The legacy of the unidentified man was placed in a Sheriff's Department property envelope.

When Sheriff Whiteaker returned from the Louise orchard to his office in the county courthouse on Second Street, there was an interoffice memo waiting for him. His secretary had taken a call from the Marysville Police Department. They had heard about the second body from the police radios and thought Whiteaker should know they had a missing person report on a wino named "Pete" Peterson or Sigurd Emil Beierman.

A friend of Beierman had reported him missing about the first of the month. Beierman usually ran out of money near the end of the month, waiting for his next pension check. Now there were two checks waiting for him at the Day Center in Marysville. Beierman's friend, Roy DeLong, didn't know where the old man had gone. Guys on Skid Row don't keep that close track; besides, those wino types were liable to pick up and go at any moment. The Marysville Police Department had booked Beierman on January 24 and had gotten a good set of prints on him. He should be easy to identify; he was missing the tips of his left thumb and index finger.

The secretary's memo added, "Also, [the Marysville Police] have a report of about a year and a half ago wherein there was a cutting and the weapon was a machete. This happened at Guadalajara Café. If you would like this file, it may have some bearing on our 11-44, and 187 PC," the memo concluded.

This was the second time that Marysville had called about the Guadalajara incident. Whiteaker decided he wanted to take a look at the file; a cutting with a machete was close enough to the head wounds on the two dead men. You never could tell.

Whiteaker spoke with the Marysville Police Department. According to Roy DeLong, Beierman was last seen going off with a Mexican labor contractor. DeLong couldn't identify the driver but the vehicle was a yellow Chevy van. Ronald Huff, a Marysville patrolman, had run a field interrogation on May 4, around eight-thirty in the evening when DeLong had pointed out the van. The driver said he didn't know the missing man, and the officer had waved him on. The driver of the yellow van though was the same man who had been a suspect in the cutting at the Guadalajara in February of last year, a farm labor contractor named Juan Corona.

Marysville would send over a copy of their investigation reports right away. In the meantime, they would pick up DeLong as a material witness and hold him for Whiteaker.

Like Purcell and Gregory before him, Whiteaker now had a suspect.

At three o'clock that afternoon, a second local doctor, Charles Clement, performed the autopsy on the still unidentified body. His first task was to remove the fingers from the body, then turn them over to a deputy, who would in turn ferry them forty miles south to the fingerprint laboratory of the state Department of Justice in Sacramento. If the Department's Criminal Identification and Investigation Bureau (CII) didn't have his prints on file, they could try the FBI in Washington.

Doctor Clement's autopsy was comparatively difficult. "There were marked postmortem changes of degeneration. The tissues were swollen and the skin was beginning to slip, and there was a large amount of gas in the abdominal cavity and chest cavity."

Clement was unable to determine which wound had killed the man. The victim had been stabbed once in the left chest, the force of the blow shattering the fifth rib, the knife blade penetrating the left lung. He had been slashed twice across the face—once over the right cheek, once from the top of the left ear down across his left cheek. A third slicing wound was discovered at the nape of the neck.

There was blood in his bronchial tubes from the base of the lungs up through his throat. Whether the blood there had come from the knife wound in the lungs or whether it had come from the multiple wounds across his face, Doctor Clement could not say. In any event, the victim had strangled to death, drowned in his own blood.

Skid Row killings are common. Five dollars will buy a lot of wine, with enough left over for a room for the night and some cold pancakes in the morning. Cheap whiskey and raw muscatel fray the temper; arguments are frequent in the raucous Outlaw, Manuel's Place, the Pago Pago, the Guadalajara, or Little Harlem.

The sheriff's deputies investigating the death of Kenneth Whitacre at first were inclined to treat it as another Skid Row killing; the police science books were full of them, even if they were rare in the Marysville-Yuba City area. But finding the second body changed that. The unidentified man in the Louise orchard and Whitacre had been killed in almost the same way; the killer's *modus operandi* linked the two deaths.

Sheriff Whiteaker, his undersheriff, and Detectives Purcell and Gregory discussed their next move. At the moment, they had little to go on, nothing to link anyone to the crimes. But Purcell and Gregory both suspected that Juan Corona might be involved. He had contracted labor at the Kagehiro place and Whitacre was found there. He contracted labor and worked himself on the Sullivan ranch; now there was a second body.

Whitacre, obviously, had been killed sometime between ten and six o'clock the day before the body was uncovered. This one, though, had been dead for some time. How long they didn't know, but the stench was enough to tell them he had been dead for a week or two weeks or longer.

It seemed logical that if Corona were the murderer, he would bury his victims where he worked, where he knew hidden places or little-traveled orchards. The Sullivan ranch, large as it was, would be a good place. And Corona had been on the Sullivan place much of the time before Whitacre's body was found.

In the period between the time the unidentified man had been killed and the time Whitacre had been dragged into the hole on the Kagehiro ranch, had the killer, Corona, murdered anyone else?

Calling the department's reserve officers in and borrowing men from the Yuba City and Live Oak Police Departments, Sheriff Whiteaker organized a foot-by-foot search of the Sullivan ranch. Later that afternoon, Ray Duron saw the police sweep of the orchards. Surprised, the foreman asked what was going on. "They told me that they were going to cover as much ground as possible looking for further indentations in the ground, or other suspicious markings that would indicate other grave sites," Duron said later.

The police combed the groves west of the freeway that bisected the Sullivan ranch, sweeping in wavering rows through the dry orchards. Reformed on the other side of the freeway, they swept east, towards the Feather River bank, which marked the edge of the Sullivan property.

It was after six in the evening of May 25 when the lines of uniformed deputies reached the eastern edge of the Sullivan property, still without finding anything. The day was fading to twilight as Deputy Sizelove drove the jeep from the ranch headquarters, up the dirt road over the levee, past the garbage dump, and right at the fork in the access road.

The men would have to hurry if they were going to complete the search before the light got too dim to see well.

Sizelove drove south along the narrow track, the ribbon of trees and underbrush lining the Feather River bank at his left, a young prune orchard on his right. One of the deputies in the jeep shouted for him to stop. There was something over there in the brush on the riverbank. It looked like a cleared out area there.

The deputies shoved their way up the bank, through the thick growth, to what Sizelove described as a "dome-like clearing in the underbrush" under the trees. The ground in the clearing by the bank of the river had been turned up, the rectangular shape and dimensions about the same as the first two graves, Sizelove thought.

At six-fifteen in the dusk of a spring day, the murmuring of a quiet river accompanying the scratching of their shovels in the loose, sandy soil, Sizelove and Undersheriff Cartoscelli began excavating a third grave.

While the undersheriff and Sizelove were digging, spelled by Detective Jerry Harrison and Deputy Sheriff Bob Pihera, Gregory arrived. He would be the recording officer, and his report was to be crucial in the court trial later. Gregory searched the immediate area around the grave, scanning the ground in semicircles eddying from the bank of the river, ten feet from where the deputies were digging. A few minutes before seven o'clock, Gregory crossed the hard-packed dirt access road that bordered the raised bank. In the dry grass of the prune orchard immediately west of the road, he found a large splotch of what looked like blood in the fading light. It was dry, "not what you would say real dirty black," but "still red-colored." From the splotch smeared on the grass, the blood trailed in a straight line fifteen or sixteen yards across the field, the dirt road, up the bank to the grave underneath the trees along the river.

On the access road, Gregory noted shovel marks where the killer had taken dirt to sprinkle on the blood staining the grass. He had apparently worked quickly, not bothering to do a thorough job in covering the bloody trail, perhaps working in daylight fearing he would be seen, perhaps failing in the darkness to see all the blood draining from the body.

In the meantime, Detective Denver Duncan had poured a plaster cast of a possible footprint, the only other evidence found in the area surrounding the grave in the dense copse.

Shortly after seven o'clock, Sizelove found a cigarette butt in the grave some thirty inches below the decaying leaves on the surface. Five minutes later, Duncan held up a small dark feather he had winnowed from the dirt in the hole.

At thirteen minutes after seven o'clock, the Sutter County Sheriff's Department made its case against Juan Corona. In the third grave, Sizelove and Cartoscelli spotted the folded pink papers at the same time, the undersheriff reaching for them before Sizelove. Cartoscelli unfolded the pink papers, read them quickly, and handed them to Gregory. The first piece of paper was a receipt for $78.35 dated Friday, May 21, 1971, just four days before, from the Del Pero Bros. and Mondon meat market. The second was a sales slip totaling $25.63 for twenty-five pounds of tongue and seventeen and one-half pounds of spare ribs. Both were made out to Juan V. Corona.

At seven-thirty-five, according to Gregory's report, the third body —that of a nine-fingered man—was lifted from the ground onto the tarpaulin beside the grave. The man had been wearing a long-sleeved plaid shirt, green work pants, loafers, and white sox. Like the bodies found earlier, the man had been stabbed in the left chest, and the back of his skull had been slashed repeatedly with what looked like an ax or machete. The wound in the chest appeared to be fresh, and to Sizelove, it seemed "he hadn't been in the grave over twenty-four hours." While Deputy Mason took photos, Cartoscelli told Sheriff Whiteaker about the two receipts found in the grave of the nine-fingered man.

Whiteaker now had a good deal of circumstantial evidence pointing to Juan Corona's involvement in the three murders. Corona knew both farms. He was a labor contractor and had been seen going off with a man who was now missing. There was that cutting in the Guadalajara Café; no charges had been brought since the victim couldn't or wouldn't identify his assailant, but Corona was suspected. And, finally, there were those two slips from the meat market, one made out to Corona, the other signed by him.

Whiteaker and Cartoscelli discussed it between themselves. Aside from the two pink slips of paper, there was nothing much in the grave of the nine-fingered man: a blue baseball cap, a Prince Albert can, a set of dentures, an almost empty package of Pall Malls, and a letter dated "Saturday 1, 1971."

Sheriff Whiteaker decided to put a tail on Corona. The first body —Kenneth Edward Whitacre—had been killed last week, this third body looked fresh, and you never could tell. The whole thing looked like the work of a homicidal maniac; he could kill at any time. And there was one other thing: Purcell had learned from Ray Duron, the foreman on the Sullivan ranch, that Corona had spent some time in a state hospital sometime around 1956.

Whiteaker decided to talk with the district attorney, Dave Teja, a close friend who understood the problems of law enforcement. In Teja's office in the courthouse annex, the two men weighed the information they had accumulated. Most of the evidence was pretty tentative, they agreed. The first thing to do was to verify the receipts. Teja asked his deputy district attorney to get hold of someone from the Del Pero and Mondon market. Even with the receipts, there was really nothing to tie Corona direcly to the dead men.

Rather than just make an arrest, the cautious thing to do would be to get a search warrant. Corona had to keep records of where his crews worked, Social Security payments, financial books. If Whitacre's name was there, it would tie Corona to him. The warrant could cover weapons —it looked like the murderer was using two—bloody clothes, or maybe something from the dead men: money, well, they didn't have much; a wallet or identification of some kind; clothes; anything, you never know.

Teja and Whiteaker were understandably shaken. About 100 yards north of the nine-fingered man, they had found another grave in the trees and brush lining the riverbank. And there was a group of what looked like three graves 250 yards farther south, near the property line. The whole bank of the Feather River was a goddam graveyard.

By seven forty-five that evening, deputies were digging under the trees and underbrush at four different graves. Sergeant Purcell and two deputies were at the grave labeled "victim number two." (While it was the fourth body to be discovered in the case, it was the second to be uncovered that day—May 25—hence the numbering.) Some 360 yards south of them, another group of police officers was digging in a cluster of three graves. Another deputy was taking Instamatic pictures while Mason was busy at the graves of the first two victims found along the river.

It had begun to drizzle, the rain silencing the crickets in the prune orchard and undergrowth. In the narrow-eyed glare of floodlights and automobile headlights, the deputies dug in relays, shoveling the loose soil out of the holes until overwhelmed by the cloying stench of decomposing flesh. A few puffed on cigars as they dug, the aromatic tobacco momentarily masking the stomach-churning odor from the ground beneath their feet.

The drizzle turned to rain—the first there had been in some time—the rain drops splattering on the trees overhead and into the river. Here and there flashlights bobbed off the access road into the underbrush on the edge of the river, will-o'-the-wisps marking the way as men in dirty brown uniforms looked for more graves. North of the fork in the road leading from the ranch headquarters on the far side of the levee, they found two more graves laid out almost foot-to-foot.

As each succeeding body was lifted from its grave, the deputies moved on to another. Going from site to site, Gregory logged the evidence and took notes for his later report. When he finished, the two crews from the Twin Cities Chapel removed the body. Later they would drive to the mortuary and leave the bodies on the garage floor to return to the riverbank.

As bodies were uncovered, the character of Gregory's report changed. The notes became more terse, the entries fewer for each grave, the description decreasing progressively as the night wore on. The report on finding Whitacre's body the week before had taken eight single-spaced typewritten pages; Deputy Mason had taken twenty-three pictures at the time and had later drawn a well-defined map of the grave site.

But on May 19, the Sutter County Sheriff's Department had had only one body and no suspect. Tonight they had seven, but they also had a suspect. The rain coming harder, Gregory was merely inventorying bodies by the end of the night.

According to his later report, drafted from the notes he made standing in the thicket, the fourth victim was wearing a gray coat, a green sweatshirt, and a gray shirt. The shirt and sweatshirt had been pulled up over his face and outstretched arms. He was trouserless, his penis exposed through his shorts. Purcell and Gregory looked at the face of the "slightly decomposed" body; he was wearing a full beard.

The body of the next victim was discovered at eight o'clock, Gregory's report noted, but not lifted from the grave for another hour and twenty-five minutes. Like the bearded man, his shirt too was pulled up over his face and arms.

Detective Harrison took more detailed notes as he dug out the fourth grave of the day, logging fresh leaves, a cigarette butt, a bar of soap wrapped in newspaper, a shoe, a small jar, a large section of newspaper, a razor, and a gray knit cap—the detritus of a life lived in flophouses and cheap bars. Harrison's shovel accidentally severed two fingers from the victim's body as he dug; the detective carefully placed them in a plastic bag, marking it for identification.

The third of the three bodies found in this cluster—the fifth, sixth, and seventh victims in the case—was so badly decomposed the morticians recommended bundling it into a body bag before lifting it from the grave.

It was raining harder, the tired deputies trying to work faster. Ten minutes after eleven o'clock, another body was lifted from its hole in the riverbank. He had been stabbed through layers of shirts and coats, but was not wearing pants. Like the bearded man recovered earlier, his penis was exposed. At twenty minutes past midnight, in the raw white of the floodlights, the last body to be exhumed that night was removed from the grave. Three more possible grave sites, found after the digging had begun, would be left for the morning.

Standing in the partial shelter of a tree, Gregory entered the last victim of the day: "2420 hrs. Grave located and victim removed from grave. The thumb and forefinger were missing at the first joint." They had found Pete Beierman, the man who had failed to pick up his checks at the Day Center in Marysville.

Five miles from the rain-wet bank of the Feather River, Sheriff Roy Whiteaker and District Attorney G. Dave Teja were attempting to comply with the Fourth Amendment's constitutional mandate that "no warrants shall issue, but upon probable cause, supported by oath or affirmation, and particularly describing the place to be searched, and the person or things to be seized." By law, their request for a search warrant could be granted only by a judge, and the legal petition, which Teja's secretary was typing, had to be accompanied by the affidavit of the peace officer requesting the warrant.

The first problem was to locate a judge. Usually, a justice court judge granted the warrants and accepted return on them; however, there had been a legal challenge to the practice of nonlawyers sitting as judges in even the minor matters that justice courts routinely handled. What might have been necessary in the nineteenth century—when judges were few and far between on the frontier—was an anachronism in the twentieth. Teja elected to ask Superior Court Judge John Hauck, a lawyer, for the warrant.

The judge agreed to be available when Teja and Whiteaker finished the affidavit and compiled the supporting documents. That would take care of that problem if a conviction were appealed.

As the night wore on, the two men revised the affidavit to fit the changing number of bodies on the Sullivan ranch. According to Whiteaker's affidavit, he began "the actual physical mechanics of preparing this affidavit and attached search warrant at 10:45 P.M. of [*sic*] May 25, 1971," an hour and thirty-five minutes before the body of Pete Beierman was lifted from its now muddy grave. The petition and supporting affidavit asked the judge to grant legal authority to search the Corona home; the small cookhouse Corona used at the Sullivan ranch; and a pickup truck, van and bus all owned by the labor contractor. Whiteaker's deputies would be seeking "knives, axes, machetes, shovels or any other cutting or stabbing instruments or weapons, personal effects of Kenneth Edward Whitacre, Sigurd Emil Beierman, also known as Pete Peterson, and those homicide victims identified herein as John Doe 2, John Doe 3, John Doe 4, John Doe 5, John Doe, 6, John Doe 7, and John Doe 8, bloodstained clothing, bloodstained weapons of any sort, bloodstained vehicles or part thereof, a black oxford shoe belonging to John Doe 2, and any other evidence including but not limited to payroll and employment records associating Juan V. Corona, or any other person, with the death of said Kenneth Edward Whitacre, Sigurd Emil Beierman, also known as Pete Peterson, and John Doe 2, John Doe 3, John Doe 4, John Doe 5, John Doe 6, John Doe 7, and John Doe 8."

To support his affidavit, Whiteaker and Teja attached copies of the death reports of Whitacre and the man discovered in the Louise orchard. Corona was twice mentioned in the first investigation; to tie him to the second victim, Whiteaker's affidavit stated, "Mr. Duron advised that Juan V. Corona had worked for the J. L. Sullivan Ranch as a labor contractor and was familiar with the orchard in which John Doe 2's body was discovered." It was a tenuous link, but all that Whiteaker had to go on at the time.

While Whiteaker was preparing the document, Deputy District Attorney John Winship was verifying the meat receipts found in the grave of the third victim, the nine-fingered man. Shortly after eleven that night, Donald Frazier, a butcher at the Del Pero Bros. and Mondon meat market, identified the receipt and the sales slip; he had given them to Corona the Friday before. Another paragraph was added to the affidavit.

District Attorney Teja supplied the next link in the evidence. Corona was supposed to be mentally ill—Purcell had said Duron had told him—and had spent some time at a state hospital. Searching through the Superior Court records, Teja turned up the involuntary commitment file. On January 11, 1956, Corona's oldest brother, Natividad, had asked the court to commit his brother to a state hospital for the mentally ill; Corona had spent three months there before being released.

Whiteaker added that information, then concluded: "In my opinion, the nature of the wounds and their savagery, and the shear [sic] number of victims indicate that the perpetrator of these offenses is at least seriously mentally ill and probably a homicidal maniac."

At two thirty-eight in the morning of May 26, Judge Hauck signed the warrant to search the bunkhouse at the Sullivan ranch and the "single family dwelling house with attached garage also described as 768 Richland Road, County of Sutter, State of California."

3

The House on Richland Road

May 26, 1971

It was drizzling when Juan Corona pulled into the driveway of the cream-colored stucco house in the new housing tract on Richland Road. Corona shook his wife awake, gruffly whispering in Spanish that they were home. Gloria stirred, then sat up.

A good woman, Gloria, Juan thought, smiling. She cooked for the men, and they saved the money he would otherwise have to pay for a cook. And she took good care of the four girls, dressing them, like all the other children in the neighborhood, from Montgomery Ward. They would go to school and learn to speak good English and be citizens.

Juan chuckled as he unlocked the front door. It would be good for the girls to be citizens; he would like to be a citizen too. This was a rich country; a man could work hard, make money, and live good. Their house proved that. One good summer in the tomatoes in Meridian and he had enough for a cash down payment. Five thousand dollars. And they had made enough money to buy good furniture and a refrigerator too.

Gloria looked in on the children while Juan put the groceries on the kitchen sink. A man prospers little by little. The peaches would be good this year—maybe two, maybe three crews working. Then he would take a crew up to Corning to pick the olives; Mr. Johnson wanted him to pick and maybe Mr. McFarland would be able to pay more money this year and he could run a crew there too.

In the bedroom, Juan emptied his pants pockets, throwing a crumpled meat receipt from Del Pero and Mondon in the bureau drawer and his checkbook in the three-drawer file cabinet in which he kept his business records. Mr. Karnail Singh had paid him $280 today; he would have to take that to the bank tomorrow to have enough money to pay the crew on Saturday. Juan smiled to himself; he enjoyed going to the bank, making a loan or depositing money. He was a businessman with good credit; people respected him at the bank. They knew he was a hard worker, a man who paid his bills.

Marysville and Yuba City were a lot different from Autlan, his birthplace. In Autlan—120 miles south of Guadalajara—there was only the sugar mill and crop picking, no chance to make money in such a small place. But in the United States, even in the small towns, a man could work hard and prosper. He had done it.

Juan Vallejo Corona first crossed the United States-Mexico border in 1950, a sixteen-year-old wetback illegally following in the footsteps of his older brothers, Natividad and Felix. "For a long time I didn't know nothing, not even a word in English, you know." He needed little or none, working for bilingual labor contractors who got him jobs, hanging around the grimy bars and cafés where English was a foreign tongue. He went from crop to crop with other workers; someone in the car always had enough English to read a map or a road sign.

Corona picked carrots and melons in the Imperial Valley for three months before following the crops north to the Sacramento Valley, picking cherries around Stockton and grapes in Lodi. The following year he first visited his older half-brother Natividad. (Natividad had come to the United States in 1944 when World War II's draft had stripped California farms of their cheap labor, those dirt-poor Okies and Arkies who had followed the crops since the Depression.) Natividad liked to work in the Sacramento Valley part of the year, then return to Mexico in the winter where it was warmer.

Juan decided to leave the crops to work as a laborer in a Sacramento construction project in 1952. After two months, he took a job on the massive Folsom Dam project, hauling gravel for cement from the plant to tunnels boring into the hills. The job paid well; the seventeen-year-old Corona made enough money to send something home each week and still have a good time on the weekends. Dancing he liked especially, and the dark-browed Corona was popular with girls.

In January 1953 Juan Corona met a Sacramento girl he liked and began to see her. Then "we got in a little trouble and we got married. I took her out sometimes and we got home pretty late, around one o'clock, and her mother was mad, very mad, and said, 'You're going to have to get married.' " The boy and girl—one a wetback, the other educated in Sacramento's public schools—were married in Reno.

The marriage didn't last long. The young bride did not like living near the Folsom construction project, away from her family and friends. She began badgering Juan, finally persuading him to give up his job in the gravel plant and return to Sacramento. They could rent a house from her mother for $30 a month. The girl found a typing job in an office; Corona got work as a construction laborer. "So pretty soon, we didn't get together too good, you know. She was working and I was working. And she had some friends. I had different friends. The family start talking about not getting along too good." Natividad, too, wanted the marriage ended before the girl became pregnant; a love match it might be, but Juan should have married a girl who could help him prosper. Under pressure to remarry in the church, Juan and his bride talked to the parish priest. He advised that the couple separate "because pretty soon you guys in worse trouble."

The marriage ended after three months; Corona felt he had to leave Sacramento. He went from crop to crop again, then took a job in a Nevada gypsum plant during the winter. In May 1953, Corona returned to the Marysville-Yuba City area at his half-brother's suggestion.

The two brothers lived together for two and one-half years, Natividad contracting labor for ranches in the area, Juan acting as foreman of a second crew elsewhere. It was from Natty that Juan learned the contracting business. In the winter they would vacation in Mexico, visiting Autlan, their father, and Juan's mother; "Juanito" was Candida Vallejo's favorite of the ten children she bore Sebastian Corona after his first wife died.

The two brothers had bought a truck in the winter of 1955 to make the thousand-mile journey to Autlan when the big rains began. It rained for two weeks while the brothers waited impatiently for it to stop. Around midnight, December 23/24, 1955, the rain-swollen Yuba and Feather Rivers tore a 2,200-foot gap in the west levee near Shanghai Bend. Thirty-eight people drowned in the first rush of water which flooded 150 square miles in the southern portion of Sutter County and left the city of Marysville an island. Two others died later from injuries, and for months after there were rumors of uncounted bodies left unidentified, buried in the muck, Mexican farm workers who would never be missed except in some small town in Jalisco, or Sonora or Baja.

Nineteen days later, as the first evacuees returned to the mud-filled streets of Yuba City, Natividad Corona filed a petition in the Sutter County Superior Court asking that his twenty-two-year-old half-brother be committed to a state mental hospital as "mentally ill and in need of supervision, treatment and care." Natividad's petition complained that Juan "believes that everyone in this area was drowned in the flood. He reads the Bible and writes all the time." Afraid of water all his life, Juan Corona believed that people he met on the street were dead.

The following day, two local doctors—neither of them psychiatrists or psychologists—examined the young farmworker. The doctors decided after an hour's conversation with Corona that he was suffering from "delusions" and was "confused," recommending he be institutionalized with a tentative diagnosis of "schizophrenia." Five days later, the handcuffed Juan Corona was delivered by three deputy sheriffs to DeWitt State Hospital in Auburn, California.

The medical records at the hospital state that Corona was agitated upon his arrival, and was said to have been "combative prior to his being admitted." The tentative diagnosis by a doctor—who conceded communication was difficult because of a language barrier—was that Corona was suffering from "schizophrenic reaction, paranoid type." The doctor wrote a prescription for a massive tranquilizer, then coming into wide use in mental hospitals, and a request for "emergency ECT"—electro-convulsive shock.

The first shock treatment was administered, without anaesthesia, on Wednesday, January 18, 1956. It was followed in the next eight weeks by twenty-two others, given routinely, the clinical changes written in by a bored technician who simply placed ditto marks under earlier entries. Within a week of his arrival, having received three such "treatments," Corona was demanding to be released. The entry from the hospital files reads in its entirety:

> 1-21-56 thru 1-22-56: Ward 202. RESTRAINT ORDER AND REPORT
> 8:00 P.M. Restraint: Secluded in side room. Patient came to the office and stated he wanted to go home and he would kick the door down if he was not let out. Went to front door and began kicking the door. When asked to stop he became combative. Was then placed in seclusion. Tried to reason with patient but to no avail.

On January 22, Natividad Corona signed a consent for medical, surgical, and dental treatment of his brother. His signature was witnessed by an older friend, Raymond E. Duron, soon to be Natividad's partner in a café and bar, later to become a foreman on the Sullivan ranch.

Throughout the month of February, Juan Corona underwent the Monday-Wednesday-Friday shock treatments. On the last day of the month, nine doctors decided in a staff conference that Corona was suffering from "schizophrenic reaction, catatonic type." The prognosis was "guarded." They recommended continued "hospitalization."

For another month the shock treatment continued. Six days after they ended, the doctor handling the Corona case wrote in the file: "The undersigned feels that it would now be possible to inform the deportation authorities that the patient would probably be ready to leave the hospital within about three weeks. Bureau of Immigration has been contacted."

Corona spent first a weekend with his brother, then a one-week leave. The hospital file noted that immigration authorities approved Natividad Corona's plan to return his brother to Mexico when Juan was released from DeWitt. On April 18, 1956, three months after he was first admitted, Juan Corona was "discharged as recovered" from the hospital.

Corona thought little about that now. He knew he had been sick, but could recall nothing of the illness itself or the treatment. The shock therapy, as it usually does, had wiped clear his memory of the period. It had happened "a long time ago"; there had been no recurrence of the illness. Fifteen years later, it was all but forgotten.

For Corona, those fifteen years had been a time of growing prosperity. He returned to the United States late in 1956, this time legally, with the green card that permitted him to work. Living again with his brother in the Marysville-Yuba City area in a house they were jointly buying, Corona grew more serious. He gave up drinking. If he went to bars, it was only to hire the day laborers who hung out there; the bartenders in lower Marysville came to know him as "a coffee drinker, all business."

At the same time, he made no close friends, only acquaintances. Though widely known, he was not well known. He was friendly and always polite, his manners those of the old country, surprisingly formal. Perhaps it was this sense of formality or respect—especially for older people—that kept him a man apart, or perhaps it was the unspoken drive to succeed. All the Corona brothers had it; the rigid confines of Autlan could not hold them nor provide enough opportunity.

One spring he had played baseball with casual friends, but his awkwardness in the field was matched only by his strength at bat—when he hit the ball. When he failed to make the team, his entertainment was limited to television and Mexican movies in Marysville with occasional dates.

Determined to succeed, he worked. There was a little pruning in March, thinning peaches in April and May, hoeing tomatoes in June, peach picking from July 18 through August, then a month of picking grapes in Lodi or maybe picking prunes, picking the big olives in Corning in October, and then the winter. When there was no work in the fields, he would take odd jobs; a man could always get along. If he made enough during the year, he would drive to Mexico with Natividad, at least for Christmas, visiting the family in Autlan.

For three years the brothers lived together, their relationship growing further and further apart. In 1958, Natividad decided to give up full-time labor contracting. He was making money, enough to open a café in Marysville with his old friend, Ray Duron, as a silent partner. Running a café was easier than working in the summer sun. For a percentage, Natividad permitted Juan to use his state license to contract labor.

The following year, Juan met Gloria Moreno, another green card, who was working as a cook with her mother in a labor camp near his home. The two women were cooking for 200 men, three meals a day, working from five o'clock in the morning until sunset. The courtship was more practical than romantic, Corona still a man of the old country. "I long time been single, you know," he explained later, "and I figured somebody the same—we could get together, see. So we can share the work." If it was practical, it was also successful. "We got together pretty good after that, you know. I used to farm in this camp and she cook for the men."

Corona took his responsibilities as a husband seriously. Protective of his new wife, he did the shopping and made the major decisions. Guarded by her mother until she married, Gloria Corona was now sheltered by the handsome, stocky man with whom she lived. She was greatly to regret that she learned so little English and never learned to drive.

With the marriage, Juan and Natividad parted. The older brother insisted the younger buy their home in the town of Live Oak, a business arrangement that still rankled Juan thirteen years later. "I had to buy his part of the house, the truck and the car. He charged me too much but I had to take it because I was broke."

Marriage and the birth of the oldest girl, Martha, in 1960 made Juan Corona even more determined to succeed. Working either as a laborer himself or as a contractor from early dawn to after dark, he also studied English and American history and institutions at Yuba Community College in Marysville. Across the hall, in another classroom, a Yuba City policeman by the name of Roy Whiteaker was taking classes in the techniques of law enforcement.

By the mid-1960s Juan Corona was considered a respected businessman in the community. It was a position he cherished. In 1970 he joined La Associacion de los Charros, a nominal horseman's group patterned after similar organizations in Mexico which ostensibly promoted riding skills. Corona was less interested in riding a horse than he was in giving his growing family the cachet of membership in this most prestigious of Mexican-American associations.

The contracting was often hard, the hours always long, but the Coronas were earning middle-class respectability. Corona was proud of his reputation, both with the growers for whom he contracted labor and with the workers who year after year came back to sign on to his crews. He was succeeding, largely by hard work in an occupation fast disappearing.

Automation had reduced the need for large manpower pools in California's farmlands. Federal legislation had restricted the number of green cards in order to make available more jobs for American citizens who tended to settle in one area rather than follow the crops. Still, when the harvest came, the growers had to work quickly. And no worker was as good as the Mexican national, the green card. Juan Corona worked only green cards; he had learned that after handling crews for his older brother. Natividad had used the derelicts and fruit tramps from Marysville's Skid Row, and Juan had found them unreliable. "Too much trouble. They pick box, maybe box and a half, and they want to quit, want to go to town." And unlike many of the 900 contractors holding licenses, Corona would not use women and children. The growers didn't want them, fearing accidents; Corona didn't want men traveling with families because he could not house the women in the bunkhouse with the rest of the crew.

By 1966, Corona was well established. That year, for the first time, he obtained the contract for the Sullivan ranch, and the free use of the large bunkhouse and kitchen for his crews, whether they were working on the ranch or not.

Now, five years later, on a rainy night in May, the reputation of the ambitious Juan Corona would be destroyed. While newsmen and cameramen questioned an evasive Sheriff Whiteaker, Undersheriff Frank Cartoscelli was organizing two search teams. Captain John Littlejohn led a group of five men, joined later by two other deputies, to the Corona home; at the same time, Cartoscelli himself would take a second team to search the barracks and cookhouse on the Sullivan ranch.

Because he had to get up at four-thirty that morning to work, Corona was sleeping on a mattress thrown on the floor of the bedroom when Captain Littlejohn knocked on the front door. At three-fifteen, the Corona's maid, Graciella Carlos, opened the front door, the sleepy Corona following her, a blanket over his shoulders.

Captain Littlejohn handed the frightened Corona the search warrant as the five officers entered the living room. Deputy Robert Wilcox, armed with an M-1 carbine, guarded the door. Corona looked at the papers and, hapless, shrugged. He couldn't understand the rococo cant. Littlejohn began reading the search warrant aloud.

Meanwhile the searchers were combing the house and garage, ignoring the crying children and the terrified Gloria Corona. One of the deputies telephoned for a translator while Littlejohn frisked Corona, removing a pocket knife from his pants.

Deputies confiscating knives from the kitchen, clothes from both the house and garage, and an array of tools, the search continued. Among the twenty-seven items booked as evidence were: a two-foot crowbar "rusty with possible bloodstains"; a posthole digger with "possible bloodstains" and "mud and hair on digging portion"; two pairs of men's shorts, "one with possible bloodstains" stuffed in a zippered bag under the front seat of Corona's Chevrolet van; and a "wooden club with possible bloodstains found at the southeast corner of [the] back yard." The deputies located an axe in the garage, a meat cleaver near the chimney, and a bolo machete under the driver's seat of the van. In the master bedroom, Detective Duncan ransacked the green filing cabinet in which Corona kept his business papers, taking two ledgers, four bundles of check stubs, and a checkbook. One of the two ledgers was to become a major element in the case against Juan Corona.

While Littlejohn's deputies picked through the Corona home, the second search team had surrounded the cook shack and mess hall Corona used at the Sullivan ranch. Several workers were sleeping in the barracks when the deputies entered, and a small, dark man was asleep in the adjacent cabin. Deputy Rodemaker talked to the man briefly, learned he could speak only Spanish, then ignored him to turn his attention to the desk in the one-room cabin.

Deputy Sizelove was boosted through an open window of the locked mess hall. In the left bottom drawer of a desk Corona used, Rodemaker discovered a knife in a sheath, a nine-millimeter Browning automatic pistol, and a box of cartridges. Deputy Mason put down his camera long enough to unload the rusty pistol of the three rounds remaining in the clip, then handed the weapon and the sheathed knife to Cartoscelli. The undersheriff in turn passed them on to the evidence officer, Detective Gregory, who was to tag the weapons, pointing out a stain that looked like blood on the slide under the barrel of the pistol. From a shelf in the kitchen area another deputy found a second knife, stamped "Tennessee Toothpick" on the blade and rolled up in a magazine. It, too, had small brown stains on the guard. The knives and the pistol would be significant in shaping the prosecution's case against the farm labor contractor.

In the mess hall, one of the deputies snuffed out the religious candle left carefully burning in the sink, then began picking up the larger knives in the kitchen area of the building. A quick search of Corona's pickup parked next to the mess hall yielded nothing.

At four o'clock, the interpreter arrived at the Corona home on Richland Road. According to Corona, the young man, Jesse Escovedo, told the bewildered contractor "it would take all night, all day to read those papers." Escovedo, speaking in Spanish, read to Corona from a card, detailing his rights to counsel and to remain silent, what law enforcement officers call "the Miranda card" after the 1966 United States Supreme Court decision in *Miranda v. Arizona*. Corona remembered only that the interpreter told him, "You have to get an attorney," and that the deputies "had to go to the river and dig for about seven men."

Forty-five minutes later, Captain Littlejohn and Detective Sergeant Purcell, according to the captain's written report, placed Juan Vallejo Corona, thirty-eight, "under arrest for Section 187 PC, nine counts" on the basis of the evidence seized under authority of the search warrant. Moments later, he was handcuffed and led to the patrol car outside. It would be the last time that Juan Corona would ever set foot in the house on Richland Road of which he was so proud.

The Sutter County jail takes up the back portion of the courthouse, a Greco-Roman relic of the last decades of the nineteenth century when civic pride demanded brick and plaster imitations of marble and stone antiquities. The interior of the building had been progressively remolded through the years; the courtroom upstairs had new oak paneling; air conditioners squatted on the window sills.

The sheriff's office on the side of the building was crowded with reporters when Captain Littlejohn and Detective Purcell led the handcuffed Corona through the side door into the tiny reception area. The photographs of twelve former sheriffs glared at the intruder. Corona was led through the room, past the staring desk clerk and the still-muddy deputies who had dug earlier that night on the western bank of the Feather River. There was none of the good feeling, none of the self-congratulation and pride that usually accompanies "the good pinch," the difficult investigation concluded by an arrest. The enormity of the crime was numbing.

Corona was fingerprinted, then photographed, front view and left profile, the booking number propped below his chin. His pockets were emptied —with wallet, keys, and change placed in a property envelope. He was permitted to make a telephone call. Unable to remember the telephone number of his younger brother Pedro, Corona finally dialed Ray Duron's home. He asked the ranch foreman to tell Pedro what had happened and to look after Gloria and the children. The call completed, Corona was led to one of the four cells in the women's wing of the small jail.

About five o'clock in the morning, the barely comprehending Corona was locked up. "I couldn't sleep. I was thinking, you know. Pretty bad, pretty scared." As a man who respected authority and was deferential to police officers, Corona was doubly terrified. For an hour and a half he sat in the barren jail cell, a guard watching him, worrying about his family. Gloria and the girls would have to move if he was locked up; the house payments were $150 a month and he couldn't work in a jail. This was big trouble.

Corona didn't know the tall man with the sharp nose standing on the outside of the barred doors, his eyes still puffed with interrupted sleep. The man introduced himself as an attorney, Roy Van den Heuval, the public defender. As public defender, Van den Heuval had not been officially informed that he had a new client; he only went to make certain Corona had an attorney and to advise him of his rights.

"Do you have an attorney?" Van den Heuval asked.

"Yes, my family's getting one," the dark man said through the cell bars. Van den Heuval told Corona to be sure he talked to his attorney before he talked to anyone else, handed Corona his card through the bars, and left.

Roy Van den Heuval had been the Sutter County public defender for seven years, representing at public expense those people indicted on both misdemeanor and felony charges who were unable to pay for private counsel. The job was his on a contract basis, a supplement to his income from the private practice of law. The workload not overly demanding, in many counties the appointment was considered a choice political plum.

Outside the cell area, Van den Heuval saw District Attorney Dave Teja. Though they met in the courtroom frequently, the two men were not friendly; playing out their adversary roles, they were civil to each other, respectful of one another's skills as a lawyer, but distant.

Teja told the defense attorney that Detective Purcell was drawing up the complaint charging Corona with nine counts of murder. It would be ready for the arraignment around noon that day. Just to play it safe, Teja said, it might be wise for Van den Heuval to be there. Teja was going to ask Judge John Hankins to come over from Marysville to arraign Corona since the justice court judge here in Yuba City was not a lawyer. This case was too important to have it screwed up right at the start by a mistake like that. A non-lawyer might be all right for a traffic ticket, but not for a case involving nine murders.

While the sheriff answered reporters' questions, Undersheriff Cartoscelli was organizing a detail of six men to excavate the three possible grave sites left undug the night before. By eight-thirty in the morning of May 26, 1971, the seven men were digging once again on the riverbank south of the fork in the dirt road on the Sullivan ranch. It took an hour to expose the body; Reserve Deputy Ernest Johnson's report, completed six weeks later with the aid of Deputy Lester Perrucci, noted blandly, "Victim was face up in grave. He was wearing a shirt which was pulled up over his head and his arms were crossed above his face, not touching his face. Victim was also wearing shorts and socks."

Half an hour later, the sweating deputies had moved 400 yards to the north to dig out the next body. While other deputies came and went, five rotated the shovels to dig out the hole, piling the wet topsoil, then the drier earth below, alongside the excavation. It took them nearly an hour to uncover the body. Once again, the victim's arms were crossed about his head, his shirt pulled up to cover his face.

Fifteen yards from the grave site of the eleventh victim, the twelfth was found. Nearby were the empty graves of the first two victims dug the night before. It took only half an hour of digging to exhume the body, Reserve Deputy Johnson's report stated. Once again, "victim was face up in grave. He was wearing a shirt which was pulled up over his head, arms were crossed above face, but not touching face. Victim was also wearing shorts."

When the bodies had been removed to the Chapel of the Twin Cities, Cartoscelli returned to the courthouse. He had been on duty now for more than twenty-four hours and he was tired as he sketched in the details of the morning's digging for Sheriff Whiteaker. Because Detective Sergeant Purcell's complaint charging Corona with nine murders was already written, the sheriff decided not to add further counts to the complaint. They could amend it later; the nine counts they had would be enough to hold Corona anyway.

Fatigue and the sheer number of bodies had dulled the officers' senses by then. None of them had heard of, let alone experienced, anything like this. Some who had been in the military had experienced sudden death, but a war in the South Pacific or in Korea was not a quiet May in Yuba City. The shock was numbing, and only the fact that they had the killer locked in a cell lifted the pall.

While Detective Gregory completed his three-page report on the excavation of the seven bodies of the day before, Detective Sergeant Purcell telephoned the state Department of Justice's Criminal Identification and Investigation division. CII promised a man from the Latent Prints Section and a criminalist from the lab to assist in the investigation.

Purcell then took a statement from Roy DeLong, the man who had first reported "Pete" Beierman missing three weeks before. DeLong had spent the night in "protective custody" in the Marysville jail and had been brought across the river earlier that morning.

DeLong, fifty-two, resident of the Wicks-Worley Hotel in Marysville, told the detective, yes, he knew "Pete," last saw him "right about six weeks" ago at the "corner of D and Third. We were standing on the corner talking."

"Did you see Pete leave with anyone?" Purcell asked.

"A guy walked up to us, but I didn't pay any attention to him, I think it was a Mexican, and asked Pete if he wanted to do a little work. Pete said yeah, he'd work a few hours and they walked off."

"Did you see if they left in a car," Purcell asked.

"They left in a yellow looking panel," the stubble-faced DeLong answered, confirming the earlier report from the Marysville Police Department.

"Could you recognize this man?"

"No sir, I couldn't."

Purcell sighed. There went an eyewitness to tie Corona to one of the dead men. Well, they still had enough to go on, the receipts in that first grave, the bloodstained weapons they had found this morning, the fact that Corona was around where the dead men were found. They would need more, but it would hold up for a while anyway.

While Purcell, Gregory, and later Littlejohn worked on their reports, the sheriff was talking to the press about the killings, the search in the rain the night before, the lightning arrest. No, he didn't know much about Corona. He was a contractor, worked on the Sullivan ranch. They'd have to get what they could from Corona's family. His wife was in there now with him.

Gloria Corona had called Pedro—Juan's younger brother and the closest to him—when the deputies left the house on Richland Road earlier that morning. Frightened and crying, she told him what had happened. Now after breakfast, Pedro had brought his sister-in-law to the jail to see her husband.

The meeting was difficult. Gloria cried as she talked to her husband, the jailer looking on as the frightened man in the rumpled clothes tried to calm his wife.

Corona was worried about his wife and the four girls. Through the twelve years of their married life he had protected Gloria, fulfilling a man's responsibilities to his family. Now he could not. Natividad was in Mexico, and Felix had left for Phoenix a month before. That left only Pedro, the youngest brother in the United States, to take care of Gloria and the girls for him—and Pedro had Lencha and his own children to worry about. It was a lot to ask of his brother, who had only his own labor-contracting business in the Yuba City area to support them.

Calming his wife, Corona told her to ask Pedro to visit him. There was some money in the bank and maybe Pedro could help him find an attorney. There was an attorney fellow there that morning already, but he didn't know how much that man would charge.

His wife gone, Corona returned to the stripped down bunk in his cell to worry about his family.

4

"A Totally Unreal Case"
May 26, 1971

State Highway 70 runs due north from the capital, barren asphalt cleaving the fertile Sacramento Valley. In the northeast, the cumulus clouds gather in the afternoon over the foothills of the Sierras, enticing billows shrouding thunderous downdrafts—a pilot's nemesis for all their beauty. Westward lies the distant coastal range, worn down by erosion, plow, and subdividers.

For forty miles the highway splits rice paddies, stoop crops, orchards of prunes, plums, peaches, and pears. The tar softening in the hot sun, it pauses at the crossroads junction of East Nicolaus, then runs on, paralleling the Feather River.

Then the highway encounters a few scattered houses clustering in small communities—first Olivehurst, then Linda, finally the Beale Air Force Base turnoff. Just beyond, the asphalt tops the bank of the Yuba River a half-mile from where it flows into the Feather, the bed of which is more sand than water since the dams were built. On the other side of the river, Marysville, California—population 10,400, elevation 61 feet—hunkers in the lee of the 100-year-old levee.

On May 26, 1971, the cumulus clouds growing darker with the threat of more rain, the morning sun barely felt, the out-of-town reporters drove over the bridge and into Marysville, past the restored Chinese Joss House. They were from Sacramento bureaus of the two major wire services, from the three television stations, and the two daily papers, the *Bee* and the *Union*.

They drove through Marysville, ignoring everything but the highway signs, following Route 70 through the town, past the out-of-date store windows and the State Theatre. The highway was now called E Street, its rural freedom bounded by traffic lights and pedestrian crosswalks.

The reporters knew little about the story, just what the desk editors had handed them from the first wire service copy that morning. A local correspondent, what the wires call a "stringer," had called the Associated Press and United Press International bureaus in Sacramento. He had quickly dictated stories based on the information the sheriff had given him early in the morning. Nine bodies found in an orchard, a suspect in custody.

The wire services were not interested in a single murder in some little town nobody had ever heard of, especially when the dead man was only a bum; the death of Kenneth Whitacre had gone unnoticed by everyone except the local Marysville *Appeal-Democrat* and the Sacramento *Union*. But nine murders, that was big news—too big to be left to stringers for long. The wires, the papers, the television stations were on their way.

The TV station wagons drove west on State 20, through the gauntlet of prefabricated take-outs and drive-ins, over the long bridge above the Feather River bed separating Yuba county on the east from Sutter on the west. Midway across the bridge, they passed the sign reading "Yuba City, Pop. 14,002, Ele. 62."

The courthouse lawn was crowded, the curiosity seekers and doom sayers there to catch a hoped-for glimpse of the man who had murdered nine people. While the cameramen set up their equipment, the reporters went around to the side entrance and the sheriff's department. It was chaotic inside the small reception area.

Was the sheriff there? No. A P.R. man? Don't have one. Well, anyone who can give us some information? Only the sheriff can give out any information. As the morning wore on, the woman at the desk became more cross in her answers. She had taken calls from all over—Los Angeles, San Francisco, Chicago, New York—everyone wanting to know about the killings and Corona. The first ones she had given to the sheriff, until he told her to stop ringing him.

Now Sheriff Whiteaker was talking with the district attorney in the courthouse annex, complaining that the press was badgering him. He didn't want to give out the wrong information, but he wanted to help. Did Teja have any ideas?

Between them they settled on some simple guidelines. Tell the press the facts of the crime, the facts of the arrest, but discuss nothing that might be used as evidence—not the receipts, not the weapons with bloodstains, nothing about the information he had put into his affidavit early that morning. Essentially they were using standards put forward by a joint committee of the California Newspaper Publishers' Association and the state bar association, guidelines formulated in the wake of the precedent-setting Sheppard case.*

* In 1966, the United States Supreme Court ruled in an 8–1 decision that Cleveland osteopath Sam Sheppard had been denied a fair trial because of "the carnival atmosphere" generated by sensational press coverage of the case, both before and

The wire service reporters and those writing for afternoon papers were forced to work quickly, taking what information they could get, and dictating stories over the telephone in order to make early editions. As the tenth, eleventh, and twelfth bodies were found, they rewrote the leads for subsequent editions—time enough for a write-through later. The Sacramento *Bee*'s first edition reported nine dead,. relying on the wire stories; the second edition had eleven victims, the last edition twelve. In Los Angeles, the Hearst flagship *Herald-Examiner* progressively reevaluated the breaking story, each time increasing its importance. The first edition carried the story of nine dead, from the UPI wire, in column one on the front page, the spot usually reserved for the second most important story of the day. With more time to make up the second edition, the story was moved to columns one through three; the third edition bannered "11 Machete Murders," and to give the story an immediacy, the desk editor wrote a subhead: "Calif. Victims Found in Orchards." Ultimately, the Sunset, or last, edition trumpeted "12 Machete Murders."

As the death toll mounted, so did the number of reporters. By midmorning, newsmen from San Francisco, 120 miles southwest of Yuba City, had joined the early arrivals. More reporters from the Sacramento bureaus of the wire services and men who normally covered legislative affairs were detailed by their editors to the story. Three-man television crews from San Francisco's stations clustered in front of the courthouse, jostling with wire service photographers for the best vantage point.

There is an excitement that accompanies a large gathering of newsmen. Competitors they may be, but on a story emanating from a single source, they become allies. Individually, they are a nuisance—necessary, but annoying; collectively, their presence generates heavy pressure for information. Only the most experienced people—national politicians and entertainers are best at it—can handle a badgering press. Neither District Attorney Teja nor Sheriff Whiteaker was experienced.

Having finished his talk with the district attorney, the tired Whiteaker agreed to answer questions. He described Corona briefly, stating that the labor contractor "speaks little English." In response to another question, Whiteaker assured the reporters, "We're certain he committed the murders."

There were twelve bodies found on the Sullivan ranch. All were "killed

---

during Sheppard's trial for the murder of his pregnant wife twelve years before. Justice Tom C. Clark's decision noted that the trial court judge might have "proscribed extrajudicial statements by any lawyer, party, witness or court official which divulged prejudicial matters. . . ." In the intervening years, courts across the country had come to routinely issue so-called "gag orders" in those cases which provoked widespread press coverage. Whiteaker and Teja were anticipating there would be a similar prohibition on public comment in the Corona case; additionally, their self-imposed restraint, before a gag order was issued, would minimize chances of a reversal on Sheppard grounds.

by the same person over a period of five or six weeks," the sheriff said. He described the wounds, adding, "I would rule out an axe as the murder weapon; it could have been either a machete or a large, heavy knife." Two of the graves, Whiteaker said, were "probably dug within the last forty-eight hours."

The reporters were plainly impressed with the worn young sheriff trying to answer the four or five questions shouted whenever he paused for breath. Whiteaker was nothing like their concept of the rural law enforcement officer; he dressed well, spoke quietly, and sounded as if he knew what he was doing. Apparently he ran a pretty good department; they had this guy Corona fast enough. Thirty-one years old—that would probably make him the youngest sheriff in the state, a good angle for a later story maybe.

It was Sheriff Whiteaker's moment of national attention. The district attorney was asked little; his only reported comment was to say that the case "was totally unreal. I still can't comprehend the totality of the crime." Then the balding lawyer went back inside the sheriff's office to make arrangements for the arraignment.

Under California law, a person arrested for either a misdemeanor or a felony must be brought before a judge within forty-eight hours of his arrest, unless the time expires when the court is not in session. In those cities with heavy criminal calendars, law enforcement officers usually take the full forty-eight hours to prepare their case.

Teja and Whiteaker decided, however, to arraign Corona immediately, and to have the judge advise him of his rights, thereby avoiding a possible appeal on the grounds he had been denied constitutional protections. He discussed the matter with Van den Heuval and Judge J. J. Hankins, who suggested that Corona be arraigned in the sheriff's office rather than in the justice court down the hall. That way the labor contractor would not have to walk a gauntlet of cameramen anxious for pictures of the mass murderer.

At five minutes past noon, less than eight hours after he was arrested, Juan Corona came before the bar for the first time. Satisfying himself that Corona understood English, Judge Hankins asked, "Do you have an attorney?"

Unsure, Corona paused, then said he did not. "Have you been in contact with an attorney?" Judge Hankins asked.

"Well, this man," Corona answered, pointing to Van den Heuval. "He come and see me."

"The record will show that the defendant is handing me a piece of paper with the name of "Van den Heuvel, 431 Center Street, 673-9515," the judge said. "Mr. Corona, do you have funds to hire an attorney?" Hankins asked.

"I think so."

Judge Hankins was unsure. "Okay, when you say you 'think so,' we are talking about an attorney's fee of probably not less than $5,000 and maybe as high as $20,000. Now, do you have any kind of cash available for any attorney?"

Corona conceded he did not. "All right. It's going to be the order of the court that the public defender will be appointed to represent the defendant. The record will show that Mr. Van den Heuvel, the public defender, is present in court."

The proceedings to that point had been staged by the district attorney. They had a good case, and needed nothing from Corona. It was better, for all concerned, that he have an attorney right now; the judge's appointment, even when Corona had indicated he had some money with which to hire a private attorney, would effectively nullify a number a possible grounds for appeal. If Corona wanted a private attorney, he could always hire one later.

Van den Heuval immediately postponed for one week Corona's actual plea to the nine counts of murder contained in Sergeant Purcell's complaint. He needed time to study the complaint and the available police files, he said.

Then the district attorney raised the question of pretrial publicity. "The case has gained nationwide notoriety. The sheriff's office has been bombarded by requests for interviews and information. . . . We feel that so far he has managed the problem of prejudicial pre-trial publicity very well. . . .

"However, he's being badgered right now for permission by various news photographers, both television and wire service, for photographs of the defendant. He's being asked for mug shots. He's denied this so far." Teja had no particular court order in mind, he told the judge. "I bring this to the attention of Mr. Van den Heuval so that if he cares for some order protecting his client's rights we can get it at this time and avoid any change of venue."

Judge Hankins took it upon himself to issue what was to be the first of four so-called gag rules in the Corona case. The district attorney, the sheriff and his deputies, and court attachés were ordered "not to discuss this case and not to give any information other than that information which is public record and in the records of the court and are not to discuss any of the evidentiary things or matters that could be considered evidentiary." The order also applied to Van den Heuval.

Judge Hankins also agreed to go out into the courthouse hallway, where the growing number of newsmen waited, to tell them of the gag rule and to outline the legal procedures.

With Corona again in his cell and the newsmen scattered to telephones and portable typewriters, the Sheriff's Department settled down to the drudgery of law enforcement. Deputy Mason drove out to the garage of the Twin Cities funeral home to take pictures of the wounds on the victims dug up the day before. All but one had been stabbed and hacked; The eleventh victim found that morning had been shot. Don Stottlemyer, a criminalist for the state's Criminal Identification and Investigation Division, arrived from Sacramento; Detective Jerry Harrison took him in tow.

Harrison turned over to Stottlemyer fourteen items gathered up by deputies at the Corona home and Sullivan ranch early that morning, including a hatchet, the posthole digger with possible bloodstains, a hoe, a Levi's jacket found on a shelf in the rafters of the garage at 768 Richland Road, three butcher knives, a meat cleaver, a hunting knife, the "two-and-one-half-foot wooden club with possible bloodstains," the machete found under the floor mat of Corona's Chevrolet van, a leather bag found under the front seat of the van containing the two pairs of men's shorts, one with possible bloodstains, and six nine-millimeter Luger shells. It would be Stottlemyer's task to analyze the bloodstains on these items and to compare the weapons with the multiple wounds on the bodies.

An hour later, Harrison and Stottlemyer went over two of Corona's vehicles which the sheriff had impounded at the A-1 Towing Service and Body Shop. Harrison found a strand of red hair in the trunk of Corona's Impala, while Stottlemyer scraped off samples of red stains from the trunk latch and the rubber molding on the turtle deck. A black belt, the floor mat, and two throw rugs were taken as evidence. From the interior of the van, Stottlemyer scraped six small stains, the flakes carefully placed in pliofilm plastic bags and labeled; a seventh stain was scraped from the rear of the vehicle. Stottlemyer also removed a pair of rubber boots from the van while Harrison watched.

The Sheriff's Department was operating with a skeleton staff—the deputies who had dug the night before finally relieved from duty—when the telephone call came. It was Ray Duron asking for Jerry Gregory, the detective with whom he had had the most contact since the day Whitacre's body was found. Gregory was home, sleeping, and Duron's call was transferred to Detective Denver Duncan. The foreman was half apologetic. He had just come from the Ferrie block; it looked like there was another body buried there.

Duncan and Detective Cochran drove to the Sullivan ranch to meet Duron and the owner. The two detectives took a quick look at the depression Duron pointed out to them in the orchard and, in the formal cant of police reports, "determined at this time that this was another grave site and the grave will be dug in the AM of 5/27/71."

The decision to delay digging until the next day was made for three reasons. It was getting late in the day—almost four o'clock—and the normal day-side crew would not return to duty until tomorrow morning.

The sky was heavy with the threat of more rain. Corona was in custody; whatever evidence they were to find in the thirteenth grave would only reinforce the case against the murderer.

While the deputies tramped through the humidity and mud of the Ferrie block, Doctors Connolly and Clement were working in the embalming room of the Chapel of the Twin Cities. Armed with an array of surgical and carpenter's tools, the two men worked at the stainless steel tables—shallow sinks actually—taking on the ten bodies found along the riverbank in the order in which they had been numbered.

The autopsy procedure was routinely quick. As each dirt-coated body was placed on the table, the doctor surveyed it for visible wounds. These he marked either on preprinted diagrams of the human body or in notes, the rubber-gloved fingers probing crushed skulls, the steel ruler thrust into hack wounds to measure the depth.

The two doctors then attempted to wash some of the dirt from the bodies, the water sluicing off to run down a drain in the embalming table. Their gloves and aprons fouled with mud and flecks of rotting flesh, they used electric saws to cut through the sternum, then scalpels to slice open the abdomen. The flesh peeled back from the ribs, they examined the organs: circulatory system, respiratory system, digestive and genito-urinary tracts. The ten bodies no longer needed privacy, no longer had secrets.

John Doe 1, the first body found on May 25 and the third murder for which Juan Corona was arrested: "The body is that of an apparent white male; approximately five feet six inches in height. External examination of the body reveals a massive skull fracture immediately above the right ear. It measures fourteen centimeters in its greatest diameter. The exploring hand can be admitted through the area of the skull fracture. It involves the temporal and the lower portion of the parietal lobe on the right side. External examination of the body reveals no other trauma." The cause of death, Doctor Connolly wrote in his report that day, was "skull fracture, massive, compound, right temporal parietal bone."

John Doe 2, the fourth victim of the case, had been stabbed in the left chest, the knife entering below the fifth rib to sever the pulmonary artery.

The next body autopsied was identified by papers in his wallet and a savings account passbook from the Roseville, California, branch of the Bank of America. Donald Dale Smith, age sixty-one, had hoarded $255.22 by the time he died of a stab wound in the right chest and a skull fracture.

Number 4 had been bludgeoned to death, Doctor Clement's report noting: "Compound fracture right vertex and lacerated cerebrum." The formality of a doctor's Latin depersonalized the death of the man tentatively identified as John J. Haluka. Number 5 similarly had been stabbed in the right side between the sixth and seventh ribs, the blade puncturing the lung; death, however, could have resulted from either of two skull fractures, Doctor Connolly wrote. Number 6 had died like number 5, a stab wound in the left chest, with multiple skull fractures. "Pete" Beierman, number 7, had been stabbed in the heart, then hacked about the head. In death, the doctors located the gallstones which had given Beierman so much trouble in life.

The eighth body to be autopsied that day had similarly died of a massive skull fracture. As with two others before him, his pants were pulled down around his thighs. The body was described as that of "an apparent Negro male" by Doctor Connolly; the fracture was ten centimeters wide, and extended through both layers of bone in the skull.

The ninth body to be autopsied in the embalming room of the Chapel of the Twin Cities was identified by a Social Security card and temporary driver's license as William E. Kamp. He had died, at the age of sixty, of what appeared to be a skull fracture large enough to "easily" admit Doctor Connolly's hand into the skull cavity. Still unidentified, the last victim washed down and slit open that afternoon had suffered a fractured skull and a stab wound in the left chest. He too was not wearing pants when he was found, Purcell noted.

In another room of the mortuary, Sergeant Purcell and employees of the funeral home inventoried the clothing and property found on the dead men. As chief deputy coroner, Purcell would be legally responsible for its delivery to the next-of-kin, or to the county if the dead man had died without heirs. There was little of value, but enough for the investigators to begin drawing some tentative conclusions.

The John Doe 4 had seven dollars in his pockets, the ninth a total of $8.96. Robbery was not a motive then, even if the killer, for some strange reason, thought that these winos had any money on them. Six of the victims were not wearing pants when they were buried, and one was naked from the waist down. Whatever it meant, it suggested that the dead men knew their killer well enough to be partially undressed in front of him.

Purcell considered the case against Corona to be pretty good, but he knew that with circumstantial evidence only, the jury—if there was one —would want a motive. Purcell knew from his classroom work at Yuba Community College that there was nothing wrong with circumstantial evidence; it was as valid as direct evidence in a court of law. The trouble was, juries didn't always think so; they wanted a motive, some explanation that would make all the circumstantial evidence fall into place.

The lack of a motive would trouble Purcell and his superiors for the next seventeen months.

5

A Rainy Day's Toll

May 27-28, 1971

It was not going to be a good day. It had rained on and off through the night and the dark clouds were still there this morning. Sheriff Whiteaker and Undersheriff Cartoscelli struggled over the assignment of their men. Purcell, Harrison, and Gregory would stay with the follow-up investigation. Mason had to soup the pictures he took the day before. It didn't leave them much, not with all the paper work that had to be done. They would need some help, especially experienced investigators.

By nine o'clock, Cartoscelli and his digging party were at the Sullivan ranch, standing in the muddy soil of the Ferrie block. A large group of newsmen had followed to watch the excavation with Sheriff Whiteaker's permission. As Sutter County backhoe operator Jim Kilmer started his machine, Deputy Sizelove waved the press back. He drew an imaginary line in the air some forty feet from the trench and warned, "Anyone crossing that line spends the night in jail. We're not kidding. We'll book all you guys." An Associated Press reporter later noted laconically, "No one crossed the line."

While the backhoe operator dug in the wet soil to remove the first two or three feet of earth before the deputies carried on by hand, Roy Van den Heuval was hastily preparing an order to be signed by Judge Hankins. Van den Heuval was angry; the day before he had been barred entry to the Sullivan ranch at the California Highway Patrol roadblock; he would be angrier still when he learned that the sheriff had permitted the press onto the ranch while he remained barred.

Sheriff Whiteaker now realized just how big his case was, how much national interest there was in the multiple slayings, the accused killer, and his victims. If he had not understood yesterday's rush of reporters, this morning's San Francisco *Chronicle,* sold in Yuba City, told him. A banner across the front page read, "12 Bodies in Orchard Graves—A Mass

Murder Mystery." There were two Associated Press photos on the front page, Corona's mug shot, which the sheriff had finally released yesterday afternoon, and an aerial photo taken from a low-flying airplane showing the riverbank graveyard. The *Chronicle*'s reporters, George Draper and Paul Avery, had written the lead story, basing most of it on the press conference Whiteaker had held the day before. In addition, the editors used five other stories and six more photos. The *Chronicle*'s play was larger than most, a prelude to the continuing story that was to be on the paper's front page for the next nine days.

The deputies' shovels replaced the backhoe. Whiteaker went off to talk with Ray Duron. The digging went slower than it had with the machine, but the deputies now were looking for evidence in the grave as well as ex-huming a body. At nine-forty-five they had cleared away the dirt around the corpse and had retrieved two pieces of evidence: a half-empty wine bottle found near the dead man's right knee, and an inexplicable, empty Friskies dog food bag on top of the victim's feet.

As the morticians removed the dirt-caked body, Whiteaker held the second of what was to become a morning routine, the daily press con-ference. His deputies would continue to search for victims, he told the reporters clustered around him, "until we quit finding bodies." He ex-pected to uncover at least one, possibly two more today. How many, he couldn't say for sure.

Fettered by the court-imposed gag rule, Sheriff Whiteaker inadvertently provoked speculation in the press that was to have a major impact on the case of the *People v. Juan Corona*. The reporters had heard rumors of a map of the Yuba City area with hand-drawn Xs, a "death map" as it was quickly labeled. Did the deputies find it when they searched Corona's home? Whiteaker declined to comment on the ground that he could not discuss evidentiary matters. In fact, there was a map, but it had been roughed out by the Sheriff's Department after discussions with Ray Duron.

It was Duron who gave the sheriff's deputies the rough map of the Sullivan ranch which they normally used to plan dusting flights and irriga-tion checks. On it Duron marked the places where some of his ranch workers had seen Corona alone. Whiteaker had assigned Cartoscelli to be responsible for digging any graves they located from the map.

The rain began falling again at midday, first a drizzle, then a harsh storm. The search was momentarily suspended while reporters and law enforcement officers ran for cover to the ranch headquarters on the western side of the levee.

In the courthouse, the clerks could not hear the rain falling, but they could feel the gray damp warping the old building. The air in the small offices grew musty from drying raincoats and umbrellas. In Judge Hankins' temporary courtroom on the second floor, the attorneys exchanged terse comments on the weather while waiting for the court reporter.

Van den Heuval had filed his affidavit and petition asking a court order to allow him and his investigator, Norman Hull, onto the Sullivan ranch. District Attorney Dave Teja was opposed to the motion on the ground "that the on-going investigation conducted by the Sutter County Sheriff-Coroner's Office is not doing anything directly to the defendant at this particular time."

Ultimately Judge Hankins worked out a compromise. Van den Heuval might have access to the Sulivan ranch, but if either wanted to see the actual grave digging, he would have to be accompanied by a deputy. Van den Heuval had won a minor skirmish.

In the sheriff's office downstairs, Detective Sergeant Purcell and Detective Harrison were busy turning over more evidence to the CII criminalist, Don Stottlemyer. Their immediate problem now was one of identifying the bodies. They had names for five of the victims; two, Whitacre and Beierman, were positive. The other three were tentatively identified by papers in their pockets: the fifth body as Donald Smith, the sixth as John J. Haluka, the eleventh as William E. Kamp.

For the first time Purcell and the morticians began using a new numbering system for the bodies, a system devised so as to label the victims not only in the order in which they were found, but in the approximate location. Bodies from west of the freeway were prefixed with a "W," bodies east of the freeway with an "E." This was followed by a number denoting the order in which the body was located on the west or east side, and that by a second number denoting that body's overall order among the graves found on both sides of the freeway.

Kenneth Whitacre thus became W-1-1, the first body found on the west side of the freeway, and the first body found. The unidentified corpse discovered in the Ferrie block on the Sullivan ranch became W-2-2. John Doe 1, the first corpse found in the thicket along the bank of the Feather River was renumbered E-1-3; the second (John Doe 2) E-2-4; the third, now tentatively identified as Donald Smith, became "victim East No. 3" on a report signed by Stottlemyer. The confusions caused by this new and more complicated numbering system would dog the prosecution's case from beginning to end.

There were also all the leads that came in by telephone from people who had read about the case in the newspaper; the more publicity there was, the more people came forward. The trouble was that most of the callers were either cranks looking for a little notoriety or people whose imagination was out of control. Still, some were asking about missing relatives or friends, any one of whom might be among the unidentified bodies lying on the floor of the mortuary's garage. You had to follow up, even if it only meant writing a report and letting Jack Purcell decide if it was worth looking into.

The rain slackened, then stopped. On the Sullivan ranch, the small digging party followed Ray Duron from the labor camp over the levee, then turned south at the fork. It was out there, near the property line separating the Sullivan and Prindeville ranches that the men had seen Corona. As they'd told Duron, it was strange the labor contractor was there at the time; there was no work going on.

The deputies swept the orchard while backhoe operator Jim Kilmer waited beside his machine. At one-thirty that afternoon, near the northeast corner of the orchard, they located the grave of the fourteenth victim. With the help of Kilmer's backhoe, it took just one half-hour to unearth the body and bring it to the muddy surface of the orchard. Deputy Steve Sizelove, the reporting officer, picked through the dirt-caked pockets, looking for some identification. The dead man's name apparently was James Howard. He was carrying two bottles of pills dated April 30, 1971, and a Greyhound bus ticket made out the following day. Welfare papers in a pocket indicated that Howard too was one of the drifters who spent their days in Wino Park in Marysville.

A half-hour later, Cartoscelli's crew began digging at the south end of the orchard in the grave of the fifteenth victim. With Kilmer's backhoe doing most of the excavating, the deputies located the body in just eight minutes. The dead man was fully clothed, but his trousers were unzipped. Once again Sizelove gingerly poked through the clothing, gagging at the sickly sweet smell of the putrified body. A set of dentures, four food stamp books, and a food stamp application form all had the victim's name, Jonah Smallwood. The food stamp books indicated the victim was on welfare, another of the fruit tramps who drank up what they earned.

It took longer than they had expected to find the next group of victims. Duron led the deputies north on the muddy track that paralleled the riverbank, past the fork in the road, the trash dump, and the irrigation pump house. The party drove in a sweeping arc from the fork out onto a finger of low-lying farm land formed by a hairpin bend in the rain-swollen river's course. The riverbottom orchard in the northeast corner of the 600-acre ranch could be easily missed unless one knew it was there.

At five-thirty on the afternoon of May 27, the searchers located five depressions in the wild bracken along the western edge of the prune orchard—graves of victims sixteen, seventeen, eighteen, nineteen, and twenty. The graves were partially covered with torn shrubbery and short grass parched in the heat of a dry spring and now crushed under a ring of dirt surrounding each grave.

The first grave was in a small clearing in the wild blackberry bushes that tangled below the spring-green trees. The body was three feet below the surface, lying on its back, the legs bent at the knees and pressed against the chest. While the sheriff and undersheriff watched, Sizelove pulled on rubber gloves once again to pick through the pockets of the victim's clothing. Cigar smoke hung in the damp air, masking the odor of the decomposed body lying on the black loam of the riverbottom. A Social Security card, a jail release form and a set of dentures with a name scratched on it identified the victim as Elbert J. T. Riley.

Fifteen minutes later, the crew moved to the second grave. Within ten minutes, Deputy Bill Rodemaker had waved off the backhoe and begun scraping away the loose soil with his shovel. A little more than three feet below the surface the deputy uncovered first a wallet, then the body itself. Lying beside the body were a handful of personal papers and an eye-patch; Rodemaker handed them up to Sizelove, then turned back to look at the victim's head. The young deputy felt his stomach heave; half of the dead man's face was missing. Rodemaker could see the mottled mass that had once been the brain of Paul B. Allen.

It took another ten minutes to move the floodlights in the orchard twilight to the site of the eighteenth grave. The body of Edward Martin Cupp was three feet from the surface, lying on its back, the legs crossed. Both shoes were untied. Sizelove tagged the evidence—a receipt dated April 1, change totaling $1.81, a Velvet brand tobacco tin, and a small pile of pocket-worn personal papers.

One hundred and fifty feet from the eighteenth grave, the deputies found another body. His pockets were empty, but one of the digging party found a red hard-hat where it had been tossed in the berry bushes at one end of the grave. The hard-hat would later identify Albert Hayes, known in lower Marysville as "Scratchy."

The digging went rapidly, no more than thirty minutes for each body. The crew stopped only long enough for Deputy Rodemaker to make plaster casts of tire tracks found between graves nineteen and twenty. The twentieth body was buried in a grave more than ten feet long at the surface; the killer had started to dig, hit a hidden root, then continued beyond the obstruction.

At the mortuary, two doctors had begun autopsies on the eight bodies recovered that day on the Sullivan property. While Doctors Clement and Connolly had conducted hundreds of autopsies for Sutter County, neither was a pathologist. Furthermore, their reports were sketchy. Connolly's of the first body found on the riverbank ran just twelve lines, Clement's of the second but eleven. Scanty reports such as these might be sufficient in the case of an accidental death or an apparent suicide, but not in a homicide case where there was any likelihood of a trial.

Therefore, Whiteaker and Purcell, acting in their dual capacities as sheriff and coroner, had called Sacramento County Coroner George Neilsen asking for help. They decided to re-autopsy the twelve bodies already examined by Clement and Connolly; it would be best if they transported these bodies to Neilsen's new morgue in Sacramento. Facilities there were better, and there was ample room to refrigerate the bodies.

In the meantime, Neilsen agreed to send two of his men to conduct the autopsies on the victims dug up that day. Both Joseph Masters and his immediate superior, Pierce Rooney, were forensic pathologists, board-certified and long experienced.

While the local doctors had performed autopsies in just twenty minutes each, the painstaking Rooney and Masters took an hour for each. From eight-thirty on the night of May 27 until the early morning hours of the following day, they worked at the Twin Cities mortuary, pointing out wounds for Deputy Roger Mason to photograph or taking color slides themselves, detailing organ by organ the medical biography and savage deaths.

While the doctors worked at the mortuary, Detectives Gregory and Jerry Harrison were taking statements from potential witnesses. David B. Schmidl had called to say he had once seen Corona in the riverbottom orchard—where they were now recovering bodies. Detective Harrison asked him to come in so they could get his statement on tape.

Shortly after, Gregory interviewed two of the Sullivan ranch workers who had pointed out to Duron places on the ranch where Corona had been seen and where later bodies had been discovered. With Ray Duron interpreting, Moses and José Ramirez placed the labor contractor in the riverbottom prune orchard on May 23, four days before. They had been delivering ladders to the orchard when they saw Corona drive into the orchard, park his red and white pickup truck, and walk off into the underbrush. Corona seemed to be looking for something in the under-brush, Duron translated for Moses Ramirez—perhaps "something to cut because he kept pushing aside and moving around," José Ramirez added. It was Corona's later arrest that made the two ranch workers suspicious, Duron told Detective Gregory. Gregory was pleased; the longer the investigation wore on, the more circumstantial evidence they accumulated pointing to the man now locked up in the women's wing of the Sutter County jail.

One by one the investigators finished their reports, retrieved their raincoats and said good night, too tired to hang around the sheriff's office for the usual small talk with the night watch. The coffee grew cold; the typewriters fell silent, muzzled by plastic covers. The desk officer shifted in his chair, trying to find a comfortable spot where the police special wouldn't rub against his thigh or the holstered handcuffs dig into his back. It would be a quiet night, what with the rain and all. Funny thing though, since this body search had started, they didn't seem to have any crime reports; it was as if the one crime was more than enough for even the burglars or car thieves.

In the hotels and motels, reporters snubbed out the last cigarettes and said good night to their workaday acquaintances.

By morning, their stories and film had been printed or broadcast, their editors asking for more copy. What was this about Corona being in a mental hospital? That explained everything, how some guy could kill twenty people. He had to be a nut.

The habits of a profession foster problems. Self-protection demands that each reporter have what every other reporter has; the *Appeal-Democrat*'s discovery of Corona's mental illness fifteen years before became public property. It was impossible to deny the commitment papers; unqualified, the bald fact of the mental commitment was incorporated in the copy from Yuba City.

At breakfast the next morning—May 28—in the coffee shops along Colusa Highway, the reporters read the morning *Sacramento Union* and *San Francisco Chronicle,* favoring the latter because of its reputation, paying less attention to the more restrained *Union.*

The *Chronicle*'s banner shrieked, "Twenty Bodies—Death Map," a subhead announcing, "Suspect Has Mental Record." The story by George Draper and Paul Avery was meticulously accurate:

> Sheriff's deputies following a crude map dug eight more bodies out of Yuba City's orchards last night, bringing the total of corpses found to 20.
>
> A high county official revealed to The Chronicle late last night that "something that could be called a map" was being used to make the gruesome finds.
>
> Earlier Sheriff Roy D. Whiteaker had refused to confirm or deny that the "map" of the Yuba City area with hand-drawn X's on it had been found by deputies searching suspect Juan Corona's home with a warrant.

The gag rule, which ostensibly was to protect Juan Corona's right to an unprejudiced jury, had operated to his detriment. Though he talked freely of his case off the record, Sheriff Whiteaker had scrupulously observed the no-comment rule the day before. Still, the effect of the morning's story was to imply that the suspect now under arrest had, in fact, drawn a map of the graveyard he had dug.

The *Chronicle* was in full cry. The Draper-Avery story began on the front page, then filled three full columns on the jump. Additionally, the editors ran a "sidebar," or supplemental story, two pictures, and a map, lavishing space on the biggest news story in the nation. The two reporters had talked to Doctor Benjamin Miller, one of the two doctors who had examined Corona prior to his commitment; Miller no longer remembered the case, but conceded to the reporters that if he had used the words "confused, disoriented, having hallucinations" to describe the farm laborer's condition, "it must have been clear cut."

The morning paper also reported the announcement of Tehama County Sheriff Lyle Williams that the "Yuba City killings are similar to the slaying of an unidentified man whose brutally hacked body was found in Corning on the banks of the Sacramento River in January of 1970.

"Sheriff Williams said the body surfaced after the great winter floods," the *Chronicle* story continued. "The man, he said, had been dead about three months. In the late fall of 1969 Corona was in Corning with a work crew, harvesting the olive crop, the sheriff said."

It was raining once more as the reporters began gathering at the courthouse for Sheriff Whiteaker's third morning press conference. It didn't look as if it would be a big day, not with the rain. There were some questions they could ask about the five bodies found the night before; the reporters for afternoon papers and television stations had deadlines that precluded any report of that late night find.

Yes, they had another grave site located. No, they didn't know how many bodies were buried in the orchards; they would just keep looking until they stopped finding them. No, he wouldn't comment on any map, period. They would try to dig up the body, if that's what it was, when the rain let up. Once again the young law enforcement officer handled himself well, a number of reporters deciding they would hang their stories that day on the sheriff himself.

While the sheriff talked to reporters, Detective Jerry Harrison was typing up the list of evidence seized the morning of Corona's arrest to present formally to the court. That so-called return of the warrant would be filed with Sheriff Whiteaker's original affidavit and request for the warrant along with all the supporting documents Whiteaker and Teja had appended three days before.

Word that Harrison was to return the search warrant had leaked to a handful of the reporters. A group was waiting in the courtroom temporarily occupied by Judge John J. Hankins when a clerk brought the documents in. The waiting reporters clustered around Hankins' desk, telling the balding jurist, "This is what we're looking for." The judge shrugged and pushed the file across to them. State law provided that once a search warrant was returned, it became a public record, open for inspection. "Go ahead, look at it," Hankins told the reporters.

Looking at it and taking notes from it were two different things. Hankins quickly realized that one copy was not enough for the small group of reporters who had been waiting, and certainly would not be adequate for the even larger number who would want to see it as soon as they learned of its availability. In an effort to cooperate, the judge ordered his clerk to make copies of the warrant, the affidavits, and the return. She could hand them out to anyone who asked.

Not having read the documents, Hankins did not at first realize he might have made a serious mistake, one which Juan Corona's attorney would later claim denied Corona any possibility of a fair trial in Sutter County. Left to their own devices for the past four days, denied any information of evidentiary value by Hankins' own gag order, newsmen were suddenly handed sixty-five pages of material constituting the state's case against Juan Corona. While some reporters were skeptical about using it, knowing full well that it incriminated the labor contractor, there was no way not to. If they didn't, somebody else would; pleading Corona's right to a fair trial was not likely to impress an editor who had been beaten by the opposition. The reporters grabbed for copies of the warrant and fled to telephones to dictate stories.

Whiteaker's affidavit detailed the case against Corona: the Marysville Police Department missing-person's report and the subsequent field interrogation of Corona; the two receipts found in the first grave dug up on the riverbank; notice of Corona's earlier mental commitment; and the Marysville Police report of the assault in the Guadalajara Café fifteen months earlier.

Reporters fastened on the mental commitment, and Whiteaker's sworn statement, "Raymond Duron, 1830 Romero Street, Tierra Buena, who is general foreman of the Jack Sullivan ranches in Sutter County and personally acquainted with the said Juan Corona, has advised Detective Sergeant John Purcell of my office that the said Juan Corona is mentally ill." The newsmen now could understand why the confident Whiteaker had repeatedly insisted that Corona was guilty.

In addition, they now had the thirteen-page report of the investigation in February and March 1970 of the assault with intent to commit murder in the Guadalajara Café. A young man by the name of José Romero Raya had been discovered in the rest room of the café around one o'clock in the morning of February 25. He had been hacked about the face and head and when transported to the hospital, the investigating officer wrote, "victim's brain was leaking from one cut on top of his head." Apparently Raya had been hacked with a meat cleaver, the doctors told police, something heavier than a knife anyway. Typically, no one in the bar had seen anything.

The owner of the bar, Natividad Corona, finally had admitted that it was he who had called police. A week later, Natividad Corona showed up at the police station to report he suddenly remembered who had told him about the injured man in the rest room. It was Natividad's younger half-brother, Juan. Juan, the older brother offered, had had a "mental breakdown" and was committed to DeWitt State Hospital.

If the reporters had any doubts about the swift arrest, their reservations were overwhelmed by the list of evidence seized at Corona's home and at the Sullivan ranch. There were possible bloodstains on a crowbar, a posthole digger, and a wooden club. And there were all those weapons, including a machete and meat cleaver that could have been used to hack the skulls of the victims. Off the record, Whiteaker had told some of the reporters that they didn't have a confession; with all this evidence, it didn't look like they would need one.

While the reporters dictated stories based on the return of the first search warrant, Detective Denver Duncan was drafting an affidavit in District Attorney Teja's office for a second. Duncan had remembered that two of the men whose bodies were dug up last night, Paul Allen and Jonah Smallwood, were listed in the ledger he had picked up at the Corona house the night before; the second victim, just identified as Charles Fleming, was also on the list. Apparently they had worked for Corona.

A further search of the house on Richland Road, the Sullivan camp, and the house Corona owned in Live Oak purchased with his brother Natividad might turn up other business records. They would also check with the Live Oak Bank of America for any checks in Corona's bank account. Furthermore, Allen's grave had had an adding machine tape in it; it might match the adding machine left behind at the cookhouse when that building was searched two days before.

Meanwhile, two detectives took inked impressions of the tires on the two vehicles in which blood had been found. (Detective Duncan concluded that the pickup's tires matched the cast made of the track between graves nineteen and twenty.) Captain John Littlejohn, momentarily relieved of his duties as commander of the department's patrol division, delivered to the Sacramento laboratories of CII tree branches that had been strewn over the graves in the north riverbottom orchard; blood samples from the victims; and fingertips excised by the morticians for fingerprinting the ten victims still without any identification. It was a distasteful but necessary business, Littlejohn thought as he drove to Sacramento, the severed fingers wrapped in plastic bags in a box beside him.

The district attorney's office was busy, too. There had been a phone call from the county welfare department. In March 1971, with little farm work available, Corona had applied for the first time in his life for welfare under the Aid for Dependent Children program. Two social workers had visited Corona's home, one of them telling investigators "she noticed something odd about him and that was that every few seconds he would get up and go out in the living room apparently with no motivation except wandering off back and forth." Corona's application had ultimately been turned down because he had, by law, too many assets—the two houses and some cash in the bank.

As the late afternoon rainstorm slackened, Undersheriff Cartoscelli led a four-man digging party back to the Sullivan ranch and the grave of the twenty-first victim. Raindrops brushed from the wild grass soaked their pants as they made their way to the solitary grave at the eastern end of the dirt road which led into the north riverbottom orchard. Ten minutes after they started digging, the deputies uncovered a floodlight bulb, then a small glass bottle, and finally a three-inch piece of rubber which appeared to be carpet padding. Just below the refuse, Deputy Sizelove reported, the body of John Henry Jackson lay jammed against a rolled up sleeping bag.

The dead man was bundled in clothing, wearing his entire wardrobe —Navy peacoat, sweater, two nylon jackets, two shirts, and bib overalls. The deputies couldn't be certain because of the wasted condition of the body, but it appeared the dead man was a black.

6

The Guests of the Community
May 1971

The buttes loom on the horizon, at two thousand feet the most prominent landmarks in the valley. They jut up from the floor of the valley, purple and gold in the late afternoon sun, dominating the flatlands, the lava core of some eons-old volcanoes eroded to landmarks. The Maidu and Wintun Indian tribes had named the buttes "Breathing Spirit" and chiseled precarious handholds and stairs into the third highest of the six peaks. Sky Chief formed the buttes while waiting for his son, Nose Walker, in the antiquity of Maidu oral tradition. The two-thousand-foot range was there when the first of the nomadic bands of hunters and gatherers wandered into the northern valley.

Kenneth Whitacre could see the buttes shimmering in the bright sun as he walked along Colusa Highway on May 19, 1971. Not that he cared much about them, or anything else. Things had been slow around here, he hadn't seen many familiar faces, and work was scarce. He decided to return to the Bay Area, if someone would just put him on the right road. Didn't matter much whether he made it to his sister's in Palo Alto or his brother's in Alameda tomorrow or the next day or the day after that. He didn't have to be anyplace at any time, not since he gave up his truck-driving job with the telephone company.

Forty years old, unmarried, Kenneth Whitacre was labeled a transient in police records—with six arrests for being drunk in public since 1959 and a robbery conviction in Oakland in 1966. Since then he had stayed out of jail, reading his Bible a little and working just enough to pay for a meal or a room in the Grand Hotel on First Street. Diffident or unconcerned, Kenneth Whitacre lived from one day to the next, until the afternoon of May 19, 1971.

Like Whitacre after him, John Augustus Sutter was a wanderer too.

Born in Baden, Germany, in 1803, the restless Sutter had become a Swiss citizen, then served as a captain in the French army. Unsatisfied with military life, he married, launched the first in a series of disastrous business ventures, and eventually fled bankruptcy by sailing to New York in 1833.

It took five years for Captain Sutter to reach San Francisco, where he rented a steamer to sail up the Sacramento River. At the confluence of the Sacramento and American Rivers, on the site of what is now the state capital, Sutter laid out a stronghouse, quickly dubbed Sutter's Fort, and a small colony which he named New Helvetica.

Two years later, the Mexican government gave Sutter a massive grant of land that included most of the northern portion of the fertile Sacramento Valley. In 1847 John Sutter planted the first peaches near his hop farm in what is now Sutter County, importing the fledgling trees from China.

Charles Cleveland Fleming was found buried in a prune orchard twenty miles from John Augustus Sutter's first orchards, on land the Swiss adventurer had used to graze his horses and cattle. The sixty-seven-year-old Fleming had been stabbed and hacked, then dragged to the grave in the Ferrie block and buried hastily.

Fleming was never missed. A wanderer who apparently shifted from place to place as the mood struck him, Fleming had few friends in Marysville and Yuba City. He would be cremated and buried in a pauper's grave at county expense, half a continent away from his native Louisiana. Beyond a World War II Selective Service folder, a Social Security record and a one-page death certificate, he left no tangible evidence of his itinerant existence.

John Marshall inspected the millrace he had designed for the new sawmill on the American River, thirty miles upstream from Sutter's Fort. Kicking through the gravel and sand alongside the millrun, Marshall spotted a shining stone on the bank. The foreman picked it up and, in doing so, started the greatest mass migration of speculators, adventurers, ne'er-do-wells, thieves, and malcontents in history, the rush to the western goldfields.

Despite an effort at secrecy, word of the gold find trickled to San Francisco and into the dry goods store owned by Sam Brannon. It was Brannon who cannily accepted the metal flakes in payment for goods the overlander wanted, and Brannon who ran through the streets of the city shouting that gold had been discovered on the American River.

Within weeks, the city of San Francisco was stripped of everyone strong enough to carry a pack. By boat up the meandering Sacramento

River or overland when the boats ran out, these adventurers made their way to the banks of the American River to stake claims.

Crafty Sam Brannon, the man who had set off the panic, decided against staking his own claim. After all, he was a dry goods merchant, a respected member of the community, not a quick-rich rapscallion. In July 1849, with two other investors, Brannon laid out a townsite where the Yuba flowed into the Feather River. It became a wide-open checkerboard of tents and false front stores, saloons, and wagon-bed whorehouses cheek-by-jowl—dusty in the summer, swamped in mud during the winter. Brannon optimistically called his instant shantytown Yuba City.

A hundred and twenty years later, the whores were gone, long since run out of town; the clapboard saloons had been transformed first into taverns, then into bars decorated in red plush and brass to imitate a Forty-Niner era that never was. The gold was panned out, but a man could work in the orchards where ranchers raised a wealth ten times greater than all the gold shipped to the banks of New York, London, and Geneva.

Melford Sample came to Yuba City looking for work first in 1969, staying two weeks at the U.S. Hotel, one dollar a night, sharing the creaking bed with a man known only as Ford. Sample had worked during May and June thinning peaches, then moved on to other crops, other jobs, other towns.

Fifty-nine years old, separated from his wife, Virginia, twenty years ago, he was free to come and go as he pleased. He had little contact with his son Bernard, a policeman in Sunnyvale, California, and wrote infrequently to his sister who lived in Escondido, near San Diego. A laborer since his discharge from the Army at the end of the World War II, Sample only had to set his blue baseball cap for the next town to be gone.

He died of a skull fracture, his brain crushed by six blows, his body dumped into a grave beside the river where Forty-Niners had mucked for tiny flecks of golden metal.

Naming the new town across the river from Yuba City was a problem. A ragtag collection of miners' tents when Charles Covillaud arrived in 1849, it didn't need a name. But the following year, when Covillaud laid out a tract map, a more formal name than "The Flats" seemed called for. At a mass meeting called for the purpose of naming Covillaud's tract, the Reverend Mr. Wadsworth suggested the new town be named "Marysville, in honor of the most beautiful lady of the place, Mrs. Mary Covillaud." As one local historian put it, "At the time, being the only lady of the place, and her husband being one of the founders, the name seemed particularly appropriate."

Within five years, the town named after one of the handful of survivors of the Donner Party, Mary Murphy Covillaud, was the third largest in the state. First a ferry, then a toll bridge, linked the two towns, but it was Marysville that dominated the area.

Some of the first buildings erected on lots sold by Covillaud still stood 120 years later. They clustered along D Street, First, Second, and High, their ornate brickfronts painted, faded, painted again, then forgotten.

The oldest part of town had become the poorest. Carpenters' Gothic scrollwork was tinned over with Coca-Cola signs. The better stores moved uptown, or across the river into Sutter County where there were more people. Lower Marysville was left to the workers who drifted into town, then out again when the work petered out; or to the old men augmenting meager Social Security checks by hiring out as day laborers; or to the winos who worked to drink and drank to live. Charles Covillaud's real estate venture had become Skid Row, a place for men like Donald Dale Smith.

The restless Smith had been on the road since his graduation from Frankfort High in 1928. There was nothing in the small Kansas town to hold him, even when he periodically returned to visit his brother and sister. He started drinking while in high school, leaving a trail of drunk and misdemeanor arrests, ninety-seven of them, across the West.

June 4, 1952, arrested for drunkenness by sheriff's deputies in Shoshone, Idaho, given ten days' suspended jail sentence on condition he leave town —unconstitutional but effective in keeping the unwanted out of Shoshone. September 16, 1952, arrested for being drunk on the highway by the sheriff's office in Red Bluff, California, sentenced to seven and one-half days or a $15 fine—a drunk's time worth only $2 a day.

The arrests came more frequently. Colusa, Alturas, Oroville, Red Bluff, Willows, Auburn, Tracy. He paid for his wandering in jail sentences for drunkenness, petty theft, vagrancy, loitering, even burning a campfire without a permit. Woodland, Stockton, then down south to the Imperial Valley to pick winter lettuce, Barstow, finally in 1965 settling on an annual round within the northern Sacramento Valley. Seven arrests in 1966, twelve in 1967 for drunkenness, nine in 1968, twenty-five in 1969 for drinking and panhandling, seven in 1970, never long in jail, never long out of it.

There was only one entry for 1971 on this ten-page rap sheet: "May 26, 1971, Sheriff's Office, Yuba City. Donald Dale Smith, Deceased." The onetime combat infantryman, cited for action in North Africa and Sicily, had been found buried in a grave overgrown by the bracken along the Feather River bank.

The flood of 1853 ruined a badly overextended John Sutter. Squatters jumped his claims at Coloma, carved up his property at New Helvetica.

The courts turned him aside, pettifogging lawyers picking apart the validity of his land grant from the Mexican government.

Although he had lost his lands, Sutter had proved that the unfamiliar Chinese fruit could grow in the Yuba City area, and Dan Provost had proved he could can and sell fruit grown in California. But it was not until 1860, fourteen years after Provost opened his cannery in San Francisco, that the first commercial peach orchards were planted in Sutter County.

In the next hundred years, growers in Yuba, Sutter, and neighboring Colusa Counties would earn a half-billion dollars growing peaches, eventually planting 18,000 acres and producing forty percent of the world's largest selling canned fruit.

The peach orchards meant work for John Joseph Haluka, $1.25 an hour, $10 a day. It wasn't much, but it was enough to get a room, three meals, a drink now and then, and even save a few dollars if you were careful. Haluka was a careful man who liked to stay out of trouble; he always had a few dollars in his wallet so he couldn't be pulled in for vagrancy and he didn't drink enough to get drunk. He stayed away from trouble, and trouble stayed away from him.

Oh, he'd had some run-ins with the law, but he had wised up since 1942 and '43. He had been, what?, twenty-four then, fresh from his hometown of Perth Amboy, New Jersey, when San Diego police picked him up for vagrancy. He got ten days, but escaped from the county jail after serving three. The next year he had served ten days on a Modesto work gang for vagrancy. That was enough; for seventeen years he had stayed clear of the law, roving up and down the state, picking crops here, pruning there, sometimes visiting friends on Los Angeles' Main Street.

Marysville was just another temporary stop on his perpetual itinerary: April and July, 1969; February, May, and June the next year. He last dropped off the Western Pacific freight outside of town in March 1971, with enough money this time to stay at the Golden West for a couple of nights and get cleaned up.

Shortly after, fifty-two-year-old John Haluka was dead of a skull fracture, the sixth victim to be found. He was identified by papers in his pocket and an old letter addressed to him from his sister, who had died in the past year. No one was officially notified of his death. If anyone wondered, they could read his name in the papers.

The placer mining along the riverbanks played out eventually, the yield too poor to make a living. The Forty-Niners were replaced by hydraulic miners, their powerful water hoses literally washing entire mountains away, making it profitable once again to work the Mother Lode—if you didn't care what you did to the land or to the rivers.

But flatlanders did care, and they brought legal action against the hydraulickers who had ruined the rivers. The courts agreed, handing down a permanent injunction which shut down the massive hydraulic hoses.

In their place came the gold dredgers, buying up land on both sides of the Yuba and its tributaries. The last of the great, ungainly barge operations in the contiguous United States shut down in October 1968 as the government-pegged price for an ounce of gold rested at just half what Yuba No. 21 needed to stay in business.

It is easy to slip by the watchmen the company has posted, to poach fish in the Yuba, and to sleep out; so no one really bothers the tramps and hobos who camp along the river nine months of the year. The victim identified only as East-5, the seventh to be discovered, might have camped up there, ten miles from Marysville; none of the men he would have met in town came forward to identify him. Wearing only under-shorts and socks, he had been dragged to his grave along the Feather River; there was nothing to identify him. Deputy Coroner and Sheriff's Sergeant Purcell arbitrarily listed his occupation as "farm laborer" on the death certificate. The label lent a bit of dignity to a government form otherwise filled in with "unknown."

As mining declined, agriculture increased in importance in the northern Sacramento Valley. Where Marysville had dominated the mining-based economy, Yuba City across the river in Sutter County became the economic center of the surrounding farms. Ultimately, the population center shifted west, across the river, from Marysville to Yuba City, from Yuba County on the east to Sutter on the west.

When the merchants crossed the river to open new stores in the shopping centers along Colusa Highway, they left behind the swaybacked buildings, the paint flaking in the hot summer sun. Lower Marysville became a tiny urban slum in the heart of rural California.

As the stores closed, the bars opened, selling bar whiskey at 35¢ a shot. The bar maids and waitresses grew older and thicker around the middle, their tight sweaters sweat-stained under the arms and frayed at the wrists. The farmers and townsfolk stayed away, except to make furtive visits to the whores, leaving D Street to the migratory workers.

Warren Jerome Kelley had drifted into town from Arizona, where he usually spent the winters. He hung around the park at the foot of D Street, waiting for someone to offer him a job. He hadn't worked much since getting out of the Bakersfield County jail in the middle of March but Kelley was about as used to the long periods of idleness between drunks as a man could get. Sixty-two, he had been on the road since the 1940s, long since having left his wife Ruby behind in his native Texas. Kelley was a loner; no one missed him when he disappeared.

His body markedly decomposed, the fingerprints illegible, Kelley was identified by the multiple tattoos on his arms and hands. T-R-U-E had been etched on the fingers of the right hand, L-O-V-E on the left; the sentiment had been duly recorded by CII under "identifying marks and physical characteristics." Kelley was buried in Sutter County, his wife declining to claim his body, the eighth victim found in the orchards he had sometimes worked.

As casually as they came into town, they left. "You see somebody go for a little walk. Maybe somebody offers 'em a job, pickin' an' thinnin'. Maybe in two or three months they come back and say they were in Oregon, Washington, up by Oroville. Anywhere," the black woman told the reporter who bought her a drink. "They just come and go, git a little stake an' they're gone again. They drift in an' they drift out. The wind come along and blow an' that's the size of it."

Sigurd Beierman was an exception. He had lived in Marysville for twenty years; his wife had died there after a long illness. Now he loafed in Wino Park when there was no work or when he still had money from his Social Security disability check. There were a couple of checks waiting for him at the Day Center, a three-room hostel where the drifters could get a free meal and coffee, his friend, Roy DeLong, noted.

In those twenty years, Beierman had made a few friends, including DeLong. Not close enough for DeLong to know that Beierman needed those checks to supplement what he could make scrubbing out the Orchard Club. It was DeLong who realized he hadn't seen Beierman around town for two weeks, maybe three, when he reported the old man's disappearance to the Marysville Police Department.

Of the twenty-five victims eventually recovered, number 9, Sigurd Emil Beierman, nicknamed "Pete," was the only one ever missed.

Bhagat Singh Thiara called his Men's Day Center a "rescue mission." Unlike most rescue missions however, the Day Center did not require attendance at a religious service in exchange for a free meal; Thiara, an East Indian Sikh who had come to the Marysville area in 1932, found it handy for recruiting casual laborers. Thiara paid the rent, sometimes bought the groceries, and let the church install a manager, Chris Bergtholdt; Bergtholdt ran the center.

It was at the Day Center in the latter part of September 1970 that Thiara met William Emery Kamp. The sixty-two-year-old Kamp said he was willing to work, so the grower hired him to do odd jobs on his Live Oak ranch. Kamp worked steadily, either for Thiara or for nearby growers. A man who kept to himself, Kamp had only a few friends; Thiara remembered once or twice a car came to the ranch to pick up the farm worker. By and large, Kamp spent the rainy days and evenings reading a much-thumbed, spine-worn Bible, copying biblical homilies into a small dime-store pad, or discussing religion with his employer.

Kamp had not always been so reliable. Born in Wisconsin in 1907, he had been a casual worker for forty years. Between 1931, when he was first booked for drunkenness in Marquette, Michigan, and January 1961, when Oakland, California, police charged him with public intoxication, he had been arrested fifty-eight times. Suddenly the arrests stopped; William Kamp gave up drinking and turned to his Bible.

Kamp worked for Thiara or on other ranches in the Live Oak-Yuba City area until January 23, 1971, the morning he told Thiara he was going into Marysville. Kamp never returned. He was found on May 26 in a grave on the riverbank, a bullet fired through his brain, his head hacked four times. In his pockets sheriff's deputies found $8.91, a bottle of aspirin, a pocket watch, a gold religious medal, and a clutch of religious tracts.

There were few places for the drifters to stay in Sutter County, and a hostile police department in Yuba City hustled them out of town at the slightest excuse. The "unattached males," as they are known in the social workers' jargon, helped to swell Yuba County's welfare bill to $3.8 million while Sutter County taxpayers contributed only $1.4 million to their impoverished neighbors. Sutter had one of the lowest tax rates in the state; Yuba was second highest.

The people of Sutter County meant to keep it that way. Larry Mark, the fifty-five-year-old meat cutter serving his third term as mayor of Yuba City, told reporters on May 31, "Our police department does not tolerate 'winos' in Yuba City. Chief Garcia takes them down to the railroad depot and tells them to get on a train and leave. We just don't allow them." The Constitution's prohibition against banishment did not extend to winos and fruit tramps in Yuba City.

"This is unfortuate that this would have happened on our side of the river," the mayor continued. They have bad problems on the other side of the river, but we have a real clean town. No Skid Row here, no winos; our chief gets rid of them."

The publicity surrounding the bodies lying on the floor of the Chapel of the Twin Cities mortuary, the mayor complained, "gives us a really black eye. The unfortunate thing about it is that this fellow Corona lives in Yuba City." The image of a progressive city, festooned with new shopping centers and take-out food franchises, had been damaged.

Clarence Hocking usually avoided Chief Garcia and Yuba City. Since he had first come to California in 1962 he had wandered up and down the interior valleys from Blythe on the south to Oroville on the north, then on to Oregon and the crops there. He apparently had been passing through when he was offered a ride or a job, something to earn a few bucks before quickly moving on to someplace with more work.

Hocking didn't stay long in any one place, hadn't, in fact, since 1940 when he first hit the road. That was the year he was arrested for petty theft by an Illinois Central railway detective. There had been other arrests since then, mostly for vagrancy or sleeping, as they called it in the midwest; at fifty-three, Hocking was not what you would call LaSalle, Illinois' brightest product.

There was just one entry on his arrest record from the city Hocking had avoided all those years: "May 26, 1971, Deceased." The careful man was the thirteenth body on the floor of the mortuary garage.

There are contradictions in Sutter County. The Board of Supervisors is growth-conscious, anxious to stimulate new building, new industries. The general feeling in the county is that new homes, new residents, new shopping centers represent progress.

At the same time, the brightest of the Union High School's graduates leave Yuba City, seeking opportunity and schooling in Sacramento and San Francisco, dissatisfied with dropping pills or smoking pot for kicks during the lunch hour. In more ways than one, the big city has come to Sutter County.

The ambitious ones who went off to college or jobs elsewhere left behind the timid or the content, the more conservative ones who would inherit their fathers' land or business, snugly fitting into the settled social order of a stratified society in which class and position were surely fixed.

Migratory workers such as James Howard ranked at the bottom of the social scale, below the regular Mexican-American farm workers. Howard might have liked to stay a while in one place—eight years in Amarillo, nine in Los Angeles, a year in Sacramento—but he was still a day laborer. No matter that he was a good worker or that he was quiet; he was outside the established order. Howard divided his time between Marysville and Sacramento, where he stayed with a brother, sometimes working on farms, sometimes on construction jobs.

Partially supported by his $109 disability check, Howard usually had some money on him. If he ran short at the end of the month, he borrowed some change from Clarence Darling, the manager of Joe's Number Two; it was 30¢ the last time, on May 11, 1971, a few days before he was murdered. Mr. Darling would have to write off the 55¢ in outstanding loans he had made to sixty-four-year-old James Wylie Howard.

The news reports of the multiple slayings had a curious effect, or lack of it, upon the residents of Sutter and Yuba Counties. No one had much to say about the murders or the dead men, reporters quickly learned.

"It isn't that the people of Yuba City are more callous than anybody else. The murder of twenty-three local farmers or merchants or housewives would throw the whole town into a state of shock. The slaughter of twenty-three pet dogs would arouse the community to fever pitch," George Draper wrote in the San Francisco *Chronicle* before all twenty-five victims had been found. "But these weren't their people who turned up in those anonymous graves out at Sullivan's. They weren't anybody's people, alive or dead."

The deaths of twenty-five hobos and tramps and drifters affected very few. Chris Bergtholdt, director of the Day Center, tried to defend them, angry that they were all dismissed as alcoholics. A Marysville housewife, Mrs. Judy Freeman, organized a memorial fund for the victims to buy gravestones. The total cost was estimated at $5,000; Mrs. Freeman's committee collected $732. But for most people in the Twin Cities, the slaughter was a remote matter, of little more personal interest than a devastating tropical storm in Florida or an airplane crash in the Peruvian Andes. There was little or no fear, and no hysteria; Corona's arrest was announced before panic could ignite. Few people knew the dead men; few people were concerned by their deaths. Fewer still were touched beyond a *pro forma* regret. It was too bad it had to happen here.

The dead men were invisible, nonpeople, marginal men who had little contact with the townsfolk. If, like Jonah Smallwood, they had made a few friends, the friends too hung out in lower Marysville.

Ken Busby was one; he and Smallwood spent days together at the Day Center when they weren't working. Busby had nicknamed his friend "Driftwood" because wherever Busby seemed to go, as far away as Reno even, Smallwood would sooner or later turn up too. It didn't take much money—a couple of bucks for food and a bus ticket if you couldn't get a lift—and Smallwood liked to have a "front," a few dollars tucked away in his wallet in addition to the $5 in food stamp books he carried. The old 'bos like Smallwood always did; "the front" was a bit of insurance against a vagrancy arrest, that and a quick story. You couldn't count on it to work; Smallwood had been arrested ten times on vagrancy charges since he hit the road after getting out of the Navy in 1952. But it was better than nothing, especially if it seemed the cops were always down on you, like they were on Smallwood.

Smallwood wandered up and down the interior valleys, as far north as Portland, Oregon, sometimes alone, sometimes traveling with a friend like Elbert J. T. Riley. The two of them met in Modesto, after Riley got out of jail on the drunk driving charge. It was early in May, they could get work thinning peaches in Marysville, so they decided to drive together.

Like Smallwood, Riley had been on the road most of his life. According to his sister, Riley periodically disappeared from the family home. "He gets fed up with the family and just takes off." A niece defended him too. "He wasn't a tramp, a drifter to any of us here. He was one of the best guys I knew." Riley just couldn't stay long in any one place. He would live with his wife in rural Farmersville, go to the Pentecostal Church services faithfully, work as an electrician or carpenter—using skills he had picked up in the Army—and pay his bills. Then one morning, he would be gone. The family got used to it. "He'd get in touch with us if he got into trouble," his niece said. There was a lot of trouble—114 arrests over a twenty-three-year period.

The last one took place on May 9, 1971, when the highway patrol picked him up for intoxication and impounded his car. Released the next morning, Riley borrowed the twenty-seven-dollar impound fee from a labor recruiter for a local ranch. The recruiter, Byron Shannon, also loaned Riley and his companion, Jonah Smallwood, $15 to get a meal and a room. The two promised to begin work for J. V. Johnson, Shannon's boss, the following week in order to repay the loan. Shannon last saw them getting into a pickup truck owned by another labor con-tractor, he told sheriff's deputies—a blue-and-white pickup with the name Juan V. Corona painted on the side.

For the people of Yuba City and Marysville, the mass slayings had taken on a carnival aura. For the first time since 1955 and the Christmas floods, the area was in the news. You could see pictures of the court-house and the silver water tank at the corner of Plumas and Colusa, even a quick look at a friend's back on Walter Cronkite. As the story wore on, the combination of court-ordered gag rule and rain forced newsmen to turn to the people of the area—first for the obligatory reaction piece, then for investigative leads of their own.

The friend's back became the friend talking, right there on the television, telling some reporter that folks around here were really good people and, no, he didn't know any of the dead men. Sure, he had seen Juan Corona around town driving his pickup; no, he didn't know Corona. It was just too bad that those television people and newspaper fellows had to talk to all those bums in Marysville; it gave the area a bad name.

When the rains let up, the sightseers came, driving out the freeway to the Sullivan ranch, stopping at the Highway Patrol roadblock to watch sheriff's vehicles and the mortuary's station wagons come and go. They perched on the fenders of their cars, necks craned, squinting in the overcast—vultures picking at the carrion of gossip and rumor.

There were even motorboats heavy with laughing people, drinking beer as they cruised along the river, straining to see sheriff's deputies in the thicket on the western bank or heard the sound of shovels. Overhead, an occasional private plane swooped in under the rain clouds, banked in wide turns, and roared back over the trees, one wing dipped to offer a better view of the riverbank cemetery.

A few of the curious drove slowly past the Chapel of the Twin Cities where Sergeant Purcell was working with the undertakers, cataloging the bodies and inventorying personal possessions. East-14, the seventeenth victim found, was identified by a Social Security card and a crumpled booking slip from the county jail in Oroville. At the time of his death, Paul B. Allen's worldly possessions consisted of the clothes he was wearing, a patch to cover his missing right eye, a pair of gloves jammed into a pocket, a padlock, a can opener, and $2.17. They would ultimately become the property of Allen's brother in Forth Smith, Arkansas, who was to claim the body for burial in the military cemetery there.

Sergeant Purcell counted out the $1.81 in change rifled from the front pants pocket, the sum of Edward Martin Cupp's life on the road. When he could find jobs, Cupp had worked as a roofer on construction projects, but there wasn't all that much, not for a man with his record. Even the nonunion scab work went to others if the bosses found out he had done time as an army deserter, for grand larceny, and for escaping from a Jefferson, Missouri, prison farm. That had been a long time ago, and there had only been a string of drunk arrests since then, but those first entries on his rap sheet hurt. So he stayed on the road, mostly in California, picking up what work he could, in and out of jail, twenty days in Los Angeles, forty in Sacramento, then another fifty, then four in Santa Paula, five in San Jose. The last time had been on May 8, 1971, in Sacramento when he was sentenced to forty days in county for plain drunk; if he hadn't gotten off with good behavior, he would not have traveled to Marysville, and he would not have been buried in a shallow grave in the riverbottom orchard sometime before May 27.

While Mrs. Freeman contacted churches in the Marysville-Yuba City area, asking them to take up collections for her memorial fund, Oakridge Holdings, Incorporated, publicly offered to supply and pay for the setting of markers on the graves of the twenty-three victims then reported. The Chicago firm, which dealt in cemetery and funeral supplies, was the only corporation to see an obligation that "Scratchy's" life somehow be remembered.

His real name was Albert Leon Hayes, but the men in lower Marysville knew him as "Scratchy," the guy who always wore that cracked red hard-hat. He was fifty-eight years old and had been wandering from place to place for twenty years. At one time he had applied for a job as an apprentice forest firefighter with the state, but had decided not to take the job, telling the clerk he was "no longer interested." For fifteen more years "Scratchy" had shuttled between Los Angeles on the south and Roseburg, Oregon, on the north, a loner looking for work or a drink or a place to sleep without getting busted by some eager rookie cop.

"Scratchy" was the nineteenth victim located. The cracked red hard-hat he was never without was found in the bushes near the foot of the grave where evidently the murderer had pitched it.

Father Bishop's decision to hold a memorial mass for Corona, his family, and the twenty-three victims was not well thought of in Yuba City. If he wanted to say some prayers for the dead men, okay, that's his job. But for Corona, the murderer? (It didn't matter that Corona had been a member of the father's congregation.)

There were 250 parishioners at St. Isidore's, lost in the pews that normally seated 1,500 for a Sunday service, uncomfortable before the television cameras given permission by Father Joseph to film the service. Speaking in Spanish to his Mexican-American congregation, the priest quietly offered the mass "for the repose of the men who have been found murdered. We beg God to give them in the future life, and the life they are now enjoying, the joys, the happiness that they obviously missed during the last sad years of their life here on earth."

Outside the drizzle filtered down on the parked cars, the cruising police, and a pair of newsmen huddling uncomfortably in the lee of the church, preferring not to transform a private thing into a public spectacle. A baby whimpered while Father Joseph spoke: "I wonder if anyone here could really say they experienced anything remotely near the suffering that must be in the hearts of the family of Mr. Corona during these days. I don't think that any of us could possibly imagine the anguish that these people feel."

The sun guns on the television cameras bored through the damp gloom. "In her matrimonial bond, Mrs. Corona vowed to take Juan Corona for better or for worse. In this tragedy we see to what point her love has been tested. We also ask this community not to be guilty of an even greater crime by judging indiscriminately."

The priest cleared his throat. "Juan Corona is the *accused,*" he said, stressing the last word. "Obviously none of us at this point knows who is responsible for the tragedy that took place in our community."

One by one the television lights went out, leaving the nave darker than ever.

Raymond Muchache never strayed far from northern California. He had been born in Fall River near Susanville, a member of the Pit River Tribe who could not stay on the tribal lands long. Perhaps it was whiskey —he drank a lot of it—perhaps his reputation as a troublemaker, but Muchache kept on the move, traveling from Alturas in the Sierras down to Sacramento, but rarely farther south. He worked, drank, and was arrested; released from jail to work, drink, and be arrested once again. He was booked eighty-seven times for public drunkenness or driving under the influence of alcohol by Sacramento police in the last ten years of his life. In one six-week period he was hauled in five times; in a four-month period in 1970 another twelve times.

Muchache didn't come to Marysville very often and he rarely stayed very long. The last time was on May 17, 1971, when he showered and shaved at the Twin Cities Rescue Mission. Ten days later his body was lifted from the grave in the riverbottom orchard, rolled into a body bag, and loaded into the rear of the blue station wagon from the Chapel of the Twin Cities.

Lying beside Muchache's body in the garage of the mortuary was John Henry Jackson, male Negro, sixty-four years old, born in New York, dead of cranio-cerebral injury due to incised wounds of cranial bones in Sutter County, California, on or before May 28, 1971.

Jackson too was a loner; though he had been coming to Marysville periodically since 1940, no one seemed to miss him. Perhaps it was because he was black, perhaps because he preferred it that way: no family, no ties, his next-of-kin listed ten years before as a friend, Anna Lishinsky. Perhaps it was Mrs. Lishinsky who had taught him Yiddish.

It was to have been a massive gesture of sympathy, a memorial service jointly sponsored on June 8 by the Marysville and Yuba City Ministerial Fellowships. The service would be held under the arc lights on Yuba City Union High's football field, the only place large enough to hold the expected crowd.

Fifty newsmen and television crews stayed for the event, wringing from the Yuba City mass murder case one more front-page story, one last thirty-second film clip on the networks.

Six ministers from local churches spoke on the program, including the Reverend C. W. Renwick, director of the Twin Cities Rescue Mission. The victims "were not bums. A bum is a man who does not want to work, and these men wanted to work." The Reverend Howard Alexander, pastor of the Marysville First Baptist Church, described the men whom Police Chief George Garcia ran out of town as "guests of the community." The minister's voice rose in the warm spring evening, "We are our brother's keeper. We should be more concerned about men such as these, who have contributed to the economy of our community. These men have now passed beyond any help we can give them, so it is for us, the living, that we have this service tonight."

Two hundred citizens of Yuba and Sutter Counties, total population 81,000, attended the memorial service.

7

A Matter of Convenience
May 29-June 2, 1971

The rain stopped on Saturday, May 29, leaving the lawn in front of the Sutter County courthouse a sodden sponge of green. In his office in the rear of the damp building, Sheriff Whiteaker huddled over a duty log, working on assignments for the day.

Gregory, Harrison, and Cochran had to interview a dozen people; Whiteaker was anxious to canvass Skid Row for possible witnesses. In the meantime, Whiteaker would continue to deal with the press and with the district attorney; there were some wrinkles he and Dave Teja had to iron out.

The biggest problem was to get out a revised list of the victims. There had been some mistakes on the tally released to the press yesterday: victim number 2 had been listed as "unidentified" though they had a name for him now; John J. Haluka had been placed in the third grave when he should have been either number five or six; "Pete" Beierman was reported in the seventh grave when he was actually the ninth victim; Jonah Smallwood was first called victim number 11, then 12; he belonged in grave number 15.

What was really screwed up was the third victim, the first dug up on the riverbank three days before. Gregory claimed he had tagged the body of a nine-fingered man as the third victim the night the body was dug up. Inexplicably, the tag had been lost. The two receipts, just four days old when they were uncovered, had been located in the grave of the third body found. With the confusion of bodies though, the four-day-old receipts were recorded as being in a grave with a body dead as long as thirty days. Those receipts had to be in a grave with a fresh body; recent receipts with an old body suggested that the man in custody had been deliberately set up, the incriminating receipts planted by the killer long after the dead man had been buried. The only fresh body recovered along the riverbank was that of the nine-fingered man, but Purcell himself had already marked the rolled fingerprint impressions of the nine-fingered man as the second recovered on the riverbank, not the first—as victim number 4 not 3.

Purcell was going to have to get it organized at the mortuary, and straighten out the mistakes now, before the bodies were shipped for safe-keeping in the Sacramento coroner's office. The two doctors had finished autopsying the bodies dug up yesterday; they would reautopsy the first twelve in Sacramento.

Those newsmen were damned anxious to get hold of a list of victims; it would be a big help too when they published it. The next-of-kin would call, which saved the police the time spent trying to trace the families of the dead men. It also meant that the county wouldn't have to pay for the burials if the families claimed the bodies. Trouble was, the phones rarely stopped ringing; the girls had lost track of the number of calls they had taken from people inquiring about missing people. And a number of them were cranks or troublemakers.

Before holding his regular morning press conference, Sheriff Whiteaker decided to move Corona from his cell in the men's wing of the jail to more secure quarters. The threatening phone calls bothered him enough to consider special protection. Whiteaker didn't want some nut taking a shot at Corona. He didn't need another Lee Oswald–Jack Ruby case on his hands. Whiteaker called the Yuba County Sheriff's Department across the river; they had a new jail facility in Marysville where they could hold Corona easily, thereby sparing Whiteaker that worry.

The morning *Chronicle* had two lead stories on the case—one describing the return of the first search warrant and the finding of the receipts in the grave of "John Doe Number Three"; the second based on an interview with the sheriff himself. The *Chronicle* reporters wrote that Corona became very angry when his family was denied welfare assistance in March. The front-page story speculated that Corona "may have been triggered into a schizophrenic rage late in March when his appeal for Aid to Dependent Children was turned down by the Sutter County Welfare Department." The story continued:

> When authorities rejected his appeal, Corona flew into a rage at the welfare office and "became loud, belligerent, and hostile." He indicated at the time he was being discriminated against because he is a Mexican.
>
> Investigators are believed working on the theory that Corona, who was committed to a state mental institution in 1956 as a "dangerous schizophrenic" and released as "cured" after three months of observation and treatment, may have turned in fury against white Skid Row drifters and alcoholics, most of whom receive some kind of welfare aid or pensions.

In less than a week the sheriff had become adept at handling the press.

By granting not-for-attribution interviews, he was able to fill reporters in on developments in the case while appearing to abide by the court-ordered gag rule. The rules of the game required the reporters to take full responsibility for the story, relying on such opaque ascriptions as "it was learned" rather than attributing the story to even "informed" or "highly reliable" sources.

Whiteaker had quickly picked out a handful of newsmen he deemed most friendly, and to those favored few he gave exclusive information. After the Sacramento *Bee* linked Corona to one of its own crusades—for stronger laws governing farm labor contractors—the *Bee's* correspondent, Bob Williams, was welcomed in the sheriff's office. On June 3, Williams learned of the nine-millimeter pistol found in the mess hall on the Sullivan ranch, linking it to the bullet found in William Kamp's brain. In subsequent days, Williams was to obtain a copy of the ledger with its so-called "death list"; was to learn that "Blood Is Found on Weapon from Home of Accused Sutter Mass Slayer Corona"; and was to be told that the tire tracks found near the graves matched those on Corona's car.

Corona's court-appointed attorney, Roy Van den Heuval, was frustrated; the newspapers knew more about the case against his client than he did. Some of the published information he knew was erroneous, but how much he could not yet say. The district attorney had still not turned over copies of the first police reports to which the defense was entitled by law. Beyond his conversations with Corona, conversations which didn't help much to explain how or why the contractor was linked to the dead men, Van den Heuval had little to go on.

It was difficult formulating a defense in such circumstances, worse still when there was so much going on at once. "It was hectic," Van den Heuval recalled later, with three investigators working on the case, his law office all but closed down so he could concentrate on the Corona case, his client in jail, no official reports, and deputies out there still searching for more victims.

It was hard to know what to do first, and Van den Heuval was overwhelmed. Further, it seemed futile; from all Van den Heuval could learn from the district attorney, and especially from Sheriff Whiteaker's affidavit for the first search warrant, it didn't look good for Corona. He would have to get hold of the records from DeWitt State Hospital.

Based on the possibility that the prosecution did not have a solid case—however unlikely it looked—Van den Heuval took the first steps in preparing an affirmative defense. Knowing the risk, he elected to hire two psychiatrists, Joseph Catton and Walter Bromberg, to interview the quiet labor contractor. Bringing a psychiatrist in to see his client would certainly make the papers—Teja or Whiteaker would see to that—and the publicity would only reinforce the earlier stories about Corona's mental illness. Still, that was hardly his biggest worry; it wasn't likely that this case would ever get to a jury.

It was one thing for Corona to say he was discharged from DeWitt as cured; it was another for a psychiatrist to certify him sane now. Van den Heuval had to know for sure; if there were any doubt at all, or if he could raise a doubt, he might be able to make a deal with the prosecution. If Teja's case had any holes in it—it was apparently all circumstantial right now—Van den Heuval could ask the prosecutor to go along with a plea of mental incompetency. Backed by a psychiatrist, Van den Heuval could claim Corona was incompetent to stand trial, unable to understand the proceedings brought against him, and incapable of assisting in his defense. That would send him to a state hospital for the criminally insane until he was able to stand trial; conceivably, Corona could die there, without ever coming to trial at all. They would just never cure him. It was a lot better than the gas chamber.

By the end of the first week in June, Van den Heuval had written a memo to himself on the penal code section authorizing pre-trial hospitalization for mental incompetents. He would have to raise doubts in the judge's mind about Corona's present mental state, arguing that the state penal code's section stipulated that an "irrational man cannot aid his counsel in preparing a just and rational defense." To support any mental incompetence plea, he could argue Corona's previous state hospital commitment, the odd behavior reported at the welfare agency, and the fact that the crimes had been committed by an irrational person.

Van den Heuval went to talk first to Gloria Corona to get her assent to put Juan under psychiatric observation, and then, in the wash of her teary refusal, with Pedro, the younger brother with whom Gloria and the four children were staying. As Pedro remembered the three conversations he had with Van den Heuval, translated by Raul Ybarra, "He say, 'One hundred percent better to send Juan to the hospital. Don't send him to the gas chamber or to the jail for the rest of his life.' He say, 'Okay, you sign those kind of papers okay to send Juan to the hospital.'"

Like Gloria, Pedro Corona refused, despite Van den Heuval's repeated efforts. "I never think, I am sure one hundred percent that Juan is innocent. There is no way to convict him because he don't commit the crimes."

It was a disappointment for Van den Heuval; the mental incompetency ploy had been the best possible. True, he could still pull it off, if he got the judge to go along, but none of the locals were likely to go for it without Teja's tacit agreement. If the district attorney wanted a conviction, the mental incompetency thing rarely stood up.

How good a bargain Van den Heuval could strike he didn't know. There were twenty-some dead men just then; Teja could hardly let Corona plead to killing one while ignoring the others. Even so, there seemed no doubt that these were all clearly first-degree murders; conviction would certainly mean life imprisonment, more likely the gas chamber. The law might permit parole of "lifers" in seven years—the average murder sentence in state prisons was fifteen years—but the parole board would never let Corona out, not with all those other dead men charged to him. But again, if the prosecution's case were weak, Teja just might go for a deal, one that would at least save Corona from the gas chamber.

Van den Heuval knew that Teja, like most district attorneys, preferred to plea-bargain. Teja was a good politician and a shrewd administrator. His briefs were workmanlike, but his trial work was rusty; he just might want to close the Corona case the neatest way possible if the evidence were not entirely good. Van den Heuval had to take a hard line for the moment to appear ready to go to trial for his client; there was plenty of time to compromise later if he had to.

Right now though, Van den Heuval and his investigator had a couple of tips that there were bodies buried somewhere besides the Sullivan ranch. If they were to find one, it would help to turn the suspicion away from Corona. There were also those kids who said they saw a car near Bear River, blood dripping from the trunk, two days after Corona's arrest.

While Van den Heuval sought bodies elsewhere, Undersheriff Cartoscelli and a digging team were unearthing the twenty-second victim. It took the digging party a little less than one hour to locate the body of Lloyd Wenzel. Like the others, he had been stabbed, then chopped about the neck and head. The body was partly decomposed, in the words of the autopsy surgeon, "showing moderate putrefaction." Working quickly, Deputy Sizelove plucked from the mud-caked clothing a Yuba County welfare document dated April 14, 1971; food stamp books worth $28 in groceries; 6¢; a stub from a Sacramento-to-Marysville bus ticket dated May 14, 1971; and a tarnished, dented harmonica.

While Sizelove inventoried the property in Wenzel's pockets, Duron was reporting yet another possible grave site. The week before, Jim Cummings, a carpenter hanging new doors on the Sullivan barn, had spotted Corona backing his van up to the edge of the orchard adjacent to the camp area. It didn't seem like much at the time, Cummings told Duron, but perhaps it would be smart to check.

They found number 23 about 600 feet from where Cummings had seen Corona park his van the week before. Mark Beverly Shields had been stabbed twice in the left chest, the knife blade entering his lungs, then hacked once behind his right ear. Shields had died of a crushed skull, the heavy blade crashing through the bone into the skull cavity. Sizelove gingerly fingered in the victim's pockets, locating a blue plastic comb and a bottle of pills with Shields' name on the label and the date the Oroville doctor had prescribed them—February 1, 1971.

It would be six more days before the last two bodies were dug up. The twenty-fourth victim was Sam Bonafide, a fifty-five-year-old itinerant farm laborer who had worked his way up and down California's interior valleys since the end of World War II. The right side of his head had been caved in, the brain crushed by three massive blows.

Joseph Maczak's was the last body found, located in the northernmost of Sullivan's orchards, buried under the fruit-heavy peach trees.

Ray Duron had called once again to report that another worker on the ranch, José Breceda, had told him that tractor driver Ernesto Garcia had seen Corona come out of one of the orchards at ten o'clock at night in January 1971. Corona had told Garcia that he was looking for his dog, though the animal had been frolicking behind the mess hall the entire night. Thinking back on it now, especially with everyone else finding bodies on the ranch, Garcia and Breceda decided to tell the foreman. Duron had sent the two men into the orchard; together they had found the telltale depression in the muddy earth.

Maczak's life had been destroyed in a fury of three stab wounds in the chest and seven hacking blows to his head, his body dragged to the grave and buried amid a scattering of rubbish. Sizelove recorded the trash as it was recovered from the grave: grass cuttings; a scrap of upholstery fabric; a broken mirror; a child's knee-length stocking; a shattered glass candle-holder inscribed "Our Lady of Guadalupe"; a sodden shopping news dated April 21, 1971, still folded with a rubber band around it; and two crumpled Bank of America blank deposit slips with Juan V. Corona's name and his Richland Road address printed on the face. The deposit slips all but made the district attorney's case.

Rain or no rain, the investigation continued, Sheriff Whiteaker using all the available people he could muster. Detective Duncan interviewed Corona's mother-in-law, Lupe Moreno Gravell; Mrs. Gravell described her son-in-law as "a good father and a good provider for Gloria and the children," Duncan wrote in his report. "She also stated that in regards to the incident where the knifing occurred in the tavern in lower Marysville, that Gloria had never mentioned Juan being implicated or involved in this incident in any way."

Duncan was more successful with Chain Singh Khera, a grower with orchards that adjoined the Kagehiro property. Corona had supplied crews for Khera in the past and had repeatedly sought work again this year. Khera was able to provide another increment in the circumstantial case against the farm labor contractor. Khera "stated he had seen Juan Corona in the area . . . where the graves were located two or three days before the bodies were picked up. He stated it was approximately 200 yards southeast of where the first body was located and Mr. Corona was driving the same van truck at this time," Duncan concluded in his summary of the interview.

If it was to be a case based upon circumstantial evidence, Teja and

Whiteaker believed they would need more witnesses who could directly link Corona to the victims. They had Roy DeLong's two-page, rather vague statement asserting that "Pete" Beierman had driven off in a "yellow-looking" panel truck, a vehicle similar to Corona's van. They needed a fuller, more definite interview, Teja told Whiteaker.

DeLong, however, had dropped from sight, according to Men's Day Center director Chris Bergtholdt, because of the newspaper publicity he had received. "He was more or less running scared," Detective Gregory wrote in his report on May 29. "Mr. Bergtholdt also advised that Mr. DeLong had commented he was thinking about leaving the area while he could." The following day, DeLong was picked up as a "material witness" and booked into the Sutter County jail.

Bergtholdt himself had never seen Corona around the Day Center, and "would not know him if he did see him," Gregory's summary of their conversation continued. But there were others in lower Marysville who had. Ishmuel Kenneth Walton told detectives Corona had offered one of the identified victims, Donald Smith, and him a day's work. Walton was unsure of the date, right around a month before. He and Smith were in front of the Golden West Hotel on Second Street, talking, when a Mexican in a pickup asked if one of them wanted "to dig a hole to bury garbage in." The color of the pickup? Walton was unsure. "I think it was yellow. I could be mistaken. I wouldn't swear to it." Walton didn't want the job and told Smith not to take it either. The Mexican man had driven off with another laborer, forty to fifty years old, a white man, around ten o'clock in the morning. Walton knew it was Juan Corona because "some of the other boys that worked for him before told me."

Detective Duncan spotted James Pervis at the intersection of Second and D Streets in lower Marysville on the night of June 2. In an interview recorded there on the street corner, Pervis told the detective he had been offered "a couple of hours of work, cleaning up around the camp" by Corona. It was about April 10, around four o'clock in the afternoon, Pervis said. Because he was working on his car, Pervis did not take the job. He was certain it was Corona; after all, Pervis had seen him around town for "eight or nine years that I know of. Kind of a heavy set man, kind of bushy haired, you know, kind of dark complected." At that time he had offered the work to Pervis, Corona was driving a pickup, a green "two-tone job."

A surveyor for the state, Jacob Compton, had been working in the riverbottoms along both banks. On April 29, he had twice seen "a van type vehicle which was light colored, either light yellow, white or beige, and I would say it was beige. There was a lot of dust so it may have been white or yellow." The van was on the access road to the north riverbottom orchard, the first time some one thousand feet from where Compton was resting, the second time just across the river. He had been too far from the van to get a look at the driver. It wasn't a perfect identification, but it helped place Corona in the orchard about the time the men were buried there.

Three days later Duncan was to be assigned the best lead they had had. Mel Hodges, the foreman for Del Monte Corporation's California Packing Corporation ranch, had called the Sheriff's Department. One of his employees, a Juan Mosqueda, had told him "that approximately two months prior he [Mosqueda] had met with Juan Corona and the two of them had picked up a wino in Marysville and transported him to the Jack Sullivan ranch. . . . Corona had dropped him [Mosqueda] off at the bunkhouse and had taken the wino individual in an easterly direction from the camp and was gone for quite some period of time and upon his arrival back at the camp Mr. Corona did not have the individual with him," Duncan wrote in his summary report.

Getting the story from Mosqueda would be difficult. He had heard a newscast of Corona's arrest on a portable radio, and just as suddenly had told Hodges he was quitting immediately. They could forward the $5 the company owed him to his home in San Bernardino. Hodges doubted the man would be at that address; Mosqueda had said something about leaving Sutter County to pick apricots.

It took two days of tracking by Detectives Duncan and Cochran to find the fifty-year-old Mosqueda while he was picking up his mail at the Stockton, California, post office. Booked as a material witness, the fretful Mosqueda waited twenty-four hours before the detectives interrogated him. Then through five hours of questions, the farm worker denied he had been with Corona when they picked up a "wino-type." The two disappointed detectives secured permission to take Mosqueda to Oroville for a lie detector test. Hodges could have it all wrong or Mosqueda could be lying; the Butte County district attorney's polygraph might solve the conflict.

The lie detector test was inconclusive. Polygraph operator David L. Dansby—whose report was withheld from Corona's attorneys for more than seventeen months—was asked to determine if "subject told . . . CPC [California Packing Corporation] foreman Mel Hodges that he had been with suspect Corona when he picked up a wino in Marysville and transported him to the camp at the Sullivan ranch. Corona then left with the wino and came back without him."

After three hours and twenty minutes of questioning a tired, nervous Mosqueda and struggling with his limited English, Dansby concluded:

Subject's negative answers to the following questions produced responses indicative of deception: "Did you ever see Juan Corona pick up a wino?" "Did you ever tell anyone that Juan Corona picked up a wino?" "Did you ever go to the Sullivan ranch with Juan Corona and a wino?" "Do you know if Juan Corona left camp with a wino?" "Did you lie to the police officers?"

These results suggested that Hodges had been relaying the story accurately. But two other questions raised the possibility that Mosqueda had made up the story:

Subject's negative answers to the following questions produced responses indicative of truthfulness: "Did Juan Corona leave the camp with a wino and come back without him?" "Do you know who killed the winos?"

Dansby summarized the three-hour test so as to negate his own findings. "The subject's responses indicate he definitely had knowledge of Corona's activities and may have some knowledge of the crime. Due to the limited information in a short verbal statement by Det. Duncan available for testing, I feel I was unable to reach the area where the subject's relevant knowledge actually lies."

While the frustrated Duncan and Cochran struggled with Mosqueda's denials, Detective Jerry Gregory was interviewing a far more cooperative witness. Byron Shannon, the labor recruiter for the J. B. Johnson ranch, hung out a lot in Wino Park; apparently he knew a number of the dead men, and had seen Corona with them.

Shannon, a black friend by the name of Willis Lasby, and three of the men whose bodies were later found on the Sullivan ranch had been idling time away in Wino Park about eleven o'clock on the morning of May 12. According to Shannon, Corona and a second man—an "Italian-looking fellow"—had driven up in a blue pickup and offered them work.

Shannon, who had a job with J. B., declined. Lasby asked if he could go too, but the men in the truck said they didn't want "no colored." Shannon told the investigators that he had seen Elbert Riley, "a one-eyed fellow," and a third man he later identified as "Jack" Smallwood get into the back of the blue-and-white pickup. He never saw them again.

Why had Shannon waited since May 26 until now, twelve days later to "contact the authorities?"

"I was in jail—with Corona."

"You was in jail with Corona?"

"Yeah, on the eighteenth I went to jail and they brought him over there while I was in jail and put him in Yuba County jail, see."

"When did you get out of jail in Yuba County?"

"The second of this month."

The detective pressed Shannon. "You haven't seen a list of names of possible victims of Juan Corona?" The contents of the ledger had been leaked to the press. If Shannon had been reading the papers, presumably he would have seen the so-called "death list."

"No, I haven't."

"You haven't seen this on television?"

"No, I haven't. I haven't been watching TV."

"Are you lying?"

"No. I'm telling the truth."

"And this statement is on your own free will?"

"This is on my own free will. If I wasn't in jail, well, I would have testified they—Corona and his recruiter—picked him up before then, see. When it come out, see, 'cause I was in jail then, see."

By three o'clock that afternoon, Shannon had located the shoe shine boy at the Harlem Café. Willis Lasby, identified as William Lasby in the transcript of the interrogation, confirmed he was with Shannon "betwixed the eleventh and twelfth, over there in the park," and had seen Corona "looking for a few people to take to work."

"What type of individuals did Mr. Corona pick up, sir?"

"I don't know what they was. I guess they was mostly Mexicans or Indians, I think it was."

"Mexicans or Indians?"

"Yeah."

"And how many men did Mr. Corona pick up on this date?"

"I couldn't say exactly. I would say about twelve." Pressed, Lasby was sure it was "about twelve." Later that day, he had seen Corona "get some men out of the Day Center there on Second Street."

There were three men, two and Corona, in the front of the truck, a red-and-white pickup, Lasby thought, and six or eight in the back. "I couldn't say exactly. That's about what I figure he had, 'cause he had a load." It had been around two or three in the afternoon when Corona had stopped to load workers at Wino Park before driving on to the Day Center.

Lasby insisted the passengers in the truck were all Mexicans. Lasby didn't think he had ever seen Corona pick up workers before in lower Marysville, but he was able to describe him. "A full faced man. I'd say he weighed about 180, 185 pounds. Somewheres like that. About five ten, five eleven." Driving a red-and-white pickup truck.

"Well, could you identify Mr. Corona?"

"No, not positive that I could identify him." Lasby paused. "No, not positive."

"In other words, you are not sure that the individual you are referring to that was driving the pickup was Juan Corona."

"No, not positive."

"And you couldn't testify in court that this was Mr. Corona?"

"Yeah. If I do, I'd be lying."

"Why do you think it was Mr. Corona?" the detective asked.

"He said it was him."

"Who said?"

"That's what Shannon said that's who it was." Lasby paused, then explained. "See, we was over there sitting in the park and I said, 'Who is the contractor there?' and he said, 'That's Juan Corona.'"

As a labor contractor, Corona hired men, but he also worked for farmers and ranches, at one and the same time both employer and employee. While other detectives scoured the Marysville-Yuba City area for itinerant farm workers who might have worked for Corona, Detective Duncan was talking to the ranchers who had hired Corona.

Duncan's interviews vaguely troubled him. He didn't know anything about psychology and that sort of thing, but it just didn't fall into place. Everyone they talked to said that Corona was a good worker—conscientious, honest. No one had seen him use Anglo workers with the exception of Ray Duron, the foreman of the Sullivan ranch, and that was only during the peach picking season, in August and September, when help was always short. Duncan had also talked to a casual laborer, a Filipino named Aguinalbo Baclaan, who had worked for Corona at the Sullivan camp. Baclaan rode out from Marysville one day in the middle of May alone with Corona in a van, either light yellow or light tan, he couldn't remember which. They had driven straight from the Brunswick Hotel to the camp, and at the end of the day, from the camp back to Wino Park.

According to Baclaan, they had taken no detours. "During the day that Mr. Corona took you to work at the ranch north of Yuba City, did he in any way make any advances or say anything out of the way to you?" Duncan had asked.

"No, he didn't say nothing. He was quiet." Moody maybe. They knew that about Corona. Maybe Corona was a nut, a psycho, but if ever a guy was set up to be a victim, it was Baclaan. Picked up alone, early in the morning, sometime before seven o'clock. Alone together in the truck. Yet Corona brought Baclaan back to town, paid him $10 cash, and said good-bye.

Even as the detectives worked in the field, the investigative leads piled up on Sergeant Purcell's desk. Someone said that Corona had beaten his wife; Harrison was assigned to run down the rumor, contacting Corona's doctor and the Sutter County Hospital.

It didn't pan out, but Detective Harrison did learn that from April 19-26 Corona had "an infection on his feet." He had seen the doctor four times in that period until the infection cleared up. Apparently it was a recurring thing. In March, when he had no money, he had gone to the night clinic at the county hospital. Harrison was unable to interpret the copy of the medical records provided by the director of nurses and asked the medical director, Doctor Thomas Leavenworth, to explain them. According to Harrison's summary, in the middle of March, Corona "complained of a sore on his right leg and he was treated for possibly a boil or infection. The infection of this sore had traveled up his leg and he was having problems in the groin area." He returned twice, the last time on the first of April; the leg appeared to be healing, Leavenworth told the detective.

For every good lead, there were two or three bad ones, each requiring time. Yet despite the false starts, the myriad rumors, slowly the detectives were amassing evidence for possible use in court. No matter how much evidence they gathered, though, District Attorney Teja was certain that the crucial element in their case was the three pages in the ledger containing the names of some of the victims. The first ten names and dates were neatly entered. With the eleventh listing, the handwriting became erratic, some portions of the list an illegible scrawl. The first ten names were in a cursive hand, the balance partially in script, partially in block letters. There were few immediately apparent similarities between the first ten entries and the last twenty-five, a problem for the handwriting examiners at CII to solve. Handwriting changed under stress, sometimes drastically; it might well be that Corona made the entries in the ledger immediately after killing his victims.

Ultimately, the ledger would list eight identified victims among the thirty-four names, with dates presumably corresponding to the day the men were killed:

Warren Gerome [*sic*] Kelley, March 30, 1971 S.R. [Sullivan Ranch?]
John H. Jackson, April 15, 1971
Mark Beverly Shields, April 28, 1971
Sam Bonofiede [*sic*], May 6, 1971
Smith Camino Rio Oso [Bear River Road], May 9, 1971
Charles Lenil Fleming, May 11
Jona [*sic*] Smalwood, May 12
Paul B. Allen, May 15

A ninth name on the list, William Earl Vaughan, with the date of April 5, 1971, was that of a man whom the regulars in lower Marysville said had dropped out of sight. The disturbing factor to Sheriff Whiteaker was that only eight of those on the list had been discovered; there might well be another twenty-six bodies buried in the orchards of Sutter County.

Alternatively, District Attorney Teja argued, "Some names in these lists may merely have been victims of assaults of one degree or another and not murder victims." The first entry on the three pages of presumed victims was "José Romero R Med————," "obviously" the name of the assault victim in the Guadalajara incident, José Romero Raya "in the common and ordinary Mexican fashion," Teja wrote in a memo to the sheriff. The entry in the ledger was dated "Fev 24 1970"; the brutal hacking in the rest room of the café had taken place between twelve-thirty and one-fifteen on the morning of February 25, 1970, or, as commonly thought of, the night of February 24.

Granting that the list might contain "mere" assault victims as well as actual murdered men, Sheriff Whiteaker decided he could not cancel the search for more bodies. He elected instead to arrange for two aerial reconnaissances, the first by a private firm, the second by Navy jets from Los Alamitos in southern California. The Navy planes were equipped with sophisticated cameras and sensing devices which had been employed in Vietnam to scout the Ho Chi Minh Trail. The aerial photos turned up nothing resembling a possible grave.

Although the People's Case Against Juan Corona was not yet ready for trial, by law Teja was required to initiate legal proceedings against the man now fretting his days away in the Yuba County jail across the river in Marysville. At Corona's first court appearance on the morning of his arrest, he had been advised of his constitutional rights and given an attorney. Roy Van den Heuval had waived an immediate arraignment, the formal pleading of guilt or innocence to the nine counts of murder for which Corona had been arrested. The arraignment had to be done now.

Reporters, cameramen and photographers were waiting when Captain Littlejohn, Sergeant Purcell, Detective Gregory, and Deputy Mason backed up to the door of the Yuba County jail. Scrambling around the car, the photographers grabbed what pictures they could before Corona was bundled into the back seat between the slight Gregory and the hefty Mason. The photographers had not been able to get a good head-and-shoulders shot because Corona had covered his face with his jacket.

Five minutes later, the patrol car pulled into the rear of the Justice Court building. Again one of the officers whispered an order to Corona who then pulled his jacket up around his head; the still photographers and television cameramen took what pictures they could. Though there were no good head shots, the resulting pictures—the first of Corona since his arrest—portrayed the farm labor contractor with his face covered, as if he had something to hide. It was a picture familiar to the public from gangland arrests in the East, of evil men hiding guilty faces. Experienced defense lawyers know this and advise their clients not to hide.

Corona did not utter a word at the short arraignment; Van den Heuval entered a blanket not-guilty plea for him. While a covey of artists from television stations and networks stood on chairs outside the courtroom to sketch the scene inside through the transom—Judge Hankins having barred the press and public from the hearing the day before—Teja and Van den Heuval sparred over a critical legal question.

The courts of the State of California have, in a long series of legal decisions, substantially opened the prosecutor's files to defense counsel. Grounded on the Due Process Clause's guarantee of fundamental fairness in criminal proceedings, the concept of discovery was formulated to equalize the gross imbalance of resources between the government and the defendant in a criminal case. Prosecutors have an enormous array of investigators, police agencies, crime laboratories, and experts qualified to testify on scientific matters. The district attorney can also call upon the office of the state attorney general for help in preparing legal briefs, especially on extraordinary matters. He has recourse, if necessary, to an almost unlimited budget. It is, in sum, what Supreme Court Justice Felix Frankfurter once called "the awesome machinery of the law."

In contrast, most defendants in criminal matters have limited amounts of money, certainly not enough to hire an attorney, pay for experts of their own, and retain private investigators.

To balance this, California's law of discovery requires the prosecution to turn over to the defense, in ample time for the documents to be used, all reports, interrogations, laboratory studies, investigations, and arrest records of prospective witnesses. Discovery, then, has the effect of revealing to the defense the prosecution's evidence, before that evidence is presented in court, so that the defense can build a rebuttal or prepare a cross-examination. Discovery also removes to a great extent the element of surprise from the prosecution's case; evidence withheld by the prosecution cannot be used in court, no matter how damaging it is to the defendant.

Van den Heuval had filed with the court a motion for discovery, seeking reports, photographs and transcriptions of any and all interviews. District Attorney Teja was opposed to granting the order, "largely as a matter of our own convenience at this time." The reports were voluminous, many still unfiled, the typists working full time just to keep up with the detectives, yet still two days or more behind.

Pleading with Judge Hankins, Van den Heuval argued, "We are asking the court and we are asking the district attorney to be allowed to get these reports and the witnesses' [statements]. At times it seems that the newspapers have more information than I do; the newspapers have more access to the various activities and the scene than I do." Van den Heuval's investigator had been barred a second time from the Sullivan ranch by a highway patrolman, though Undersheriff Cartoscelli was on the ranch at the time and knew of the earlier court order giving Van den Heuval access. Moreover, it rankled Van den Heuval that newsmen had been given a guided tour of the Sullivan property by Sheriff Whiteaker four days earlier, the sheriff pointing out the grave sites and detailing the search for more bodies. Van den Heuval could get no such cooperation.

Judge Hankins ruled that Van den Heuval could have access to the police reports in forty-eight hours, giving Teja time to sort through the accumulating material before duplicating it for the defense. Twenty-seven minutes after the arraignment began, it was over, Corona escorted back to the patrol car, the newsmen elbowing each other to get a look at him, photographers cursing the crush of competitors. His jacket once again over his face, Corona stumbled once on the stairs; two officers grabbed him by the arms to steady him.

Outside the small Justice Court, Van den Heuval was surrounded by reporters. "Does the not-guilty plea mean you are going to force the prosecution to prove its case?" one of them demanded, thrusting a microphone in front of him.

"That's right. You're damn right," he snapped. That extrajudicial comment would be Roy Van den Heuval's last as attorney for the defense.

8
El Gavilan
May 26-June 18, 1971

Richard Hawk had missed the major news story of May 26. Flying his single-engine plane to the Orange County Airport in southern California, Hawk was much more interested in the three-day ground school he was to attend than in his law practice or the news of the day. The Federal Aviation Agency's written examination for instrument flying was every bit as difficult as the state bar exam, or so it seemed; if he was to pass, he would have to concentrate in these classes.

It was not until seven o'clock on the morning of Thursday, May 27, that Hawk learned of the mass murders in Yuba City and of the arrest of a farm labor contractor by the name of Juan Corona. Eating breakfast in the coffee shop of the hotel, Hawk read the lead story in the Los Angeles *Times*. Like millions of others who skimmed the papers that morning, Richard Hawk, an attorney, drew the obvious conclusions:

The dead men were described as transient farm workers, Corona as a farm labor contractor; consequently there was a link between the dead men and the accused murderer. The men had been found hacked to death by "what apparently was a machete or large knife"; unconsciously, Hawk ruefully would concede later, he equated "machete" with Mexicans. Most of the bodies had been found on the Sullivan ranch, where Corona had access. Though the sheriff had admitted there was "no motive that we can discover," the killings were "sadistic," and, the young law enforcement officer added, "we are certain he committed the murders." The cumulative effect was damning, even on a lawyer who had come to specialize in criminal defense. Well, it wasn't his problem; he had this damn instrument flying test to worry about.

That evening Hawk took his two children to dinner at an expensive restaurant that looked out on the even more expensive yachts docked in Newport Harbor. He could always lose the weight later; he took it off as easily as he put it on. The kids deserved it, especially Cristi. Ever since the two of them had decided to leave their mother in Oregon to live with him, Cristi had had to be a little of everything—housekeeper and cook, high school student and adolescent, baby-sitter and dishwasher. It wasn't easy for her, especially when he got involved in a trial; there wasn't even time then for him to do the shopping. He'd come home worn out and fall asleep on the couch, heedless of the television set. Long since having plucked the car keys from his pocket to do the marketing, Cristi would be in bed when he got up to fix some leftovers into a midnight sandwich.

Still, he didn't think he had done too badly in the year since Derek had joined his sister in Concord. Cristi was an attractive girl; in a couple of years she would be a real knockout. Derek was all arms and legs, enthralled by the 'cycle in the garage Hawk had taken as a fee some months before. Oh, girls were all right, more fun than they used to be, but nothing compared to a Honda or Harley or Kawasaki. Almost couldn't blame the kid; there was nothing quite like riding a hog on an open road.

After dinner the youngsters agreed that the Long Beach pier would be all right; it would be fun to see the place their father had gone when he was a boy.

The pitch-and-toss games, the baseball-throwing booths, the stuffed pandas and plaster panthers poked at Hawk's memory. All this time and the pier hadn't really changed much; maybe amusement parks didn't. It was about as he remembered it. The big roller coaster—biggest on the West Coast, maybe bigger than any in the country—gone now, like his father, dead these many years, lying beside his mother in a cemetery in Walla Walla.

Hawk was proud of his father. His old man had done pretty well. Twenty years a cop, Clarence Hawk had retired from the department to buy a bar for $2,500. The war came along, and business boomed. Two years in that tavern, with his wife helping him, and they sold the place for $50,000.

With the money, Clarence Hawk bought a beer distributorship in the Walla Walla area, raised a son, and sent him off to the most socially prestigious school on the West Coast, Stanford. He didn't want his son to become a Model-T mechanic or a cop. A degree from Stanford would open doors for the eighteen-year-old boy if he decided he didn't want to become a partner in the beer distributorship.

Stanford hadn't been much different from high school, harder, but only a little more interesting. He liked political science—enough to get through school with acceptable grades—but he was still undecided about a job or career.

Hawk was graduated from Stanford in 1954 with a bachelor of science degree and a fiancée, a girl he had met at a New Year's Eve party. Marrying Marilyn, he spent the summer after his graduation back in Walla Walla, driving a beer truck. Two months of delivering Olympia, High Life, Heidelberg, and Acme in the summer sun convinced him he didn't want that. If there *was* anything that interested him, it was law school.

With the fall semester only weeks away, he applied for Stanford's law school and was accepted. The putative beer salesman and his new wife returned to Palo Alto, he to work forty hours a week as a bellhop and spend the rest studying, his wife to work until she got pregnant during his second year of law school.

Responsibility had helped to settle him down—that and the threat of returning to Walla Walla. Law school wasn't easy, but he had found something he liked to do. If legal research was boring, he did like trial work. He realized that quick thinking—an ability to make fast decisions —was the stuff of a good trial lawyer. That and an ability to make practical decisions. Like writing liberal-oriented exams for Democratic law school professors and conservative exams for Republican professors. He graduated in the top third of his class in 1957.

He'd never gone back to Walla Walla to sell beer. Instead, he had joined a Burlingame law firm, as a junior attorney in the probate department. The whole job consisted of writing wills, lifting the boilerplate from the form books, and filling in the blanks. Those blanks were big enough to be sure; Burlingame was then and is now an exclusive residential community on the San Francisco peninsula, full of wealthy widows with trivial problems. Five file cabinets full of wills waiting to "mature." Someone died, the will "matured," the firm took its cut, and two more open files replaced that of the old widow with a thousand shares of Standard Oil or five hundred in Ma Bell.

It was dull and frustrating. Hawk asked to be transferred to the firm's trial department. For a while he had followed a senior partner around the courthouse, doing nothing more responsible than running errands. At the end of a year, the partner told Hawk that he "would never make a trial lawyer." Hawk was dispatched back to probate, once again to hold old ladies' hands, to cluck sympathetically when a favorite lap dog died or a maid quit, to find a new dog or maid.

Six more months of writing fill-in-the-blank wills and he had quit. There had to be something better. Checking at the law school, he learned that an attorney in Pittsburgh, up on the Sacramento River, was looking for an associate. The job didn't pay much at first, $600 a month when he had been making $1,000. With two kids now it would be hard to make the change, but poverty was better than stagnation.

The Pittsburgh attorney had given him trial work all right—every dog he had. The first case should have been a tip-off. Two counts of armed robbery, eight witnesses—the guy was a goner, Clarence Darrow couldn't have saved him. The senior partner had surrendered the guy and gotten all the publicity, but when it came time to take the lumps, he had turned the case over to Hawk. Hawk had had the jury out eight hours.

Hawk's salary, dependent upon his senior partner for cases that could be won, plummeted. Financial problems led to marital problems; Marilyn finally took the two children and left for her family home in Oregon. A divorce followed.

That was rock bottom. Hawk took an apartment and learned what loneliness was. He shuttled from the office to the courts—winning maybe one in four of the cases his partner sent his way—to the bars of West Pittsburgh. The Okie music on the juke boxes there suited his mood, maudlin ballads of truckdrivers and trainmen and country girls. His stomach forever in knots, he had chewed three, four packs of Rolaids a day. It hadn't helped, not with all the booze.

The financial arrangement never improved. Two and one-half years after moving to Pittsburgh, he quit, and for the next six months he did as little as possible. There were days when he didn't have the price of a pack of cigarettes. So he moved television sets for a while, just to help a friend. His nerves settled down, and he began thinking about practicing law again. On his own.

The time spent hadn't been a total waste: he had learned how to be a trial lawyer. He had mastered all or almost all of the tricks of the trade. He had also learned from watching older lawyers how to influence a jury. God only knew what led a jury to a verdict—it wasn't the facts half of the time—but he had some ideas now. Simply enough, juries went for equities.

If the defendant was clean and a likeable guy, the jury would bend over backwards for him. If he wasn't, well, you had to show the jury someone worse, to put someone else on trial, to make the prosecutor defend someone he might not even know instead of prosecuting your client. It could be the police, or a screwed up investigation, an unfaithful wife, anything to deflect attention from your client.

A dozen murder cases in six years. Most attorneys wouldn't get even one in their entire careers. He had a good reputation in the county, and with it came the hard cases. Contra Costa, half a million people now, didn't have a public defender when he first got there. Members of the local bar were put on a list; when someone couldn't hire an attorney, he got the top name on the list.

Hawk had put his name down—it was a good way to earn a couple of bucks–and that was how he had gotten that first case—a murder the D.A. tried as an assault because the doctors weren't sure what had caused the woman's death, the beating or the bad heart. Gene Davis had beaten up on his girlfriend, then blanked out; that was his only defense. He probably had killed her, but he didn't know it if he did. Had blood all over him. Type AB. Her type was AB. That's the way the cops picked him up. He admitted he had been with her, but couldn't remember. Hawk got a hung jury the first time, and a not-guilty verdict when the D.A. refiled. Davis claimed he couldn't remember, the cops admitted he had said that, so Hawk had played the tapes of the police interrogation in court. Told about the death of his girlfriend, Davis had broken down and cried, right there on the tape. That convinced the jury.

There had been a lot of publicity locally on that. Enough to get Hawk going. Now he had all the work he could handle. Fifty felony cases, fifty misdemeanors cases a year, an income in mid-five figures. He won a lot more than he lost, and he tried more cases than most, refusing to bargain pleas with the prosecutors. This year he would try two or three heavy felonies, crimes with five-to-life sentences riding; he couldn't take more than that, not with four- or five-week trials. Too much preparation, investigation. But it was enough.

He had most of the things he wanted: a second marriage, the two kids with him now, a nice house, his own private plane. He was even toying with the idea of getting a Cadillac, one with all the options GM offered, something with a little class. If there was anything missing, well, sooner or later he and his new wife, Geneva, would get it together. They had their problems, Lord knows.

He liked to think that the old man would be pretty proud of him now. Pop had said if he was going to be an attorney to be a defense counsel. Strange, the old man had been a cop, but he liked defense attorneys better than prosecutors.

He had become a pretty good attorney—a defense attorney—even if he didn't read all the advance sheets. You didn't have to read all the goddamn things because a high percentage of the time the law followed what your common sense told you. He read the important cases, but a man could spend his life reading advance sheets, with all the appeals being filed now. Law books didn't do it for you; you became an attorney, really an attorney, when you sat at the counsel table and first realized you were the the only person standing between your guy and the gas chamber, when you felt the full weight of the state of California coming down on you.

Over breakfast the morning of May 27 Hawk read the mass slaying story. Somebody else, Corona and his attorney, the public defender, would be feeling the full weight now. By noon, when Hawk picked up the early edition of the afternoon paper, the mass murders were widely discussed by the ground school student pilots. There were fifteen bodies at the time, but the bigger story was about Corona's prior mental disturbance.

As an attorney, Hawk was offended by the release of the DeWitt hospitalization record. Corona's mental condition was admissible as evidence only under certain narrowly drawn conditions. It was one thing for people to gossip about the case during a coffee break, somehow finding in the mental commitment an explanation for the otherwise senseless murders. It was something else if the prosecution tried to use that as a motive. The trouble was, if they were talking about it at the Airporter Inn in Newport Beach, they were sure as hell talking about it in Yuba City, and that was where Corona would stand trial. Publication of that story had, in effect, introduced Corona's mental condition into the trial even before the trial began.

The following day's story was even more dubious from a legal stand-point. The fact that the sheriff claimed to have found bloodstained weapons was news, but the sheriff should have known better than to say that. Whether or not dried blood was present was something that could only be determined by a laboratory technician. And even then, two of them could disagree whether the blood was human or animal. Hawk might have his doubts about the propriety of the way the sheriff was releasing information, not to mention the judge, but it looked like Sutter County had Corona cold. There were the meat receipts found in the grave, the arsenal of weapons, the nine-millimeter pistol, the earlier assault on Raya at the Guadalajara Café, statements by the ranch foreman and another informant that Corona was nuts and sometimes had to be tied up because his temper was so bad.

The weekend was crammed. The ground school completed, Hawk had to take the written examination offered by the FAA on Sunday, yet still find time to take Cristi and Derek to Disneyland. On Monday, May 30, Hawk was back in his office, settled in the routine of his law practice. The Corona case was forgotten; he had his own problems to worry about.

Sutter County District Attorney G. Dave Teja had problems too. They had enough evidence to hold Corona for trial, especially if Van den Heuval was considering an insanity plea; the public defender would be so busy with that he wouldn't have much time to check anything else. But Teja still had loose ends to tie down. The lab reports weren't in on the weapons; the machete and the gun would be especially important. He had to make sure that Don Stottlemyer, the criminalist CII had assigned to the case, did that first; then Stottlemyer could work on the tire tracks, to see if they matched Corona's vehicles, and on the blood they had scraped from Corona's van and Impala.

He also needed the handwriting analysis on the ledger; if Terry Pascoe could make that as Corona's handwriting, it would prove that the ledger was, in fact, the "death list" the papers were calling it. Pascoe was having problems there; it didn't look like an easy match. Pascoe needed more samples of Corona's handwriting.

In his eight and one-half years as district attorney, a year longer if you counted the time he had been the part-time deputy, Teja had never encountered an investigation as complex as this. The sheer number of bodies still seemed unreal to him, but the number of victims by itself made little difference. Instead of one autopsy report there were twenty-five, twenty-five coroner's reports for Jack Purcell to prepare instead of just one.

No, that wasn't the problem. The trouble was the amount of evidence they had to sort out. It was difficult to tag the stuff properly they had gotten from the graves, let alone the bloodstained weapons, the pistol, the ledger with its death list, the receipts in the third grave, and other evidence. They had a half-dozen statements from witnesses putting Corona near where bodies were found or recruiting the bums in lower Marysville —he would have to watch that; calling the victims "bums" wouldn't be a good idea in front of the jury.

There were other problems too before the case could be ready for trial. José Romero Raya, the young man who had been cut in the Guadalajara Café, still insisted that it was Natividad Corona who did it, not Juan; they would have to reinvestigate that, and see if they could get Raya to change his story. The hacking wounds on the twenty-five dead men and on Raya were just too similar to ignore.

They would also have to talk to some witnesses again; a couple of them had not described Corona's pickup very well. They still had a dozen bodies unidentified and hundreds of inquiries about the victims from families looking for missing husbands and sons. (Eventually, the sheriff's department would sort through 1,550 telephone and mail inquiries.)

If nothing else, being shorthanded permitted Teja to take a hand in the direct investigation, like analyzing the contents of the ledger. Teja liked to be involved; he liked law enforcement. From the time he had gotten out of the Army and come back to Yuba City to practice law he had had the idea of running for district attorney. That was why he had gotten that certificate in police science administration at Sacramento State College even before he passed the bar. And why he had jumped at the chance to be John Hauck's deputy D.A.; when Hauck went on the bench, Teja had campaigned for his old boss' job.

He was twenty-eight when he was elected district attorney in 1962, the first East Indian to be elected to anything in the county. He was pretty proud of that. His father, an immigrant who managed to save enough money to buy an orchard, had gone a long way. A successful orchardist— the son liked that title better than "farmer" or "rancher"—B. S. Teja had really launched his second son on a political career. The father had been a wheelhorse in the Democratic Party locally, one of the few; Governor "Pat" Brown had appointed him to the Board of Governors of the county fair as a reward. The son wanted to go even further.

Dave had done pretty well for himself already: a good-looking wife he had met while attending law school at the University of Arkansas, a commission in the Army, two nice kids, an important job. Maybe it didn't pay as much as he would like or he and Billie Ann could use; $21,000 was pretty good money though, and the Board of Supervisors came through pretty steadily with raises. In just five years they had increased his pay from $13,000 to $21,480; they knew he was doing a good job and worth every penny of it.

Teja's conviction rate was right around ninety percent, as good as any prosecutor in the state most years. He bargained pleas a lot but never settled for any time less than he thought the judge would give anyway: a year in county instead of one-to-five in San Quentin. Summary probation for first offenders in misdemeanors.

His opponent in the last election, George Lane, had blown that up all out of proportion. It was Teja's first real campaign; he had run unopposed twice and didn't really know what to expect. Damn foolishness for Lane to claim that he was undermining the system of justice by plea bargaining, that it demoralized law enforcement.

Hell, he could hire a half-dozen young lawyers as deputies to try the cases if he wanted to; that's how he had started with Hauck. That wasn't the issue. But he might just as well save the county's money since the sentences wouldn't be any heavier after a trial than the ones he settled with defense attorneys in exchange for pleas of guilt. Lane should have known that.

Anyway, he had gotten reelected, by 500 votes out of 12,000 cast. It was closer than he had expected and he didn't intend to let it happen again; he'd do his fence-mending and political homework now, before the next campaign.

It rankled him though, he had to admit. Just barely beating an attorney backed by all those John Birch nuts. Teja wondered if that was why the reporter from the Sacramento *Bee* had asked him if he intended to call in the state attorney general's office to try the Corona case. Or maybe he had been tipped off in Sacramento. Teja had answered it pretty well. Yes, this would be his first murder prosecution, but he had tried about 175 cases before this and he intended to talk to other district attorneys, to get their advice. And he had just gotten convictions in a $3 million forgery ring, so he knew how to handle big cases.

He hadn't called the attorney general; they had called him, gingerly asking if he needed some trial help. He had turned them down, probably, he had to admit, because he guessed he felt pretty much like Roy Whiteaker did. Besides, he and Roy had to stick together; they were about the only Democrats holding elective office in this county. Teja would be damned if he'd help a Republican attorney general gild his reputation in order to run for governor in three years.

Teja wasn't always sure of his cases—no attorney can be—but he was sure about this one. Corona was guilty as could be.

The Corona family didn't agree. The shock was slowly wearing away; there were moments now when Gloria even smiled a little. The girls were confused, wondering where their father was, but it didn't seem to bother them too much. Children were good that way. They had a letter from Juan today from the jail in Marysville explaining the visiting hours. The sheriffs had told Juan to explain why they had not been able to see him. Gloria had read the first line of the letter, "My Esteemed Wife," and had started crying again.

Pedro did not wish to seem cruel, but this was not a time for tears. There were worse things to cry about. Juan was in bad trouble; the television said he was crazy, and the attorney was ready to send him to the hospital. Van den Heuval was a gentleman, but Pedro wasn't sure he was good enough to handle that bastard Teja. Van den Heuval didn't seem to do anything except ask them to send Juan to the hospital.

Pedro wanted to get another attorney. He had already driven to Sacramento and talked to the Mexican lawyer, who wanted $25,000 to represent Juan. That was a lot of money; even if they sold Juan's two houses they couldn't raise that kind of money. Felix didn't have it, and Natividad, he wouldn't give that much money to Juan, even if he did have four million pesos and all that property in Guadalajara. Natividad was not that close to Juan.

If Pedro had the money, he would be glad to give it to Juan, but Pedro didn't. Money was a problem now; here it was June and he couldn't get work for his crews. The ranchers who had hired him and his crews before now were telling him they wouldn't need him to thin or pick peaches this year. Only Mr. Robert Berg had stuck by him, and let him continue to use the camp there. Berg was the only one with *cojones*. He would have to find something, even if it was only picking fruit himself. Gloria and Juan's four girls were living with him and Lencha and their six children now. And *La Doña* Candida, his mother, had come from Autlan to be near Juan. That was fourteen people to feed, and Pedro had no job. Friends, a few, would help, but it wouldn't be enough when his savings ran out.

Right now Pedro had to talk to Tony Diaz, a kid who used to work for Felix on one of his crews. Diaz had called him up to tell him about some attorney in the Bay Area. Diaz had gotten into some trouble, bad trouble it seemed, and this attorney had helped him. He wasn't a *chicano,* but he was married to a Mexican-American. Diaz assured the younger brother if anyone could help Juan, this was the man.

At his camp at the Berg ranch, Pedro talked with Diaz, a green card with a wife and children in Jalisco, near Autlan. Diaz had been arrested in Pittsburgh, charged with two counts of attempted murder and one of assault with a deadly weapon. A policeman had lied and said that Diaz stuck a pistol in his face and tried to shoot him, but the gun misfired. The attorney had gotten him out on bail which meant he could work and earn money for his family instead of rot in the jail. He could have spent ten years in the penitentiary, the attorney told him, for assault on a police officer. But the attorney got him off. Even though Diaz didn't have much money, and would have to pay the attorney a little bit at a time, the attorney spent eight days in trial. He made the policeman out a liar, and the jury believed Diaz. They had deliberated less than two hours before bringing in a verdict of not guilty on all three charges.

So, if the Coronas needed a lawyer, Diaz assured them, he knew just the attorney for Juan. He would even phone him.

The call came through the answering service, the girl explaining that Tony Diaz wanted to talk to Mr. Hawk. Neither Hawk's Spanish nor Diaz' English had improved over the months, but the attorney understood well enough. Juan Corona's family wanted to talk to him. It was Tuesday, June 8.

On Sunday, June 13, Richard Hawk met with Juan Corona, Spanish Bible in hand, in the Yuba County jail. The thirty-eight-year-old labor contractor made an immediate impression on the attorney with his formal manners. A year later Hawk would recall, shaking his head slowly, Corona's refusal to sit down until Hawk and the bilingual Geneva had taken the chairs; his standing immediately when Hawk rose to walk around the small interview room. Corona apologized for his appearance. He had lost a lot of weight; the clothes they made him wear—wash-worn dungarees and a faded blue shirt—didn't fit. He hadn't had a haircut. That bothered him. He liked to be neat; before all this he had gone to his barber, Al Alvarez, every two weeks. A man had to look good if he wanted to get ahead.

They had little trouble understanding each other. When Corona spoke in Spanish—it was sometimes easier to answer difficult questions in Spanish —Geneva translated. Neither Hawk nor his Mexican-American wife would ever be able to define it, but both recognized that there was something in Corona's manner which convinced them the heavyset contractor was telling the truth. Hawk could only say, "You just had to believe the guy."

An attorney must be skeptical—of the police version of the facts, of potential witnesses, but most of all, of his client. Most people arrested for crimes are guilty, perhaps not of the crime with which they are charged —prosecutors like to pile on the charges in hope of securing a bargained plea to a lesser offense—but they are guilty of something. An attorney's job is to defend his client, to compel the prosecution to prove his client's guilt beyond a reasonable doubt, with what the judge's instructions term "a moral certainty." Some guilty men go free because their attorneys can establish that reasonable doubt in a jury's mind, even when the attorney himself knows, or believes, his client is, in fact, guilty.

But most do not, Hawk knew. You didn't win all that many big cases when you went to trial. Look at Percy Foreman; you didn't see him try that guy who shot Martin Luther King, Jr. He took a deal and ran. A smart criminal lawyer tried the cases he thought he could win; otherwise he tried to work out the best deal for his client he could. Maybe that would be all he could do for Corona, but it was better than nothing.

In an abstract sense, a defense attorney did not defend his client, he tested the system, forcing the government to follow the rules embodied in Constitution, law, and case book. Contrary to public opinion, the attorney who successfully defended a guilty man was not immoral, not unethical. A client's immorality had nothing to do with his attorney's ethics.

Hawk had no such problem. Within an hour he was convinced that Corona was innocent. They had talked about Corona's life in the United States, discussed superficially the charges and the evidence (Hawk knew only what he had gleaned from the press, and Corona little more), and, finally, whether the attorney from Concord would represent the nervous man locked in the Yuba County jail's padded cell. Corona didn't know about money; he didn't have much. His brother Pedro had told him it would cost $25,000.

Hawk agreed, but added that he didn't think money would be much of a problem. Juan had the houses; if he sold them he would make something on the deal, enough to get started on. After that, Hawk thought he might be able to start a defense fund. If every Mexican-American in the state gave just one dime, they could raise $25,000. The Corona case would be every bit as important to *chicanos* as the Angela Davis case was to blacks.

That was to be Hawk's first mistake. The Juan Corona Defense Fund was never to raise more than a few thousand dollars, despite repeated efforts by Hawk, Corona's family, and a handful of supporters. The Mexican-American community, unlike the black, was neither militant nor organized. Furthermore, Hawk was never able to demonstrate that Corona was arrested the way he was—in the middle of the night, without opportunity to explain the receipts—because he was a Mexican. Beyond that, there would not be enough to galvanize the largely somnolent, fragmented, and constantly bickering Mexican-American community to the cause.

Even if he had known that, Hawk was prepared to take the case. Such sensational cases, with all the publicity surrounding them, were rare. Just one, even an unsuccessful one, could make a lawyer famous, could guarantee him a succession of clients. If he were successful, Hawk would be in a position to pick and choose from the clients who sought him out, raise his fee from $1,500 for a routine felony to $5,000. He didn't need more money, but he wouldn't have to work as hard.

The Corona case is one any lawyer would have taken.

Even if he was never paid for his time, Hawk did have to consider the problem of money. He and Geneva—she would be needed as an interpreter —would have expenses. The $25,000 the *chicano* attorney in Sacramento wanted was only the half of it. Usually the guy who wants his own attorney never has the funds to pay for anything more than that, with nothing at all for investigators, expert witnesses, or psychiatric testimony.

Corona's defense would need $20,000 at least, even if Hawk was never paid a cent. But Hawk couldn't say no. How could he say no to a man like Pedro? Juan had left the decision to his younger brother, saying simply, "I trust you."

As nominal head of the family now, Pedro's approval of Hawk was decisive. Hawk was aggressive, Van den Heuval taciturn. The new lawyer talked about what he was going to do for Juan; Van den Heuval had only told them what Teja and Whiteaker were going to do to Juan.

That evening, Hawk, his wife, and the Corona family met with Van den Heuval in the public defender's law office. Van den Heuval was both relieved and disappointed that he was losing the case, relieved because of the very magnitude of the defense's task, disappointed that the big one was not to be his. They talked for a while, Hawk arranging to get from Van den Heuval reports and photographs he had already obtained from the sheriff through his motion for discovery. Whatever his investigators had, Hawk wanted. Van den Heuval agreed to type up the substitution of attorney papers and ask the judge for an immediate hearing.

Hawk already had formulated some plans. The first thing to do was to get Corona out of that cell, and quick. If Corona was crazy, he sure didn't act it. And also about the haircut: he wanted his client to look presentable; he had already told Corona to disregard Van den Heuval's order to cover his face in public. He also wanted to raise hell in Marysville about the jailers not feeding his client once; Corona hadn't complained "because he didn't want to make no trouble." All Corona wanted really was to see his family. He would have to get Archie Gore, his investigator, to work as soon as possible. They would have to double-check all the people who had given significant statements to the sheriffs. He would have to do a lot of reading, just to catch up, and a lot of talking to the family and to Corona himself. There were any number of things he had to know about —the Guadalajara axeing or knifing or whatever it was, whether or not Juan did have a temper, the business at the welfare office. He, Geneva, and Gore would have to find character witnesses for Juan, and maybe someone besides Gloria who could substantiate an alibi. It would be worthwhile too to visit the sheriff and the district attorney, just to find out what they were like.

It wouldn't mean too much right away, but Hawk was curious about the two men responsible for the jailing of his client. Hawk couldn't spring Corona on bail, but there were a number of things he could do for Juan. If it was as bad as he thought it was around here—Marysville and Yuba City were not that much different than Walla Walla—he would file a motion for a change of venue. There was no way Juan could get a fair trial in Sutter County, not now, not with all the publicity. It wasn't his responsibility really, but he could take Gloria down or ask Geneva to get Gloria on welfare. The fucking state had locked up her husband; they could support her and the kids. Pedro might not like that, if Hawk read him right, but fourteen people was a lot to feed with no money coming in. He would just have to convince Pedro that it was for the children; otherwise he would say no, just out of pride.

The first chance he got he was going to file a civil suit on Juan's behalf asking damages for slander and false arrest. He could even make it a joint suit, with the kids and Gloria also suing Sutter County. It might not be a good suit, not right now, but it would cheer up the family, make them think he was up here doing something, not just holding their hand. A suit would also be good for a headline or two, he thought, and if there was one thing Juan needed, it was some good press. As he had said about the newsmen in the jail cell, "Those bastards convict me." They sure had.

At three-thirty in the afternoon of the following day, Richard E. Hawk substituted for Roy Van den Heuval as defense counsel in the case of *People of the State of California v. Juan Vallejo Corona*. The seven-minute hearing took both the prosecution and the press by surprise; in time, Hawk would learn how to vex one while satisfying the other.

District Attorney Teja was concerned about the substitution; it was one thing to deal with a local attorney like Roy, a man you knew. With Roy, Teja knew where he stood. Not so with this stranger, though. Up here from the city or someplace like that. His card had listed only a post office box in Concord, a suburban community north of Oakland in the Bay Area. Teja smoothed back the thinning hair over his ears, and pulled his sports jacket down over the holstered pistol he liked to wear. Having a stranger defend Corona would make it more difficult. Teja wondered if the new attorney, Hawk, was any good, or if he had just sold the Coronas a bill of goods. Matter of fact, Teja was a bit surprised that there hadn't been more attorneys trying to get the case from Van den Heuval. Maybe the publicity scared them off; Corona was obviously guilty; who would want to take on a loser?

On Tuesday, Richard Hawk met the press for the first time, at the end of second short court session, this to postpone the preliminary hearing until July and to file his own motion for discovery. Hawk enjoyed talking with the local newsmen, but missed the national press people who had left town a week before. No, he wasn't changing Corona's plea. Juan was innocent. "Corona is trying to be brave," Hawk added. "Mexican men have a lot of pride, but he's damned concerned, as well he should be. The state of California is trying to put him in the gas chamber."

Blinking in the bright sunlight in front of the courthouse, Hawk continued. "A lot of people believe he's innocent, including me. They've got the wrong guy." To another reporter he said, "There is no reason to plead not guilty by reason of insanity." So much for that trial balloon launched earlier by Van den Heuval. Hawk conceded he was considering a change of venue. "In any case of this magnitude, the farther away a defendant gets from the immediate area in a trial the more likely he is of getting people who are objective."

Within forty-eight hours of taking the case, Hawk had outlined his defense; it would be a year before he could claim even a small victory in court.

If there was nothing he could do for his client right away in court, he could, at least, make Corona's living conditions a bit easier. Abrasive, even contemptuous of the law enforcement officers of the two counties, Hawk accomplished what he intended, threatening court orders when sheriffs were slow to comply. The calculated troublemaking heartened Juan; it also earned the attorney the nickname *"El Gavilan,"* The Hawk, among family members. Some of the tactics were petty, but they had the effect of letting both Teja and Sheriff Whiteaker know a new boy was in town.

On the morning of June 18, Hawk was lying on his bed in a Marysville motel, wearing undershorts and bathrobe, working through the Sheriff's Department reports for the first time. He was perplexed, first of all, by the superfluous nature of much of the material he had been given. Maybe it was just his attitude to begin with, being suspicious of cops and their motives, but Whiteaker's affidavit for a search warrant seemed very tentative, hardly the kind of thing an experienced cop would have relied upon to claim he was certain he had the right man. Leaving that aside, it provided Hawk with a lot of opportunities for cross-examination.

According to Whiteaker's affidavit, Purcell had told him that Ray Duron, the Sullivan ranch foreman, claimed Corona was crazy. That would be easy enough to check. And where did the sheriff get off using that kind of evidence anyway? Corona's mental condition could not be used in court unless the defense raised it first. Whiteaker had also relied upon a confidential informant who claimed Corona had to be tied down by the family when he lost his temper. There was no way they could keep that informant's identity a secret.

The big question was why had they snapped Corona up so fast, without getting better evidence? What was the big rush if they kept him under surveillance?

The telephone startled the attorney. Juan had been taken to the emergency room of Sutter County General Hospital at eleven o'clock that morning complaining of chest pains. The doctors thought he might have suffered a heart attack.

9

An Abandoned and Malignant Heart

June 18-July 12, 1971

For the moment, Juan Corona was resting comfortably, relaxed by a massive dose of Thorazine, a potent tranquilizer. The county medical director, Doctor Thomas Leavenworth, wasn't certain of his diagnosis. It could be a heart attack—Leavenworth would have some specialists in San Francisco read the ambiguous EKGs—or it might be nothing more than tension.

Obviously, Corona had reason enough to be tense, and he complained of being nervous, unable to sleep. He had apparently lost a lot of weight too, twenty-five pounds since last March when he was treated at the hospital's Migrant Clinic for a leg infection. Still, the burning pains he described in his chest and the flattened T-wave on the EKG suggested something more than a case of nerves. Cautious, Leavenworth insisted on admitting Corona to the hospital for further diagnostic tests though there seemed to be no immediate danger.

Corona stayed in the hospital for three weeks, the doctors unsure of their diagnosis, two deputies posted as guards around the clock at the door of the private room at the end of the new hospital's wing. His hospitalization would be a major concern for the next two months—Sheriff Whiteaker forced to deploy scarce manpower in order to keep Corona under guard, District Attorney Teja and defense counsel Richard Hawk alike pondering the strategic advantages and disadvantages of an ill defendant, Doctor Leavenworth unsure of the proper therapy, and County Administrative Officer Larry Cilley fearful that Corona would die in custody, making the county liable for a wrongful death suit.

Corona's illness gave the district attorney more time to prepare his still incomplete case. Two days before, Hawk had postponed the preliminary hearing until July 13, on the ground he needed the delay to familiarize himself with the case against his client. He had stormed about the courtroom, demanding enlargements of the photos Mason had taken, copies of the ledgers now at CII, all but claiming that Teja was deliberately withholding evidence. And then when the district attorney told the judge he was "a little disturbed, frankly, at this particular moment about the obvious publicity and photographs, the coverage that this particular proceeding will receive in the news media," Hawk had gone out of his way to be snide. "Mr. Corona is innocent of any charges brought against him. He has nothing to hide. I will look out for Mr. Corona's interests." All Teja was really suggesting was that it might be possible to waive Corona's presence at some of the procedural hearings, and thereby cut down on any prejudicial pretrial publicity.

The district attorney now had until July 13 before he would have to present the People's case at the preliminary hearing before Judge Hankins, his onetime boss. He and Whiteaker might be able to whip things into shape in that time, but Teja was skeptical. Hawk appeared to be experienced; and a good trial lawyer, Teja realized, could punch holes in the case the way things stood.

They still had no written reports from CII on the physical evidence; Stottlemyer made the bullet from Kamp's head as a nine-millimeter—that fit Corona's pistol all right. There was a lot of blood, but the machete didn't match. So far as they knew, there was no motive for Corona to kill those twenty-five men. A lot of witnesses helped tie together a reasonable circumstantial evidence case, yet it was not airtight. Some of the witnesses were vague, or obviously confused.

Teja had one good option open to him. He could avoid the preliminary hearing, and especially the cross-examination by a hostile defense attorney, by convening the grand jury, presenting the case there, and getting a true bill.

The nineteen members of the Grand Jury of Sutter County, drawn by a clerk from the forty names placed in the century-old jury wheel by Judge Hauck, were neighbors of the district attorney. Without legal backgrounds, they trusted Teja, their friend and neighbor, to do what was right.

In theory, the Grand Jury is to be an independent tribunal, convened secretly to weigh the evidence in a criminal matter, as a judge would do publicly at the preliminary hearing. The panel of citizens is to stand between the police and the public, scrutinizing the actions of both. In practice, the Grand Jury more often than not stands shoulder to shoulder with the prosecutor, arm in arm with the police.

California law stipulates the Grand Jury is to "find an indictment when all the evidence before it, taken together, if unexplained or uncontradicted, would, in its judgment, warrant a conviction by a trial jury." But the district attorney alone chooses which evidence the grand jury will hear; even when invited to testify, as Corona would be, defendants rarely appeared or stood upon their Fifth Amendment right to silence. They would have to answer the prosecutor's hostile questions without benefit of counsel—when the prosecutor, by going to the Grand Jury in the first place, had elected to seek an indictment.

The Grand Jury of Sutter County met on Thursday, July 1, to hear the first of fifty-seven witnesses that Teja and his deputy, Thomas Mathews, were to call. Insurance salesman Robert Hunt, the jury foreman, called his sixteen colleagues to order—the two absentees presented no problem since only twelve votes were necessary to return an indictment—warning them that any member "who has a state of mind in reference to the case or to either party which will prevent him from acting impartially" should withdraw. Additionally, Hunt reminded them, "Dave has already talked to you about not discussing it with anybody, and that means anybody."

Teja began with three of the four doctors who had performed autopsies on the victims, routinely taking them through their reports: how many wounds, size of lacerations, depth, cause of death. The most difficult problem was keeping the numbers of the victims in order; Doctor Charles Clement had autopsied two bodies numbered "2," one from the west side of the Sullivan ranch, the other the second body tagged at the mortuary as coming from the eastern portion of the ranch.

To clarify the confusion, Doctor Clement's second "number 2" was relabeled as "East-2, Number 4," the second body from the east side, the fourth found overall.

To identify the victim, Teja asked, "Is there anything distinguishing about the left hand of the individual in this photograph?"

"The left fifth finger has been amputated—old, not recent," the local internist answered.

Teja then raised a question that television-primed laymen expect doctors to answer, one which qualified pathologists would prefer to avoid. "Could you approximate a time of death for this individual?"

"I don't think so," Doctor Clement said, shaking his head.

"Okay. Could you put it within any particular time limit?"

"Based on the amount of change in the body, I would say that it was a matter of a few days or a few weeks."

"Doctor," Deputy District Attorney Mathews interjected, "You mentioned this one, the body was moderately well-preserved. And this is in comparison to the last body you testified about?"

"That's right. The degree of degeneration or decomposition had not progressed as far." Beyond that, the doctor could not say; the first body was older, dead longer than the second. "It is very difficult because of circumstances. It depends upon heat, moisture, the conditions surrounding the body at the time and where it's been stored."

"Other than saying that this one is a newer body, in other words, shorter length of time dead, you couldn't make an actual time factor then?" the deputy persisted.

"I could within very broad limits, but I can't really tie it down as to a day or so many hours."

Doctor Pierce Rooney, the chief forensic pathologist for the Sacramento County Coroner's Office, was far more thorough. He had reautopsied fourteen of the victims, including the man found in Goro Kagehiro's peach orchard, Kenneth Whitacre. Hacked about the head, Whitacre's skull was to provide the prosecution with an important piece of evidence. Doctor Rooney had removed a portion of the skull and sent it to the criminalistics laboratory of CII. The minute striation marks in the hard bone along the edge of a hacking wound were to be compared there to the knives and machete found in Corona's possession.

"In your opinion," Teja asked the doctor, "what sort of weapon would make that type of wound?"

"It think it has to be a fairly heavy cutting instrument," the doctor answered, "and I think that a machete, meat cleaver, scimitar, those kind of things can do this." An axe was not likely. "I don't think an axe would bounce off as readily as this did, number one; and, number two, I haven't seen axe wounds with this smooth of an edge."

"Did you ascertain from your examination a tentative or actual time of death?"

"He was in excellent shape. A person that's dead over twenty-four hours is not in excellent shape, so I would say probably he was dead under twenty-four hours."

Of the other victims, Doctor Rooney was less precise. "In a decomposed body the best way to determine when somebody died is to have a reliable witness see them alive. Scientifically speaking, there is no real good way that one can come close to telling when someone has been buried." Rooney could only estimate that the bodies he had examined had been dead as long as three months. The minimum time, "again a rough estimate," was a week, "maybe a little less than that."

The following morning, Teja brought on Doctor Joseph Masters, the second of the two Sacramento County pathologists who had reautopsied the victims, beginning with the case, as he told the doctor, "that I believe has been recently identified to you as Sutter County's E-1-3," the first body found on the riverbank, the third overall. "Decomposition was only moderate in this individual. There was still some slight rigidity remaining in this body. There was, however, some detachment of the skin, and there were postmortem degenerative changes."

"Was there anything obvious about this individual before death that would have been an identifying feature?"

"There had been a prior amputation of the left fifth finger, yes, sir."

"That would be the little finger of the left hand?"

"The little finger of the left hand," Doctor Masters agreed.

Teja then introduced a series of witnesses who formed the bulk of the circumstantial evidence case sheriff's deputies had amassed. A gaunt Roy DeLong said he had known Pete—"I never did know his last name until this came up"—for eight to ten years. He hadn't seen his friend around since the middle of April. He had been with the victim identified as Sigurd Beierman, standing on a Marysville street corner, when "some man walked up and asked Pete if he wanted to do a little work. Pete said 'yes' and went down Third Street with him" to ride off in a yellow panel truck.

"Would you recognize the man if you saw him again?"

"No, sir, I couldn't say that I would—"

Shortly after the first of May, DeLong had stopped Marysville police officer Ronald Huff to tell him that Beierman was missing. As they were talking, DeLong spotted the yellow van in which Beierman had driven off.

Officer Huff remembered more than did DeLong. "He stated the last time he had seen him he got in a van with a Mexican subject and that was the last time that he had seen him."

"Okay. Who was in the van?"

"Juan Vallejo Corona."

"Smokey" Brbora had lived in Marysville all his life, forty-five years. He stayed at the Golden West Hotel in lower Marysville, working at odd jobs, for a period sweeping out the Guadalajara Café, owned by Juan Corona's brother, Natividad.

In the middle of May, Brbora had been offered a job by Juan Corona. "He asked me if I wanted to dig some holes. I told him no."

James Pervis too was a longtime resident, and like Brbora had swept out the Guadalajara for a while. He too was offered work by Juan Corona, "clean-up work around the camp." Pervis too had declined, concerned about getting his car fixed.

"Do you ever spend any time over in Marysville, Mr. Pervis?"

"Well, that's my hangout when I am not working."

"Have you ever seen Juan Corona over there?" Teja asked.

"Well, yes," Pervis nodded. "Off and on, picking up guys around there."

"Okay. What sort of people were these who he picked up over there, Americans, Mexicans?"

"Yes. Mostly Americans."

"What sort of men, young men, old men?"

"Middle-aged. You know, runs around thirty to fifty, sixty, something like that."

Pervis had been well primed. "Did you know any of them?"

"Oh, yes. One he got, I know."

"Who was that?"

"Earl William Vaughn." The missing Vaughn's name had been found in the ledger in Corona's bedroom. Vaughn might well be one of the four still unidentified bodies, or one still lying out there in some shallow grave.

Byron Shannon, the labor recruiter, testified that on May 12 he, a friend nicknamed "Cleanhead," Riley, Smallwood, and a fourth man he thought might be the twenty-second victim, Lloyd Wenzel, were in the small park at the foot of D Street. (Earlier, Shannon had described the third man as the one-eyed Paul Allen.) "Around about eleven o'clock, Mr. Corona and another fellow in the pickup drove up. They was in a blue-and-white Chevy pickup, and he said he wanted to work us. So Willie asked him could he go to work for him, and he said he didn't want no colored. He taken Smallwood and Mr. Riley and put them in the pickup and he left with them."

"Did he say where?"

"He say, 'Out to the Sullivan ranch there.' "

The man with Corona, Shannon testified, was about forty years old, not too heavy, a Spanish guy wearing a straw sombrero. Shannon was certain of his description of the pickup, "a blue-and-white Chevy, a late model."

Deputy District Attorney Mathews pursued the identity of the man with Corona, showing Shannon a photograph.

"Yes, I seen him about three or four weeks ago. I seen him in the pickup with Corona."

It was a photograph of Juan Mosqueda, the farm worker who had suddenly left the California Packing Corporation ranch the day news of Corona's arrest was broadcast and had been located later in Stockton by Detectives Duncan and Cochran.

"At the time with Smallwood and Riley?"

"With Smallwood and Riley when I seen him." Shannon was excited, delighted to be of use. "He is the one sitting in the pickup."

The following day, Shannon appeared a second time before the Grand Jury to identify the man he had seen "with Juan Corona on May 12 when he picked up Riley, Smallwood, and the other fellow.

"Is he the Mexican man sitting out in the hall?"

"Sitting outside there," Shannon agreed, nodding. "I seen him sitting out there a while ago."

Shannon was excused, and Juan Mosqueda was brought into the Grand Jury room. It was a clever bit of staging, but Mosqueda, unlike Shannon, did not seem to know his part.

The man tracked down in Stockton because he was believed to have been with Corona when someone was killed shifted nervously on the witness stand. He admitted he spoke English "a little bit, but it's better with an interpreter." Teja brushed it aside, telling foreman Hunt, "We believe Mr. Mosqueda speaks English to get by well enough without an interpreter."

Mosqueda had first met Corona in 1962 when he signed onto the contractor's olive picking crew in Oroville. He had last seen Corona between May 8 and 12 in front of a bar in Marysville. He had thought to ask the contractor for a job, but did not.

"What was he doing?" asked Teja.

Mosqueda shrugged. "I just saw him. There was some guys getting into a green or bluelike bus, wagon, or something. I cannot remember. I cannot remember what kind of vehicle it was."

"Okay. What kind of guys were these?"

"I just saw the hats. They were Mexican hats."

"Do you recall an incident on the twelfth of May where you went down to the park on D Street in Marysville near the Guadalajara with Mr. Corona?"

"No. I never been there with Mr. Corona."

"Okay. Never ever?"

"No." Mosqueda was firm.

"What sort of hat do you wear, Mr. Mosqueda?"

"When I work I use that kind of small hat, cloth hat."

"Do you wear a Mexican straw sombrero?"

"No."

"Never?"

"Never."

Working from a prepared questionnaire, Teja shifted now to the incident which had ultimately led to Mosqueda's arrest as a material witness. "Have you ever been with Mr. Corona when he picked up somebody to work for him?"

"No. Never."

"Where were you when you heard that he had been arrested?"

"I was driving my car from the CPC [California Packing Corporation] Camp to the job."

"And what did you tell Mr. Hodges that day?"

"I tell Mr. Hodges I be—I been a little surprised, because I—when I saw Mr. Corona I intend to ask for a job, you know. And then I say, 'Maybe if I ask to him for a job maybe I be the ones that be in the—' I mean, dead."

Mosqueda was not being helpful. He claimed he had never ridden with Corona, not in the van, not in the pickup. He had last worked for Corona in August and September of 1970, picking peaches at the Sullivan ranch. He had driven each morning to the job there in his own car, a 1963 Chevrolet. No, he had never owned a pickup. As far as Mosqueda knew, Corona hired only Mexicans, no Anglos, no winos.

Teja was nettled. If Hodges was telling the truth—and why would he lie?—if he hadn't gotten the story confused, then Mosqueda was lying. The lie detector test suggested something was screwy.

"Since you heard that Mr. Corona was arrested, have any of his family or friends contacted you, Mr. Mosqueda?"

"No." Mosqueda shook his head.

"Have any of his friends talked to you about this case?"

"No."

Teja changed tack again. "Why did you quit working for Mr. Hodges?"

"Because the cherries, I make more money there."

"But you just quit during the middle of the day, didn't you?"

"Yes. They was not working." Mosqueda paused. "Was it raining?" he asked, then nodded to answer his own question.

"You took off without even picking up your check, didn't you?"

"Yes. I tell to him send me to the address I give him."

"You were afraid, weren't you?"

"No, I not afraid."

Trying to shake Mosqueda's story, Teja challenged the farm worker's manhood. "When the officers contacted you in Stockton you were very frightened, weren't you?"

"Fright?"

"Afraid."

"Afraid, no." Mosqueda stammered to explain, but failed for a lack of English.

"Isn't it a fact that you lost control of yourself and messed your pants when the officers took you into custody in Stockton?"

Mosqueda winced. "No."

"You didn't mess your pants?"

"No. No. I tell to him, I—when I was going to my car, I–I going to go to the rest room, but I don't do it, no."

"Okay, Have you ever gone out and actually solicited people for Mr. Corona, asked people to go to work for him?"

"No, I never." For another ten minutes, Teja and Mathews alternated questioning Mosqueda, reluctant to let him go, unable to tie him to Corona through his own testimony. They dismissed him finally in favor of Melvin Hodges, the foreman at the CPC ranch.

Hodges was reluctant to be involved. He had earlier told Detectives Duncan and Cochran "that he had been contacted by a high official from CPC Packing and advised that they were a packing company and not a police agency. He was also advised that anything concerning this case that he might have heard it would be advisable for him to keep to himself and not relay any information to the Sheriff's Department. Mr. Hodges advised at this time," Duncan wrote in a report dated June 9, "that from the conversation with the high official it was indicated that if he became involved in this incident that he would be replaced."

A twelve-year employee of the ranch owned by the Del Monte Corporation, Hodges was now involved. "Me and the crew boss were going through checking the thinning job, and this one particular fellow was very nervous. And he [was] actually shaking. I thought maybe he had been injured or something."

It was Mosqueda. "I asked the crew boss what was the matter with him, and he said he had just heard over the news that a fellow had been arrested, this Juan Corona. . . .

"He was nervous about it because he had been with Corona one time when they picked up a fellow in Marysville and went out to the Jack Sullivan ranch. And the guy said, 'Gee, this could have been me out there if this guy was the one doing all this.' "

Byron Shannon's lead had evaporated, Teja reluctantly realized. In the first place, the lie detector test was inadmissible in court; they couldn't use that to impeach Mosqueda. Secondly, Hodges' testimony was inadmissible hearsay; his crew boss, not he, had talked with Mosqueda. Hodges was merely repeating what he had been told; there was a good chance that either the crew boss or Hodges had misunderstood Mosqueda's story about taking someone out to the Sullivan ranch with Corona.

Willis "Cleanhead" Lasby, the shoe shine boy, was no help either. He had been in the park with Shannon "and a couple of other guys," but "I am drunk. I don't know exactly what happened."

A man had come up and asked them to work, but Lasby didn't remember what the man looked like. He had made a mistake when he earlier described the vehicle for the two detectives, he really didn't recall what it looked like.

Ishmuel Kenneth Walton, like his friend Donald Smith, was a wanderer, but unlike Smith, Walton did not work in the fields. Instead, he was a house painter, a craftsman among unskilled laborers.

Walton had last seen Smith on April 30 just before leaving for a month-long stay in Oregon. He and Smith had been sitting around the Day Center "waiting on something to do" when they were approached by a man offering them work—two or three hours' work digging a hole to bury garbage.

So I told him I wasn't interested. Then he asked Don to go. So when he asked Don to go, I told Don not to go, so he didn't go."

"Why did you tell Don not to go?"

"Well, you know, normally, a man ain't going to dig a hole to bury garbage; too many garbage dumps around."

"Just sounded a little suspicious to you?" Teja asked, smiling faintly at his leading question.

"That's right."

Corona had left, according to Walton, to pick up "American people, white people, I mean. Just one. Right there by the Day Center. It's where he came down every day and picked them up. He always just picked up one man at a time."

Teja and Mathews had now established that there were twenty-five dead men and Corona had either offered jobs or had been seen picking up some of them about the time they were killed. With twelve additional witnesses—eight of them employees of the Sullivan ranch itself—he was able to place Corona at various times in the vicinity of a majority of the graves.

Ray Duron, an excellent witness, was to tie the loose ends together. Born in Mexico, long since naturalized in the United States, he spoke impeccable English. An employee on the Sullivan ranch since 1944, Duron was named foreman in 1969. Both ambitious and hard-working, Duron had been elected president of the local chapter of a far-flung Mexican-American benevolent society, and had become the announcer on a one-hour Spanish language radio program broadcast on Sunday mornings. A home owner, a taxpayer, Duron was prosperous enough to afford a European vacation, a trip that set him off from most of his neighbors. In the Marysville-Yuba City area, he was considered "a responsible member of the Mexican community." The district attorney called him Mister Duron, but what he most sought, social acceptance by the majority, eluded him.

The cooperative Duron's testimony was wide-ranging. He had been there when Detective Gregory came around with the photo of the first victim, Kenneth Whitacre, and had shown it to Corona. "He looked at it, and he told me in Spanish, 'This fellow looks like he is dead already.' To which I replied, 'As a matter of fact, he is. That's a picture of a dead man.'"

"Was this done matter of factly, or did he appear to be surprised or upset in any way?"

"Nothing at all. Very matter of fact about the whole thing."

"Calm?"

"Very calm," Duron agreed.

Corona, he said in answer to a series of questions from the district attorney, during the April–May thinning season used Mexican laborers.

"Did he ever hire wino types to work in his crews in the orchards?"

"Yes. During the peak of the harvest season when help is hard to get he would hire anything that came out looking for a job: wino types, drive-ins, families."

The contractor had exclusive use of the large bunkhouse, the cook house or mess hall, and a small shack adjacent to the two larger structures. Because all of the buildings on the ranch had a common lock, Corona with a "Twenty-Twenty" key, as it was called, had access to most of the ranch.

Did Corona ever complain of any heart trouble? No. In April, "he had a boil on one of his feet that kept him off the job for two weeks or more."

"Did he stay completely away from the ranch during that period of time, did he take a lighter job, or just what did happen?"

"He was off the job, but he wasn't completely off the ranch. He would come and go. He would visit the bunkhouse or the cook house often. And he asked me if I had a job that he could perform such as driving a tractor, something that would keep him off his feet." Corona worked a day and one-half driving a tractor, fertilizing young trees.

"Was he actually able to walk during that period of time?"

"Well, he had a real soft slipper on and he said he couldn't walk."

"Did you see him walk at all?"

"Yes."

Coolly, Duron agreed that during April and May there was nothing to take Corona to the orchards of the Sullivan ranch alone.

Using an aerial photo, Duron reviewed the ten graves uncovered by ranch employees. "Juan Sanchez found this one," the foreman pointed out. "And I found this one myself. This is the one that the ranch carpenter—his name is Jim Cummings—had told me about a suspicious incident that happened the Saturday before. So we went out there, walked five minutes and we found this grave right here. And this one right here, we found it because of another incident that one of our employees told me about. And this one up there was found because I had sent José Ramirez out to flag some trees off for greendrop in that particular peach orchard. And in the process of flagging off the trees he found that grave."

Duron's testimony was compelling. Teja hammered it home. "So this one in the corner was the only one of these four here in the orchards west of the levee that didn't result from some suspicious circumstance" of seeing Mr. Corona alone in an orchard.

"That's right."

"At one time, Mr. Duron, you related to me an incident that occurred when a group of employees of the ranch or, perhaps, of Mr. Corona's, were harvesting pears. I believe this was probably last year. Something about the workers telling you about Mr. Corona coming out and checking their work while they were filling bins."

"Yes. It wasn't his crew. It was our crew. And Mr. Corona came out there where they were and began to look, and instead of looking at the trees or the bins he kept looking at the ground. The crew boss remembers this because now he thinks that there might be somebody else buried out there, as they remember distinctly a depression or an indentation in the ground that looked very, very much like the ones we have been finding at the ranch later."

"But it has not been uncovered since this all came up in May?"

"No." Duron shook his head.

In a courtroom, a defense attorney's objection would have prevented such testimony—both because it was hearsay and because Corona would not be charged with a twenty-sixth murder. Evidence about a presumed twenty-sixth victim could not be used to convict on twenty-five other counts.

The next witness, Chain Singh Khera, had known Corona since 1962 when the labor contractor first supplied workers for Khera's sugar beet farms. Like Teja a member of the county's East Indian community, Khera now owned a group of prune and peach orchards along Larkin and Eager Roads, one stand adjacent to the Kagehiro property.

Khera had seen Corona on a dirt access road between orchards "about two day, I think—I don't know for sure—two or one day before they found the body on—right close to the body—where the first body they found it."

"How close was he to the place where they found the body?"

"Oh, maybe about two hundred yard."

The two men had approached each other along the dirt track, and had stopped their vehicles. From the driver's seat of his car, Khera had asked, "What you be doing?"

"What did he say?" Teja prompted.

"Well, he say he come—he say, 'Please give me job for thinning.' He say, 'Help me out.' I told him, 'I told you too many time I don't want to start here. I want to start other place, finish other place first.' " Khera had promised to let Corona know when he would need a crew, and the two had parted.

Teja called three other witnesses to place Corona in the north river-bottom orchard during April and May at odd hours. David Schmidl and his girlfriend Sharon Reeves had driven through the camp and over the levee on May 19—"approximately between 8:30 and 9:30, around there"—to fish for catfish in the night waters. "Well, we first pulled up, we didn't see him at all, just his pickup. And Dave got out of the pickup and walked over to the river, and I was sitting in the pickup, and Mr. Corona came out of . . . the other side in the bushes, and he had a shotgun or a rifle. And he got in his pickup and left," Miss Reeves said.

"You are sure it was not a shovel or something?"

"No," Miss Reeves shook her head. "It was a gun."

The next witness, Jacob Compton, the civil engineer for the state Department of Water Resources, was surveying the Feather River in late April. On the 28th or 29th, he twice saw "a light-colored" van driving on the curving access road that led into the river-eroded orchard. He was too far distant to identify the driver.

James and Wilma Huff lived next door to the Coronas on Richland Road, neighbors but not friends. Mr. Huff knew a bit about Corona's cars. "He had a new Chevy panel, yellow panel. He had an older Chevy pickup, red and white. And then a Chevrolet sedan, two-door hardtop."

"Did you ever see anybody drive a blue or a blue-and-white pickup around there," Teja asked.

"No." Huff was unable to tie Corona to the truck others had said he had driven.

"Did you ever have occasion to watch Juan Corona wash his cars?"

"Yes." Huff nodded.

"Did he do this regularly?"

"Pretty often."

"The panel truck?"

"Yes. I saw him on one occasion."

"The pickup itself?"

"Not that I can recall on the pickup."

"Was there anything unusual about his washing cars? Did he do it with unusual frequency or—"

"At the time," Huff broke in, "no, didn't seem to me."

Huff also noted that Corona would frequently be home at seven-thirty in the morning; "I figured he was getting ready to leave." He also was at home during the noon hour, when Huff came home for lunch. Huff himself hadn't noticed it, but his wife, Wilma, "asked me several times and mentioned it several times about the odd hours that he would keep at night, but I did not ever observe it myself."

Mrs. Huff explained. "Well, we don't usually go to bed, you know, until late, like eleven or so, and I would hear him some time after that leaving, and then I wouldn't usually hear him returning. But it would be anywhere from, say, midnight on that I would hear him get up and leave during the night."

Thomas Leavenworth, the medical director of the county hospital, was asked to review Corona's medical history. On March 1, Corona was treated at the hospital Migrant Clinic for pains in his back and shoulders. The examining physician diagnosed it as "primarily muscular pain from straining." At the time, the doctor also noted Corona had a mild hypertension. A week later, Corona was "somewhat better"; the musculoskeletal ache had eased with a pain killer and rest.

On March 15 Leavenworth treated the contractor for a small circular infection of his right calf which had spread to the lymph nodes in his groin. His entire leg infected, Corona was to take an antibiotic, rest, and apply compresses. Three days later he was to return to have the infected area opened up. On April 1, Corona had returned to the clinic, his leg healed.

"Just for our own interest at this particular time, what is his present prognosis?" Teja asked.

"Well, Mr. Corona has electrocardiographic evidence that he has either had a coronary or came about as close as you can and not have one," the doctor began.

"I don't think you could undergo the rigors of what it sounds like your preliminary hearing is going to be. If it's going to be a stressful, tough two-to-four-week program, I just can't see how he can do it. Stress and pressure, internal emotional pressure, seem to be more of a problem to this man than physical exertion from what I can tell. It would seem that he might respond to a court hearing even worse than he would, say, mining coal."

William J. Vasquez, Corona's personal physician, testified that Corona had been in to see him on April 19, suffering from an infected right foot. "He was unable to bear weight on the foot because of the pain and swelling. The infection had apparently started from a blister on the end of the toe, and then as the germs got into the tissue they spread throughout the soft tissue of the foot."

"Was he able to walk on the foot?"

"With extreme difficulty. As I remember, the first day he came in he hopped in on one foot because it was too painful to bear weight on it." The infection was "practically well" by April 26.

"How long was he incapacitated so that he either had to walk or suffer a severe limp during this week-long period?"

"Oh, I would say practically the entire week."

Teja was disappointed. Theoretically, some of the twenty-five victims had been killed during that period. "Okay. But he was able to get around?"

"Well, yes. I think after about the twenty-second he was able to get around, but he was still favoring his foot."

"Okay. How long had he had this infection, in your opinion, before he came to you on the nineteenth?"

"Oh, I'd say probably a few days."

Teja changed the subject. "During the period of time when he has been coming to you, has he ever complained to you about his heart?"

"No. I have nothing in my records about his heart."

The district attorney had two witnesses to link Corona to some of the evidence found in the graves. Meatcutter Donald Frazier verified he had given Juan Corona a receipt and a sales slip on May 21 at the Del Pero Brothers meat market—the two pink slips found in the third victim's grave along the riverbank.

Eleven-year-old Mark Sustrick testified that he delivered a hundred copies of the weekly Twin Cities *Shoppers' Guide* in the Richland Road neighborhood. A folded copy of the April 21 issue, a rubber band still in place, had been found in the debris of the twenty-fifth grave. The young man wasn't sure, however, if he had delivered the throwaway paper to every home. "I would just go up and down the street, zigzag kind of like, to each house."

The next witness was Don Stottlemyer. It was only common sense that Stottlemyer be assigned to the Corona case by his superiors at the state's

Criminal Identification and Investigation bureau. For ten years a criminalist, he also owned a ranch near Marysville, knew the area, and was familiar with many of the local law enforcement officers. His task was to provide the technical expertise the Sutter County Sheriff's Department lacked to analyze the physical evidence.

For over an hour and one-half, Teja and Stottlemyer reviewed the evidence gathered by sheriff's deputies at the Richland Road house and the Sullivan ranch. There were human bloodstains on the right sleeve of the Levi's jacket found on a shelf in the rafters of the garage at Corona's home. There was blood on the fly of one of the two pairs of undershorts found in Corona's van. The species test failed, "quite possibly due to the age of the stains." There was blood too on both knives found in the mess hall at the Sullivan ranch. The silver-and-black "Tennessee Toothpick" taken from the shelf in the mess hall had thin smears of blood on the handle and guard; Stottlemyer also had found dirt on the blade, as if it had been stabbed into the ground as hunters frequently do to clean a knife. The second knife, found sheathed in the desk drawer, also had human bloodstains on the blade and handle; it too had apparently been hastily cleaned by a thrust into the ground.

A number of blood-flecked items had been found in Corona's two-door hardtop. But the amount of blood, or lack of it, was disturbing. Stabbed in the chest, hacked about the head, the dead men would have bled profusely. Even after they had been dead for some time and their hearts stopped pumping, blood would have spilled from the wounds as they were transported to the Sullivan ranch graveyard. "Suppose, Mr. Stottlemyer, somebody had gotten blood in the trunk of his car such as appears on this floor mat or trunk mat, whatever you want to call it, and he washed the automobile out with water, would you still be able to determine the presence of blood as you have in this particular example?"

An experienced witness, Stottlemyer refused to overcommit himself; a copy of the Grand Jury transcript would routinely be given to Corona's defense. "It would depend on how thoroughly it had been cleaned out. If the blood was real fresh it would probably dissolve in the water quite readily. As blood gets older, it doesn't dissolve as readily. Here again, it would depend on the amount of cleaning, that sort of thing."

"Did you form any opinion as to whether this had been disturbed by washing or anything else?"

"A number of the stains don't appear to have been, no."

From the yellow van, Stottlemyer had retrieved a number of human bloodstains, the largest outside the van, behind the rear bumper.

From the inside of the van, Stottlemyer had scraped flecks of blood into pill boxes: small stains from the roof near the rear door; from the left wheelwell; from the left side between the wheelwell and the rear door; from the right side over the wheelwell, and in front of the wheelwell on the interior paneling; from the spare tire on the right side; eight in all."

"Which was the largest of the eight you described?"

"The largest I would say was that on the outside of the van that ran down to the gas tank. This was the largest in diameter. The others appeared to be just spots. Maybe splatters."

Inside the van Stottlemyer had found a pair of rubber boots with human blood on each of the boots, spots large enough to be seen with the naked eye.

The criminalist had also completed his examination of the bullet recovered from the skull of the eleventh victim, the Browning nine-millimeter pistol found in the desk in the mess hall, and the loose cartridges retrieved from the gun case and the van.

The bullet which had killed William Kamp, Stottlemyer said, was jacketed, indicating it had come from a revolver. From the weight of the bullet and the lands and grooves, "I determined that it was a nine-millimeter bullet."

The bullet had been badly deformed and corrosive acids formed by the decomposition of the body had attacked the jacket. "I could still see coarse lands and grooves impressions on the bullet, therefore I know that it was a bullet. However, all the fine striations"—the characteristics which would have established that the bullet in Kamp's skull had come from Corona's gun—were missing.

"What possible types of automatic might it have been fired from," Teja attempting to tie bullet and gun together.

"One is a Browning nine-millimeter automatic. There were others, but I don't have them written down, and I don't recall just now."

"But it could have been fired from a Browning nine-millimeter automatic pistol?"

"Yes. It corresponded with the Browning."

Stottlemyer had also examined the automatic, scraping flecks he later identified as human blood from the muzzle and from under the slide on the barrel.

Cumulatively the district attorney had presented a substantial amount of evidence which apparently linked Juan Corona to the mass murders: weapons, bloodstains, and most damning, the receipts found in the third grave. The confident Teja made but one mistake during the six hearings before the Grand Jury; he called Ruby Virginia Adams Lillard.

Detective Gregory and one of Teja's investigators had talked to Mrs. Lillard in her Santa Rosa home the day before. Though the interview had not been transcribed, Teja did listen to the tape recording the two excited investigators had taken. "Some of her testimony," he warned the Grand Jury, " is going to be in the nature of hearsay, but she does have information which is relevant to this particular inquiry. I haven't had an opportunity to interview her myself, but I am going to be finding out a lot of what she says myself when I interrogate her before you."

Mrs. Lillard said she had first met Juan Corona in 1957 at the snack bar she managed for the state Division of Highways. "Juan came in alone, introduced himself, and said Natividad, his older brother, sent him. "I couldn't understand what he wanted until he began saying he was sick, 'Call doctor. Call police.' "

"Did you call a doctor or the police for him?"

"No. He would say, 'Sick in the head.' He said his 'heart turns over.' " Mrs. Lillard said she had done nothing for Corona, who had gone back to work as a laborer.

A year later, sometime in 1958, "He found me in town and wanted to talk to me. He said he was troubled. Said he was still sick. He said he 'thinks bad things.' "

"Did he say what sort of bad things he thought?" Teja was pleased with Mrs. Lillard's testimony; she would make a good rebuttal witness if Hawk tried to prove that Corona had had no mental problems after leaving DeWitt in early 1956. Right now, of course, she was establishing a motive for the killings as the work of a homicidal maniac.

"He drew pictures, and he would say 'Man' and then he would cross them up and give them to me."

"And how did he cross them up?"

"With the pencil across the head. It was all directions." Corona had not explained what the figures represented, Mrs. Lillard testified. "He only said he 'thinks bad things,' and he had been hospitalized at DeWitt by his brother."

Mrs. Lillard was anxious to be helpful, smiling on the witness stand, an old woman for a moment the center of attention. She had more to tell.

At a third meeting he had asked her to walk with him to the small park at the end of D Street in Marysville. They had talked, she said. "In very broken language I understood that he couldn't understand why people would not listen to him. He turned around and said, 'I am sick. Sick, sick. Get police.'

"I talked to a police officer. They said he [Corona] didn't want to work. They want welfare. So he said, 'We can't do anything unless they commit a crime.' "

"Did Juan Corona say anything to you about bodies or death on that particular occasion?"

"Yes, he did. I couldn't understand it, but he said, 'Maybe they get him doctor if maybe he kill someone.' I said, 'No.' He said, 'I kill everybody.' I laughed at him. I said, 'Juan, what would you do with the bodies?' he said, 'Don't know.' And he asked, 'What they do?' And he said, 'What bodies?' And I told him, and I said, 'They bury them.' "

Mrs. Lillard had next seen Corona, she said, in 1960 or 1961, at a bar she had purchased in Marysville. She hadn't recognized him. "I don't know, but he looked different. He was talking about him working hard, he had a nice home, he had nice furniture. He said, 'I buy nice home. I get married.' Said, 'I go to church. I take up money for father.' He said he 'had to do everything right. His wife leave him. He get married.' " And I asked him where his wife went. Said, 'He don't know. She took all of his money and left.' " After impulsively offering to give her his "nice home," Corona had left.

To return the next day. "He talked to me, told me he was still sick, 'need the doctor.' He asked about help again, and he asked our ways in the United States. And I told him, 'When you need help you go to the welfare department.' He couldn't understand that," Mrs. Lillard assured the grand jurors. "And he said, 'They help?' I said, 'Yes, they will.' Then he laughed and he said, 'I go.' Meant he would go talk to them."

According to the smiling woman in the witness box, she had next met Corona in 1963 when "his brother Natividad came and asked me to talk to the family" at a celebration at the Guadalajara Café. Corona "had a heart attack, or something, while I was there. Juan had something wrong, and they told me, 'He sick.' He came in, and he sat in a chair a long time, and he went to the doorway, Juan did, and he stood at the door sniffing, and I knew he was sick."

"Sniffing?"

"Sniffing in the air like he couldn't breathe," Mrs. Lillard assured the puzzled district attorney, holding her head back and snorting loudly. "He stood there, but soon he seemed to be alert, and he turned around and said, 'Nothing no one can do.' He turned back around to the door, started gasping, and he went out."

On yet another occasion she had met Corona who told her again and again, "No one listen. Must see doctor." She also recalled that on another day Gloria Corona came into "one of the places there on D [Street]," and "kept on saying, 'Juan's sick.' "

"Where did she take you?"

"Juan was slumped over the fender of an automobile."

"On the street?"

"Yes." Mrs. Lillard remembered it all clearly. "Two police officers came up and one hit him in the stomach and the other one hit him someplace else. Then I screamed at them and asked them—I told them, 'Stop!' I said, 'He is not drunk. He don't drink.' And they said, 'Wait a minute.' And I said, 'This is his wife. She came after me.' So they talked to him a minute, and they stood there, talked to him. And I said, 'Are you taking him in?' And they said, 'No. Take him to the hospital.' "

"Did they actually take him away?"

"They did. They took him somewhere." It had taken place in 1965, according to Mrs. Lillard. The woman didn't know the names of the officers, but if they had taken him to a hospital or to the city jail, it would be easy enough to check. Wherever, Corona hadn't stayed long; Mrs. Lillard claimed he had taken her home that day.

The woman had been with Corona one additional time. He had asked her to go with him, she told the Grand Jury, while he dumped some "garbage" one night. They had ridden in his panel truck to Yuba City from Marysville, "down to the levee, out on Sullivan's ranch, or along there."

They had parked near a stand of trees, she recalled, and Corona had gotten out of the panel truck. "I heard absolutely no sounds. Death quiet. Then I heard a piece of paper, maybe, or cardboard, just move lightly.

"Then only a minute later I heard a terrible blow, a thud, hit the bottom of the van."

"Inside the van?"

"Inside," Mrs. Lillard assured the staring members of the Grand Jury. "There was no way to see. I was sitting in the front seat."

"Well, you were in an enclosed cab then?"

"Yes. And when I heard this, yes, it frightened me, because I listened for more noise." Mrs. Lillard was caught up in her story now.

"What do you mean by 'terrible thud'?"

"Sort of concussion, knocked me off my equilibrium. And the springs of the truck you could feel it go down, but I didn't feel it come up. But I didn't hear not another sound for at least five minutes."

"And then what did you hear?"

"I hear a sniffing. Like an animal and it was in the van. It was outside and came near the driver's side. I locked the door."

"Could you see anything at all outside the van?"

"No. So it went back around the truck, came to the other side of the other door, and I locked it. I was locked in. I laid down and held both doors, and I was frightened, because I thought he was down in the woods and an animal came up, and I don't know what kind.

"Then I listened. I didn't hear any noise whatsoever. I wished he'd come back. And then I looked again and I saw a shadow, and it went into the trees, behind this tree. Then I heard nothing for quite a while. In fact, it was breaking day before he came back to the truck."

"Juan Corona?" Mrs. Lillard was quiet, lost in her recollection. "Juan Corona?" Teja asked a second time.

"Juan Corona." Mrs. Lillard nodded. "So he drove away. He asked me where I lived. I told him. He drove up in front, and he set there. He said, 'I no let you go. You tell my brothers.' I said, 'No.' I thought his brothers had been mean, so I thought he was worried about—they told me if he said anything or did anything I didn't like that his brothers would take care of him."

The district attorney shuffled through the notes he had taken while listening to the tape recording. "Did Juan Corona and his brothers ever talk about garbage?"

"No. I heard them talking about wino garbage."

"Had this expression 'wino garbage' ever come up before?"

"Well, I have heard the Mexican group mention something about wino garbage, but I don't know what they mean."

"Okay. Did anything occur to cause you to associate wino garbage with the incidents you have described out by the levee?"

"No. It seems to me I asked Juan what kind of garbage he was dumping and he said, 'Wino garbage.' "

The district attorney took Mrs. Lillard through portions of her testimony, then paused again to look over his hastily scrawled notes. "Did he ever explain to you why Natividad had him sent to the DeWitt State Hospital?"

"He did. He said he was sick. He is 'sick in the head.' He said he worshipped his brother, and he said his brother liked men, wino men." Teja had stumbled upon another possible motive for the slayings.

"Juan said Natividad liked wino men?"

"Yes. He said he liked men."

"He was a homosexual, in other words?"

"Yes."

"How did this relate to Natividad having Juan committed?"

"He seemed to think his brother put him in a mental hospital because he didn't want him to tell his other brothers that he caught him with this man."

"Did Juan say that he had caught Natividad with a man?"

"Yes. Juan told me. He didn't say, 'I catch him with man.' That was in 1957, the first visit."

"Okay. He had already been to DeWitt and back when you first met Juan Corona then?"

"Yes. He was also worried that he would hurt someone while he was in DeWitt."

There was one more point Mrs. Lillard had told the investigating officers the day before. "Did you have a conversation with Natividad a year or so ago?"

"Yes. He told me he was in trouble, and I asked him what was wrong. He told me there had been a fight or an accident in his place of business and he was worried about being sued."

"Was this at the Guadalajara Café?"

"Right. I didn't talk to him very long. I just asked him, 'Well, what happened?' And he said a man got hurt, hurt bad, and I asked him who. He said he 'don't know, but he think Juan.' And I said, 'Do you know that?' And he said, 'No.' "

Mrs. Lillard's testimony was compelling, even frightening. Apparently she had innocently witnessed a murder, perhaps even planted the idea in the mind of a maniac. She had helped to stitch together the case against Corona by providing possible motives—motives of a maniac perhaps. From her testimony apparently Corona was still mentally ill when he was released from DeWitt in 1956. Furthermore, she had brought in the Guadalajara Café incident, effectively linking Juan Corona to the savage assault on José Raya.

Late in the night of July 12, just hours before the preliminary hearing had been scheduled to begin, the Grand Jury voted to indict Juan Vallejo Corona for twenty-five violations of Section 187 of the Penal Code, a felony. Grand Jury foreman Robert Hunt endorsed the indictment as a true bill, charging Corona did unlawfully kill twenty-five human beings, with malice aforethought, in circumstances which showed an abandoned and malignant heart.

10

A Little Drop Here

June 19-August 27, 1971

It was a heady experience. As Juan Corona's attorney, Hawk was automatically news, sought after by the reporters who came to town periodically for scheduled hearings or to do a story from the defense point of view. There had been more of these lately, the newsmen solemnly assuring Hawk they wanted to be fair and present both sides. After all, he was the only one visibly doing anything.

Actually Archie Gore, his investigator, and Geneva were doing most of the outside work, interviewing witnesses, taking photographs, pulling together the material he would need for the trial. With Juan in the hospital, the doctors watching to make certain he didn't become too excited, it was difficult to organize an affirmative defense; Hawk really needed to talk to Juan a lot more than he had.

The tranquilizer that they had given to Juan kept him relaxed, but it had some serious side effects, what Doctor Leavenworth called Parkinson's disease symptoms. Corona's thinking was all right, the doctor assured Hawk, even though his speech was sometimes chopped into small phrases, his answers to questions slow, and his rigid walk the gait of a man who didn't know how far the floor was from the bottom of his shoes. The Thorazine had turned him into a zombie; he sure couldn't be brought into a courtroom looking like that.

If getting information from Corona was difficult, he could still work on the case. He had George Loquvam examine the bodies at Sacramento. As one of the best forensic pathologists in private practice in the Bay Area, Doctor Loquvam had a big reputation in the profession. A week before Hawk had retained Loquvam, Pierce Rooney, the Sacramento pathologist, had called to ask Loquvam's opinion about fixing a time of death for the victims. They had agreed it couldn't be done with any precision, but it would be nice at the trial to ask the state's expert if he hadn't called the defense's expert for advice; whose opinion then would carry more weight with the jury?

There were a lot of little ploys like that he could use. It all helped, Hawk knew. A long time before, an older attorney had told him, "You win criminal cases like filling a glass of water with an eyedropper. A drop at a time, drop by drop."

They already had a few drops in the glass. On June 21 Hawk, Geneva, and Gore had toured the Sullivan ranch with old Jack Sullivan and his foreman, Ray Duron. Duron had pointed out the grave sites and showed them about the camp area, Hawk asking questions, Gore taking notes. Gore had asked Duron in front of them all if the foreman had ever made a statement to anyone to the effect that Juan was mentally ill. Duron had strenuously denied talking with anyone about it, insisting he had never told Purcell or any other cop a thing about Corona's hospitalization or illness. That raised some question about the validity of the search warrant affidavit Whiteaker had sworn out the night Corona was arrested.

That, along with all the other mistakes in that affidavit—the hearsay, the reliance on a confidential informant—would provide damn good grounds for challenging the search warrant on its face; with luck, he might get the first warrant quashed and with it most of the real evidence they had on Juan.

It was hard to tell just how much evidence they did have. The Sheriff's Department reports were slow in coming, and Hawk would not get a copy of the grand jury transcript until Juan was indicted on July 27. In the meantime, he was going to prepare a fuller motion for discovery; they were so slow Hawk wondered if Teja wasn't holding out on him. It had been done before. Right now, if you could stand back, they didn't really have very much from all he could see.

Their big mistake, as far as Hawk was concerned, was the failure to talk to Corona before arresting him. Juan had a pretty good alibi for the time when Kenny Whitacre had been killed. Whitacre's was the only one whose time of death could be closely fixed—sometime between one o'clock when Gina Cross Chapman had seen Whitacre alive and six o'clock on May 19 when Kagehiro had seen the grave closed.

Corona had been with his wife most of the day, helping her in the morning to clean up the camp, then traveling alone to Kagehiro's orchard to pick up his crew at noon. They had had some beer and potato chips to celebrate finishing the thinning—Kagehiro substantiated that—and had left around twelve-fifteen o'clock. Corona had returned the crew to the Sullivan ranch camp where he and Gloria had served lunch around twelve-thirty. The two of them had then cleaned up the mess hall, and around two o'clock had gone out to the house they rented to Mrs. Sara Vallejo in Live Oak to fix the screen door.

Juan had told them he had purchased a new screen door for Mrs. Vallejo the day before; Gloria was unsure of the date, remembering only that they had bought the screen door one day and hung it the next. Gore had tied it up nicely though, first by visiting the local lumber company where Corona had bought the screen and getting their copy of the May 18 sales slip. Then a week later he had found Corona's crumpled copy of the sales slip on the Sullivan ranch, not far from where it had been windblown from the garbage pit between the levee and the riverbank.

Gore had found some other papers in the garbage pit area—one with Ray Duron's name on it—a couple of hundred yards from where the two meat receipts had been located in the first grave. Conceivably those receipts could have been blown by the wind into the grave, but more likely —especially with that mess of junk found in the twenty-fifth grave—they had been picked up around the garbage pit, like the household trash, and deliberately dumped in a grave.

Gore had also made a tape recording of the interview he and Geneva had with Mrs. Vallejo, the renter. She told them the Coronas had been there from after lunch until three-thirty. She knew the time they left because Gloria was anxious about the children coming home from school. The Coronas didn't like to leave their four girls alone with the maid without checking constantly.

After visiting with the children at the house on Richland Road, Juan and Gloria had returned to the Sullivan ranch to make dinner and serve the crew. They hadn't finished until after six, about the same time that Goro Kagehiro spotted the filled-in grave.

Hawk shook his head slowly. You'd think they would have tried to check it out before arresting Corona and flashing his name around the world. Apparently they had jumped on those two receipts found in the third grave without stopping to think about it. The receipts plus Corona's mental commitment plus the Guadalajara Café incident was the gut of their case, or at least the basis for the arrest.

Corona told a reasonable story about the cutting in the Guadalajara. He had been in the place that night, but had left around ten-thirty, at least two hours before the kid, José Romero Raya, was cut. Juan had been a suspect, at least momentarily, but apparently had been cleared by Captain John Gust of the Marysville Police Department. According to Captain Gust's report, dated March 5, 1970, "Natividad Corona had been interviewed on three prior occasions to this instance without revealing any more information relative to the case.

"At this time he came to the station and stated that he suddenly recalled who the person was who had told him about the injured person being in the lavatory." It had been Natividad, sole owner of the club now that his silent partner, Ray Duron, had been bought out, who had first called police to tell them the kid was lying in a pool of blood in the can. When they had first talked to him, Natividad Corona had said it was a person "unknown and unrecognized by him" who had told him of the cutting.

Now he claimed he had suddenly remembered. "He stated that the person was his half-brother, Juan Corona, who lived in Yuba City. Also that his brother had a mental breakdown and was committed to DeWitt State Hospital shortly after [the flood of] December, 1955."

The following morning Captain Gust and a policewoman-interpreter, Mary Guerrica, had interviewed Juan. "Subject had been contacted by phone and requested to come to the station. He was asked if he had any knowledge why officer wished to speak to him and stated that he did not.

"He was then advised that it was in regards to the cutting that occurred at the Guadalajara and was asked if he was there that night.

"He stated that he was in Mexico visiting his mother who had an injured leg, and knows nothing of the cutting at the Guadalajara."

Hawk stopped and reread the sentence. At first reading, it sounded as if Corona denied being there, claiming he was in Mexico. (Juan had returned from visiting his mother three days before the cutting, and was in the café telling Natividad about his visit on the night of the assault.) In fact, the police report did not state that Corona denied even being in the café that night. Whiteaker must have misread it too.

A bit later in the interview, Corona had conceded he was in the bar, "but that he was there before the cutting." Advised that he had a right to remain silent and to have an attorney present during the interview, Corona had shrugged. Offered a polygraph examination "in order to ascertain his truthfulness," Corona agreed to take it.

Captain Gust had then called CII in Sacramento only to learn that a lie detector operator would not be available for two weeks. The matter had been dropped, and according to Corona, Captain Gust had even given the farm labor contractor his card when Corona had asked, "What I do if people say I cut Raya?" Tell them to call the captain, was the advice.

Two weeks later, Mrs. Guerrica and Captain Gust had talked to a Fidel Juarez Lopez. Around ten o'clock the night of the cutting, Lopez had met Corona in the Guadalajara and asked if he had any work for his three brothers. Corona had told him he did have something and at five o'clock the next morning would pick up the three men at the labor camp run by Pedro Corona, where the three were staying. If they needed lunch, Corona would provide it.

"Juan then left the counter, leaving his cup of coffee, and Fidel saw him go to the rear of the premises toward the lavatory. . . . About three minutes after Juan left the counter, he noticed Juan going out the front door, leaving the place." According to Juarez Lopez, the whole thing had taken about twenty minutes, which was pretty close to the time Corona had said he had gone home.

As Hawk read them, the Marysville Police Department reports made Natividad Corona out a better suspect than Juan. The Marysville police had taken two calls, one anonymous, fingering Natividad, and then there was Natividad coming into the police station and pointing the finger at his brother. Apparently Juan didn't even know that it was Natividad who put the heat on him.

Raya had told the police he didn't know who hit him. He had been struck from the rear, and never saw his assailant. But that hadn't stopped him from going into civil court and filing suit against Natividad for a quarter of a million dollars later that year. Natividad had quickly sold off his property and his blue panel truck to Pedro Corona, then had skipped the country. Raya had won a default judgment against Natividad in Superior Court for the quarter-million. Maybe they knew more than they would admit—as the senior male in the family Natividad was to be protected—but the Coronas all claimed that Natividad hadn't been back since October 1970.

Now, something like eight months later, Raya was still insisting that it was Natividad who had cut him in the Guadalajara. Detective Gregory, with a friend of Raya's translating, had interviewed the sadly scarred Raya on June 7, trying to get him to change his story.

"Mr. Raya, are your past charges against Mr. Natividad [*sic*] Corona the correct charges or was it someone else who actually did the cutting or the damage to you?" Gregory had asked.

"Yes, it is correct, Mr. Nativida Corona is the one that cut me and hurt me. He is the only one that I saw, I only saw him and since I didn't turn I only saw him. So it must've been him. . . ."

"Have you at any time had any trouble with Mr. Juan Corona?" Gregory had persisted.

"No." Raya had talked to Corona that night in a little bar next to the Guadalajara, asking for work. Corona had said he would use both Raya and his friend, Nick Ramirez, and wanted to meet him at the Sullivan ranch in the morning. When they said they didn't know where it was, Corona had offered to drive them out there that night to show them the way; they preferred to stay in town and continue drinking, finally arranging to have Corona pick them up in front of the Tower Theatre early the next morning.

Given the amount of evidence they had, Hawk was confident he could have successfully defended Juan in Yuba County on the cutting charge. The problem was that Teja wasn't going for a charge of assault with a deadly weapon, or assault with intent to commit murder; he had twenty-five murders and he was going to try to dirty up Corona by dragging the Guadalajara incident in. Hawk would have to fight to keep it out; under the law's common scheme and plan theory, Teja wouldn't have to prove Corona actually cut Raya—after all he wasn't on trial for that—but only establish the similarity of the wounds on Raya and the twenty-five. The similarity would help to establish the identity of the mass murderer. The prosecution's argument—Hawk could write it himself—would be that the man who cut Raya was the man who killed the twenty-five. The similarity of the wounds proved that, or so Teja would argue. Since Juan was a suspect in that case, he was guilty in this.

Corona's mental illness really didn't bother him too much. It could become a problem if he introduced a lot of character evidence on Juan's behalf—they had a half-dozen statements from ranchers who had used Corona's crews and from business associates and friends willing to testify. In rebuttal, the prosecution then could bring up his mental condition. But they would have to do it without having a shrink talk to Corona—Hawk would never waive the doctor-patient privilege—relying on nonexperts who had heard this or seen that. Those kinds of witnesses Hawk could handle on cross, he was sure.

There was nothing wrong with Corona mentally, and he was damned if he would try to cop him out on an insanity plea as Van den Heuval had been thinking. Maybe for the first time in his career, Hawk ruefully smiled, he had a client who was innocent. The question in Yuba City wasn't "my-guy's-guilty-but-can they-prove-it?" The supposition here was "they got the wrong guy."

Hawk believed it, and the more he talked to his client, the more convinced he was. Thorazine and all, Corona just came through. Geneva and Gore believed it too, and Geneva especially was nobody's fool. Not only did she talk to Juan in Spanish, and get even more than he and Gore did, but she was sharp. Ten years with him, and a lot of time dealing with the junkies and hookers in West Pittsburgh, and she knew when someone wasn't telling the truth.

Released from the hospital after twenty days, Corona patiently went through everything with them: his private life, his shopping habits, where he had credit, whom he had worked for, his relationship with his brothers, especially with Natty, as he called him.

Oh, he liked Natividad, but they were not too close. "He's not around too much. Most of the time he stays over there, in Marysville."

The favorite brother was Pedro. "He's been doing too much for me. Looking for people to come to the court. Walking about the court. He bought the shoes for me, you know, he bought the shoes." Hawk sighed quietly. Even the closest brother, the one who did most for Juan, didn't want to talk about Natividad.

In English, Hawk asked Juan quietly, "I understand Natividad is a homosexual."

Corona looked at his slippered feet. "Uh huh," quietly assenting to the accusation. Resignation maybe, acceptance, but otherwise nothing.

"What do you think about that?"

Corona shrugged, "Yeah, it's true."

"How do you know?"

"By talking, you know," Corona answered quietly.

"You only hear. You've never seen?"

"No, I haven't seen it."

"How do you feel about it?"

"Well, not so good. But what's a guy going to do?" Again Corona shrugged, curling his lower lip in disapproval.

So much for that anonymous informant who claimed Corona got violently angry when the subject of Natividad's homosexuality was brought up.

For hours Hawk, Geneva, and Gore talked to Corona, picking through his life. Corona was more than cooperative—he enjoyed the company far more than old magazines and books they allowed him in the Yuba County jail. His memory for detail was astounding, a memory he sharpened apparently by taking notes on everything. Whenever possible, they would check his story; they had yet to catch him in an error. Nor would he lie, even to help himself.

"Juan, the police found blood in your van, and in the Impala. How did it get there?"

He remembered taking a worker to the doctor on May 12. Carlos Leon Sierra had fallen from a ladder while thinning at the Sullivan ranch. Bleeding from a superficial cut over the right eye, Sierra had ridden in the van to Doctor Vasquez' office. Gore would later get a copy of the doctor's records and report from the State Compensation Insurance Fund; contusions on his back had prevented Sierra from working for two weeks.

Okay, that took care of the van. What about the Impala? "I don't know," with a shake of the head. It was Gloria Corona who helped them there. One of the daughters had nosebleeds, the chronic kind that came suddenly, then stopped. The child had even been treated for them. Could she have had a nosebleed in the Impala? Gloria was certain she had.

"The Levi's jacket found in the rafters, there was blood on it. Were you wearing it when Yolanda had one of her nosebleeds?"

"I don't know," Corona half smiled.

Hawk was impressed. Juan might easily have lied; they couldn't type the blood so who could say he was lying? Juan just wouldn't.

"Who has access to the camp besides you?"

"Everyone. It was open most times during the day."

"Was it open when you and Gloria weren't there?"

"No. We locked it."

But someone who wanted to could get in. One of the doors had on it the ranch's standard lock. Anyone with a Masters brand "twenty-twenty" key—and that included most of the people who worked for Sullivan the year around—could get in. And if they didn't get in that way, they could easily pry open a screen. There were also times when the mess hall was open and the Coronas were not there, shopping usually, sometimes picking up the children. Corona even kept a piece of paper tacked to the wall for workers to chalk up IOUs when they took a soft drink from the Pepsi-Cola cooler.

"You slept there. Gloria slept there sometimes. Who else?"

"Emilio Rangel."

"Who's he?"

"My crew boss." Describe him. "Short, maybe five feet, maybe five feet six inches tall, strong—"

"You mean stocky?"

"Yes, stocky. Maybe forty, maybe fifty." Rangel had worked for Juan's brother Natividad until the older brother had given up his contractor's license. When Juan took over the license, Rangel went along with it. He didn't live in the Marysville-Yuba City area. His home was in Mexico. He came for the thinning and then picking. Rangel used the red-and-white pickup truck to recruit workers or to pick them up in town. Rangel slept there, usually in the little shack behind the mess hall.

Bit by bit, they were filling in the details, organizing the facts necessary for a defense. There was still a lot Hawk felt he needed to know, especially about the prosecution case. By the middle of July he had received more than 500 pages of reports from the Sheriff's Department and 300 photographs. But they were still slow in coming; the district attorney had held onto one large batch for damn near five weeks before turning it over. It had finally taken a court order to speed things up.

First, Hawk had to disqualify Judge J. J. Hankins on the usual grounds of prejudice. Hankins probably wasn't any more prejudiced against Corona than any other judge around the area, but Hawk had caught him in a private meeting with Teja and Whiteaker. Hawk didn't know what it was about, but Hankins was now suspect. To replace him, the state Judicial Council had assigned a Butte County Municipal Court judge, William M. Savage.

Savage was everything Hankins was not. At the age of sixty, he had almost nineteen years' experience as a judge, knew the law, and better yet, had no axe to grind. Plainly enough, he didn't give a damn about local opinion. Hawk was only sorry that Savage would not be presiding long; once the Grand Jury returned its indictment, the Corona case would be kicked up to the Superior Court.

Judge Savage was a no-nonsense sort. He had immediately ordered that Sheriff's Department reports be turned over to Hawk within twenty-four hours of their completion.

When Hawk had complained that CII was slow in reporting on the evidence seized—"to the point where it becomes almost a denial of due process"—Savage had permitted Hawk to send his own criminalist to inspect the evidence.

The return of the Grand Jury's indictment had solved another problem for with it had come a copy of the transcript of testimony, as the law required. As far as Hawk could tell, the only item of incriminating evidence he couldn't explain was the pair of receipts found in the first grave on the riverbank.

Even that didn't look too bad. The Sheriff's Department was all screwed up on the numbering of the bodies. Hawk had almost missed it in reading the Grand Jury transcript, the point where Teja had asked Dr. Masters about "a case that I believe has been recently identified to you as Sutter County's E-1-3." Teja was referring to the body of a nine-fingered man, stabbed in the left chest. It had been the freshest of the bodies found along the river, only moderately decomposed, even some slight rigidity remaining in the body.

Doctor Clement, though, who had performed the first autopsy on the nine-fingered man stabbed in the left chest, had the victim numbered E-2-4. There could be only one reason for the switch in bodies: the two receipts were written on May 21. If the body had been badly decomposed, obviously buried prior to the day the receipts came into existence, then the Sheriff's Department had to explain why Corona had been arrested. And who was framing him.

The easiest thing to do was to switch bodies, Hawk realized, taking the freshest body, that of the nine-fingered man, and moving it to the first grave found on the riverbank.

The switch had come, Hawk theorized, the day after the bodies were dug up, as Detective Gregory was writing his report. That must have been when they realized they couldn't have an old body with recent receipts; they had merely moved the freshest body into the grave with the receipts. The body switch was to become a crucial part of the defense case.

That wasn't the only numbering confusion out there, Hawk knew. On May 28, both the *Appeal-Democrat* and the *Bee* had published a list—made up and mimeographed by the Sheriff's Department—of the twenty victims found to that point. The first ten were:

1. Kenneth Whitacre
2. Unidentified
3. John J. Haluka
4. Donald Smith
5. Unidentified
6. Unidentified
7. Pete Beierman
8. Unidentified Negro
9. Bill Kemp [*sic*]
10. Unidentified

A month and one-half later, the Grand Jury indictment charged Corona with killing, in order:

1. Kenneth Whitacre
2. Charles Fleming

3. Melford Sample
4. John Doe E-2-4
5. Donald Smith
6. John J. Haluka
7. John Doe E-5-7
8. Warren Kelley
9. Segurd [*sic*] "Pete" Beierman
10. John Doe E-8-10

The tenth victim was the unidentified Negro formerly number eight. Bill "Kemp" was no longer number nine, but William Emery Kamp, the eleventh victim found. In all, eight of the first ten victims had been shuffled around.

The more Hawk investigated the case, the more tentative the evidence against his client. The Grand Jury transcript hadn't revealed much he didn't already know from reading the sheriff's reports. And the more he talked about the case—especially with newsmen—the more confident he became.

Until now unexperienced in handling the media, Hawk was quickly to learn, playing newspaper off against television station and the two of them against radio. Consciously he ignored the court order issued by Judge Hankins which prohibited extrajudicial comments by attorneys to talk with reporters at every opportunity. The more he spoke, he reasoned, the more favorable attention Corona got. At the same time, he had to admit, he enjoyed it.

Actually he had done pretty well, Hawk believed. He had arranged a jailhouse interview with Corona despite Sheriff Whiteaker's objections. It had taken three days' persuasion to get Jerry Cohen of the Los Angeles *Times,* Vic Biondi of Sacramento television station KCRA, and Wayne Kint of the Sacramento *Union* into the jail, but it was worth the effort.

The result had been national play, the first good publicity Corona got, the first to counterbalance the awful stories that had appeared in the first weeks before Hawk entered the case. The interview was a way of righting the balance; wherever the case went on a change of venue he had to counter as much as possible the impression jury panelists might have of Juan Corona as a nine-foot tall, two-headed monster.

Some things he could arrange; others just happened. After the arraignment on the grand jury indictment, Juan's mother, *La Doña* Candida, had clutched Juan's shoulder and asked him in Spanish to kneel and receive a blessing. Corona had dropped to his knees, blue suit and all, clasped his hands and closed his eyes. It had taken Whiteaker's deputies by surprise. So *La Doña* had blessed her son and prayed silently with him for a minute, and everyone had stood around uncomfortably watching. Hawk had made damn certain the reporters unable to get into the crowded hearing room knew about the blessing.

Spurred by the publicity Hawk generated, Teja asked Superior Court Judge John Hauck, his former boss, for another gag order. Hawk had argued futilely against it, telling reporters at a recess angrily, "As long as the sheriff can make statements that he's got the right man, then Juan Corona damn well can say he didn't do it."

He had no intention of honoring an order that barred him from even saying his client was innocent of the charges. He had the press listening to him now—not always believing him when he tried to describe just how lousy the evidence was—but paying attention. If he could convince them, sooner or later they would convince the public—and his potential jury.

Judge Hauck did agree to Hawk's request to seal the Grand Jury transcript, so that the press wouldn't have access to even more prejudicial testimony.

By the end of August a confident Richard Hawk was firmly in control. Gore had interviewed Mrs. Ruby Lillard, the woman who had testified before the Grand Jury that she was with Juan when strange things were happening on the Sullivan ranch. The woman was badly confused. Now she claimed that it was Natividad, not Juan, who took her out to the ranch and went sniffing around like an animal. She also had a dozen other strange stories about the Coronas, all safely on Gore's tape. Like being married to one of the brothers, and never being sure which one. And being kidnapped seven times by the Coronas, none of whom seemed to know her at all. Everything factual she knew about the Coronas and the case she could have gotten from the papers. The more she talked the more confused she was. Any kind of cross-examination would turn her into a hopeless snarl of deranged stories.

If there was any real problem at all, it was Corona's health. On August 7 he had been hospitalized a second time, complaining once again of chest pains and an inability to sleep. The diagnosis this time was more certain; Juan was suffering from a chronic coronary insufficiency brought on by emotional strain. The muscles of his heart were not getting enough blood. It was as close as you could come to a heart attack and not have one. Next time he might not be so lucky. It definitely was not physical in origin, Doctor Leavenworth assured Hawk. It would take at least three weeks of rest in the hospital, nitroglycerine for his heart, and massive doses of Thorazine for his nerves to get Juan in any shape to stand trial.

Thomas Leavenworth was really a godsend, an unusual man to find in Sutter County. He had gone there, he told Hawk, in 1960, fresh out of medical school, just for a year to earn some money before going back for training in a specialty.

He never left. "I sort of got involved in the patients I was taking care of," Leavenworth explained.

Now he was tagged "the doctor for the defense." He liked Corona, and he insisted on giving him the best care he knew how. "The thing that struck me—it seems like Corona has been very considerate of me. Which is sort of amazing. In August I had an ear infection, and was off about a week. When I came back he was very much concerned about my health, how I felt. He's always been very polite. He always thanks me for the very minimal things I do."

Despite crank phone calls and obscene letters from as far away as New York, Leavenworth persisted. Even his wife complained—about the time he spent at the hospital, about the years of evening meetings, and now, about the Corona case even interfering with their weekend at Lake Wildwood. The nervous doctor and the anecdote-spinning Hawk met often for dinner, friendly beyond their professional relationship, two outsiders in a small town who believed in Corona's innocence. Later, Leavenworth said privately: "There probably was one man braver in town than I was, and that was Hawk." Hawk at another time would shrug and smile. "I admire him. I'll be gone, but he has to stay."

Leavenworth's friendly attitude was a matter of concern to Sheriff Whiteaker. He began keeping a private file on the doctor. Sergeant Purcell contributed a memo noting that the doctor had asked Corona how he felt while standing on the sidewalk in front of the courthouse "crowded with members of the news media." Whiteaker himself wrote a memo that Leavenworth had sedated Corona so that Corona could be interviewed by the press. Captain Littlejohn noted: "Dr. Leavenworth then followed Corona down the stairs and stuck his head in the squad car window and said, 'How are you feeling, Juan?' all the while the press was taking pictures."

District Attorney's investigator Leonard Brunelle in a "Memo to Sheriff Whiteaker" noted he had talked to a woman who said that a friend of her mother's had overheard "a certain party employed by the Sutter County General Hospital discussing privileged and confidential information to a group of people at a resort in California. This individual (assumed to be Dr. Thomas Leavenworth) was extremely intoxicated at the time." Sergeant D. D. Everhart's contribution was a conversation with Leavenworth's barber who had told him "he had recently received a call from a doctor at Sutter County General stating that he needed to get his hair styled right away as there were numerous TV cameramen and press personnel at the hospital and he needed to look good." Sergeant Everhart added that he "did notice a marked improvement in [Leavenworth's] manner of dress, no longer sloppy, but always a tie being worn, and also more modish clothes were evident." Even facts about the doctor's private life found their way into the police file.

If Doctor Leavenworth seemed uncooperative, hospital administrator Robert Moss was not. In the third week of Corona's second period of hospitalization, Moss called Undersheriff Cartoscelli to advise him that Leavenworth was out sick and another doctor was handling Corona.

Mr. Moss advised that part of Dr. Larive's treatment consisted of a psychiatric examination by a Dr. Andres. Mr. Moss stated that Dr. Andres' report indicated that subject Juan Corona was not a sane person. He stated that the doctor's diagnosis was extreme paranoia—not capable of standing trial.

According to Cartoscelli's memorandum dated August 25, 1971, and labeled "an extremely confidential report,"

Mr. Moss stated that I could read this report or he would prepare a copy of it for the Sheriff. Mr. Moss was advised that it would be picked up this afternoon.

Moss' willingness to release the possibly privileged information was throttled. When he got to the hospital, Undersheriff Cartoscelli met Moss and Leavenworth who "advised they would not be able to release the report without [a] court order. Both Doctor Leavenworth and Mr. Moss appeared to be extremely concerned over what Mr. Hawk might do if a report was released concerning Mr. Hawk's patient [sic]."

Anxious to help, Moss had exaggerated the finding of the psychiatric examination. Doctor Andres' entry in the case record said, "Mr. Corona states that he [is] always thinking about his return to jail. It is his understanding that at the end of three weeks he will be returned to jail. He states he is afraid he 'will go crazy' as 'I did in 1955.' "

Andres also noted that Corona was slightly withdrawn, his thinking at the moment tangential and paralogical, concerned that "being in hospital will make it bad for me." His mood was anxious, his insight slight, his judgment impaired, the doctor noted.

Ten days later, Doctor Andres found Corona "oriented and spontaneous, his associations logical but constricted. Patient talks about reality problems (e.g., four children and wife have no income, he feels he must sell his house to pay legal fees, children going to school without new clothes, etc.)." Corona was now only "moderately depressed and anxious."

Months later, the prosecution was still attempting to get information, protected by both the patient-doctor and attorney-client privileges, on Corona's physical and mental condition. At District Attorney Teja's request, three investigators visited the hospital on February 29 only to have Doctor Leavenworth again refuse to turn over the records without a court order.

Ultimately, the sheriff's prying became petty. Sergeant Purcell reported that a nurse at the hospital had said Corona's blood pressure was higher than normal after visits with his attorney. A special officer, admitting Father Bishop to Corona's cell in April, "observed Corona crying. No one was in the cell with Corona at this time." Copies of the reports by an occupational therapist—not covered by the doctor-patient privilege—found their way into the sheriff's files.

Hawk's cocky attitude grated harshly on the sheriff and district attorney. In violation of a gag rule, he had traveled to Fresno at the end of July and had given a speech to the Mexican-American Political Association convention about the case. When the trial was over, the contempt of court would cost him some jail time and a fine. He or his investigator were running around town, interviewing Teja's witnesses; Teja had to remember to file his own motion for discovery in order to get a copy of the interview Hawk had with that damn Lillard woman.

Judge Hauck had given Hawk everything but the courthouse doors on August 30—expanded visitation rights and an order for the sheriff to pay the storage charges on two of Corona's vehicles so the family could claim them. He even allowed Leavenworth to testify, laying the groundwork, whether the doctor knew it or not, to get Corona out on bail.

If the prosecution had had any satisfaction at all in the past ten weeks since Hawk got into the case it was in the rumor that Hawk was getting out. Rumors circulated at the end of July that Melvin Belli was interested in handling the case. Then on August 27 someone on Belli's staff or his representative called Deputy District Attorney Tom Mathews claiming they would be taking over the defense.

As Mathews had told the *Appeal-Democrat,* it would "be interesting on Monday to see who is the defense attorney." At the moment, no notice of a substitution of attorneys had been filed.

One never would be. Hawk had first been tipped off that the silver-haired Belli was interested in the Corona case at the Mexican-American Political Association convention on the last day of July. Hawk laughed it off; he had a newly signed statement in both English and Spanish saying Juan wanted only Hawk as his attorney. He wasn't about to give up the biggest case a man could have to some guy with a big reputation and fancy offices. With Geneva back at home with the kids, he guessed he hadn't spent as much time as he should have explaining things to the family. It didn't look like much was happening, that he was doing anything for Juan. Well, the claim for damages had changed that.

Psychologically, it was a good move, Hawk thought. It gave Juan and Gloria especially the feeling that they were doing something, striking back, by asking for all that money from the county. As he had told the Coronas, even if they didn't win the suit, it would give Teja and Whiteaker something to worry about.

Hawk had to admit they hadn't worried long. Mostly the claim for $350 million for slander and false arrest had drawn a lot of laughs. One hundred million for Juan and fifty million for Gloria and each of the four kids; that was more than four times the assessed worth of Sutter County. If he won it, Juan would be king of Sutter County.

Well, that was sometime off. He first had to get Juan off on the criminal charges before the civil suit would mean anything. And before he could do that, he had some problems to take care of by filing motions with the court. The first was to get Juan someplace where he could get better, to get him out on bail. The next was to change venue, to get the trial out of Sutter County entirely.

11

A Kind of Subtle Salesmanship
August-October 1971
March-April 1972

Christ almighty, the change of venue hearing was dreary business, Hawk thought, listening to the fifth day of Teja's cross-examination of the impeccably groomed Norris Robert Heyer. The dignified vice-president of the Field Research Corporation was unruffled by the prosecutor's questions, answering patiently, sometimes at length. Hawk wasn't the only one bored by it all; the statistical theory, probabilities, sampling techniques, coefficient of error. The few reporters left had given up taking notes. The Corona family, sitting impassively in a row on the right side of the courtroom, understood none of it. Hawk wasn't sure how much Juan grasped; he would have to remember to explain it to him. Even Judge John Hauck seemed to spend more and more time leaning back in his swivel chair, fighting off the sleep that followed a full stomach on a warm day.

Teja was doing well. The survey of the potential jurors in Sutter County by the most prestigious of poll takers in the state was good, but it was not error-free—not by any forensic standard. The mistakes were small, an interviewer who failed to time the telephone calls, another who consistently asked a question she should not have, an occasional answer filled in wrongly. None of them invalidated the poll; even collectively they didn't amount to much. But from a legal viewpoint, the effect was damning.

The Field Research Corporation had an impressive list of clients along San Francisco's Montgomery Street: Bank of America, Standard Oil, Weyerhauser, Sears. Equally important, Mervin Field conducted the syndicated California Poll, far and away the most accurate barometer of voter sentiment in the state. Field should have been able to measure or sample public sentiment about the Corona case in Sutter County without any problem. But here was this district attorney, patient, thorough to the point of tedium, sharpshooting holes in the forty-page report the Field Corporation had produced. Teja seemed to have some understanding of statistics himself, and he had a prepared list of questions from the attorney general's office to guide him.

Hawk had decided to survey public opinion in Sutter County after reading the most recent of the change-of-venue decisions of the state Supreme Court. The court had suggested such a poll to measure community antagonism to a criminal defendant. In Hawk's mind, the poll was actually for the appellate courts; Hawk himself was certain Juan Corona could not get a fair trial in Sutter County. Too many people had made up their minds. In July Hawk had decided a poll would provide the extra proof of prejudice; now, sitting in the courtroom in October he wasn't so certain.

Hawk had paid $7,500 for the telephone poll of 411 registered voters in Sutter County, money out of his own pocket. Heyer's bill eventually would come to more than $3,000. Hawk had believed it a worthwhile investment; Corona certainly didn't have it to lay out, so the attorney had paid for it himself. But that $7,500 had strapped him; money was getting to be a problem now. Archie Gore had returned to Contra Costa long since, leaving behind a bill for some $4,000 Hawk couldn't pay. He had a big bill at the motel, the manager carrying him until he could scrape together the money he owed. His practice had all but disappeared; would-be clients thought him too busy, or maybe too important now.

District Attorney Teja had no such problem. He was spending a good deal of the county's money in an effort to keep the case from leaving Sutter County. He had used two detectives for a couple of weeks reinterviewing people, and conducting his own poll. Teja had done a good enough job questioning the Field survey that Judge Hauck felt it necessary to appoint two impartial masters to reinterview some of those people Field had contacted originally. A hearing that should have taken a day, two at the most, was now in its eleventh.

Despite the errors, the Field survey had confirmed what Hawk sensed; the taxpayers of Sutter County had already made up their minds. Not surprisingly, 65 percent believed the mass murders were the most outstanding thing to take place in the area in the last six months. Specifically asked who had been accused, just short of nine out of ten had given Corona's name, ten percent more than the people who could name the sheriff.

Even with the five percent plus or minus error of the statistical sampling techniques, Heyer testified, "I would not expect at this point in time the community awareness level to be as high as this."

"Why is there more awareness, in your opinion, in this county than there would be in a metropolitan area?" Hawk had asked on direct examination.

"Well, the event happened here. It has a much higher salience for people here. It is a relatively smaller community, so that intervening events are less likely to have captured people's attention than would be the case in the large metropolitan areas." Eighty percent of those polled said they had talked about the case, eight percent told the interviewers they had discussed it with people connected with the investigation. As many as 500 people may have visited the grave sites, or driven by the Sullivan ranch out of curiosity, if the poll was accurate.

Idle conversation and pretrial publicity added up to a massive feeling of prejudice, Heyer testified. Fewer than two percent of those polled said Corona was even probably innocent. At the same time, almost one out of five insisted he was guilty.

Even this did not measure the full extent of those who had actually formed opinions, Heyer said in response to Hawk's questions. People did not always admit their prejudices; three additional questions drafted by the Field staff were to probe for the prejudices of those who said they had not yet formed an opinion about the case.

The first asked: "Some people have alleged that Juan Corona has a history of mental illness and emotional instability that could have led him to commit the killings. Is this your understanding of his mental condition or not?" Just over forty-one percent had said it was, yet over half of these claimed to have no opinion of his guilt or innocence.

The second question asked: "It has been alleged that Juan Corona made a map or list of the location of the graves and the bodies of the dead men. Is it your understanding that this map or list is a part of the evidence in the case or not?" Twenty-eight percent of the respondents said there was such a map, half of these still maintaining they had formed no opinion of Corona's guilt or innocence.

Finally, the interviewers asked if Corona should be freed on bail? Sixty-two percent said he should be denied bail—because he had a violent temper and might murder again, because the crime was simply too great, because he had not been proven innocent, because "it was a valid arrest, and we feel he is guilty because he had been arrested."

The district attorney frantically scribbling notes, Heyer summarized his $7,500 poll. "We found earlier that over twenty-six percent acknowledged that they had formed an opinion about his guilt or innocence, and of the remaining seventy percent who claim not to have formed an opinion, almost forty-three percent of them made what we have classified here as a prejudicial response to these additional questions."

Roughly seventy percent, then, of the voters held prejudicial opinions, or 10,000 of the 14,000 people who might be called for jury duty in Sutter County. Hawk's twenty-five preemptory challenges would not last long, even if he managed to excuse for cause those who had already formed a definite opinion about Corona's guilt. In Heyer's opinion, moving the case to a big city would improve Corona's chances for a jury without preconceived opinions.

Days later, Teja was still plodding on, nitpicking his way through the 411 interview sheets, the survey his office had conducted, and the court-ordered resurvey of the Field poll. The district attorney's long cross-examination seemed too plodding to be effective; Hawk now felt he had a chance for a favorable decision on his request for change of venue.

The motion to grant bail was something else. Hawk had not seriously believed the judge would grant it. The motion had been a ploy to get some favorable testimony into the record and publicity for Juan. Hawk had borrowed the brief he filed—"a work of art, a masterpiece"—written months before by Angela Davis in the Marin County jail where she was being held on charges she was implicated in a conspiracy to free three prisoners from custody. Hawk had met one of Miss Davis' attorneys, Howard Moore, to exchange information: Moore to ask about the validity of a poll to help his client get a change of venue, Hawk to discuss the problem of bail. Angela had a sizable defense fund; the blacks were really organized, Hawk said wistfully. If they wanted to poll potential jurors, money was no problem. He had Juan Corona, damn little money, and even less public support.

Maybe the bail hearing would change that a little. Doctor Leavenworth's testimony that Corona's health would improve outside prison was helpful, but not enough in itself. The four character witnesses Hawk had called on Corona's behalf were good, but Corona would need twenty-five times that to convince any judge. Real estate broker Tom Nevis and Fred Montez, a local *chicano* businessman and about the only friend the Corona family had right now, both testified that if Corona gave his word, he would appear for trial. Father Joseph Bishop described Corona as a regular communicant at St. Isidore's—one who had even invited the priest out to his labor camp to say mass for his workers. The father would put up the money if he had it, but Catholic priests didn't ordinarily have $100,000 for bail. John Sullivan, on whose ranch most of the bodies had been found, was an important man in Sutter County—at one time he had even been mentioned as a possible Republican gubernatorial candidate—but even Sullivan's recommendation of Corona would not be enough.

The district attorney was more worried about the bail motion than about the change-of-venue question. On the one hand, if Corona were granted bail, he might flee the country. On the other hand, if he walked into court, facing twenty-five counts of murder, it would be tantamount to a not-guilty verdict. What jury would believe him guilty if he were so obviously willing to lay his life on the line?

Teja's concern had already led him to commit one mistake, upsetting Judge Hauck. The district attorney had argued in chambers a week before that he should be permitted to put the county hospital's psychiatrist, Doctor Valentine Andres, on the stand. Teja wanted to open up the records to determine "whether or not his release on bail would be dangerous to himself or to society."

"How do you know these things, what he is going to testify?" a surprised Hawk had asked, grinding his cigarette into the ash tray.

"Hospital records."

Angrily, Hawk snapped, "How did you see the hospital records?"

"The sheriff got them Monday," Teja answered, unperturbed.

"By what right, may I inquire?"

"Superior Court order."

"Order?" Hawk was startled. Unilaterally, Teja had sought a court order from a Yuba County judge temporarily sitting in Sutter County who obligingly complied, without ever notifying Hawk. His anger barely suppressed, Hawk protested, "This is complete news to me. It is outrageous that they go out there and paw through his medical records without any release from the judge who is on the case." Hawk lashed out at Teja, "Have you talked to Andres? He says these things to you? He told you these things?"

"Andres came in and asked [sic] me when he would be testifying and what the gist of his testimony would be."

"Did he discuss Juan Corona with you?"

"He didn't discuss Juan Corona with me. I discussed what he had written in the hospital records with him. I guess he nodded his head," Teja answered impassively.

Outspokenly upset, Judge Hauck barred Andres' testimony. It didn't matter much, Hawk believed, except to maybe make the judge throw a bone his way. The bail motion was down the tubes anyway, but Hawk believed the change of venue motion could be salvaged. He had certainly established there was a reasonable likelihood that Corona could not get a fair trial in Sutter County—all the law required he do in order to have the trial moved. A good argument for the judge to hang his opinion on would win it, Hawk felt certain.

It wasn't one of his better efforts, Hawk would acknowledge later. His summary was long and rambling, Teja's longer but more coherent, more methodical, Hawk speaking only from a handful of quickly written notes, Teja reading most of his argument from a prepared script.

Hawk reviewed the law, relying heavily upon the United States Supreme Court's *Sheppard* decision and a pivotal 1968 holding by the California high court: it was the obligation of the trial court to transfer the case to a county where Corona could receive a fair trial. "We don't have to actually prove that people are prejudiced against him; we only have to raise a likelihood, a showing that there is a reasonable likelihood that they are."

The publicity about the mass murders and the arrest of his client was inevitably prejudicial. The use of the word "machete," Hawk argued, was "a kind of subtle salesmanship." Because Juan happens to be a Mexican, it happens to be a machete. I think the murder weapon could well be a meat cleaver, a bowie knife, a large axe, a lot of things."

Hawk continued: ". . . an incredible amount of inadmissible evidence . . . has been disseminated to the press, apparently by Judge Hankins. The issue of Juan's mental condition is of no consequence in this trial unless Juan enters a plea of not guilty by reason of insanity. He is not going to ever enter such a plea. He is not insane, he is not psychotic, he is sound as a silver dollar. Nevertheless, it was flashed across the press—and I saw it in Los Angeles—that people here talk about how Juan has a history of mental illness. And for many people, when you have got a case where there is no motive apparently, the information which is disseminated in this community that Juan has a history of being in DeWitt State Hospital supplies a motive. If you have got a nut, you don't need a motive."

Other prejudicial information, Hawk insisted, included the nonexistent "death" map; twenty-eight percent of the people in the county believed such a map existed. The Guadalajara incident, too, was not admissible, though it had been disseminated and was voluntarily mentioned by a number of those surveyed by the Field Corporation. Stories of Corona's temper—that he had to be tied down, that he was brutal to his wife and children—had also been in the press, all untrue but seemingly believed.

Of the Field survey, Hawk offhandedly concluded, "The court either credits the survey or not, and I will only say to that that they come in with pretty imposing credentials. If you do credit it, you just have to find that people are universally aware. Mr. Teja's survey shows the same thing. You have one person out of four who admits to having an opinion and you have got, roughly, about forty-three percent who don't admit that but will say he shouldn't be released on bail because he probably killed the people, or is insane, or he drew a map, or various things."

After a recess, Teja began his closing argument. Sitting hunched over the counsel table, reading from the script in front of him, the district attorney opened by conceding that there had been enormous publicity in the case. He argued, however, that since the publicity had been so widespread, and had infected the trial wherever it might be held, a change of venue would accomplish little.

Teja was not a man whose oratory took imaginative flight. He came as close to passion as he was capable in discussing Hawk's quest for favorable publicity, what the law books call "invited error." Sheriff Whiteaker, Teja argued, had made some statements upon Corona's arrest "and then, obviously, said no more. He cooled the public off by making these statements. But, nonetheless, we keep hearing them and where do we hear them? We hear them from Mr. Hawk, Your Honor." Teja paused to sip water from a paper cup on the counsel table.

"We submit to you that the doctrine of invited error prevents the defendant from fanning the flames of publicity and seeking to reap the benefits thereof by seeking a change of venue." Teja and Hawk were antagonists now; the abstract pursuit of justice had become for both men a personal struggle. Theirs was a mutual contempt, and, for Hawk, a distrust of the district attorney. For another fourteen months they would barely bother to hide their animosity behind courtroom formalities and arm's-reach manners.

Acknowledging the Field Research Corporation's reputation, Teja criticized the poll. There were errors in the survey process, he argued, errors which Heyer had failed to explain away. The sample was not representative of all prospective jurors, but only of those with telephones. Two smaller directories were not used. There was a disproportion of women and older people in the sample, beyond the error of tolerance. The interviewers were not all experienced; some did not follow instructions; supervision was scanty. Nearly 100 of the 400 questionnaires contained some sort of error.

"The purpose of the poll was obvious. Mr. Heyer and Mr. Hawk are very adamant about the fact that this wasn't a fixed poll. We didn't suggest that there was an outright collusion here, Your Honor. . . . Mr. Heyer ultimately admitted that there is such a thing as subjective or implied bias and I submit, Your Honor, that just as his employees are biased in favor of their employer, so is he and Field Research Corporation, as Mr. Hawk's employee, biased in favor of Mr. Hawk. They knew what Mr. Hawk wanted."

Teja picked up after the noon recess, detailing methodically the faults he saw in the poll. Hawk listened, fighting off the afternoon's drowsiness by playing with his pen, occasionally taking a note for his rebuttal argument. Despite all of the publicity, Teja pointed out, almost half of the people in Sutter County had not prejudged Corona's guilt, even if they held prejudicial opinions. While Heyer had implied a continuing community concern with the case, "his whole opinion in this particular area was admittedly subjective. He goes on further, then, to say that the mere passage of time without public discussion would not alleviate the prejudice."

At one point, after citing three pages of the lower court proceedings in which Hawk had objected to imposition of a gag order, Teja said, "We find Mr. Hawk advising Judge Hankins; in effect, he wanted publicity for the defendant who had nothing to hide."

Roused by his name in the midst of the droning recital, Hawk objected. "That is completely out of context, completely misleading, and since I have been called a liar, and Mr. Heyer has been called a liar, I say Mr. Teja is a liar when he reads that in that respect." Openly angry, inwardly

Hawk was also thankful for the opportunity to break in, to stand up and stretch.

Judge Hauck was upset. "I don't want anybody called names. I presume Mr. Teja is reading from the record; whether it is a complete record I don't know."

"That is my point. It isn't," Hawk said.

Stung, the district attorney countered. "In effect, since that time, Your Honor, Mr. Hawk and the defendant have proceeded to get publicity. I even believe that Mr. Hawk has been cited for contempt of court as a result of violating your order." Point for the prosecution.

There was also the matter of convenience, the prosecutor pointed out, one of "many more factors than the mere ease or difficulty in the selection of a jury." Where were the witnesses? Would they have to be transported all over the state? It would require one or more views of the crime scene to try the case properly, one or more trips by the judge and jury back to Sutter County. Expense too was certainly a consideration; neither his office nor the sheriff's had budgets sufficient to allow travel.

The real purpose of the change-of-venue motion, Teja told the court, was "putting the district attorney off balance and getting him out of his own office and away from the courtroom that he is familiar with."

Teja finally closed the loose-leaf notebook, three hours after he began reading.

Hawk's rebuttal was short, keyed to notes he had jotted on his legal pad as Teja spoke. "He says that I have generated all the publicity, but, Your Honor, Judge Hankins made an order May 26 at nine o'clock in the morning and you have got film where the sheriff of this county, after the order was made, stood out on the banks of the Feather River with his sunglasses on like Captain Midnight and says, 'Juan is the man. We are certain.'" Hawk punched again, "After the order was made," his voice rising to emphasize the word "after."

"When the information was released to the press and the public in this court that Juan had been in a mental hospital, when it was released that the sheriff said he was guilty, when they talked about bloodstained machetes, and bloodstained this, and they found this in the house, and they said that he went over and hurt somebody across the river a year or so ago before he was arrested, I was in Los Angeles taking a ground school course for instrument flying.

"I didn't have anything to do with releasing that information. He did, the sheriff did, Judge Hankins did. Not me." Hawk was quick in his rebuttal, far more effective than he had been in opening, a defense attorney again on familiar standing.

Teja was not really worried about a fair trial, Hawk charged. Instead, the prosecutor was concerned about leaving behind in Sutter County "an awful lot of advantages that he has, not just the logistic advantage of the case being tried here and his office being in the same building, but he loses an awful lot of advantage in the fact that the people know Sheriff Whiteaker, people are going to know witnesses."

Cost was of no importance in the law. "If Dave Teja is going to kill Juan Corona, then it seems to me that he at least ought to do it through twelve people who don't know anything about this case and do it on the evidence and not what they heard about this case before or how they feel about the cost to the county, or something else."

Judge Hauck took a week to write his opinion, then notified newsmen he would file it on October 8. Three television crews were on hand to film the judge walking from the courthouse, opinion in hand; crossing the street (front and rear views on the same film); opening the door to the clerk's office (close-up of his hand on the knob); and filing the opinion (front and rear views again). The shots were so patently staged, Hawk believed, that he reopened the record to include copies of the subpoenaed television stories.

The defense attorney had deluded himself. Judge Hauck denied the motion for a change of venue. Affirming the integrity of both Heyer and the Field organization, the judge discounted their poll. Mistakes were minor, he agreed, but ambiguous questions tainted the result. "The biggest defect was that the poll developed by Field and defendant's attorney was designed to prove a point, i.e., that defendant could not have a fair trial [in Sutter County]."

Further, Judge Hauck held that there was no proof that the prejudicial opinions—if, in fact, they were prejudicial—could not be put aside by jurors.

The district attorney and the sheriff "have scrupulously conformed with orders on extrajudicial statements," the opinion continued. "Unfortunately, the same cannot be said of defendant's present attorney." Point by point, Judge Hauck agreed with the district attorney's arguments.

There was an ample record of invited error by the defense, while the prosecution had remained silent. "The defendant cannot now attempt to take advantage of his own doing."

While the case was more deeply imbedded in the minds of potential jurors in Sutter rather than in San Francisco County, Judge Hauck wrote, "This court finds that there will be no difficulty in getting an unprejudiced jury in this county. The defendant has not shown 'even a reasonable likelihood that he will not receive a fair trial' in this county."

As a disappointed Hawk drove back to his motel, impatiently punching buttons on the car radio for the first news stories reporting the denial of a change of venue, he heard a local radio station broadcasting a recording sung by a rock 'n' roll band from nearby Chico:

> They've unearthed twenty-five this day.
> How many more no one cares to say.
> Itinerant workers, all those lives,
> Ended sharply by a knive.
>
> CHORUS: Stop. Tell us more. Tell us more. Tell us more.
>   What's the score? What's the score?
>   Can you help us get the facts?
>   We will help you all keep track.
>
> The old man, he cries by me,
> He was so good to his family.
> The sheriff says yes, his lawyer no,
> But up 'til now just those twenty-five know.
>
> You have just heard of a terrible plan,
> Twin City madness, uneasy at night.
> Now it's done; they've planted the spring.
> Who knows what next harvest will bring? *

"What's the Score" was a modest local hit, though Mary Perry at Sievwright Music Store in Marysville refused to stock the record, feeling it was in bad taste.

Turned down by Judge Hauck, Hawk now appealed the decision to the three judges of the District Court of Appeal in Sacramento.

Adding to his written petition seeking a review of the trial court's ruling, Hawk's oral argument dealt with the difficulties of picking an unbiased jury, pointing out that potential jurors frequently lied in order to serve in notorious trials. Furthermore, the community had a vested interest in repairing its reputation by solving the crime. Hawk believed his oral argument one of the best he had ever given. It convinced the three judges.

In his opinion for a unanimous court, the acting presiding justice, Leonard M. Friedman, agreed. Highly publicized arrests might infect the community with hostility toward the suspect. "But this is not such a case. The news coverage was voluminous but not inflammatory."

However, the nineteen-page opinion went on, there was still the reasonable likelihood of unfairness. "When a spectacular crime has aroused community attention and a suspect has been arrested, the possibility of an unfair trial may originate in widespread publicity describing facts, statements and circumstances which tend to create a belief in his guilt."

A trial verdict was to be based upon evidence produced in court, and on that evidence alone; pretrial publicity about the "facts" of a case threatened the fairness of a trial. "The prosecution may never offer the

* Words and Music by Craig Strode, as sung on Peach Records 101. © Copyright 1971.

'evidence' served up by the media. It may be inaccurate. Its inculpatory impact may diminish as new facts develop. It may be inadmissible at the trial as a matter of law. It may be hearsay. Its potentiality for prejudice may outweigh its tendency to prove guilt. It may have come to light as the product of an unconstitutional search and seizure [and was thereby barred from court no matter how incriminating it was]. If it is ultimately admitted at the trial, the possibility of prejudice still exists, for it entered the minds of potential jurors without the accompaniment of cross-examination or rebuttal."

In a footnote, Justice Friedman pointed out the limited usefulness of gag orders and suggested ethical codes for the bar and the press intended to curb pretrial publicity. "When a newsworthy crime story breaks, these high-minded declarations fall flat before the competitive onslaughts of resourceful newsmen, bent on producing profitable merchandise wrapped in the gilt of constitutional freedoms."

Few possible jurors in Sutter County, the opinion continued, could deny some sort of knowledge about the case. "In the minds of many, the media have stripped [Corona of the presumption of innocence], and he must now disprove his guilt." The three judges had read the Field poll.

The case had to be moved, said the District Court of Appeal, to a large county where the "memory of harmful publicity will be relatively blurred by the passage of time," where "lack of a sense of community involvement will permit jurors a degree of objectivity unattainable in that locale. Potential jurors in an urban area will be less vulnerable to claims of insensitivity toward migratory farm workers."

Hawk had won a big victory. The case of the *People v. Juan Corona* would leave Sutter County. The only question was where to send it.

12

The Foolish Woman

December 1971-April 1972

It just wasn't going well. In most criminal investigations, once you settled on a suspect all the evidence fell into place neatly; there were no extra pieces for your puzzle, nothing you needed missing. Not the Corona case.

Dave Teja was working almost full time on it. He had an assistant now, a deputy hired just for the case, preparing for the trial. Brunelle and Gregory did nothing but Corona-related work, and for four months they had had Dave Perales from the Sacramento Police Department in to help. And still it wasn't coming together.

Some of it was just dumb bad luck. Roy DeLong, the man who had seen Corona drive off with Pete Beierman, was dead. He had gotten into a fight with some other resident of the Golden West Hotel. Two weeks later DeLong had died at Yuba General of pulmonary edema in the aftermath of a heart attack.

Juan Mosqueda had been less than useless. Kenny Walton was missing, off to God-knew-where, leaving behind a forwarding address that might or might not be good. That left them with James Pervis and Byron Shannon out of the group of laborers who had testified before the grand jury. Pervis was all right, but Shannon was in and out of trouble. He had been arrested a couple of times in the past months. If those charges stuck, it would look bad to a jury to have a witness with a felony record testifying. Teja would have to see what might be done with those charges across the river; if they were handled as misdemeanors, Hawk would not be able to use them to impeach Shannon; if they went as felonies, Teja could kiss Shannon off as a credible witness.

Sergeant Perales, a Mexican-American who spoke Spanish, had been a big help. His first task was to reinvestigate the Guadalajara Café incident, interviewing the people in the cafe in Spanish. If Perales could get enough on Corona there, Teja planned to move to introduce it in the trial. Perales had found some people who placed Corona in the café around midnight, close to the time of the assault. He also found someone who said Juan was as queer as his brother Natividad—pure hearsay, but interesting.

The trouble was that the witnesses contradicted each other. Two of them said Fidel Juarez Lopez found Raya in the rest room, that it wasn't Juan as Natividad had claimed. Lopez denied it, but said Corona was in the rest room just before Raya was cut. Lopez claimed he was certain; he had been talking to Juan, getting work for two cousins and a brother in the country illegally. And Lopez later told his ex-wife that Juan had done it. One of the women who worked behind the bar there said she had talked to Raya who told her "it was three guys that did it," and Natividad wasn't one of them. A couple of others had hinted that Raya was cut by a jealous rival because Raya had been dancing with the guy's ex-girlfriend. That man had been seen with spots of blood on his shirt.

That whole thing just wouldn't sort itself out, and the girlfriend, Chavela, getting herself killed hadn't helped any. She apparently had had Raya's confidence; at any rate the kid had asked her to translate for him in his civil suit against Natividad. No transcript had been made of the trial, so her testimony would have been helpful. Then in April an ex-boyfriend pumped nine twenty-two-caliber bullets into her; that meant Perales and Gregory would have to work on Raya without any help.

If anybody could do it, Perales could. With the help of a Federal Bureau of Narcotics agent in Guadalajara, Mexico, Perales had done a damn good background investigation on Natividad. There didn't seem to be much question that the oldest brother was a homosexual. On more than one occasion, he had registered in the run-down hotels of lower Marysville—one for as long as a week—when he owned a $20,000 home a few miles from town. He admitted his homosexuality during an interrogation by the state prosecutor in Jalisco in 1971, when a woman charged that Natividad and another homosexual had kidnapped her teenage son, Efren. Natividad had told the state prosecutor, "I paid fifty dollars to Efren for his services rendered"—quaint phrase that—"and I have not seen him since that time." Corona had denied coming to the United States after December 1970.

Perales would need more time to work with Raya. The police had no close ties with the Mexican community, yet they were certain that the true story was there, somewhere. It was the old story of "I-don't-know-nothing" whenever the authorities came around. Even after all the time that Perales had spent with him, Raya still insisted that it was Natividad who had assaulted him in the bar.

Sergeant Perales wasn't the only one working under pressure, though. Investigators were having trouble with Mrs. Lillard. Everytime they talked to the woman she came up with another nutty story. She had even asked to be taken to a psychiatrist or hypnotist. They had a shrink working with her now, if only to see if she was competent to testify, and maybe—just maybe—to help them figure out what was true and what wasn't in what she told them.

The district attorney's new deputy needed all the time he could get, too, just catching up on the 850 pages of police reports. Bartley C. Williams had had almost five years of trial experience as a deputy district attorney in Santa Clara County since graduating law school in 1965. Bart wasn't the most sophisticated of attorneys, but Teja considered that an asset; Sutter County was a small place, wary of big-city types. And the two of them got along well together; they were both the kind of guy who bought a new suit once every year, wore the old one out, and didn't worry about it; the kind who went to the barber shop for a haircut every three weeks, though the fast-balding Teja hardly needed one then.

That sort of thing wasn't much of a problem anyway. Hawk was hardly a fashion plate. In fact, he kept trying to pass himself off as a country boy —ducking the big-city-lawyer tag whenever he could—wearing the same two suits to court, yanking off his tie the minute court was over. Well, Hawk might not be a stylish dresser, Teja realized, but he was far more experienced, far slicker than any attorney in the Twin Cities area. Bart's thirty-five or forty felony trials as a prosecutor would help to balance things.

Williams had moved with his wife and small daughter to Gridley, a small town about ten miles north, to go into private practice. Things had been slow for him there; Teja had approached him at an opportune moment after checking around the Marysville and Yuba City courts about Williams. Their interests meshed nicely: Teja would handle the legal research and pretrial maneuvering with the help of the attorney general; Bart was to be responsible for preparing the case for trial.

The crew-cut Williams had come up with a lot of good ideas. First, he had located Doctor Ruth Guy at Parkland General Hospital in Dallas, a hematologist who had perfected a method of typing old and even contaminated bloodstains. If she could match the blood found in Corona's van and Impala, on the weapons and on the Levi's jacket with blood from the victims, they would have a direct link. Don Stottlemyer at CII had not been able to do it, claiming that by the time he had gotten around to it, the blood was just too insoluble. Doctor Guy's process was slow-going though, and there was a lot of blood they needed to have typed. You couldn't just drop a few chemicals in a test tube and shake them around as she had done in her demonstration in Yuba City on January 20.

Stottlemyer's failure on the blood hadn't been the only disappointment at CII. The fingerprint man, Russell Parmer, had failed to get any identifiable prints from Corona's cars.

Far more important, the handwriting expert, Terrence Pascoe, had not been able to make Corona as the author of the names in the death ledger. The first nine entries were by one writer, the balance of the names on the three critical pages by one, maybe two others. Pascoe's report had been a real blow; without those ledgers, the prosecution's case would come apart.

To shore up that aspect of the case, Teja had contacted a private handwriting examiner in Los Angeles, John J. Harris. On the basis of a limited number of exemplars, fewer than Terry Pascoe had, Harris had been able to conclude that "one person did substantially all of the writing," but doubted "it could be demonstrated" in court without more samples.

Handwriting examination was an equivocal business, more art than science. No two examiners could ever quite agree on the details. Not so laboratory analysis of striation marks. Stottlemyer had spent every spare minute over a period of four months trying to match the machete found in Corona's van with the wound on Kenneth Whitacre's skull. The best he could do was say that "either this tool did not make the striations on the skull or that it did make the striations and the cutting edge was subsequently altered."

Only two of the dozens of Corona's knives and tools had blood on them, Stottlemyer's final report in December had noted. There was nothing on the club—which wasn't a club but a two-by-two anyway. The posthole digger from Corona's garage had two human hairs on it, embedded in the dried mud, but no blood. The tire impressions taken near one of the graves and the photographs of tire tracks did not match Corona's vehicles.

Reluctantly Teja had turned over Stottlemyer's last report to Hawk; it was as if he were conceding that they had no evidence, that the case, which had once looked so good, had evaporated.

The experts' reports were at one and the same time depressing and maddening. Teja was convinced Corona was guilty; he knew it, felt it. There was so much pointing in the direction of the labor contractor. If this wasn't the machete that killed those men—the district attorney was not ready to concede that yet—then there must be another one somewhere. After all, they hadn't found the murder scene yet, only the place where the victims were buried. Or some of them. Somewhere in Sutter or Yuba Counties there was probably a slaughterhouse, maybe more than one.

Everything the prosecution seemed to touch right now turned to dust. The adding machine tape found in the grave of the seventeenth victim had not come from Corona's adding machine. Another direct link shot. Bart had started working through the evidence they had and found it all screwed up, evidence tags missing, or the tags not signed or dated, or things associated with the wrong graves—just everything that could go wrong. The whole evidence locker in the basement of the courthouse was mixed up, no master log of who went in and out, who took what and where they took it, just chaos.

Williams had complained. You couldn't blame him, Teja had to agree. He just hadn't known things were in such bad shape. The cases Teja had had up till then had never raised any evidence problems, no real question about the chain-of-possession. The upset Williams had argued that he couldn't put the evidence in order and do everything else necessary to get ready for the trial.

Teja had reluctantly agreed to ask the county Board of Supervisors for the $2,000 a month it would take for George Roche, a criminology instructor at Sacramento State College, to come up and straighten out the chain-of-possession. If the chain-of-possession wasn't cleared up, Hawk would have half of their evidence thrown out of court.

Williams was too busy to help Roche conduct his investigation of the investigation. As the witnesses became less secure, the more their chance for a conviction rested upon scientific examination of the physical evidence. It was the hair on the posthole digger which had given them the idea of attempting to match hair from the victims with loose hairs found in Corona's cars and on his clothes. Stottlemyer had vacuumed both vehicles —bagging lint, hair, dirt, a few bits of screen wire—then had sent it off to Washington, D.C., to the crime laboratory maintained by the Alcohol, Tobacco and Firearms Division (ATF) of the Internal Revenue Service.

The well-funded ATF lab had the most sophisticated devices, including a neutron activator, with which to analyze evidence. Not only could the lab compare the hair, but it would also analyze the bullets found in the mess hall, comparing them spectrographically with the slug taken from Kamp's skull. The ATF lab also maintained an extensive file on ink formulas; their expert thought it was possible to match the colored ink found in Kamp's notebook with that in the death ledger and both of them with an unusual Italian ballpoint pen that wrote in six colors which Corona had kept in the mess hall. The ink and pen, overlooked in a first search and picked up later when someone realized the ledger was in three or four colors, was a major piece of evidence.

The ATF lab was a great find, Williams was certain. The lab had its own handwriting examiner, Sidney Goldblatt, a real pro apparently. Howard Hughes had even sought to hire Goldblatt on a private basis in the McGraw-Hill and Clifford Irving thing. Goldblatt had turned the job down because of the press of work; if Hughes wanted him, he must be as good as his colleagues claimed.

There was a little problem with Goldblatt, Detective Gregory reported, after returning to Yuba City from the East. Goldblatt didn't want to be in conflict with an examiner from another agency, and did not "want to become involved in these type arguments in court," as Gregory put it in his memo. The detective was higher than a kite on Goldblatt though; "Goldblatt has a very, very good reputation on the East Coast." If that were the case, Williams and Teja would have to either convince him or get his superiors to order him to take the Corona case on. He wouldn't be that much in conflict with Pascoe, and if it were necessary, they could always drop Pascoe from the witness list and use Goldblatt.

While Williams was busy with the evidence, Teja was struggling with a snarl of legal problems. He had filed a motion for discovery to obtain a copy of the interview Hawk had with the strange Mrs. Lillard. Now the bail question, buried in October, was alive again, far more serious than ever. On February 18, 1972, the California State Supreme Court became the first high tribunal in the country to rule that capital punishment was cruel and unusual, a violation of constitutional law *per se*. Lawyers all over the state—including both Hawk and Teja—had been watching the case brought by the NAACP, waiting for the inevitable. Year by year the state's Seven Wise Men had inched closer and closer to an outright ban on the death penalty with successive decisions; it had finally come with the *Anderson* decision.

With the *Anderson* case ending capital punishment, Corona would be eligible for bail. State law had previously guaranteed the right to bail before conviction in all except cases punishable by the death penalty "where the proof of guilt was evident or the presumption thereof great." Now, with the filing of the *Anderson* opinion, this single exception to the right to bail also fell since there no longer were any capital cases.

The capital punishment opinion enraged Teja. At the same time it delighted Hawk. Corona no longer faced the death penalty, the court making its holding fully retroactive. Simultaneously, Corona became eligible for bail, but if he were to file a new motion for bail, Hawk had to make a critical decision.

Judge Hauck had once denied bail. Supreme Court ruling or no, he was not likely to reverse himself, loosing a suspected mass murderer in Sutter County. He could ignore what was happening all over the state— judges granting bail to murder suspects—ignore the fact that Angela Davis herself was admitted to bail five days after the *Anderson* decision. Hauck would just shrug and say, "Take your appeal, counselor," making it necessary for Corona to spend another six months in jail before his case came to trial.

If it were not for the question of bail, the defense attorney would have liked to hang on to Judge Hauck. Though Hawk had lost the motion on change of venue, the judge had seemingly given the defense a fair share of the rulings on what was inadmissible. Hawk believed that the judge would be extremely cautious during the trial, letting in much Hawk wanted as evidence, blocking prosecution evidence that looked troublesome or problematic legally.

If Hawk were to get bail set for Juan—Hawk and the Corona family had secured pledges totaling $200,000 in title-free property to post as bond—it meant that Judge Hauck would have to be disqualified, using the one peremptory challenge for prejudice Corona had on the Superior Court level. The state Judicial Council, the housekeeping arm of the judiciary, would then assign a new judge. There were 300 Superior Court judges in the state; Juan Corona would be taking potluck. It could be any one of them, though, most likely, it would be a judge from a less burdened rural area, not someone from crowded Los Angeles where there were no judges to spare. It was a chance Corona had to take unless they wanted to delay the trial another six months to wait for a favorable ruling from the District Court of Appeal.

On February 22, Judge Hauck was automatically disqualified by the affidavit of prejudice Corona filed. Notified of the disqualification, the Judicial Council two days later assigned a new judge to preside, at least temporarily, in the Corona case.

Judge Richard E. Patton had been eager to accept the appointment from the Judicial Council. The Corona case was the sort upon which judicial careers could be advanced, and Patton, who had served occasionally and temporarily on the state Court of Appeal by assignment, was ambitious enough to desire a permanent seat on the appellate bench.

Nicknamed "The General" by court attachés though unrelated to the World War II military commander, Patton had frequently presided over cases in Sutter County. Severe on the bench, friendly outside the courtroom, the judge was noted for his rapid-fire decisions. Attorneys in the adjacent counties of Yuba, Sutter, and Colusa considered him fair, "an above-average judge who runs a tight ship," a "non-nonsense type" with a "disciplined mind."

Patton seemed just the sort of man to keep a tight rein on Hawk, who had already been cited three times for violating the gag order. Patton was fifty-two, with nineteen years' experience on the bench, the last ten of them as a Superior Court judge in his native Colusa County. A small-town boy who had gone off to San Francisco to get his law degree in 1948, Patton now lived on his own walnut farm, still a farmer who often drove a pickup truck to the courthouse.

March 6 was a pivotal court hearing, the first at which Patton presided. Both the law-and-order judge and the untrammeled defense attorney would be feeling their way, measuring the other. Hawk was anxious to make a good impression; as far as the bail question was concerned, he had everything going for him—the law, the facts, and even a little more favorable press. The reporters were coming around more frequently for a drink, listening to him, interested in his broad hints of another suspect. They were bright enough to sense a good story.

Both Judge Patton and Hawk were punctilious. "The matter before the court this afternoon is the proceeding numbered 17399, the People of the State of California, plaintiff, versus Juan V. Corona, defendant. The defendant is represented by Mr. Richard Hawk. Are you, sir, Mr. Hawk?"

Judge Patton asked with ceremonial politesse, looking down from the curved bench in the modernized courtroom.

"I am, Your Honor," Hawk acknowledged, one hand resting on Corona's shoulder.

"And I take it the gentleman next to you is your client, Mr. Corona." It was the first mark of a personal courtesy toward Juan Corona that the judge would maintain throughout the trial.

Hawk nodded. "It is."

"And I note appearing for the People is Mr. Dave Teja, district attorney of the County of Sutter." Patton and Teja were at least familiar with each other, if not friends, Hawk noted.

The judge had read everything available on the *Anderson* decision as well as the briefs written by both attorneys. (In a calculated ploy he was to repeat frequently, Teja turned over to Hawk a copy of the prosecution brief only as the hearing began, effectively denying the defense an opportunity to do the necessary legal research to rebut Teja's points.) Judge Patton brusquely dismissed the district attorney's opposition to bail. "If there is some question of mental condition, that should come before the court in the proper proceeding. It's not a matter which the court can consider in the motion for bail."

"That was going to be my argument, Your Honor," Hawk put in, pleasantly agreeable. Brownie points never hurt.

There was only a very narrow legal question before the court, Judge Patton held. Once the state Supreme Court's decision was final, once the thirty-day period in which the attorney general could move for a rarely granted rehearing had expired, Corona "will absolutely be entitled to have the court fix bail. Until that is final, he does not have that right, though." It was only a matter of waiting until March 18.

It was to be a fruitless wait. On the last day of the thirty-day period, at the urging of the attorney general, the state Supreme Court modified its capital punishment ruling with what Hawk bitterly called "the Corona amendment." The court revised its ruling and maintained nonbailable offenses by holding that the statute's provision of cases punishable by death was a class of offenses, not a specific enumeration. While the death penalty which had defined it as a class before the *Anderson* decision was no longer in effect, the class of cases remained. Therefore the standards for bail—and its denial—remained unchanged.

All Hawk could do was make a final, feeble, emotional plea. "I ask you in the name of all that's right and decent and fair to free on bail a guy who's been in jail an awful long time." Given back the former standard, Judge Patton denied bail.

There was little enough the defense attorney could salvage from the bail hearing. The Corona family was disturbed that others had been freed—like Angela Davis—while Juan remained in jail. By comparison, Hawk did

Aerial view of the Sullivan ranch looking eastward, with the Feather River at the top and U.S. Route 99 at the bottom.

The riverbank graveyard. Aerial view of the Sullivan ranch, showing locations of graves.

Pages from Juan Corona's ledger containing names of some victims in the case. "In any event, it was not possible to identify all the questioned writing as being by one person."

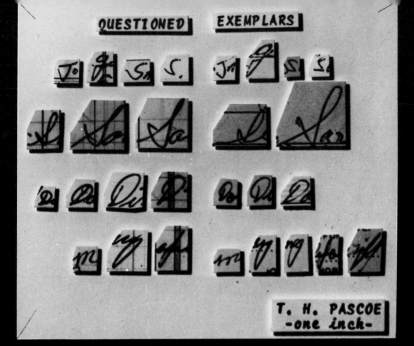

Handwriting exemplars. Those appearing under the heading "questioned" are taken from Corona's ledger; those appearing under "exemplars" were furnished to the court by Corona. "If they can't figure them out, how do they expect me to?"—Juror number 4.

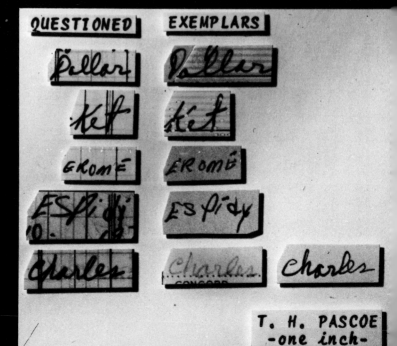

not appear to a good attorney. About all Hawk could get out of it was a couple of paragraphs in the papers that "he had evidence that indicates someone else committed the crimes." He vented his rage on the small band of *chicano* activists who had joined the Corona family to demonstrate in front of the courthouse that day. "If you people got together, this would never have happened. If you were like the blacks, you would have gotten Juan out, like Angela got out."

That night Hawk got drunk.

The bitterness didn't last long. In its place came a lasting anger—at the prosecutors, at the sheriff, and, finally, at the judge—an anger almost imperceptible in the courtroom, but barely masked elsewhere. Justice for Juan Corona was slow in coming. That Corona was being held, that they had even arrested him on the lousy evidence they had, only made it worse.

It was difficult for Hawk to face Corona, to forever explain the bad breaks; it was easier to just tell Juan what he was going to do next, then go ahead and do it. Better to drink with some reporter or Pedro Corona than to see Juan in the two-cell women's wing of the Sutter County jail, and look at the damn crucifix Juan had hung on the wall or the pictures of the four girls.

Although Hawk did not know it, Corona did have another visitor, a psychiatrist hired by the sheriff and ferretted into Corona's wing despite the court order which barred anyone from talking with the prisoner without Hawk's permission. Cooperative, an unsuspecting Corona had talked to the doctor for an hour. Conversation in the jail was rare, the days of television and old magazines long. The sheriff had even curtailed, on the grounds of security, the infrequent visits of the physical therapist and the woman who volunteered to teach him to paint by the numbers.

The psychiatrist's three-paragraph report was carefully drafted to buttress the prosecution's contention that Corona was dangerous:

> During the hour I spent with Mr. Corona I found him to be cooperative and affable, conventionally oriented, and in possession of an intact memory for both recent and remote events. He denied both visual and auditory hallucinations. No evidence of delusional thinking was elicited. His sense of humor is impaired and his mood is decidedly depressive. There is no evidence of psychosis at this time. He is alleged to be receiving heavy doses of Thorazine. He appears to be in need of Artane or similar medication to prevent the complications of extra-pyramidal symptoms [side effects of the major tranquilizer].
>
> Diagnosis: Adjustment Reaction of Adult Life.
>
> In view of the current depression it is my opinion based upon reasonable medical probability that Juan Corona does presently constitute a hazard to himself or others. It is further my opinion that he would benefit from a 1203.03 Penal Code commitment for ninety days' observation at the California Medical Facility.

The doctor had delivered upon demand, his observations contradicting his diagnosis, his diagnosis differing from that of the cooperative Doctor Andres at the county hospital.

At the same time, District Attorney Teja was also involved with a psychiatrist in his effort to rehabilitate Ruby Lillard. The doctor said he needed Hawk's interview with the woman to supplement those the district attorney had taken; and Teja himself was interested in knowing exactly what she had said to the defense. The Lillard woman had told them only that she had contradicted her testimony before the grand jury.

Teja filed a discovery motion seeking Hawk's interview, resting his brief on a legal decision which had been clearly superseded. With the exception of physical evidence, discovery flowed but one way—from the prosecution to the defense. The prosecutor could obtain physical evidence including, under United States Supreme Court holdings, samples of a defendant's blood, hair, and handwriting, but nothing else that would help prove guilt or even give them assistance.

Throughout the hearing, Teja sat expressionless, a poker player with poor cards, while his newly hired deputy polished little-used trial skills.

Williams called Leonard Brunelle as his sole witness. Three years an investigator with the district attorney, Brunelle had spent all of his time until the Corona case working on welfare frauds; Mrs. Lillard and her many problems had been turned over to him.

The slight experience was enough to qualify him in the court as an expert investigator. Under direct examination by Williams, Brunelle testified he had worked with the psychiatrist—who would be called as a witness at the trial to validate Mrs. Lillard's credibility. Hawk, more surprised than he let on, objected. "I would stipulate that Ruby Lillard gave preposterous testimony to the grand jury. But I still don't understand what Mr. Brunelle is going to say as an expert."

Ernestly, Williams explained. "The essence of our discovery motion is that we don't feel that the doctor can give good expert testimony as to this witness' credibility until all of the information concerning his patient is available. And part of that information is the statement she gave to Mr. Hawk and his investigator."

Hawk was honestly aghast at what he considered naive reasoning. "Your Honor, it appeared at one time that the appellate courts were opening up discovery as far as the prosecution getting things from the defense, but *Prudhomme,* the most recent decision, seemed to shut the door back up. And I can tell you right now that I have discussed this with my client, Juan, and that he has instructed me not to deliver the statement." Forcing Hawk to disclose the statement now, contrary to case law, would be reversible error—even before the trial began. The prosecutors should have known that.

Williams stubbornly plowed on. "Ruby Lillard gave a statement to the defense subsequent to her testimony in front of the grand jury that exonerates the defendant, that points the finger in the opposite direction or to the direction of Natividad Corona and not Juan. I am sure that Mr. Hawk will make the most of her change in story at the trial. If she is a credible witness and she has subsequently pointed her finger at Natividad Corona, not Juan, then obviously we are trying to discover information that can prove the defendant's innocence."

Hawk was amused by what he considered a beginner's error. "The serious question in my mind is whether the doctor or any other psychiatrist can get in here and after a witness has testified get up and give some professional expert opinion and usurp the function of the jury on credibility. I have never seen it done. I find it difficult to believe that somebody can be hired by the prosecutor to testify, 'This one you can believe, this one you can't.'"

Williams insisted on pressing the matter; Judge Patton, resigned, agreed to permit Brunelle to testify. The neatly dressed investigator grinned nervously.

"Mr. Brunelle, could you just paraphrase in your own words what you got out of Ruby Lillard's testimony relative to the incident that originated at the Guadalajara Café and ended up in the orchard at the Jack Sullivan ranch in 1965?"

Mrs. Lillard, Brunelle explained, had changed her story, claiming now it was the oldest brother, not Juan, who had taken her to the orchard, repeating the account she had told Hawk's investigator. She was with Natividad when she heard the noise in the rear of the van, felt the springs go down, then heard the animal-like sniffing around the outside of the vehicle.

"Did Ruby Lillard ever indicate to you why she changed her story?"

"Other than being confused, no, sir." Brunelle spoke softly, one eye on Hawk leaning back in his chair, frankly smiling.

"No pressure by Mr. Hawk's investigator?"

"No pressure whatsoever."

"How many times have you talked to Ruby Lillard since?"

"Approximately four or five times in person."

"Now, has she always maintained consistently that it was Natividad who took her out to the orchard and not Juan since that time?"

"No, sir, she has not been consistent in that statement."

Hawk interrupted again. "I haven't seen those statements. That is something that has never been given to me. I would like to see the report he wrote."

With no legal alternative, Williams agreed. "They are available to the defense when they are transcribed." Hawk would never see them.

Because of the woman's bizarre statements, often contradictory, often rambling, Brunelle and the district attorney "decided to have Mrs. Lillard see a psychiatrist in February 1972." She had since seen him twice and was still under therapy.

Some of his confidence returned, Hawk was enjoying himself. He could savor the anticipation of cross-examining a green investigator trying to defend an incredible legal theory. In point of fact, the Lillard statement he had was useless to the prosecution; Hawk could have given up the statement but for a defense attorney's conviction that he should not cooperate if he didn't have to. The prosecution had everything going for them anyway; he didn't have to help them along, not legally, not ethically, and certainly not morally.

"Mr. Brunelle," Hawk began, "if I understand what you are saying, you are spending the taxpayers' money in Sutter County to have Ruby Lillard examined by a psychiatrist?"

"Objection. Argumentative," Williams burst in. Judge Patton pursed his lips, sustaining the objection.

Hawk looked at the judge, shrugging. "Well, what are they doing with her down there?" he asked rhetorically. Turning back to Brunelle, he asked, "For what purpose did you send her down there, to have therapy for her, or what?"

"We sent her down to speak with a psychiatrist to see if her testimony, all or any part, may or may not be credible," Brunelle answered solemnly.

Hawk feigned disbelief. "You mean you needed a psychiatrist to tell you something is wrong with this woman?"

"Objection, Your Honor. Argumentative."

"Sustained." Judge Patton leaned forward. Apparently Hawk did like to belittle witnesses. The judge had been warned the defense attorney would bully law enforcement officers if he were permitted.

"But you did read her testimony, right? In the transcript?"

"Yes, sir," Brunelle responded more confidently, reassured by the deputy district attorney's protective objections.

"Wasn't it your opinion after reading that that there is something wrong with this woman?" Hawk paused to look at the investigator. "What about this creature that comes out of the lagoon down there and sniffs? What creatures do you have like that out there?"

"Objection, Your Honor. That's irrelevant."

Stifling a laugh, Judge Patton advised, "Try to make your questions a little simpler, Mr. Hawk."

An effective cross-examination could accomplish much. The defense attorney intended to prove to Judge Patton that the defense investigation was the equal of the prosecution's. "Incidentally, the lady's legally blind, isn't she?"

"That is correct. I believe so, Mr. Hawk."

"And her occupation is that she runs one of these canteens?"

"Correct, sir."

"And you checked her out here in town, didn't you?"

"Yes, sir."

"And she got fired over here because she was coming to work drunk, and winos were hanging out at the Division of Highways, right?"

Brunelle was uncomfortable again. "We didn't go that far."

"Didn't you?" Eyebrows raised, Hawk cocked his head to one side, then shrugged. "Didn't your investigation go far enough for you to find out she was a drunk and that they let her go because of that?"

Brunelle was uncomfortable. Either they should have checked or he was lying when he said they hadn't; Hawk didn't care which it was.

"Well now, she has got some kind of felony conviction too, hasn't she? Armed robbery or something?"

"No, sir."

"She said she was an armed robber, didn't she?"

"She does have a record, yes, sir."

"What is her record? How wrong was she when she said, 'I have got an armed robbery conviction'?"

"I think—if I am not mistaken—that the arrest was for disturbance of the peace."

Hawk nodded. "And she told you that she was an armed robber and you found out all she got arrested for was disturbing the peace?"

"Yes, sir," a subdued Brunelle answered quietly.

"And you need a psychiatrist to tell you that something is wrong with this woman?" There was no objection from the prosecutors this time. "Now, she related to the grand jury an incident that you kind of skipped over here." The defense attorney paused to look at his notes lying on the counsel table, and to catch a glimpse of Teja's and Williams' opaque expressions. "Something to the effect that one day she was at the Brunswick—"

"Yes, sir." Brunelle nodded gently, then swallowed.

Gloria Corona, Mrs. Lillard claimed, had come into the bar to tell Mrs. Lillard her husband was sick. The three were standing on the sidewalk talking to two Marysville police officers. According to Mrs. Lillard, one of the policemen punched Corona in the stomach, then had kicked him as he lay on the sidewalk. "Remember?"

Brunelle shifted uncomfortably. "Yes, sir, that's in the transcript."

"Is there any report on that in Marysville?"

Brunelle shook his head, "No, sir."

"Now that she's been seeing the doctor, is she straightened out about that incident?"

There was no objection. "I don't know," Brunelle admitted.

"Well now, you are an expert investigator and qualified here," Hawk said deliberately. "What do you think about somebody that tells some kind of wild tale about a couple of Marysville police officers beating a man up in the street?"

Brunelle was trapped. He could either burn away his witness or criticize fellow law enforcement officers. He tried to hedge. "I would tend to believe it until I could verify it."

"You think two Marysville police officers stomped Juan Corona, is that—"

"There is that possibility," Brunelle interrupted.

"Well, now there is no medical record of it, and there is no police report of it. Do you still believe this goofy woman?"

"It was—"

"Come on, the truth now," he prompted. "You don't believe her, do you?"

"Yes, sir, I do," Brunelle assured Hawk.

Hawk then began reading a thoroughly confused account of what Mrs. Lillard had termed a kidnapping by a brother of Juan Corona, Judge Patton interrupting to agree that it was incoherent.

"What does all that mean? What is this about this shooting in Sacramento and the kidnapping and all this nonsense? Did any of that ever happen?"

"We never verified any of it," a distressed Brunelle whispered.

"You tried, didn't you?"

"We didn't even try."

"Do you believe any of that?"

"There is a possibility, sir."

"Anything's possible. It's possible the sun won't come up tomorrow or the world may stop on its axis or maybe God will come through the wall in a moment. Anything's possible." Still no objection.

"Yes, sir."

"You are an expert. What is the probability?"

"I wouldn't say."

Without objection from the two prosecutors, Hawk continued. "How do you explain that in one moment she doesn't speak a word of Spanish, Juan doesn't speak English, but somehow she converses with him all the time, way back in 1950?"

"I have no explanation for that."

"Do you know where he was in 1950?"

Brunelle shook his head. "No, sir."

"He was in Mexico. How did she talk to him in Olivehurst when he was in Mexico? You didn't check that out?"

"No, sir."

"Why not?"

"Once again, its inconsistency."

"I see," Hawk nodded, his voice rising and falling in mock understanding. "Which you hope to salvage with some psychiatrist you have hired, is that right?"

Williams finally objected. Patton, who had been waiting for an objection to the compound questions, to the argumentative tone, to the badgering and interruptions, quickly sustained the prosecutor. Hawk had to resist the temptation to smile knowingly at the judge.

"Was that the purpose of sending her to the psychiatrist, to try to salvage the testimony of this foolish woman?"

"No, sir, that wasn't the purpose. The purpose of sending her down to the psychiatrist was to see if her credibility—to see if she was credible."

Hawk nodded. "Credible. I see. Hasn't he kind of hinted to you that there might be kind of something wrong with her mind?"

"No, sir."

"He hasn't?" Hawk's eyebrows peaked on his forehead. "Is she real sound, sane?"

"No, sir." Brunelle was barely audible.

"What did he say her problems are?"

"He said she was very confused and very frightened."

The defense attorney was elated. After months of legal maneuvering, Hawk had finally had an opportunity to use his best skill, cross-examination. In the two hours Brunelle had been on the stand, Hawk had succeeded in raising serious questions about the prosecution's case—for the judge, for the Corona family, and, most importantly, for the press. Hawk had claimed all along that they had a lousy case against Juan, and now he had proven just how bad one part of it was. After all, Mrs. Lillard had testified before the Grand Jury; presumably her testimony had helped secure the indictment.

At the same time, he had had an opportunity to test the new trial deputy, to measure the opposition. Hawk was not impressed. Williams seemed like a nice guy, a man just doing his job; he didn't have the personal involvement of Teja. But then it wasn't his political career on the line either. Even so, Williams didn't appear to be much better in a courtroom than Teja.

It would appear that Judge Patton too had weighed the effectiveness of the opposing attorneys. Hawk was quicker by far, much more experienced. Patton understood that continual objections—especially on minor points—angered judges and juries, that objections needed to be well-placed. But Williams had given Hawk almost free rein, much too much leeway in Patton's opinion. He would have to make certain that the scales were not so heavily tipped in the future, that the People were adequately represented.

The People's discovery motion was ill-advised at best. The whole matter should never have been raised, the judge thought. The statement Hawk had from Mrs. Lillard was not discoverable and the prosecution should have known it. They also had erred in insisting on Brunelle's testimony. All it had done was expose them to ridicule; surely they weren't going to rest their case on the evidence of a woman whose testimony a psychiatrist would have to certify as credible. Unheard of.

Teja too was troubled. The more nettled he was, the more impassive his face; the more embarrassed, the more expressionless, the good poker player to the end. Hawk had punched Brunelle around the courtroom. The deputies who were going to testify in the trial had damn well better read Brunelle's cross-examination, so each of them would know what he faced. Brunelle's credibility had been seriously questioned; he would testify only on a minor point later in the case. Mrs. Lillard's credibility had been totally dissolved; she would never be called.

From that point on, Hawk had the initiative.

13

The Ninth Street Barrier

June 5-July 1, 1972

Judge Richard Patton had never seen a lawyer like Hawk, an attorney who willfully disregarded the court's gag order, who deliberately asked objectionable questions or made uncalled-for remarks in court. The man was nothing so much as a courtroom brawler, a Pier Six lawyer. Hawk even said it himself. "Everytime they take a punch at me, I'm going to hit them back. Harder."

Judge Patton resented Hawk's unwillingness to admit that he was not the only one who wanted to protect Corona's rights. The judge himself wanted the same thing. He didn't favor one or the other party; he ruled as he had to, based on legal precedents, and legal precedents alone. Hawk should have realized that by now. Denying a number of prosecution motions for discovery, he had ordered Hawk to turn over only a single piece of physical evidence, some asphalt gouged from a road in the southern part of the county by Van den Heuval's investigator. Supposedly blood had dripped on it from the trunk of a car after Corona was arrested. In any event, there was no blood on the asphalt; it hardly mattered to either side.

At the same time, the law demanded that the defense obtain copies of all police resports, arrest records of prospective witnesses, any statements those witnesses might have given law enforcement officers, reports of the prosecution's expert witnesses who had analyzed the evidence, photographs—virtually everything the prosecution had, good or bad, useful or useless to either side. He had ordered it turned over, just as the law demanded. If there was one thing he could insist upon, it was his fairness to both sides.

Richard Hawk didn't agree—certainly not after the judge's ruling of June barring Hawk from presenting evidence to support a motion to quash the sheriff's search warrants. If the first warrant was invalid, then the evidence seized under authority of that warrant could not be used in court. Teja would lose the ledger, the weapons, the blood found in the two vehicles, and with it, the guts of his case.

Once again Teja had come in late with his brief, mailing it after business hours Friday night for a hearing the following Monday morning, even though the judge had his hand-delivered copy in plenty of time.

The defense attorney had contended that the warrant issued by Judge Hankins early in the morning of May 26, 1971, more than a year before, was based on an inadequate affidavit prepared by the sheriff and district attorney. Hankins had found that probable cause—the law's reasonable belief in suspecting an individual of a particular crime—did exist based on three grounds: the two receipts found in the grave along the river; allegations that Juan Corona was mentally ill; and, finally, the suspicion that Corona had assaulted Raya in the Guadalajara Café.

All three of the grounds were defective, Hawk's brief contended. Whiteaker lacked the professional qualifications to stipulate that the body in the grave had been killed after the receipts were written; the best medical evidence made it just as likely that the victim had been slain before the receipts were written.

The mental-illness allegation was fallacious at best. Whiteaker's reasoning seemed to be that Corona was mentally ill; the killer must have been mentally ill; ergo, Corona was the killer. And Judge Hankins, instead of agreeably issuing the warrant, should have asked more questions, demanded something more than he had, Hawk contended.

Finally, there was the Guadalajara incident. If there had not been sufficient probable cause to charge Juan with attacking Raya in 1970, how could that serve as probable cause for a search warrant in this case? The standards were the same.

For his part, Teja's late-filed brief argued that Hawk was attempting to look into the facts upon which the affidavit had been based. A warrant could be upset "only if the affidavit fails as a matter of law to set forth sufficient competent evidence supportive of the magistrate's finding of probable cause since it is the function of the trial court, not the justice court, to appraise and weigh evidence."

Quickly Judge Patton first ruled that Hawk could not present the expert testimony from doctors or bring Duron in to refute the statement in the affidavit. Then he denied Hawk's motion to quash the warrants.

If the judge had allowed a hearing, it would give Hawk a tremendous advantage. Even if he didn't get the warrant quashed—Hawk doubted that Patton or any other local judge had that much resolve—the prosecution would be forced to detail its case against Corona, *before the trial*. Hawk would know where their strongest evidence lay, and whom he had to present in rebuttal.

At the moment, Hawk wasn't certain what the defense case would be.

He would put Corona on, that was for damn sure. If the jurors didn't hear from Corona, they would hold it against him. Besides he was clean—he had no felony record. Who was going to hold it against him that he had been deported as an illegal alien, a guy who came to this country to better himself? Corona would be a good witness, too. Teja would not have enough sense to lay off him and would end up burying himself in the stoic Corona.

Tactically, Hawk believed he was in a favorable position. His constant hints about another suspect, coupled with the prosecution's concession that Mrs. Lillard had fingered Natividad, worried Teja and Williams. His publicity stunt—to try and shift some of the guilt from Juan—was paying off, far better than he would have imagined. How else could they explain Williams' motion for a list of the defense witnesses, supporting it with a disingenuous assertion that "the state of the law is uncertain on this particular request." It wasn't uncertain at all, Hawk snorted; the courts had not specifically said the prosecution could have such a list and Hawk was not going to give them one. More importantly, Williams had told the judge in chambers, "I might well indicate to the court that every time the defense attorney calls someone that we are completely unaware of, everything stops until we get an offer of proof outside the presence of the jury and find out what relevancy their testimony might have." It was certainly a novel theory, something the prosecution had concocted apparently because it was afraid of that "other suspect."

If Hawk guessed right, they had apparently given up their effort to hang the Guadalajara incident on Juan, probably because they couldn't line up enough witnesses and because Raya still said it was Natividad who cut him. If they were afraid of it, Hawk might consider raising it himself. That would put them in the position of having to defend Natividad, and if they were defending Natividad, they couldn't very well be prosecuting Juan.

Hawk would have to look into the whole thing more, mull it over. He reasoned that Teja would have to try to hang the Raya cutting on Juan—it was the best thing the district attorney had going for him—but to get it in, Teja would have to argue the similarity of the Raya incident and the murders of the twenty-five. The only similarity was the head wounds, and how many different ways were there to cut a guy? Not many. The differences between the Raya cutting and the mass murders were much more apparent; one was a fight in a bar, the others were stealthily done. Raya was left lying in the toilet, alive; the twenty-five victims were killed, then buried. It was a completely different set of circumstances, Hawk believed.

However, if the prosecution wasn't going to use it, he just might. A big problem there was the Corona family itself; they refused to talk about Natty, protecting him even at the expense of Juan, Pedro especially. In the end, it would all turn on Judge Patton. "I don't know how brave he's going to be about his prejudice. He probably privately believes that Corona is a spic, or maybe he's politer than that, and refers to him as a Mexican national," Hawk told an aide.

Patton, Hawk reasoned, was nobody's friend in weighing the admissibility of the Guadalajara incident. Conceivably he was worried already about appeals and his reputation. After all, the case would be picked through for years to come. Patton just might very well want to keep the incident out for fear the appellate courts would later reverse a conviction because he had let it in. "I don't really think he's got balls enough to let it in," Hawk concluded. "I might get fooled, but I doubt it."

That would keep for a while. More important at the moment was, finally, the hearing on a change of venue. Judge Patton was upset that the District Court of Appeal had ordered a hearing in the first place to find an urban area free of prejudice to farm workers; ordinarily, the Judicial Council merely looked at the case loads around the state and picked an empty courtroom. But the executive secretary this time had recommended two counties, Sacramento and Stockton, both right in the heart of the agriculturally rich Sacramento Valley, neither of them free of prejudice against Mexicans or untainted by the news coverage which had forced the change of venue in the first place. It was hard to figure out what the council was thinking of in recommending those two places.

Hawk was upset by the council's recommendation, so much so that he took the unusual step of visiting Justice Leonard Friedman of the District Court of Appeal in his Sacramento offices. Perhaps, with the justice's permission, Hawk could subpoena him to testify at the hearing as to what he meant by his decision ordering a change of venue.

The justice had been outraged by the suggestion, offended that Hawk had come to see him. Trying to soothe the judge—conceivably he could sit on any future appeals on Corona's behalf—Hawk explained. "I didn't come to offend you; that wasn't my intention. And if you feel it isn't appropriate, I certainly wouldn't think of subpoenaing you. That's why I came here, to ask you. You've got to understand. My man's been in jail for a year. Another three-month delay while I appeal a change of venue to either Stockton or Sacramento would be cruel."

Somewhat mollified, the justice insisted his opinion had left nothing unsaid. Hawk agreed with the jurist, but added that neither Stockton nor Sacramento met with the opinion's ruling that the site selected be free of prejudice. "What I had in mind was for you to explain it, to save Juan three more months of waiting. I don't think the judge understands."

They were two men bound by rules and roles. Concerned himself about an unwarranted delay, the justice's anger eased. Without discussing his opinion, Justice Friedman pointed out that the Judicial Council had power to change venue based upon the burden of the courts alone. But there was in a change-of-venue case resulting from prejudicial publicity something more than case loads and convenience to court attachés. Hawk believed the justice "was really saying, 'Don't worry about it. If they ship you to Stockton or Sacramento, take your writ, and I'll see that things are straightened out.' "

They shook hands before Hawk left the jurist to return to his legal research, Hawk far happier than when he had come, but no further along.

June 29 would be another scorcher in a summer of 110-degree days. The thermometer was over ninety as the crowd began forming in front of the small courthouse in Yuba City at nine o'clock in the morning. The Corona family straggled in a small picket line walking in a rubber-band circle on the sidewalk, forlorn signs proclaiming "*Justicia para Juan Corona.*" Newsmen clustered at the head of the steps, barred from entering the building by the polite deputies, the first sentinels in an elaborate and burdensome security system Sheriff Whiteaker had deemed essential.

It was to be the last hearing in Sutter County, called only to determine a new trial site. Hawk had worked hard preparing for the hearings, driving up and down the Sacramento Valley to interview prospective witnesses. One group would testify that there was substantial prejudice in Stockton, the other that Sacramento was similarly biased.

Teja too was disturbed by the Judicial Council's recommendation of either Stockton or Sacramento. The prosecutor wanted to move the trial to the state capital, just forty miles from Yuba City. If the trial were there, he would be able to commute, to live at home, to work out of his office in the Sutter County courthouse. Stockton, however, was too far south for that.

The district attorney secured an affidavit from the Stockton chief of police stating the department was not equipped to handle any expected public demonstration such as those which accompanied the Angela Davis trial. Teja placed all his legal eggs in the Sacramento basket, submitting a brief that contended the appellate court-ordered hearing was not legally required, and that the Judicial Council's recommendation was to be adopted.

By the noon recess, Stockton had tacitly been eliminated. If both attorneys objected so strenuously, why send the trial there? Hawk's witnesses sketched pervasive patterns of prejudice against Mexican-Americans, especially those who were no longer passive, who identified themselves as *chicanos.*

Teja was fumbling, unsure of his direction, attempting to minimize the prejudice he knew existed, which he himself could not and would not deny. The prosecutor seemed to be barging ahead, asking open-ended questions: a good cross-examiner did not leave room for the witnesses to lecture at length.

It was Teja's badly framed question in midafternoon which scuttled any possibility of the trial moving to Sacramento. The district attorney was cross-examining George Williams, the assistant city editor of the Sacramento *Bee* and a twelve-year veteran newsman, about his assertion that migratory workers were rousted in Sacramento. "Could you give me an example of somebody, a migrant farm worker, having been forcibly removed from some area of Sacramento to another area where he was expected to remain?"

Primed for the question, Williams answered, leaning into the microphone on the witness stand, "Yes. Not too long ago I was taken off the city desk for three days and I was assigned to work down in the west end of Sacramento, to dress up like a migrant worker and to do a story which would tell what it would be like for a migrant farm worker to come from outside of the community and into the community, and exactly what he would have to face.

"And during that time I observed a number of instances in which migrant farm workers would walk from the downtown area—walking east from the river you start at First Street—and when a migrant farm worker who could be identified by his appearance would get as far as Ninth Street a policeman would come up and tell him to go back the way he came."

Teja abruptly changed the subject, leaving it for Hawk to elaborate with questions when Teja's cross-examination ended. Dressed in old clothes, Williams had himself been turned back, not once, but twice. He had seen others also turned back to the flophouse district along the river.

"You mean," Hawk asked feigning outrage, "that in 1972 a man can't walk where he wants to in the capital of the largest state in the country?"

"That's correct," Williams agreed.

"You saw men turned back at Ninth Street?" Hawk rephrased the question for emphasis.

"Yes."

"And you yourself were stopped at this Ninth Street barrier?"

"Yes."

"No further questions."

Shortly before four in the afternoon, Hawk realized that Corona was tired, still feeling the strain of his heart episodes. No longer taking the Thorazine, he no longer looked and acted woodenly in the courtroom, a decided improvement over the past. But without the tranquilizer, Hawk could not be certain of Corona's condition. Thinking to ask for a recess until the following day, Hawk asked to see Judge Patton and Teja in chambers.

It was the judge who brought up the subject. "I'm satisfied that Stockton is out. I'm also pretty well satisfied that a strong showing has been made that Sacramento may not be correct." Teja's face fell. "It's geographically the county next door; I think there's probably community involvement, much the same as there is here; there's the problem of the Sacramento *Bee*."

The trial site should be close to Yuba City, convenient for witnesses and law enforcement personnel who would have to leave their duty posts to testify; it would also have to be an urbanized area. Hawk mentally thanked Bob Heyer and the Field poll for that.

The judge had settled on one of three likely counties: Solano, on the north side of San Francisco Bay; Hawk's home, Contra Costa, just across the Sacramento River from Solano; or Alameda, dominated by the city of Oakland. He would make his final decision the next day, after talking with officials in all three counties. Laughing, Hawk offered to introduce the district attorney to courthouse functionaries and show him the facilities if the judge selected Contra Costa.

The defense attorney was grinning broadly for the benefit of the Corona family as he walked from chambers; he leaned to Corona's ear and whispered, "We've won," Corona first nodding, then faintly smiling.

That evening over dinner Hawk was expansive, volubly elated. Things were equal now, or if not equal, at least a lot of the tactical advantages the prosecution had, the little conveniences of life, were gone. For him it would improve a little; he had already learned how to live in a hostile territory.

Not only had Hawk succeeded in removing the trial from the Sacramento Valley, he had learned something about the district attorney.

"God, he walked into some things there today." Hawk sipped his scotch and soda, musing, "The golden rule of cross-examination is not 'Never ask a question on cross-examination you don't know the answer to.' I even heard it on *Owen Marshall, Counselor-at-Law* last night. But that's not it. The real rule should be: 'Never ask a question when you haven't set the witness up so that common sense will tell you what the answer is going to be.' If he doesn't answer that way, he looks foolish. You got to commit him, obscurely, and then you pop the key question and he has no choice but to come your way. You can't know all the answers, but you can guide them.

"I learned a lot about Teja today. He's going to be real weak, and I'm going to be able to set a lot of traps for that guy, lots of traps." Hawk laughed.

"Teja's just liable to ask witnesses if I've talked to them. 'Well, what did he say?' " Hawk ad-libbed the cross-examination, playing both roles. " 'He said that you're a damn crook, that you've been hiding reports for the last six months.' " Hawk laughed, enjoying the prospect.

"You know, I think he'll blunder into that, and he'll jump on Juan thinking he's going to get some sort of violent reaction. And he'll get nothing. He hasn't got the faintest idea of Juan's answers, unless he makes the prosecutor's fatal error and starts believing the police reports."

Hawk leaned back. "I was on his case good today. He does a dumb thing like asking the judge for an order that the evidence, that asphalt, not be destroyed, say, and I come back, 'Well, Your Honor, unlike the district attorney who mixes bodies up, and fliply switches them from grave to grave, we take care of the evidence.'

"He may not be used to guys doing this to him. Or I make some totally inadmissible statement and the D.A. sputters an objection and I say, 'But it's true, Your Honor. How come I can't get the truth in?' When the jury's here, I'm going to pull a lot of that shit. 'How come I can't tell the truth to the jury? What is this game we're playing here?' "

Hawk was suddenly silent, the ice cubes in his glass chiming as he twirled the drink idly. "Great day. Jeez, I'm happier than I've—" His voice trailed off. "It's the major victory. To me, it's the key point in this case."

G. Dave Teja and his deputy, Bart Williams, spent an hour in their office after the hearing, rarely talking, each involved with his own thoughts. Time enough tomorrow to start worrying about moving everything, once Patton decided where the trial was going. That was going to be a mess, setting up an entire office, secretaries, investigators, files and all. Not to mention the costs.

They had already spent $140,000 on the case, and it looked as if he would have to go back to the Board of Supervisors for more. The chief administrative officer, Larry Cilley, estimated another $160,000 before the trial was over or another 10¢ tax for each $100 of assessed valuation. The state was going to pick up a big part of that, Teja knew, under the provisions of a retroactive law adopted in the wake of the Corona case; that legislation, introduced by the local senator and assemblyman, provided that the state would pay for any costs above and beyond what could be raised from an across-the-board tax increase of 5¢. Still, it was expensive; no politician wanted to spend tax money like that, not if he wanted to stay in office.

The following afternoon, Judge Patton selected Solano County, eighty miles south of Yuba City, as the site of the trial. County officials had not been pleased; as Patton put it, "No county welcomes a case that involves as much as this one." Still, Solano County Sheriff Albert Cardoza had agreed that he would hire extra deputies—he would bill Sutter County for it anyway—and lay on the security system the judge wanted. Moreover, the state prison at Vacaville, just fifteen miles from Fairfield, the county seat, had a hospital wing. Corona could be kept there and his heart condition closely watched, far better than it could be if he were in some city jail.

Of the three counties, it was the one closest to Sutter; both the judge and the district attorney could at least spend the weekends at home. It would have been nice if they could have had the remaining pretrial hearing, on the prosecution's motion for handwriting exemplars from Corona, in Sutter County, but Hawk had objected.

"I want Juan Corona moved out of the clutches of Roy Whiteaker as soon as possible." The judge smiled faintly; the boyish sheriff was hardly menacing enough to have "clutches." But Patton was not amused by Hawk's unsupported accusation that the Corona family had been "harassed and degraded" by the sheriff since Corona's arrest.

Sheriff Whiteaker was not amused, either, by Hawk's accusation. That afternoon, as his first public comment on the case since the first weeks of the investigation, Whiteaker released a handwritten statement to newsmen. "Mr. Hawk has been one of the most obnoxious attorneys that has ever been in contact with this office and the sheriff. His attitude and approach to a difficult situation and in regards to this office has been similar to the actions of a small child."

Hawk was pleased with Whiteaker's estimate. It meant Hawk had gotten under the sheriff's skin; that would make the sheriff vulnerable on cross-examination.

On July 1, Juan Corona took down the crucifix from the wall of the two-cell complex in the women's wing of the Sutter County jail to move to the state prison facility at Vacaville. He would not see Jim Liminoff finish painting the exterior of his Carpenter's Gothic home across the street from the cell's basement window.

14

Cowards and Contemnors
July-August 1972

The trial date had been set for September 5, Hawk waiving the mandatory thirty-day deadline the state had in which to begin the trial so as to complete his own preparations. Oakland attorney Charles Garry and his associate, Al Brodsky, had found time to discuss with Hawk the questions Garry had used to select jurors in the three trials of Huey Newton. The three attorneys would spend an afternoon together, going over the extensive list of questions Garry had prepared for the voir dire of prospective jurors in the murder trials of the Black Panther leader. Hawk also wanted to talk to Leo Branton, Angela Davis' chief attorney; whatever he had done, he had obviously picked a good jury, one that apparently had no trouble finding Miss Davis innocent. Hawk intended to borrow another strategy from Branton and make Corona, as was Miss Davis, co-counsel.

Hawk still had not settled two tactical problems: whether to introduce into the trial Corona's mental condition, and whether to raise the Guadalajara Café incident in an effort to shift suspicion to Natividad. The only reason for going into the question of Juan's sanity was the fear of some lingering memory of the publicity surrounding the case fourteen months earlier. He could hope to screen potential jurors for it, but he couldn't hope to find all who might have some recollections. A decision on that would have to wait until he could size up the jury during voir dire.

The Guadalajara incident was something else, the big problem there being the family's reluctance to involve the oldest brother in the case. Hawk supposed it was a cultural thing; Natividad, with the death of the father, was the oldest male in the family. Homosexual or not, he was the head of the family. That he would just have to confront; if Juan agreed, it wouldn't matter now what the family thought. It was too late to change attorneys.

For months Hawk had been pondering the motive problem; Juan didn't have one, obviously, but someone else did; there had to be some explanation for the murders of twenty-five men in April and May 1971. The sheriff's reports suggested a sex angle; a number of the victims had been undressed in some degree. The sheriff himself apparently suspected these were sex crimes; they had taken a rectal swab from Kenneth Whitacre's body. For some unaccountable reason, Detective Gregory had visited a lawyer-psychiatrist in Los Angeles who told them he believed these were homosexual killings, but apparently the prosecution had not followed this up. At least they had not hired the man.

Evelyn Hooker had been recommended by a friend of Hawk's as the foremost expert on homosexuality. A clinical professor of psychology at the UCLA Medical School, she had served as chairman of a task force studying the question for the National Institutes of Mental Health. After a long conversation, Doctor Hooker had agreed to help Juan; she would do a psychological work-up intended to answer two questions: Was Juan homosexual, and was he capable of the mass murders?

Equally important, Doctor Hooker had been able to explain the significant differences between homosexuality in the United States and Mexico. Unlike this country, as Hawk understood the woman, there were three types of homosexuals in Mexico, depending upon the roles they played in the sex act. The *activo* was the male, as she put it, "the insertor." For him there was no particular social opprobrium; in a society where the women were still closely sheltered, the *activo* was merely taking advantage of the sexual opportunities at hand. In a sense, he was asserting his masculinity, his *machismo*.

The *passivo* was the female or "insertee." He was not shunned by his family as his counterpart in the United States would likely be. Indeed, he was often protected—as was Natividad by the Coronas.

The third type was the *activo-passivo*, the ambivalent man who played both roles. If the murderer of the twenty-five were Mexican, and if the murders were homosexual, Doctor Hooker explained, the killer was likely an *activo-passivo*. He was a man driven to humiliate himself; that was why he played the female role in the sex act within a culture that considered *machismo,* manhood, so significant. At the same time, he harbored an enormous rage, as Doctor Hooker had put it, a hatred for the *activos* who were stripping him of his *machismo*. That rage could easily, and repeatedly, lead to murder.

Natividad fit, Hawk exulted. What better way to humiliate himself than with Skid Row bums, dirty some of them, poorer than Natividad himself? Natividad obviously screwed that kind of guy. The sheriff had uncovered a number of Natty's registration entries on the guest ledgers of the run-down hotels in lower Marysville. Why would a man with a $20,000 house just six miles from town spend a week in a flea-bag of a hotel unless it was for sex?

It all fit. Natty had already tried to blame his brother for a crime he, Natty, had committed—the Guadalajara cutting. Why not now? Hawk didn't know why there was bad blood between the two brothers, neither Juan nor any other member of the family would talk about it, but it was there. After all, Natividad, who was worth $400,000 earned by contracting and selling beer, had sent just $250 for his brother's defense. Big deal. Hawk made a mental note to ask Pedro Corona for some sample of Natividad's handwriting. If it matched the ledger, Juan was a free man.

Based upon what he had told her of the two brothers, Doctor Hooker agreed that Natividad was a better suspect than Juan. Hawk would have to figure a way to get that out of her at the trial, before the prosecution could object. He'd load her up on that; she could slip it into one of her answers; the judge would order it stricken, no doubt, but the jury would have heard it anyway. Teja's objection would only serve to underline the comment.

Doctor Hooker was great. She had made sense out of the case, finally, and fingered a better suspect in a way that Teja couldn't impeach—not unless he could find a bigger expert on homosexuality, and there just wasn't one. Convinced of Juan's innocence, she was volunteering, and not only that, she had passed Hawk on to a colleague, West Los Angeles psychologist Harvey Ross, who agreed to sit in on the first days of jury selection and comment on the veniremen drawn. It was a frequent ploy, especially of prosecutors, but Hawk had been unable to pay the $350 a day it cost to have a psychologist in the courtroom. Ross' voluntary appearance would give him a lot of clues about what to look for.

Like Hawk, the two prosecutors also had to make a series of tactical decisions. Hawk had refused, on July 10, to permit Corona to fill out a set of handwriting exemplars that Teja had drafted in collaboration with CII's handwriting expert, Terrence Pascoe, and John J. Harris in Los Angeles. Neither expert could firmly prove that the handwriting in the ledgers was Corona's, though Harris was personally certain it was; both needed more authenticated samples of Corona's handwriting to compare to the ledgers: examples of Corona's script and block printing, as well as copies of the three critical pages in the ledger.

Instead, Hawk had offered to the court a completed set of exemplars on forms that CII used, filled out the day before, he said, in Juan's cell at Vacaville, while a tape recorder was recording the session.

Hawk's exemplars were not adequate, Teja and Williams argued, since they had not been done in open court as Judge Patton had ordered. Hawk had dictated the exemplars, as CII procedure called for, but unlike the prosecution's draft, the completed forms did not have any of the names from the ledger. Teja and Williams wanted those names both in script and block printing, thus providing Pascoe, Harris, and the Treasury expert, Sidney Goldblatt, with A to B comparisons.

Hawk had other reasons for refusing to permit Corona to fill out the prosecution's exemplars, for "flirting with a contempt citation," as he told reporters. He distrusted any handwriting exemplar that was copied—so too did the state's examiners who had talked to him in Sacramento—but he was doubly suspicious of an exemplar form that required Corona to copy the names from the three pages in the ledger that the prosecution claimed was "a death list." Under the stress of filling in the forms in the courtroom, Corona's handwriting might become just erratic enough for the examiners to find some similarities.

Hawk did not intend to withhold handwriting examples at all. Under the law, if he did so, the prosecution was permitted to comment on it, and permit the jury to draw its own conclusions. Hawk had no intention of allowing that to happen, not when his client had not written the names in the ledger. The ledgers had been at the camp until sometime after May 6 when, his crew finished pruning there, Corona had taken them home. Corona knew nothing about the entries on the three pages. Significantly, Kenneth Whitacre, killed on May 19, was not entered; nor was Melford Sample, the victim found with the receipts dated May 21. Some of the dead men's names, not all, did appear on the list; they had been written in there either at the ranch, or at Corona's home. The only people with access to his home would be personal friends or someone in the family; the maid was in the house when the Coronas were not. Anyone— Duron, Rangel, the ranch workers, Sullivan himself—could have access at the ranch, access denied when the ledgers were moved.

The prosecution would try to claim Corona wrote the "death list," but Hawk was going to create difficulties for them. He planned to hand the exemplars over to Harris in the courtroom, and make him complete his examination there, in front of the jury. Hawk was confident he wouldn't be able to do it.

Judge Patton had spent an anxious week since Hawk had refused to comply with the court order for a handwriting exemplar. Well, not refused an exemplar, but refused to order his client to produce one as the judge had instructed. Technically, both Hawk and Corona were in contempt of court. The question, a week later, was how to proceed.

"Mr. Hawk, the court has previously ruled that the People's motion be granted and that the people be entitled to exemplars which be authenticated beyond any question. You have refused, and do you now tell your client not to comply with the court's order?"

Hawk was nervous, his speech halting, carefully chosen. "With respect to the authentication, each page is initialed and dated by me; each of the pages which would be contained in the exemplars that I am offering was filled out in my presence by Mr. Corona. In my mind, I am a member of the state bar and an officer of this court and it is authenticated as far as I am concerned and beyond that."

The issue had become a test of strong wills, the judge intent upon enforcing his order, the defense attorney resisting that order because it clearly aided the prosecution. If Patton merely wanted exemplars, he could modify his order and save a lot of trouble.

"May I point out to you as to what the effect might be? With the defendant's refusal to give the exemplars, the government can rely at trial on the strong inference to be drawn from the continued refusal by the defendant to furnish the exemplars after having judicial order to do so."

Hawk had a counter-argument. "Your Honor, it is my considered opinion that Mr. Corona has not refused to provide exemplars to the prosecutor." He would be willing to trust his chances with the jury, arguing that he had offered the handwriting but the prosecution had refused it.

The judge held Hawk in contempt, sentencing him to forty-eight hours in the county jail. He stayed execution of the order for five days to allow the defense attorney time to appeal, then turned to the quiet defendant.

"Mr. Corona, the court has ordered you to produce the exemplars of your handwriting and your counsel has advised you not to comply with the court's order. And, I ask you now: Are you prepared to give the exemplars of your handwriting as ordered by the court?"

Corona looked at the slip of paper cupped in his hand, and in a quiet voice read, "My attorney tells me I have already offered you and the prosecutor more than enough."

The judge perceptibly shrugged, asked the question a second time, and listened while Corona once again read from the yellow slip. Half sighing, Judge Patton fined Corona $250.

Hawk would serve the two days. An appeal on the ground that the law required only an authentic handwriting sample, not one prepared under specific circumstances, was denied summarily late on a Friday afternoon. Hawk was left with no opportunity to take the case to the state Supreme Court or into the federal courts.

"Actually, the jail time wasn't too bad," Hawk told his daughter Cristi. He just needed a shower. Isolated from the rest of the prisoners in the county jail—"for his own protection" the sheriff said—Hawk managed nonetheless to talk to two prisoners who sought him out. "Two writs will be coming out of there this week," he laughed.

There had been one favorable aspect to it all. He had come out looking good in the papers. The press had been on hand both for the jailing of the attorney willing to go to jail for the accused mass murderer and for his release. That gave him two more opportunities to point his finger elsewhere. "Corona is innocent. Both Dave Teja and I know who killed these people, and this will be apparent after the trial begins." Cautious for fear of the family's reaction, Hawk refused to identify the "real killer."

Teja and Williams no longer had time to worry about Hawk's constant carping, though Williams sometimes wondered about other suspects, possible killers. The trial scheduled to begin in three weeks, there were still motions to be heard, witnesses to be interviewed, and the evidence relabeled for the trial. George Roche, the Sacramento State College criminalist, had organized things for them, plugging some of the gaps in the chain-of-possession, and suggesting at their big meeting in June which items were useful, which were not, and which were susceptible to further scientific analysis. Roche had been worth every penny of the $4,000 they paid him.

Hawk too was feeling the press of time. He also had to sit down with John Thornton, a member of the criminalistics faculty at Berkeley. Thornton was privately assisting Hawk, meeting early in the morning or after dinner, far into the night. Thornton was an expert on blood, just the expert Hawk needed since the prosecution was apparently going to rely heavily on the bloodstains the deputies had found.

Handwriting wasn't exactly Thornton's specialty, but he had enough training to be able to look at the packet of old checks written by Natividad that Pedro Corona had been saving for his oldest brother. There were letters and combinations of letters in the checks that looked to Hawk identical to the writing in the ledger.

On August 14, Judge Patton heard the prosecution's renewed motion for a court order compelling Corona to fill out the handwriting exemplar. Corona had told Hawk he wanted to furnish the handwriting; he feared nothing and he didn't want Hawk to go to jail for him again. Hawk refused Corona's offer; there was both a point of law and a point of honor in it.

The district attorney was openly upset that the head of CII's handwriting lab, Sherwood Morrill, was testifying for the defense. Under subpoena or not, Morrill would have had to have talked with Hawk before the defense attorney called him to testify; Morrill was hardly innocent in all this.

Hawk had called Morrill for one purpose only: "Do you have any opinion as to whether or not Mr. Corona made any attempt to disguise his handwriting."

Teja immediately objected. After a month's reflection and conversation with other judges, Judge Patton had some doubts about his previous ruling—enough doubts so that he permitted the defense attorney to make his case. "Overruled."

"Your Honor," Morrill began with a swift look at Hawk, "in my opinion, and I examined the exhibits, the handwriting which purports to be that of one person is that of one person with no attempt to disguise whatsoever anyplace along the line."

Thirty-nine years' experience weighed heavily in Hawk's favor. Morrill testified that good practice in taking the exemplar had been followed. There was nothing wrong with the exemplars and no evidence of a fraud upon the court.

The district attorney pressed his motion on the same grounds he had earlier. "All we want to be able to do," the district attorney continued, "is stand up at the trial and be able to vouch for the authenticity of the handwriting exemplars and the People obviously cannot do that right now with those exhibits."

"That's his problem, Your Honor." Hawk smiled at Teja. "I'm not attempting to prove anything. They're the ones who are attempting to prove something. They have simply asked for an authentic handwriting sample, and according to Mr. Morrill, that's just exactly what's in front of the court.

"They haven't cited any case that says I have to do it in the presence of the court or under certain circumstances. The cases just say that they are entitled to an authentic sample of the defendant's handwriting."

Patton realized Hawk had constructed a stout box for him. It did appear from the cases that in ruling earlier on the motion, he had overreached his authority to compel the exemplar under specific circumstances. Obviously, the judge acknowledged, there was nothing wrong with the exemplars as samples of Corona's handwriting; bringing in Sherwood Morrill, an expert long familiar by reputation, Hawk had validated the documents. As Hawk argued, Teja had originally sought handwriting exemplars; now he had them if he wanted them.

On the other hand, to rule against the prosecution now would be to concede that his original contempt order had been incorrect. The advice he had received in the past weeks from colleagues was divided; it was a new situation, with no precedent in the case books.

Even before the trial opened, it appeared that Hawk had laid the groundwork for a reversal of a guilty verdict. If the judge exceeded his authority in ordering the defendant to furnish new exemplars, a higher court could overturn the guilty verdict; no one would ever know how persuasive the handwriting was to the jury.

At the same time, he could not concede his earlier order incorrect. "The court has previously held and now holds that the People are entitled to the exemplars, to be given under such methods as to assure their authenticity." Hawk sighed.

Again the attorney and the frowning Corona declined to furnish additional handwriting. Again Judge Patton found them in contempt. The sentence was three days in the county jail for Hawk, and an additional $300 for his client. At the judge's urging, the subdued attorney promised to appeal the citation immediately.

Three days later, Hawk went from depression to euphoria.

On a visit to CII's crime lab in Sacramento to discuss a report with

Don Stottlemyer, Hawk chanced to see a letterhead of the "District Attorney of Sutter County" on a desk. Over the protests of the technician working there, Hawk quickly scanned the letter, written by Bartley C. Williams, and addressed generally to "Gentlemen." Hawk snickered; he didn't qualify.

Williams' was a covering letter for a document prepared by the criminalist George Roche. Williams' letter described the document as one that "summarizes the fingerprint identification evidence that we have accumulated concerning the victims in this case. As you will also note, it summarizes some of the mistakes, errors, and omissions that have been made concerning primarily the chain-of-possession of this evidence."

Hawk read no further. It dealt with the Corona case and he wanted it. The technician was reluctant; obviously the material would help the defense. The resistance faded when Hawk threatened to file a new discovery order for the document.

The Roche Report, as it came to be called—though the criminalist had written dozens of similar analyses of the evidence—dealt with the thoroughly confused chain of evidence surrounding the victims' fingerprints. As the cover letter noted, "The identification of the persons in this case, of course, is extremely important as it goes directly to the admissibility of evidence of Juan Corona's ledger containing the names of seven of the victims. In addition it goes directly to the admissibility of evidence of those areas of evidence indicating that certain victims were directly connected or in the company of Juan a short period before they were recovered from the graves on the Sullivan ranch."

According to the Roche Report, there were problems associated with all but a handful of bodies: fingertips excised but not labeled; no notation who had excised the fingertips; records of fingertips being delivered for printing at CII as much as a week before the body was actually dug up; failures to identify the people who had delivered or received the fingertips. The chain-of-possession was a shambles, and Williams was seeking help in straightening it out.

Some of the information in the report Hawk had already gleaned from police reports; much was new. And there it was laid out point by point, grave by grave; Roche might as well have been working for the defense.

The Roche Report and Williams' letter would continually punctuate the trial of Juan Corona, provide days of cross-examination, and ultimately provoke an internal investigation of CII's crime lab.

The hearing on August 21, two weeks before the scheduled beginning of the trial, was ostensibly to be devoted to motions of discovery filed by both sides. The prosecution sought a sample of Corona's blood; Hawk was still attempting to secure experts' reports.

A nervous Bart Williams, however, took the initiative. "I would like to indicate to the court at this time, in all due respect," Williams paused, one hand in the pocket of his loose-fitting pants scrambling the change there, "that the decision has been made by the prosecution in this case to absolutely refuse to forward to the defense from this time on, any and all information, report, any discovery material whatsoever."

Having challenged the court, the apprehensive attorney plunged on. "Now, the reason for that, Your Honor, and I say this in all due respect, is that last week we brought a second handwriting motion and again the court granted this order and again Mr. Hawk contemptuously disobeyed this order and is depriving the People of material evidence."

For the first time in the long series of hearings, Hawk was speechless. The prosecutors were deliberately risking contempt citations themselves. Moreover, they could be blowing their case; if they withheld evidence to which the defense was entitled, the conviction would never stand. Obviously, they needed that exemplar; their entire case hung on making Corona the author of the "death list."

There was no legal basis for what the two of them were doing. They had two remedies if he withheld the exemplars: contempt, and the right to comment on the withholding at the trial, letting the jury make of it what it would. But discovery was not the *quid pro quo* business they seemed to think it was.

Williams sat down, closed the file in front of him, and folded his hands on the table, a contrite schoolboy waiting the rap of the teacher's ruler.

Judge Patton leaned back in his chair, looked at the paneled wall above the empty jury box—he really didn't like this courtroom, the jury was too far away—and circled his chin with a thumb. "Mr. Hawk has made reasonable argument on the point as to why the handwriting samples were not produced. He's entitled to have the matter reviewed by a Court of Appeal." The judge turned back to the attorneys ranged below him at the counsel table. "I'm not unmindful of the fact that Mr. Corona has been in custody now for almost fifteen months and it was only very recently and within the last few weeks that the People made any motion to have handwriting exemplars produced."

The judge sensed Teja was in trouble, floundering around for evidence, anything. "May I point out, Your Honor," Hawk responded, "if the district attorney persists in his attitude—now I frankly think he's just afraid to try this case—if he is going to refuse to deliver these matters, then I will have a memorandum prepared and we will file it asking this court to dismiss the charges against Mr. Corona and turn him loose."

District Attorney Teja matched and raised. "We intend on this date to make a motion for a continuance of the trial until such time as it may take the defendant to comply with your orders granting us discovery of the exemplars, *authentic* exemplars, of his handwriting. And furthermore, there's a corollary motion that the contempt order and the sentence against Mr. Hawk be imposed until such time as he purges himself of contempt by complying with the order of the court."

Hawk opposed Teja's motion on technical grounds, adding, "Besides, I think your whole motion is ridiculous and I resist it." There was not authority in the law for the prosecution to seek a delay in the trial; the very premise violated the constitutional right of a speedy trial. Only the defendant could waive time.

To avoid citing the two prosecutors for contempt and to give them an opportunity to reconsider, the judge postponed Hawk's motions for one week. Patton also needed time to weigh the prosecution's move to delay the start of the trial. The case was already complex enough without these novel legal theories adding to it.

With the first of the 300 jury panelists ordered to report in just a week, the courtroom on August 28 was tense. The picket of deputies guarding the courtroom doubled, frisking spectators with a metal detector, taking photos of each person who entered. No one was exempted from the search, including Hawk, his daughter, and the prosecutors. The number of newsmen covering the trial had also increased, filling the two rows of seats allotted to them in the seventy-seat courtroom. Immediately behind the press, the Corona family filled another row on the left side of the room. In time, that would become informally "the Corona section."

Hawk's motion to have Corona appointed as a co-counsel was to be taken up first. The defense in the Angela Davis case had used it, Miss Davis making a considerably favorable impression on the jury. The obvious advantage was that Miss Davis had, in effect, testified without having to undergo cross-examination. Corona might not be as bright as Angela Davis, but he was certainly brighter than some other people sitting at the counsel table, Hawk muttered.

The co-counsel motion was one of two ideas Hawk had to present his client in a favorable light. The other, finally approved by school authorities, was to have his daughter, Cristi, delay her senior year in high school to help him at the trial. More important, it would help Juan. Cristi would be there, talking to him at recesses; the jury would see that, and couldn't help but be impressed. Besides, Juan liked her; she helped to ease the tension, and that might avert another heart attack. If it was hard on Corona now, it would be harder later when they were in court five days a week, for weeks on end.

Hawk was frank in his argument in favor of Corona's appointment as co-counsel. The publicity alleging he was insane was "a burden he shouldn't have. He has, I think, a burden of establishing to this jury that he's a sane, intelligent, sympathetic, fine human being."

His hands resting on the padded leather back of the chair, Hawk said he would limit Corona's participation to a short opening statement to the jury, and to "direct examination of the character witnesses such as Jack Sullivan and Dave Teja's father who Juan worked for many years and thinks very highly of Juan."

Bachan Teja was no better a character witness than any of a dozen other ranchers Hawk could call, but he was the district attorney's father, and he did think highly of Corona. Announcing he would call the elder Teja was another way to needle the son.

As Hawk had expected, Judge Patton denied the motion. "It appears to me that the principal reason that the defendant wishes to be granted permission to act as his own co-counsel is in order that he may present, really, his mentality and demeanor to the jury. And certainly he will have the opportunity to do that during the course of the trial, if he desires to testify." The judge was not going to permit the defense the advantage of Corona impressing the jury without cross-examination.

If Hawk had boxed the judge earlier, the prosecution was to do it now. Williams repeated his earlier refusal to turn over to Hawk documents to which the defense was entitled. Judge Patton was perplexed by the prosecution's position; he was "rather at a loss to understand the People's attitude." It was nothing more than childish.

The district attorney pressed the judge to postpone the trial. "Just as the defendant should not be forced to trial without having all available evidence, neither should the prosecution be forced to trial without having all available evidence."

Hawk was delighted. No matter how pro-prosecution Patton was, he was too conservative to rule without some precedent. Despite Teja's long memorandum of cases, not one sanctioned postponing a trial. They had alienated the judge with a silly argument they couldn't win.

"Your Honor, I want to make it absolutely clear that we intend to go to trial on September 5. We want this trial to start September 5 because I want to see this evidence that they had on May 26, 1971, when they were shouting to the world what a killer Juan Corona was. It's some sixteen months later and now they're begging for a continuance because they're afraid to try the case. It's just that simple.

"The day of reckoning has come. The day is here. The day is arrived to produce all this evidence that Roy Whiteaker was braying about on the banks of the Feather River and I want to hear about it starting September 5."

Hawk could not suppress his enthusiasm. "He still hasn't showed you any authority that says you are supposed to continue this trial. Nothing says they can put the defendant in this position, throw his attorney in jail indefinitely, postpone the trial, and blackmail and extort him in that way. And that's what they're asking you really to do."

Shorn of precedents, Judge Patton denied the prosecution's motion for a delay. Teja as quickly announced he intended to file an immediate appeal.

The district attorney got his stay. On Thursday, August 31, after an *ex parte,* or unilateral, presentation of which Hawk was not even informed, a cooperative justice of the state Court of Appeal in San Francisco issued an order to Judge Patton to vacate the trial date, to reinstitute contempt proceedings, and to delay setting a new date for trial until Corona furnished the handwriting exemplars. The justice, whom Hawk condemned as "a perfumed dandy," had acted unilaterally, without a hearing, and still without legal precedent.

The following morning, an angry Hawk roamed the courtroom, accusing the district attorney of filing "a fraudulent and cowardly brief." It was a statement solely for his own satisfaction. Confronted with the stay granted by the "perfumed dandy," Corona was faced with a delay as long as five months while an appeal from the order was taken. Rather than wait, they would furnish the exemplar.

"We want the trial to start Tuesday morning. Whether Mr. Teja and Mr. Williams have guts to show up for trial, I think still remains to be seen." After sixteen months of his client's imprisonment, the prosecution was still attempting to prove the case against Corona, Hawk rasped. Not only did they want the handwriting exemplar—they had more already than in most cases—but there were also discovery motions for a blood sample and clippings of Corona's hair. "Was this some of the evidence they had on May 26 [1971] when the sheriff brayed Corona was the man?" Hawk asked reporters sarcastically.

Confronted by the galling order, an irritated Judge Patton delayed the trial until September 11; Corona would furnish the exemplars on the fifth.

There remained only two pretrial matters in the file, after months of legal maneuvering. Hawk wanted discovery of a series of documents withheld by the prosecution. Most important was the evidence list, which Hawk knew from the Roche Report was badly confused. "If they have broken the chain of evidence, which I know they have on many occasions the way they run that Goodwill Store, their evidence locker, that goes right to the heart of whether it's admissible."

The deputy district attorney had an exclusionary motion of his own. Sergeant Perales, unable to get a firm statement from Raya, Williams and Teja had spent coffee-flooded hours discussing the Guadalajara incident, weighing strategies to prevent Hawk from raising a straw man. All they had to do was read the papers to know that Hawk intended to try Natividad *in absentia.*

Hands plunged into his pockets, the change rattling as he spoke, a nervous Williams argued, "The People feel that it does not have any relevancy to the particular charges against Mr. Corona and therefore we'd like to have a pretrial order barring all parties from making any comments or reference to the Guadalajara incident during the trial."

Hawk bolted to his feet. "Oh, no. I will object to that. What they're saying is that they can't prove it so it's a no-no to talk about. I object."

"Pardon me," Judge Patton halted Hawk. "Let's hear the rest of your comment, Mr. Williams."

"I think the Court has to make the determination. The People believe that this particular instance does not fall under the evidentiary basis of common plan, scheme, design." Williams glanced at his notes, the change rattling loudly in the silence.

"The prosecution considers this inadmissible and therefore should not be in evidence. However, we feel that there could be a substantial reason for the defense to attempt to interject this particular evidence into the trial."

They were afraid to try this case, Hawk whispered to Corona, then stood up. "Your Honor, if you review the search warrant, you'll find they attached the Guadalajara incident, and said that this would clearly show that Juan was a homicidal maniac by common plan, scheme and design. It was Natividad and not Juan Corona that hit Raya on the head with whatever he got hit on the head with, and now all of a sudden they don't want to talk about it anymore.

"What they're in effect saying, at one point the evidence shows that Juan was a killer. Now they're saying, well, we can't prove it so we don't want it in this trial at all."

Hawk needed no notes; he had long weighed the usefulness of the Guadalajara incident. "Does this mean that if I can produce evidence of somebody killing these twenty-five people I can't get it in because it doesn't go toward Juan? That's in effect what they're saying to you."

The deputy prosecutor had had more than enough experience now to fear Hawk's courtroom tactics. Without a pretrial blanket order, Williams maintained, "We will get all kinds of comments, innuendoes and everything else in front of the jury. And then three months into the trial, the court rules it's not relevant, well, the damage has been done."

Judge Patton, too, was sensitive about Hawk's behavior. Raising the Guadalajara incident would add considerable time to what was going to be a lengthy trial; both sides admitted that. A blanket order without a hearing on the admissibility of the evidence could serve as one more ground for a reversal. Against that he had to balance his certainty that without some sort of restraint the defense attorney would continue to make comments.

Since the prosecution did not intend to raise the issue, he could postpone a decision on the admissibility question for some weeks, until the defense began its case. For the moment, the order needed to be limited only to the opening statement and to cross-examination.

"At this point, it's the proper order that before you make an opening statement, presuming you intend to make one following the People, that you disclose to the court out of the presence of the jury whether or not you intend to refer to this incident and in what manner so that the court can rule in advance before the matter is broached to the jury."

Hawk's protest was a vain effort. "Quite frankly, I think this is beyond your power. I think you're trying to censor my direction, gag me in the courtroom based upon nothing more than these two guys' representation that something isn't relevant that they spent hundreds of thousands of dollars on, spent ten months trying to prove."

The censorship order was to stand for five months, a major aid to the prosecution, and proof that Judge Richard Patton was biased against him, Hawk argued. It was a hell of a lousy way to start the biggest murder trial in American history.

15

The Voir Dire
September 11-23, 1972

The hallways of the three-story Solano County Courthouse were crowded with members of the jury panel, spectators, and reporters as the attorneys made their way through the security checkpoint and into Courtroom Number 4. Hawk joked with one of the deputies, stopped momentarily to pat Gloria Corona's arm, then dispatched his daughter Cristi for the notebook of questions he had left behind in the car.

He had done all he could to prepare for this, the most boring but most critical part of the trial of Juan Corona. He had visited Chambers of Commerce, collecting information about each of the towns and cities in the county. He had enlisted a handful of volunteers to copy out the information forms the jury panelists had filled out: address, occupation, age, name of spouse, spouse's occupation, number of children and ages, health problems, prior jury service. It wasn't much, but he would have much more before he had to exercise his' challenges. Provided with the names of the panelists drawn in mid-August, Hawk had dispatched his volunteers to copy their voter registration forms in the office of the county clerk; that added party affiliation and place of birth. A friend from Concord would tour the neighborhoods of the jurors tentatively seated; a former sheriff's deputy, Dick Davis, was to look for hints about the potential jurors: What kind of neighborhood was it? Was it integrated? What kind of house did he live in? Was it well kept? What kind of cars did they have? Any bumper stickers? Especially something like "America, Love It or Leave It" or "Impeach Earl Warren," something that might indicate the guy in the box was a nut.

Slowly the lines outside the courtroom filtered through the checkpoint, the spectators signing their names, emptying their pockets, then standing at a strip of masking tape for the obligatory photo taken by a sheriff's

Juan Corona. "The trial, you know, it goes both way sometimes. Some days are good. Some days are bad."

Defense Attorney Richard Hawk. He would never take a lawyer's word for anything.

Judge Richard Patton. He lived on his own walnut farm—still a farmer who often drove a pickup truck to the courthouse.

District Attorney G. Dave Teja. The first East Indian to be elected anything in the county.

"You can feel the cold wind coming off the iceberg."
The jury (Mrs. Underwood is in the first row, third from the left).

Hawk shook his head, trying to clear the disbelief. "Bail is denied, your honor?" The bail hearing; Hawk with hand over eyes, next to him Corona.

Deputy District Attorney Bartley Williams. The kind of guy who bought a new suit every year, wore the old one out, and didn't worry about it.

Sheriff Roy Whiteaker. "The sheriff Sutter County deserves."

"I defy you to know what is going through the mind of a man who systematically chops and stabs twenty-five men to death." Special Prosecutor Ronald Fahey making a point. Hawk and Corona are seated.

"If I had the $500,000 that they spent to produce this pitiful amount of evidence. . . ." Hawk delivers his closing argument. Williams and Fahey are seated.

matron. The two prosecutors leaned back in their chairs at the counsel table, casually discussing their weekends, circumspectly avoiding any mention of the trial, the district attorney repeatedly brushing imaginary pieces of lint from his new suit. Hawk nodded to a reporter, then walked through a side door to a small holding cell where Corona waited.

The two men talked briefly. The attorney told Corona he would be out to the Vacaville prison to discuss the jurors with him. "It's your jury, Juan. I want you to be satisfied with them." Corona nodded, fingered the rosary, then asked, "You think things be all right?"

"Things will be just fine. We're going to beat their brains out. You can bet on that, fellow." He would have to have Cristi talk with Juan, settle him down, relax him.

At two minutes after ten o'clock in the morning of September 11, 1972, on the four hundred and seventy-third day of his incarceration, Juan Vallejo Corona went to trial, charged with the murder of twenty-five itinerant farm workers.

Sixty-two of the first 100 panelists called for jury duty had appeared, the balance excused by the county clerk's office for a variety of reasons. Judge Patton first screened the remainder for reasons why they should not be jurors in a trial which could last as long as six months. Four more were dismissed—a self-employed man couldn't live on the $5-a-day juror's fee, a daughter had a medical problem, nine children couldn't be left alone, a pregnant woman was expecting in two and one-half weeks.

The balance were sworn, their names entered on slips of paper, the slips then deposited in a leather-covered jury wheel. Twelve names would be drawn, the twelve seated provisionally in the jury box under the yellow stickers bearing jurors' numbers pasted to the walnut veneer wall of the courtroom. Then would begin the tedious questioning of the voir dire —the examination of the potential juror's qualifications, essentially his lack of bias for either side.

Hawk had two distinct aims in picking the jury. He wanted intelligent people, critical people, first of all. There were so many evidentiary problems in the case that he felt he needed skeptics. Intelligence didn't mean education. "I don't want any truckdrivers. But I don't want any Ph.D. who's stupid." As any defense lawyer would, he attempted to screen out those who were rigorously pro-police, who could not admit that policemen made mistakes, who gave their testimony greater weight than that of other witnesses. Solano County's biggest city, Vallejo, was an industrial center, a blue-collar area largely dependent upon the naval shipyard at Mare Island. There were blacks there, "and if I get a chance to load up on blacks, I'll do it," Hawk promised. "They may not be the best kind of jurors in the world with black defendants, but blacks like me. They think I fight. I come in charging everybody, swinging at everything in sight, even the judge if he gets in the way. Black jurors like that. The Establishment has pushed them around for 300 years and they love to see somebody smack at the Establishment."

He would also have to weed out those who were prejudiced, especially the ones who didn't know it. The district attorney would be no help there; he would eschew any questions likely to turn up prejudice against minorities. A two-hour conversation with Angela Davis' attorney, Leo Branton, in Los Angeles two days before had been helpful there. Branton had suggested dozens of questions, one of which seemed especially useful: "What is Mr. Corona?" If the potential juror said, "Spanish," he was bending over backward to mask his prejudice. "Mexican," even "Indian" were the right answers. Branton and his colleagues had used a similar question on behalf of Miss Davis. If the juror answered "colored," they knew he or she was living long in the past. If the answer were "Negro," it was neutral. "Black" was best, an answer that suggested the would-be juror was sympathetic with current black community sentiment. The analogous word for Corona was *chicano,* though Corona himself did not identify with the nascent activist movement in the *barrios.*

Hawk had a second purpose in the voir dire. He was going to start educating the jury on the critical issues of the trial even before they began taking evidence. "I've got to have my case more than half won before I ever start the defense." Voir dire gave him an opportunity to pound the law into the jury; the entire panel was listening while he questioned each person drawn, one by one. If he could plant doubts, he was going to do it, especially about Natividad.

Hawk had finally broached the question to his client, hesitantly, in a small visitor's room at the Vacaville prison. "Juan, has it ever occurred to you—" Hawk paused. "We're going to talk to you about a subject that is maybe going to be very sensitive to you. By 'sensitive,' I mean, it's going to be difficult—"

Corona's expression was opaque. "Difficult," he agreed, memorizing a definition.

Hawk played with his cigarette. "This is, at this point, about Juan Corona's life, and his wife's life, and his kids' lives. I only care about you in this world. You're my client." Corona nodded. "You know the way I feel about you, Juan? You know that you're more than a client to me?"

Corona agreed. "I appreciate it very much."

"You're a very important man. Has it occurred to you," Hawk cleared his throat, "that there's more evidence on somebody else in this case than there is against you?" He paused. "You know who that somebody is?" Another pause. "It's Natividad."

"Oh?" The bushy-haired man in the faded prison blue denims was surprised.

"Here's the point. When the trial starts, I think it's not enough in this case—if this was just a burglary, and we get a little reasonable doubt going, the jury turns you loose. That's not going to be enough for Juan Corona."

Hawk was well into it now, rushing on, before Corona could cut off his argument with a refusal to cooperate. "There's so many bodies involved, we've got to have more than a reasonable doubt. We've got to point the finger at somebody else. I can point it at Natividad."

Corona was not really surprised; he had heard Hawk talking to a newsman about the "accident in the Guadalajara Café."

"I'm not asking you to help me. What I am asking you to do is sit still and let me do it. Okay?" asked Hawk.

"Okay." Corona nodded, staring at his folded hands in the dimly lit room.

"I'm not telling you this to make you feel bad or make you dislike Natividad. I'm telling you this to tell you what the hell's going on in this case. 'Cause your life's at stake. You understand, if you got convicted of this thing—while there's no death penalty—you'd never see the light of day again. You'd never walk out this prison door." Hawk pointed at the steel door, its mesh-and-glass window, the institutional green walls. "They would never parole you. So you've got to think about yourself. Right?"

"That's right," Corona agreed.

"You got to think about Gloria, Martha, Yolanda, and Lupe, and Victoria, don't you?"

Corona nodded.

"Natividad's down there," he began again. "Nobody's ever going to bother him, but Juan Corona's very important—to me, his wife, his kids. It's very important that this is between you and me. I don't know what the reaction of the rest of your family will be to it. I mean, I'm in a tough spot, Juan, you know, to get up and start throwing rocks at your brother."

Corona's expression had not changed except for a slight smile when Hawk mentioned his children.

"They may not like it," Hawk warned.

Corona only chuckled. They would not like it at all.

Now Hawk was about to start throwing rocks.

According to the procedure the judge had prescribed, the twelve people called by lot into the jury box would be questioned publicly. If the questions provoked a successful challenge for cause, the challenged juror would be excused, and the replacement similarly questioned. The procedure irritated Hawk, for it permitted potential jurors to hear the answers of others, "to go to school on them," as he put it; Hawk had wanted total exclusion, permitting only those tentatively seated to hear subsequent veniremen questioned.

Judge Patton had compromised. Questions regarding pretrial publicity would be asked in private, the court adjourning to a room next door.

A retired Air Force master sergeant working as a mechanic in a local food processing plant was the first prospective juror. He had been on a previous jury, a child neglect case, but couldn't remember if it was civil or criminal. His cousin was a member of the San Jose Police Department, but he didn't see him often. He had read the newspapers about the case "when it first came up." He lived in an integrated neighborhood: "just about every kind of people" lived there. "A person doesn't have to prove his innocence, but he has to convince me he's not guilty. I expect him to testify." Hawk mentally disqualified him.

The second prospective juror was Mrs. Phyllis L. Bailey, twenty-three years old, married, childless, a native of Connecticut who had moved to Fairfield, California, four years before with her husband.

"Mrs. Bailey, just before the recess Mr. Williams made the following statement to the first venireman: 'Do you understand that the duty of the prosecution in this case is to present all evidence in its control that might show Mr. Corona's guilt?' Do you think that's the function of a prosecutor in the United States?"

Before the woman could answer, Williams objected. "He is asking the juror for a legal conclusion as to what the function is or is not of a prosecutor."

Judge Patton agreed. "It is irrelevant also as to examination for cause to what the function of a prosecutor is."

Hawk nodded. "What is your reaction to a statement like that?"

"Well," Williams interrupted, "it is the same question just reworded. It's still objectionable."

"Sustained."

"Well, did it bring anything to mind?"

"Same objection."

"Same ruling. Proceed to another matter." Judge Patton frowned at the defense attorney.

Hawk closed his trap. "Do you believe that if the prosecution has evidence pointing to someone else's guilt they ought to suppress it?"

"Same objection, Your Honor."

"Why? That's what they are trying to do." It did not matter if Mrs. Bailey answered the question; the entire panel had heard, and could draw its own conclusions.

To reassert his authority, Judge Patton instructed, "The purpose of this examination is to establish as to whether or not there is any grounds to challenge the prospective juror for cause. This seems to me to be totally irrelevant to that purpose."

Hawk made a mistake at that point, instructing the judge on the law. "Your Honor, I believe under *Brady v. Maryland* there is a statement by the U.S. Supreme Court saying just to the contrary—that is, that it is the prosecutor's duty to present all evidence, no matter who it points to. I am simply inquiring as to what the juror's state of mind is as to the function of the parties here."

"Same ruling. Proceed." The judge was disturbed. Obviously Hawk would be as difficult during the trial as he had been in the pretrial hearings.

The defense attorney turned back to Mrs. Bailey, nervously smoothing her brown hair. "Do you think truth and fairness includes producing evidence that shows somebody else killed these twenty-five people?"

The judge sustained Williams' objection.

"Okay. Would you think it somewhat odd that the prosecution spent $100,000 in twelve months trying to prove something and now wants to suppress it?"

The objection was sustained. Hawk tried again.

"There is an instruction, I believe, that you will hear from the court that a trial is a search for truth. Would you follow that instruction as given to you?"

Mrs. Bailey paused, waiting for an objection. There was none. "Yes."

"Do you think that's what jury trials ought to be about, a search for truth?"

"Yes, they should be," the woman answered, pulling her white sweater tightly over her shoulders.

"So do I, but there are some people in the court that might not agree with it."

"Objection," Williams burst out.

"That comment is not proper," Judge Patton warned Hawk.

Mrs. Bailey had gone to integrated schools in Hartford, had friends among minority group members, understood that *chicano* meant "Mexican." Hawk liked her manner, soft, a little shy. He also liked the idea that she was holding down two part-time jobs, one of them as a waitress, in order to supplement her husband's income.

"The neighborhood that you live in, would you consider it an integrated neighborhood?"

"No." Hawk was surprised; she would be the only person questioned in the entire voir dire who would answer that way.

"You live where, Fairfield?"

"Yes." Mrs. Bailey hugged the sweater to her shoulders again. The air conditioner troubled her.

"In what way is it not integrated? Just that there aren't minority groups there?"

"One."

"And who is that?"

"Black."

"Okay. Do you live in a single-family residence or apartment?"

"Apartment."

"Okay. The person who is black, do they live in the apartment building?"

"Yes."

"How do you feel about that?"

"He lives with me."

Hawk was taken aback. "Pardon?"

"He is my husband."

"Well, maybe I should just pass right here. You just knocked out about twenty-five of my questions."

"Sorry about that," Mrs. Bailey smiled.

Hawk turned to another line of questions. Juan Corona was presumed innocent. Did she agree with that principle? Did she expect Juan to prove anything? If he didn't take the stand, would she hold that against him? Yes, no, no, that's his right.

Did Mrs. Bailey understand that just because Corona was indicted and that "a homicidal maniac probably killed them doesn't mean Corona did it? That Juan and I don't dispute someone committed twenty-five of the most heinous, grisly crimes in history?"

Williams objected on the ground that Hawk's questions were in actuality unsworn testimony.

"You realize that it could just as easily have been Dave Teja who might have committed these twenty-five murders for all we know? Do you expect me to produce the real killer?"

"No."

Neither did she expect Hawk to be "Perry Mason"; she understood he didn't have a script. Corona had no burden in her mind. Police officers made mistakes; she would measure Sheriff Roy Whiteaker's testimony by the same standards as she judged anyone else's.

"Your Honor," Williams stood up slowly. "I'm going to object here because I don't recall Sheriff Whiteaker being on our list of witnesses. This line of questioning is just meant to prejudice the jury." Williams spoke tiredly.

Hawk looked at the prosecutors. "Well, okay, if they don't call him, I will. I will guarantee you that."

Hawk then began a long series of questions framed to educate the jury about the law surrounding the case. "You will hear an instruction about circumstantial evidence: that while they are entitled to equal weight, direct and circumstantial, if a case is based on circumstantial evidence it must not only be consistent with guilt, but must be totally inconsistent with innocence. Do you follow that?"

Mrs. Bailey nodded, "Yes."

"Also there is another instruction which you will hear that if you can draw two reasonable inferences from a fact, that one points to guilt and one points to innocence, it is your sworn duty as a juror to accept the one pointing to innocence and reject the one pointing to guilt. Would you do that if you are a juror?"

"Yes." The white sweater slipped from her shoulders.

"Will you bear that in mind as this case goes along—one pointing to guilt and one pointing to innocence—it is your sworn duty as a juror to accept the one that points to innocence?" Repetition for emphasis; Hawk was learning from Teja.

"Yes."

When it was Teja's turn to examine Mrs. Bailey, he asked her whether the fact that the case was based on circumstantial evidence was a problem to her? No. Would she give it equal weight with direct evidence? Yes. Did Mrs. Bailey have any sympathy for the defendant? No more than for anyone else in a similar circumstance.

"I don't mean to pry, Mrs. Bailey, and I certainly don't want to embarrass you, but would it be fair for me to assume that you have had personal and social problems as a result of your marriage?"

"Yes," the woman answered quietly.

"Have any problems that you may have had, any personal problems, possibly caused you to adopt the attitude right now that simply because the defendant in this case is a Mexican he is somehow being picked on?"

"Honestly, yes."

"Would that be an overriding concern of yours in this particular case?"

"It's something that I would have to think about," the woman whispered. "It would, but to what extent, I couldn't say. I mean, it's a proven fact because of minority groups, you know. Well, maybe I am related in a closer way. It would hit harder, but that doesn't mean if I heard evidence I am going to look at him as a Mexican and not the evidence. Do you understand what I mean?"

"I think so. Your Honor, we will assign a challenge for cause." The judge denied the challenge.

Teja tried to strengthen his challenge with further questions. No, she would not place any greater burden than the law required on the prosecution. Her sympathy would not interfere with her decision. Yes, she would accept herself as a fair and impartial juror if she were in Teja's position.

For the first time in his experience, Hawk was permitted to ask questions of a juror a second time. "Whatever natural sympathy you have for Juan because he is a Mexican—your husband is black—you are not going to let that influence your judgment really, are you?"

"No."

"There was some talk about things that were omitted and excluded,"

Hawk began, referring to the questions he had asked Mrs. Bailey before. "Do you understand that Judge Patton is not automatically saying that it is not admissible that these people spent $100,000 in twelve months trying to prove something and when it proved somebody else did it they now want to exclude it?" Hawk was back at Teja again.

"Objection, Your Honor. We have already had a sustained objection on that."

"Several times," Judge Patton agreed.

"Okay," Hawk said quietly. "Do you understand that it is not automatically excluded by Judge Patton and these men here to try to hide it?"

"Your Honor, that is unfair," the deputy prosecutor complained.

"Yes, the word 'hide' is ordered stricken," the judge agreed.

"Does it puzzle you why they would spend that much of the county's money and then say talking about it is a no-no?"

"Same objection, Your Honor."

"Same ruling. I have ruled on this already about three times."

"All right, Your Honor. Thank you. That is all." The quiet woman in the white sweater leaned back in her swivel chair in the jury box. Mrs. Phyllis Bailey had impressed both the defense and the prosecution as an honest woman of uncommon courage. She was excused from the jury after the prosecution exercised one of its twenty peremptory challenges.

By the middle of the second day of jury selection, Judge Patton was no longer waiting for the prosecution's objections to Hawk's outrageous questions. Instead he was cutting the defense attorney off; announcing, "Sustained"; ordering him to another line of questions when Hawk persisted; all but ignoring the two prosecutors. Judge Patton believed himself a man of some patience, but the defense attorney sorely tried him.

On the morning of the third day, Judge Patton twice called the attorneys into chambers to warn Hawk against arguing his case before the jury was selected. It was outrageous asking a juror if he thought the district attorney would have "snapped Ronald Reagan out of his bed at four A.M. as they did to Juan." He also did not like the references to the defendant by his first name, Juan. Hawk had earlier protested when Williams used the first name, arguing that the prosecution had no right to the familiar form of address. The judge had ordered that both sides address the defendant as "Mr. Corona."

None of this seemed to stop Hawk in the least, Judge Patton fretted. Hawk had walked from chambers and told newsmen he would be "just as persistent as I have to be to get the truth before the jury."

On Friday afternoon, shortly before the end of the first week of the voir dire, Judge Patton's temper broke. The district attorney asked a venireman, "Does the presence of Mr. Hawk's psychologist here, evaluating you, bother you, Mr. Lawson?"

Though the man denied it, Hawk asked later, "Mr. Lawson, Mr. Teja here said something about this not being a question of which lawyer you liked the best, or something like that. That this wasn't a popularity contest?"

"Yes, sir."

"Well, with the question of Mr. Teja's paranoid feelings set aside, do you really think Mr. Teja doesn't hope that you like him and that I don't hope that you'll like me? Do you realize what big hypocrites lawyers are when they say things like that?"

"Yes, sir."

"Now, he made some reference to a psychologist being here, and this man sitting here, his name is Harvey Ross, from Los Angeles, he is the psychologist. Do you have any objection to someone coming up from Los Angeles for a couple of days free of charge to Mr. Corona, to help Mr. Corona select a jury, because he believes Mr. Corona is innocent?"

"That part is obviously an improper question," Judge Patton interrupted.

"No, it is not. He brought it up," Hawk retorted.

"I say it is. I order it stricken."

"That's why he is here, Your Honor."

"I don't care." Judge Patton ordered the attorneys into chambers.

Judge Patton was tired and irritated, his temper short. "This appears to the Court to be just one of numerous statements by you, Mr. Hawk, the obvious intent of which would be to inject extraneous matters into the record, to make statements of fact which have an obvious purpose solely to influence the prospective jurors. It contains two particularly objectionable aspects." The judge's voice rose with his anger.

"One, the reference to 'free of charge.' And second, that this psychologist 'believes that' your client is innocent. That is obviously so grossly improper as to be shocking."

"Your Honor, can I speak now?" Hawk asked calmly.

"Yes, please do."

"Mr. Ross' presence in this courtroom has not been before one single juror. I didn't mention it until Mr. Teja did. Am I supposed to sit and let it drop and say nothing?

"In fact," Hawk continued in a rush, "It is true. Mr. Ross has been sitting here two days not charging anything to do it. He did come because he feels Juan is innocent."

Judge Patton repeated himself. "It is so grossly improper it is shocking."

"I think Mr. Teja is just as grossly shocking as I was, because his intent was to influence the juror by making the juror think that I had somebody there shrinking his mind on him."

Privately delighted that Hawk had tripped over his own stratagem, the poker-faced district attorney said, "It has been obvious since about noon yesterday that this man was a psychologist working for the defense here. I asked about him, and he was introduced. If a juror sat there and looked at him he would probably figure it out for himself. It certainly was obvious to me." In fact, the district attorney was telling only the partial truth. A sheriff's matron, Mrs. Georgia Wallis, later confirmed that deputies, at the behest of the district attorney, were calling CII for rap sheets and identification of spectators.

A week of repetitive jury selection had worn away Judge Patton's reserves. He was angry at Hawk, but as infuriated at the prosecution for allowing things to get so out of hand. There was not unlimited time for irrelevant matters. The judge slammed his clenched fist on the desk, his voice shrill, "The court is intent in seeing that justice is done to both parties, but I think that the People are from time to time placing an undue burden on the Court in failing to object to matters which should be objected to; and certainly, when this trial gets under way I would be more reluctant to interpose as much as I have in the presence of the jury in the box; and I think the People are not performing their proper functions in this case."

Teja protested. The prosecution feared it was objecting "too darn much as it is."

Still angry, Judge Patton ignored Hawk's request to cite the prosecution for contempt as long as the defense was to be cited. Hawk, held in contempt—the sentence was two days in the county jail and a fine of $200—was elated; the prosecutors, only scolded by the judge, were downcast. The contempt charges did not bother the defense attorney; he had been held in contempt of court before and fined. As he viewed it, the sentence was a small price to pay for learning he could provoke the judge, who was already tired after just one week's work. An angry man made mistakes. He had also managed to make the judge angry at the prosecution; they were not quite the favored sons they had been.

For their part, Teja and Williams could take little comfort in the contempt citation. As they had feared, they had lost centerstage to the defense, had angered the judge because they had permitted it to happen, and yet could not regain parity.

By the middle of the following week, still far from agreeing on a jury, the defense attorney had collected three additional citations, the last when he charged the prosecutors with "an act of absolute white racism.

"I would like the record to show that the district attorney is trying to systematically exclude minority groups. He excluded Mrs. Bailey with a peremptory challenge because her husband is black and now he excludes Mrs. Jackson who is black also. I think it is improper."

In chambers again, Judge Patton charged Hawk with "speaking to the press rather than to the record in this matter. Just when I think things are getting settled down you bring out something that goes far out of line and it is disgraceful and I don't intend to have it."

Despite his warning to the prosecutors, Judge Patton did interject himself, frequently taking over the questioning of veniremen himself. His rulings became erratic; questions permitted of one juror were prohibited with another: "If experts testified these twenty-five murders were committed by a homosexual and homicidal maniac, you wouldn't discount that, would you?" Asked of one juror; out of order for another.

By the end of the voir dire, Hawk would amass contempt citations totaling twelve days and $1,200, not including the three days Judge Patton said "you owe me" for withholding the handwriting a second time. The contempt holdings were no surprise; Hawk had expected it to happen. "If I do five days for contempt and it's the difference between my guy falling on a manslaughter and a second-degree murder, it's not that big a deal to me." The Corona case was the biggest he would ever have; Hawk would risk much more than five days' jail time. "It doesn't matter how much I get, it's how much Judge Patton can make stick." The citations were all appealable.

Deputy District Attorney Williams too had been cited for contempt. For violating the court's gag rule he was given a two-day sentence after he called a press conference in his Fairfield apartment to discount the "other man" theory. The jail sentence, Williams believed, was worth the effort to circumvent Hawk's constant comments about another suspect. Hawk had deliberately used the press, especially the local papers and television, which everyone in Solano County relied upon, to plant the suspicion that Natividad Corona was the real killer. Williams and Teja had agreed on the strategy, with Williams to take the responsibility. They were now far more concerned about pretrial publicity than Hawk seemed to be. They certainly asked more questions than did the defense during the voir dire about what the jurors had seen on TV or read in the papers.

It took twelve days of detailed questioning of more than sixty prospective jurors before Williams passed up an opportunity to use one of his nine remaining peremptory challenges. Softly Williams told the judge, "The People are satisfied with the jury."

Hawk agreed. "I am, and more important, Juan Corona is, satisfied with the jury." He had six peremptories remaining.

There were twelve regular and four alternate jurors sitting in the swivel chairs of the jury box under the yellow placards with their numbers. Two of the regular jurors were women; six were retired; only one was under thirty-five, a twenty-three-year-old Vietnam veteran.

Number 1 was the only black on the regular panel. A World War II veteran, Calvin Williams was now a high school janitor in Vallejo. A resident of Vallejo, Williams was married, with one son in the service.

Number 2 was James R. Owen, a well-dressed metals inspector at Mare Island's naval shipyard. Thirty-nine years old, married, the father of four children, Owen was a member of a fundamentalist church group which had constructed a home for a Mexican family in Baja California.

Victor Lorenzo was the third juror. Forty-five, married, with three children, he had listed his occupation as "produce man" in a local market. Hawk later learned that Lorenzo was well-to-do; the produce man's job was merely to keep him occupied during the days.

Matthew Johnson, juror number 4, sat next to Lorenzo. At fifty-four, Johnson was retired from the Marine Corps after thirty years of service. Born in England, Johnson was the most unconventional member of the panel; he wore a beard, a fact which suggested to Hawk that he was independent in his thinking.

George Muller, his face puckered by a perpetual squint, was the fifth juror. He had spent twenty-nine of his forty-eight years in the military, retired from Travis Air Force Base to settle in neighboring Fairfield with his wife and two daughters. He worked at Travis as a jet engine mechanic. As did all the government workers, Muller earned his full salary while serving on the jury.

Bill Allen Hicks, juror number 6, was the youngest member of the panel. A gunner on a helicopter in Vietnam, Hicks now worked for the Solano Irrigation District. He was the only juror to concede that "I really would like to serve on this jury." It would be a new experience.

The seventh juror was the only one to survive from the original twelve names drawn on September 11. Ernest Phillips had retired from the Air Force in 1969 after twenty-nine years' service. The father of five children, Phillips lived in Vacaville.

Faye M. Blazek, juror number 8, was the oldest member of the panel. Now sixty-six, she was a retired fourth-grade teacher and speech therapist who lived with her teacher husband. She struck both the prosecution and the defense as a well-organized, thoughtful woman; her master's degree from New York University made her the best educated, in a formal sense, among the jurors.

Donald Rogers sat next to Mrs. Blazek in the front row. Rogers, sixty, was a retired machinist from Mare Island. The last juror selected, he was mild-mannered, a quiet man who rarely smiled in the box.

Frank Broksell was the tenth juror. He too was retired from the shipyard. Fifty-eight, he lived with his wife in Vallejo.

Juror number 11 was the second woman on the panel, sixty-one-year-old Naomi Underwood. A widow, she listed herself as "semi-retired" from a salesclerk's job at the shipyard. She lived alone in an old neighborhood in Vallejo.

The last of the regular jurors was Laurent Gallipeo, a shipyard worker who commuted from his home in Vallejo across the bay to work at the Hunters Point Naval Shipyard south of San Francisco.

The four alternates, one of whom would be chosen by lot to fill any vacancy caused by illness among the regular jurors, were Lloyd Shanks, thirty-eight, an employee for Union Carbide; Richard Bremen, twenty-four, a welder at Mare Island; Edward Johnson, sixty-two, a black service station owner who lived in Vallejo; and David Caldwell, forty-eight, a quality control inspector for a local manufacturer. Caldwell was a distant cousin of District Attorney Teja's deputy, John Winship, though the two had never met.

They were Juan Corona's jury.

16
The Opening Statements
September 29-October 23, 1972

At nine fifty-two in the morning, on the four hundred and ninety-first day of Juan Corona's imprisonment, the prosecution opened its case against the thirty-eight-year-old farm labor contractor. Deputy District Attorney Bart Williams stood at a lectern facing the jury, his back to the counsel table which had been moved diagonally across the courtroom to accommodate an eight-by-twelve-foot map of the area surrounding the Sullivan ranch. A yellow loose-leaf notebook with his 220-page opening statement lay open in front of him.

The purpose of the opening statement, Judge Patton explained to the jury, "is really to apprise the jury as to the evidence which is intended to be introduced, so that you may better understand and follow the significance or purported significance of the evidence. The opening statement is not evidence; the evidence which the jury is to consider consists of the testimony of witnesses and the exhibits admitted in evidence." True, Hawk thought, but a good opening statement could strongly influence just how the jury viewed the evidence. Hawk intended to put as much argument into his as he could.

"May it please the court, counsel, ladies and gentlemen of the jury," Williams began in the formalism borrowed from English trial practice. His opening statement would be long, he predicted, and apologized for reading it; it was necessary so as to keep in their proper order twenty-five victims, testimony from 200 witnesses—Hawk looked up sharply, surprised by the number—and several hundred items of evidence.

Williams' opening statement was a detailed summary of the evidence the prosecution expected to produce and the testimony of witnesses. Their case, Williams explained, was divided into ten phases. The first dealt with the victims themselves. Williams was most apprehensive about this portion of the trial. Here the Sheriff's Department had made most of its errors.

The second concerned the search warrants and the items found, the third the medical testimony from the autopsies. "The fourth phase is what we call the circumstantial evidence phase of the case; and this is probably about fifteen or twenty individual little factual situations," he had explained earlier in chambers.

The fifth concerned the physical evidence examined by CII. The sixth dealt with blood and the findings of Dr. Guy. The seventh phase concerned ballistics, "really a misnomer," he had volunteered in chambers. "There is no positive match-up between the bullet in Mr. Kamp's head and Mr. Corona's gun."

Phase number 8 rested on a single witness from the crime lab maintained by the Internal Revenue Service who would testify on the hair samples collected. Michael Hoffman, Williams explained, "was unable to compare the hair taken from the victims with the other hair in the case. However, he microscopically compared Mr. Corona's hair with the hair in these various places in the van, in the ash trays, on the blood-spotted shorts underneath the seat, and on the posthole digger; and none of this hair appears to be Mr. Corona's hair."

The ninth phase concerned the analysis of the inks found in the multi-colored ballpoint pen, the inks in the ledger—six or seven entries there were written in with the unusual pen—and the ink on a rent receipt Corona had given to his tenant in Live Oak, Mrs. Sara Vallejo.

The last phase, the handwriting, was their strongest.

The defense attorney leaned back in his swivel chair, playing with a gold pen, occasionally watching the eight artists sitting in the press section sketching rapidly. Hawk was impressed; one of the artists, pencil in mouth, was Howard Brodie, the onetime Marine Corps artist, assigned to the trial by CBS television. That meant he would be on television tonight with Cronkite.

Moments later, Hawk interposed the first of a long series of comments concerning material which had been withheld by the prosecution despite three comprehensive discovery orders. The judge permitted Williams to continue, then noted on a legal pad Hawk's protest.

One hand in his trousers pocket rattling the change there, the deputy district attorney reviewed each grave in turn, the discovery of number 1, the digging at number 2, the evidence at grave number 3. The fourth victim "was not wearing trousers; the victim's penis was lying outside of his tight-fitting shorts. We will introduce a picture of the exposed penis. The victim had a full beard and no shoes." Hawk and an aide, heads close together, whispered excitedly; they have never been given such a picture, more evidence of the homosexual nature of the murders. Equally important, the prosecution still had not straightened out the body confusion. The bearded man was Smith, whom they insisted was the sixth victim.

By ten-thirty, juror number five, George Muller, was openly dozing, lulled by the prosecutor's monotone. The *New York Times* correspondent fought off drowsiness for a while, then succumbed for a five-minute nap as Williams read on. Hawk's attention wandered to the large map which had been set up against the north wall of the courtroom. It dominated the room, lending credibility to the prosecution's case by its very size. It had already forced the bailiffs to move the counsel table, Judge Patton helping as he directed the rearrangement of the furniture. Blown up from aerial photos, then painted by the chairman of the art department at Yuba College, the map had twenty-five tiny light bulbs, one at each grave site, fixed to a rheostat. Hawk would have something to say about that; how could they mark grave sites when they didn't even know where the graves were? The sheriff's reports certainly wouldn't tell them.

The victim in the eighth grave was wearing only long underwear, Williams continued. The prosecution would introduce a photograph showing "that the penis of this victim was exposed." Hawk shrugged in the direction of an aide; it was another picture they had not seen. Victim 9 had on two pairs of pants, both pairs unzipped, Williams read. The tenth body was wearing shorts, the pants unzipped and pulled down below the thighs. The twelfth victim was without pants too. The trousers of victim number 15 were unzipped.

The trial broke for lunch at noon, Williams picking up again at one-thirty. Even in the air-conditioned courtroom, the weight of lunch on a hot day made concentration difficult. While Williams read, Hawk struggled to pay attention, three times interrupting to note for the record that documents and photographs to which the defense was entitled had been withheld.

At two o'clock in the afternoon, the deputy prosecutor turned to the second phase of the case. Captain Littlejohn, he detailed, had gone to the Corona home "for the purpose of arresting Juan Corona and searching his house, garage, and the surrounding area." Hawk smiled; Williams had inadvertently confirmed a defense contention, that the search warrants had nothing to do with the arrest; deputies had made up their mind to arrest Corona before they ever left the office.

Dealing with the third phase, Williams told the jury that the doctors would testify "based on the condition of the body, that Whitacre was dead less than twenty-four hours; that as to the other bodies, it would be pure speculation as to how long they had actually been in the ground because of the variety of conditions of moisture, temperature, et cetera, in which the victims had been buried." The prosecution was now agreeing that the sheriff could not have known the age of the third body, that the critical defect in the search warrant was there as Hawk had claimed unsuccessfully in May in seeking to quash the warrants.

The day droned on, Williams reading, Hawk more and more frequently looking at the clock, Corona sitting in his chair, hands folded on the counsel table in front of him as they had been all day. The crowd which had filled the seventy-seat courtroom in the morning had dwindled to six members of the Corona family and ten newsmen. The expected sensation that had drawn the morning's spectators had failed to materialize.

The more Williams read, the less attentive his audience. Mr. Duron would testify, Williams doggedly continued, "that the small cabin was maintained by Mr. Corona, and as far as this witness knows the lock belonged to Mr. Corona and was placed on the—

"That's an opinion, and it's not true, and they know it; and that ought to go out also," Hawk fired, objection and rebuttal in one burst.

"I don't know about that point," Judge Patton ruled.

"'As far as he knows,' it is Juan Corona's," Hawk quoted.

"Overruled."

"Will you listen to what he said, carefully?" Hawk asked the judge. "He said, 'As far as he knows,' it is Juan Corona's lock."

Now fully awake, the judge sustained Hawk's objection.

Hawk was elated with the prosecution's detailed opening statement. Williams had filled in some holes for the defense, and more important, by going into detail about each witness' testimony, Hawk had a full preview of the prosecution's case. "If a witness forgets, or contradicts himself, or contradicts what Williams said he was going to say, I'll yell, 'Reasonable doubt.'" Additionally, Williams' day-long statement contained assertions he could not prove, not if the witnesses hewed to statements given to the sheriff. Hawk intended to open his own opening statement with some comments designed to undercut the prosecution's credibility.

"It's a shame they've been holding this guy on such lousy evidence for so long," Hawk mused as he drove home over the Martinez Bridge. "Twenty to one they don't get a vote; fifty to one they can't hang the jury; and 100 to one they won't get a conviction." He laughed, then sobered suddenly. "You know, they screwed this case up so much they could just confuse the jury enough to get a conviction."

Corona too was concerned. On Monday morning, with Williams scheduled to complete his opening statement, Corona whispered to Hawk, "I guess we will be very lucky to win the case against those two guys. They had a lot of money to spend from the county."

"Yeah, but you know what, Juan?" Hawk said seriously. "Those guys never spent their money right."

Hawk wished he had had some of what they had spent. Right now he was behind in his house payment; his practice had all but disappeared. There were times when he just wanted to chuck the whole thing, moments of despair such as he had had the day before. "It's a six-attorney case," he had snarled, looking through the papers left in disheveled piles on his desk. Cristi and the Coronas were carrying four catalogue cases of files into the courtroom each day now, and there would be more if he ever got Teja and Williams to turn over all they should have. Making the television news programs, coming home and reading the day's Corona story in the San Francisco *Examiner*, all that was very satisfying, but there were days when he didn't have enough money to buy lunch.

The second day of the trial proper opened in chambers. The discovery problem was troubling Judge Patton. Hawk had listed those items to which Williams had referred which had not been turned over.

"I might interject at this point," Williams answered, "that during, especially the last thirty to sixty days, our investigators have been running around collecting information. Not all of it has been reduced to writing." It was a foolish thing to admit, Hawk believed; after all these months, they were still investigating the case.

It took an hour for Hawk to place on the record the forty-six items to which Williams had referred in the first half of his opening statement of which the defense had no copies: reports, coroner's clothing and property lists, statements, photographs.

"They refer to a picture of an exposed penis. It is a very important point, Your Honor, indicating these are homosexual murders indicating that the deceased played the active part in the homosexual relationship. I have seen none of these ever."

"All of these have been furnished to the defense, Your Honor," Teja insisted. "It's a matter of looking at them and determining."

To preserve his record for a possible appeal, Hawk moved first that the indictment against Corona be dismissed, and in the alternative, that the material withheld—"this being the commencement of the fourth week of the trial"—be suppressed.

Judge Patton denied both motions. This would be a protracted trial, he explained, "and certainly the disclosure has been made at this time sufficiently to avoid and prevent what I would consider to be any surprise on these items."

Shortly after ten o'clock, Williams resumed his opening argument, picking up at what he called the fifth phase. The criminalist from CII, Don Stottlemyer, would testify "as to the nature and purposes of striation tests, and that the results of these tests performed on the machete and the piece of skull were inconclusive; there were insufficient points of comparison between the machete and the piece of skull to either positively include or exclude the machete—"

"Your Honor," Hawk stood up. "I have got to object to such misleading statements. That is absolutely false." The objection was for the jury's benefit; Hawk intended it to challenge Williams' credibility. The protest also helped to deflect attention from the prosecutor to the defense attorney.

The blood evidence was next, the bulk of the testimony to be presented by Doctor Ruth Guy of Parkland General Hospital. "She will testify that all she can obtain from samples of blood or tissue from bodies, as distinguished from the blood of live human beings, is the basic blood groupings, to wit: A, B, AB, or O, that she cannot do anything more sophisticated than that," Williams read. Hawk made a note on his legal pad to discuss that with his criminalist, John Thornton. There were, he knew, some twenty different ways to group blood beyond the familiar A-B-O system.

Using a little-known process, Doctor Guy was able to furnish the type of blood of the person who had smoked a cigarette found in the third grave; of victim number 13, the only one shot, who had worn a glass eye; and of the defendant himself from a cup and spoon Corona had used in the jail.

Phases six through ten—ballistics, hair, ink, and handwriting ground on. At eleven-forty, after some six hours of reading over two days the deputy district attorney closed the yellow loose-leaf binder. "And that, ladies and gentlemen, is an overview of the case that the People will present."

The jury was dismissed for the afternoon so that Hawk might incorporate any of the material turned over to him that morning before he made his opening statement. The judge took the opportunity to review Hawk's intended comments.

"Mr. Corona will testify," Hawk began, ad-libbing his summary while Williams took notes. "Through Mr. Corona and others we will be able to establish that he was busy all day long and had no opportunity to kill Whitacre.

"I was going to talk about, in more detail, Stottlemyer's report concerning tire tracks. I was going to straighten out what I expected Mr. Khera's testimony to be on the basis of his previous written statement and what he testified before."

Hawk shook a cigarette from a pack, mentally checking off the points he intended to make to undermine the prosecution's contentions; no fingerprint evidence; the cut willow branches that didn't match Corona's knives or machete; Corona's illness during the period the victims were being killed.

Hawk paused long enough to puff on his cigarette. "I intend to tell them that the defense is going to show that a small shack which is out back where they recovered some things was in fact not in Mr. Corona's possession but was in the possession of one Emilio Rangel, who is a foreman who worked for Mr. Corona.

"I intend to tell them also that I expect the evidence to show that it was Mr. Rangel who drove the red and white pickup during the month of May and not Mr. Corona."

Hawk put out his cigarette, paused, then took up the question of Natividad Corona. "I intend to tell them that we hope to produce evidence that, number one, Mr. Juan Corona is not a homosexual; number two, that these crimes in all likelihood were committed by a *passivo* homosexual. I intend to produce evidence that Natividad Corona is a *passivo* homosexual." Hawk had misunderstood the psychologist's explanation that it was the transitional *activo-passivo* who was capable of repeated homicide.

"I intend to produce evidence that puts Natividad Corona in the area of Marysville during the month of May of 1971, the week that Juan was arrested." Hawk was guessing; his wife Geneva, whom he could scarcely call as a witness, had told him she was certain she had caught a glimpse of the oldest Corona brother in lower Marysville in June 1971, soon after Hawk had taken the case; others stated that Natividad was in town at the time, but no one had talked to him.

"I intend with their evidence to show that they have him checked into these dollar-a-night hotels up there staying with these winos or transient-type guys, and I would like to argue out with you, them, or someone the question of the Guadalajara incident, Your Honor.

"I believe it is admissible in this respect, that I truthfully believe that Natividad Corona is the one that killed these people and I think he is a better suspect and always was a better suspect than Juan Corona."

Judge Patton weighed the matter. The Guadalajara incident was complicated; that in itself would take many weeks to present. If he were wrong in permitting it to be dragged into this case, an appellate court would surely reverse any conviction. For the judge, those were two compelling reasons to bar it, or to put off a decision on the matter until he could get some advice from colleagues. "I will reserve final ruling on the evidentiary aspects of it, and I ask that reference not be made in the opening statement."

The prosecution had won that argument, at least for the while. Williams then tried for a second victory. "We would strenuously object to evidence on the part of the defense concerning homosexuality. We feel that there really isn't any foundational evidence that is being put forth by the People as to homosexuality or otherwise, and for the defense to raise that straw man and knock it down will certainly be prejudicial to our case.

Hawk had lost one point; he couldn't afford to lose this one. "Let me point out to you, Your Honor, it is very relevant in this sense, that by their own testimony on this point the part of the men which was exposed was the penile area, not the back ever, but always the penile area which gives, I think, an inference the jury can draw that these men were involved in homosexual acts and they were in fact what they call the *activo* or active partner in the actual intercouse and that the killer was acting out the part of the woman."

Judge Patton too was curious about a possible motive, some explanation which would make sense of the otherwise senseless killings. Hawk apparently had found one. Additionally, the prosecution had opened up the homosexual-murder theory by mentioning some victims were exposed.

Williams had miscalculated and realized it. "We went and talked to several noted psychiatrists in this field. And these people invariably said, 'I could never tell you this was a homosexual crime.' "

"Even if you can't," Judge Patton observed, "Mr. Hawk is going to offer testimony because of those exposed penises and one thing and another. He has an expert that is prepared to testify that this is a homosexual crime. That would be a proper defense, would it not?"

Williams had no answer. Instead he sought an advantage. Would the question of Corona's mental state? "We are talking about a homosexual, opening statements' comments about homosexuality open up the entire homicidal man here and we don't have much evidence on homosexuality as far as his client is concerned.

"But as far as psychotic personality and homicidal tendencies," Williams continued, "there is an awful lot of evidence involving this man from the psychiatrists who dealt with him." Williams believed it essential to their case to bring in the question of Corona's mental condition, his stay at DeWitt Hospital, Andres' notations on the hospital records in Yuba City, the report of the psychiatrist obtained for them by the sheriff.

"I don't have to rule on this now," Judge Patton delayed. Obviously the prosecution would use this in its rebuttal, after the defense case, not during its case-in-chief.

It had been a valuable two days for the defense. Hawk had a detailed outline of the prosecution's case—once the daily transcripts were completed. Moreover, he had gotten through to the judge. "I'm beginning to have a little more respect for Patton," he explained on the drive home, past the farmlands, the Humble refinery, over the Sacramento River, past the Shell refinery on the opposite bank. "Smart I thought he was, but it's encouraging to know that when you're right the guy can see it. He's not ruling all the way, but at least he's—" Hawk broke off.

"But you know, it's really not to his credit that he started off with, I think, a prejudiced point of view. He's changed his idea. I'm not sure it's anything I've done; I'd like to think it is. But it's more them exposing themselves as a couple of phonies sitting on a phony law suit."

If Hawk was pleased, Judge Patton was not. In all of his years on the bench, he had never heard an opening argument such as the prosecution had presented, detail after detail, witness after witness, even laying out the qualifications of the experts. Six hours of it. And all that evidence they intended to introduce. One cent, what did it matter if a victim had one cent in his pocket? Or a tobacco tin. It lent nothing to their case. The photographs too. Why so many, and of what significance was it to introduce a photo of a body in a body bag laid out beside a grave? All it really did was help the defense prepare its case.

The courtroom was full again on the third day of the trial proper, the reporters and members of the public there to see the "star" of the show —that's what the Sacramento *Bee* had called him, Hawk laughed. It felt good, after all this time, to have the whip in his hand. He had turned the cynical press around, he believed, and had made a lot of points with the jury already, even before a word of evidence was taken. Now he was going to make his opening statement, something right to the point, maybe an hour and one-half.

Again the attorneys met with the judge in chambers, this time to settle the question of whether Hawk would be permitted to mention Natividad Corona and the Guadalajara incident in his opening statement. Judge Patton had made up his mind.

"What you are really asking the court to do is try another very complicated litigation that has already been through the courts and would literally occupy weeks and months of time. It is collateral; it is too remote; it is too time-consuming, not sufficiently relevant to be injected into the proceedings, at least at this moment."

"It seems to me, Your Honor, that if I have evidence pointing to somebody else, that it is incumbent upon the court to allow me in the interest of fair play to introduce it. I haven't got the $500,000 to spend investigating Natividad Corona," Hawk urged. Hawk's evidence was what he had gleaned from the sheriff's files.

Judge Patton had ruled. "It has to be something more than mere suspicion or mere suggestion that someone else may be involved. You will not refer to this matter in your opening statement.

"It may be that during the course of your evidence, if you can sufficiently establish and show any competent evidence in relation to this handwriting, I might permit you to proceed on an evidentiary basis further than that, but at this point that is the only possible connecion of any kind."

Hawk was angry. A major part of his case had been taken away from him. Would the judge permit him to point out Natividad did have access to the Sullivan ranch, that he and Ray Duron had once been business partners?

Having ruled, the judge was firm. "Very well. In that same connection, the same ruling."

"What you're saying," Hawk protested, "is that I have evidence that will show he killed these men and you won't let me put it on at all."

"I am not saying that at all." Judge Patton's voice was harsh.

Hawk pushed once more. "Your Honor, may I say for the record, I think your interest in time has reached the point where you are denying Mr. Corona a fair trial? I am more interested in Mr. Corona and his rights than in how fast we get through this trial; and it is of no comfort to me that when you make a mistake and get reversed Juan Corona sits in jail for years waiting for the appeal."

The defense attorney had opened a breach that neither man would span again; for his part, Judge Patton had changed the entire tenor of the trial.

"Certainly no one here in this room is more interested in Mr. Corona having a fair trial than I am," the judge lectured the defense attorney. "And I am dedicated to the cause of justice, and I am going to do everything I can to see that Mr. Corona has an absolutely fair trial."

"Well, can I do this, Your Honor? Can I introduce evidence that these are homosexual murders and Mr. Corona is not a homosexual?"

"Absolutely. That leads to the conclusion that it was somebody else. That's my ruling; that Mr. Hawk is not to argue or state that Natividad is the one who did it or the reasonable suspect, or whatever the situation might be."

The homosexual motivation was fair game for both sides. Williams made a demand for a list of defense witnesses and for the psychiatric reports on Corona that might be in Hawk's possession. The prosecutors had no alternative other than to prepare a rebuttal based on Corona's mental state. Williams and Teja were concerned: if Hawk could establish that these killings were homosexually motivated—he really would not have to prove it—the jury might rationalize a not-guilty verdict by saying, "Look, go after Natividad or some other queer; he's the guy who killed them."

Hawk's opening statement began poorly. He was nervous, his hands shaking until he grabbed the edges of the lectern. His voice was low, directed to the jury. Marking time, collecting thoughts that suddenly strayed, Hawk formally introduced the members of the Corona family sitting in the audience, then himself. "My name is Richard Hawk and I am from Concord. I am not a big city slicker. I am not a flamboyant man, despite what the press says." He had lived with the Corona case since June of 1971 and now he was suddenly hard-pressed for words.

The G. K. Chesterton quotation, he would use that now; it was something to get going on. "It is something that I got from Richard Arnason who is a judge in Martinez. You may recall him as he was the presiding judge in the Angela Davis trial; he is an old friend of mine. It is something that I think that you ought to think about and bear in mind throughout this trial because when this case ends, the awesome responsibility that I have is going to be passed to you people and that will be the end of what I can do for Juan Corona. It is just a little quotation from a book called *Tremendous Trifles* by a man named Chesterton:

> Our civilization has decided, and very justly decided that determining the guilt or innocence of men is a thing too important to be trusted to trained men. If it wishes for light upon that awful matter, it asks men who know no more law than I know, but who can feel the things I felt in a jury box. When it wants a library catalogued, or the solar system discovered, or any trifle of that kind, it uses up its specialists. But when it wishes anything done that is really serious, it collects twelve of the ordinary men

standing about. The same thing was done, if I remember right, by the Founder of Christianity.

Some of the tension fell away. He talked about credibility, the prosecution's against his: for example, the rancher, Chain Singh Khera—a conversation was supposed to have taken place within 200 yards of the first grave. Hawk turned to the large map. "If I can find the pinball machine light. Don't be intimidated by this big board here.

"I presume that you are to draw the inference from that that Juan is very close to where Mr. Whitacre is buried, and it is about the time he was buried, May the nineteenth, the day that Kenneth Whitacre met his untimely, hideous, horrible death.

"Well, if Mr. Khera testifies in accordance with the statement that he gave, I don't expect the testimony to show that at all. He will say, 'I saw Juan two or three days before the body was dug up. Not on May 20; two or three days before is either the eighteenth or seventeenth.

Hawk paused, looking for his notes, then covered Stottlemyer's report on the striations. The machete's examination was not inconclusive as Williams claimed; Stottlemyer said either the blade did not make the wound in Whitacre's skull or the cutting edge was subsequently altered. "I don't have the burden of proving that it was not altered; they have the burden of proving that it was. And you recall that you are not to guess, speculate or conjecture about this, but he will tell you that he saw absolutely nothing to indicate that it had at any time been altered."

Hawk spoke quietly, the press leaning forward to heard him, the row of artists working quickly to meet deadlines, uncertain how long the defense attorney would stand at the lectern. Not until he began talking about the sheriff did Hawk's nervousness give way to the anger that would steady him.

"This was a case of arrest and then investigation. They had a couple of shreds of evidence and a couple of receipts and a misconception of the age of the body in the grave with the receipts. A young, green, sheriff, panicked by the press corps, snapped a man out of his house at four o'clock in the morning, and then an investigation."

Teja objected to the characterization. "It is not only inaccurate, it is prejudicial."

Hawk mentioned the injury to the bleeding worker, and transporting Carlos Leon Sierra in the yellow van to a doctor in "the presence of a great number of witnesses." They found that out after the arrest.

The twenty-five victims had been killed over a period of three months. "They found this out later. It seems that just at the tail end of March and the first two and one-half weeks of April, Juan Corona had a leg infection. He had a great deal of pain and a great deal of difficulty getting around during that three-week period of time." And for a week, during which men were presumably being killed, Corona had been home in bed, unable to walk. "The evidence will show that they didn't know this until after they had flashed Mr. Corona's name around the globe."

It was flowing now for him, all the evidence he had gathered for the past sixteen months falling into place. The shack where they found some bloodstained pants was used by Emilio Rangel, the foreman who worked for Juan, who drove the red and white pickup, who went downtown to pick up men in May.

Hawk sipped from a paper cup of water quickly, anxious to go on. Corona had no burden to prove anything, "but it should be obvious to you now that it is incumbent upon me to do everything I can to help a man who is my client and my friend. He does not have to testify, but he will testify.

"You are going to find that Mr. Corona on the only day that we know that a man died, that Mr. Corona can account for his time throughout the entire period of time in which the man could have died. This, again, is something that the evidence will show the sheriff's office never tried to develop before they arrested Mr. Corona, nor apparently have they ever, to this day. They have never really bothered to find out where Mr. Corona was that day and that afternoon. They just arrested him, and then commenced to look for the evidence to convict him."

Hawk was excited with his argument. The prosecution apparently was not going to object to the characterization; as long as they did not, he would continue.

The tire tracks didn't match. And, "you are going to find that when they went into Mr. Corona's house they handled everything in sight and never printed a thing which they picked up. When they went out to his camp with another search team they busted in there; they handled the gun, they handled the knife, they handled the pen, they handled everything out there. They didn't dust for one single fingerprint."

Hawk then turned to the aspect of his statement which was to be the day's news. They took swabs of Kenneth Whitacre's rectal area. "I think the evidence will show that the mistake they made was they assumed that these men had been attacked, or that they were in an act of anal intercourse, that they were playing the female role.

"In fact, what they should have been doing, if they had done a competent job, they should have checked the penile area to see if there was any semen in the canal, or to see if there was fecal matter on the penis itself.

"I am confident we will be able to establish that these are homosexual murders; that the act of homosexuality was one in which the twenty-five dead men were playing the part of a man; and that the homicidal maniac who murdered these men was playing the part of the woman.

"They had it reversed. In all probability, the perpetrator of these twenty-five murders is what is referred to in Guadalajara, Mexico, or in other parts of Mexico, as a *passivo* homosexual."

Teja and Williams were writing rapidly as Hawk repeated what he had learned from Mrs. Hooker, his expert witness. "The expert will tell you that there is nothing—the ultimate act of humiliation, degradation, to a Mexican man, the ultimate act of losing his *machismo*, is to play the role of the female in a sexual encounter.

"She will tell you that these men are driven by masochistic tendencies, either to have pain inflicted upon them or be degraded, that underneath all of this masochistic tendency is a boiling, bellowing rage; and that it is not uncommon at all for the *passivo* homosexual to suddenly turn in a homicidal rage to destroy or mutilate the man that he has just had intercourse with."

Hawk reminded the jury of the state of undress of many of the victims, adding who could be more helpless than a man attempting to pull on his pants.

Gloria Corona leaned forward in her seat, trying to understand. Occasionally a friend would whisper into her ear a brief summary of Hawk's statement.

"This same expert will tell you that Juan Corona is hopelessly heterosexual"—the phrase was borrowed from Mrs. Hooker who had used it jokingly to describe herself. "He has no latent desire to be a homosexual; he had a perfectly normal, happy sexual relationship with his wife. He has four children. He has no contact with this sort of thing."

Hawk went on to the Roche Report, a sensitive Williams objecting repeatedly, Judge Patton permitting Hawk to continue.

As Hawk neared his summary, he ran into problems. "It is on the basis of some of this sort of stuff that they have held Juan Corona in custody for the last eighteen months. It is on the basis of this sort of stuff that the man suffered two heart attacks."

"Objection," Williams broke in. "That is argumentative." The judge sustained Williams' point.

"If the county doctor were to testify, I would expect the county doctor to testify that Juan Corona suffered two heart attacks as the result of his arrest and incarceration."

This time Teja objected. The judge ordered Hawk's comment stricken, an attempt to prejudice the jury by eliciting sympathy.

"Let me tell you something about Juan Corona, the man, instead of Juan Corona, the killer, that everybody has been talking about for a long time."

Williams objected to the comment, the judge ordering the last phrase stricken.

Hawk tried a new tack. "Okay. Let me tell you about the man that I smuggled cupcakes into his cell up in Yuba City on his birthday in February of 1971 contrary to the sheriff's office regulations—"

"Mark the record for me, please, Mr. Reporter," Judge Patton interrupted, then called the attorneys into chambers.

Judge Patton was stoney-faced with rage. The cupcake comment. "What does that possibly have to do with any opening statement? It is contemptuous, far out of line. It is ridiculous." In his anger, Judge Patton overrode Hawk's apology. "The court finds you in contempt. Five days in the county jail. This is outrageous. You persist in this sort of conduct and you talk about your affection for Mr. Corona which I admonished you before about. It is not proper. It insinuates that you are vouching for your client's credibility." Hawk nodded his head vigorously. "And it is not a professional way to do it. It is clearly improper. It is wrong and there will probably be four or five other matters in the course of this opening statement that are just so outrageous that it is the court's feeling that it should not be tolerated."

Interrupted by the in-chambers session, Hawk had lost his opportunity for a coherent close to his statement. According to the judge's instructions, he told the jury, character evidence alone could raise a reasonable doubt; he would produce character witnesses for Corona.

There was no motive for Corona to kill the twenty-five, but there was for another person, a homosexual, "and I defy you or anybody else to make any sense out of a few fragments of circumstantial evidence without a motive."

Hawk sat down at the counsel table, the tension gone. Corona leaned over to thank him. Despite the rough beginning, it was the best opening statement he had ever made, Hawk was certain. He had held the jury's attention the whole way, making them listen. He had even gotten a little argument in, maybe even a lot.

He had also alienated Judge Patton.

17

The Blooding

October 3-6, 1972

Undersheriff Frank Cartoscelli was rattled. The first law enforcement witness, called only to verify the grave locations on the large map prepared for the trial, he had been caught in a hailstorm of objections by the defense. Hawk intended to establish his dominance of the courtroom early on. He also wanted to cut down to size the large, painted map—he had taken to calling it the mechanical monster—or, better still, have it removed entirely from the courtroom. Finally, if he could upset the undersheriff, other members of the department would be wary of Hawk's cross-examination.

Ostensibly, it was to have been a routine examination. As the officer responsible for locating and recovering the bodies, Cartoscelli had been present at all but four grave sites when they were dug out. Hawk, however, had protested; the grave sites had been affixed to the map by the civil engineer who had prepared it. Cartoscelli would be pointing to light bulbs already in place; the light bulbs, not the undersheriff, were actually testifying.

Now into the second day of his testimony, the undersheriff had conceded he had written no reports but was relying upon those prepared by other officers. With those reports in hand, in early September Cartoscelli claimed he had verified the locations of the graves. But ten of the graves in the orchards had been obliterated by the criss-crossing tractors and repeated irrigation; another had been destroyed when Sullivan cut a new road to the north riverbottom orchard. And Detective Gregory's report on the recovery of the first seven graves along the riverbank indicated no locations whatsoever.

The undersheriff was not a good witness. An eleven-year veteran, Cartoscelli had been promoted to undersheriff by the newly elected Roy Whiteaker. Hawk had expected him to know better than to argue with an attorney in court, to have to be told to speak louder in order to be heard, to be so visibly nervous, and to mistakenly locate two of the graves.

Leaning against the railing that separated the spectators from the bar, Hawk began his cross-examination on a tangential point. Did the inauguration of an east-west numbering system have anything to do with "the fact that you got E-1 and E-2 all mixed up out there?"

The dark-haired undersheriff swallowed. "You don't have to look at them," Hawk snapped.

"No."

"You do have E-1 and E-2 all mixed up, don't you, the nine-fingered man you switched all up and down the river?"

"I understand that some reports were mixed up," Cartoscelli acknowledged.

"These things you brought along with you to court. What are those called?"

"Reports. Officers' reports."

"Why do they write reports?"

"To relate information." Cartoscelli relaxed slightly; this was training academy stuff.

"Why? Why don't they just hold it in their heads?"

"Well, it wouldn't be good."

"Well now, you received a lot of training as a police officer, right? Were you ever told you were supposed to write reports?"

"Yes."

"For what reason?"

"For the information that you have received."

"Would you mind showing me reports on all these things you have been testifying to that you have done in the last sixteen months?"

"Well—" The undersheriff was embarrassed. With the normal policeman's aversion to report writing, he had consistently delegated that chore to others.

Hawk turned to the location of the five graves found in the north river-bottom orchard formed by a bend in the Feather River. "You personally verified those locations, right?"

"Right."

"With the reports?"

"Right."

"And the reports were accurate?"

"Right."

Reading from those reports, Hawk guided Cartoscelli in plotting the grave locations on a plastic overlay. Cartoscelli's black dots were at variance with the small bulbs inset in the large map. Grave 16 was 100 feet from the bulb. Grave site 17 was sixty-five feet off the mark. Numbers 18, 19, and 20 were plotted due south according to the report, not southeast, as the map indicated.

Pointing to Cartoscelli's last mark, Hawk asked, "Who owns that property there?"

Cartoscelli was reluctant to answer. "It is located in Yuba County."

"Well, according to your testimony, you dug up number seventeen here, number eighteen in the sand," Hawk jabbed at the black spot of a grease pencil perched on a sandbar at the edge of the Feather River, "number nineteen in the middle of the river," the black mark floating on the blue river glared across the courtroom, "and number twenty across the river in Yuba County. Now, explain that, will you?"

"Well, the roadway that runs through here, at least myself always considered it running south."

"Well, let me ask you, Mr. Cartoscelli, how can you check anybody's work when you don't even know which direction is south?"

"It is a southeasterly direction in my opinion."

"Okay. Well, were you wrong when you testified about it being south?"

"Yes, sir."

"Okay. What else were you wrong about on that stand?"

"Sustained," Judge Patton interrupted, without waiting for Williams or Teja to object. Hawk glanced at the jury; jurors number 6 and 11—the stocky Vietnam veteran, Hicks, and Mrs. Underwood—had quizzical expressions; Johnson, the retired marine master sergeant, was smiling. Encouraged, Hawk turned to Detective Gregory's report of the recovery of the first seven graves along the riverbank, E-1 through E-7.

"You designated Mr. Gregory as recording officer?" The deputy prosecutor inwardly winced; he had privately wondered for months why Gregory rather than someone else had been assigned that critical task. It was with Gregory's report that the prosecution's troubles began. Williams planned to take his lumps now and hope to recoup with the later scientific evidence.

"Were you concerned that he was doing a good job?" Hawk asked the undersheriff, standing directly in front of the witness stand.

"Yes."

"What is the job of the recording officer?"

"To record the information as we receive it."

"I see." Hawk's rise and fall of a mocking inflection. "And, of course, he doesn't do that on a hearsay basis, does he?"

"Normally, no."

"Then he should have been present when all of these graves were being dug; is that right?"

"That's right."

"Was he present at all times?"

"As far as I know, he was. Yes."

"I see. Well, looking at his report, may I ask you, how it is possible for him to be at two places at once. How could he be at graves one and two at 1910 hours."

"Objection, Your Honor." Williams would do what he could to protect their credibility.

"Sustained." The question asked the witness to speculate.

"When you reviewed these reports later, did you point out to anyone there were a great number of errors?"

"On some of the times that are noted?" Cartoscelli asked in return.

"Yes."

"Yes."

"You pointed that out?"

"Well, I noticed them." Cartoscelli had said nothing to either Gregory, the sheriff, or the prosecutors.

"Quite a few, aren't there?" Hawk changed the subject without waiting for an answer, his question becoming argument for the jury rather than cross-examination. "Now, the recording officer's job was to record the location of the grave and the things that came out of it."

"Yes, sir." Cartoscelli was wary; even the simple questions were suspect now.

"And you said yesterday that you verified on the basis of these reports that the grave locations were correct?"

"Yes."

"Okay. How about number one? Is there any location on number one?"

"No. There is no location on this report."

"Okay." Hawk was satisfied with the expected answer. "When you said that you verified that from the reports—the location—how did you manage to do that when there is no location put down for E-1?"

The undersheriff tried to cover his mistake. "What I meant is, that is, that I verified the locations from the reports for the grave locations in the orchards, from the tree count."

"Okay. Is it not correct that all the way through E-7 no grave locations are recorded at all?"

"No. There are no locations mentioned."

"As far as you know, the sheriff's office has no written record whatsoever of the location of these graves; isn't that correct?" Cartoscelli sat silently in the witness box, biting his upper lip. "Is that a difficult question, Mr. Cartoscelli?"

"I guess you would have to say that is correct." The undersheriff had never realized that failure until this moment.

Hawk turned to the misnumbering of victims five, six, and seven. Cartoscelli agreed the reports were incorrect.

"You got those mixed up too?"

"Our chief deputy coroner did, yes."

"Who is that?"

"John Purcell."

Hawk was disappointed in the undersheriff. As the second-ranking officer in the department, he was then-Sergeant, now-Captain Purcell's superior. Cartoscelli had reviewed the reports and Cartoscelli should have taken responsibility. Instead he had shifted it off on the deputy coroner. Until then Hawk had rather liked "old Frank." Cartoscelli had been friendly, even helpful when they were in Yuba City.

The third day of testimony and the fifth of the trial proper began in chambers with the prosecutors turning over to the defense "additional stuff that we thought had been sent out that had not." There were supplemental property reports compiled in Sacramento, a series of unimportant reports by sheriffs, and most significantly the notes of Officer Steve Sizelove written as bodies numbered 12 through 25 were uncovered sixteen months previously. "We did not realize that Mr. Sizelove actually had made any personal notes until we talked to the officers in this case, in about May of this year."

Teja apologized, then added, "We believe at this time that as a result of going through all of the files, that this gives the defendant everything that was ordered by the court in discovery."

Judge Patton puckered his lips, disapproving. "I don't have too much confidence at the moment that you have provided everything. You have made these representations to the court before. It is obvious that some disciplinary action should be taken."

Without hope, Hawk moved that the action be dismissed, or, alternatively, that the evidence contained in the reports he had just received be suppressed. Judge Patton denied both motions, leaving only a contempt of court sanction against the prosecution. They would take it up again after the noon recess.

Hawk was satisfied for the moment. The district attorney once again had been placed in a bad light. That would help temporarily with the judge, but Patton would never side with the defense completely. "He's not going to swing into the middle where he's fair!" Hawk complained to an aide as they walked back into the courtroom. There were places where Patton had ruled right, which was unusual, but not anyplace where he said, "Okay, I'm going to give you this little goodie, buddy; you've got it coming." Nothing like that at all.

This morning the large map became "Captain Davey's Electric Whizbang" as Undersheriff Cartoscelli resumed the stand. Hawk spent the first few minutes reviewing mistakes of the first two days in Cartoscelli's testimony, recommending at one point that the undersheriff not take up flying since he could not tell east from west.

The district attorney then began the grave-by-grave testimony concerning the finding of the bodies and their identification. It would take a month to complete this first phase of the trial and over 3,000 pages of testimony, much of it focused upon what the deputy district attorney had termed "the mistakes, errors and omissions" in the investigation.

Under Teja's questioning, Undersheriff Cartoscelli described the finding of the first victim, Kenneth Whitacre, in Goro Kagehiro's young peach orchard.

Cartoscelli was anxiously sitting on the edge of the swivel chair in the witness box as Hawk began his cross-examination.

The defense attorney was interested in the plaster casts of the tire tracks taken just eight feet from the grave. "Those are the ones that didn't match Mr. Corona's vehicles, is that correct?"

"As far as I know, that is right."

"Well, as undersheriff of Sutter County, didn't you consider this a pretty significant clue?"

Cartoscelli nodded. "Yes, I did consider it significant."

"Well now, considering it significant, can you tell us why it was significant?"

"Well, it certainly had been related to the grave, the victim. Could have been," Cartoscelli amended.

"What if the tire tracks had matched Mr. Corona's vehicle? It wouldn't have just been 'could have been' then?"

"Objection."

"Sustained."

"And that's the most significant clue that you had at that grave site, wasn't it?"

"I suppose so."

"Well, name one that is more significant."

"I can't." Cartoscelli was in full retreat, no longer even trying to save face.

"That's right. That was the only clue you had, wasn't it?"

"That is correct."

"And it was a good one, wasn't it?"

"Yes, I suppose so." Cartoscelli left the witness stand with a wan smile for the prosecutors.

In chambers after the luncheon recess, Judge Patton attempted to regain control of the courtroom. "I notice, Mr. Hawk, very persistently on many frequent occasions you have several little remarks after a question is answered. It is not proper, and I warned you and warned you; and I honestly don't see why you persist in this." The longer he talked, the more enraged Judge Patton became. "It upsets me, such as I stated many times, your complete disregard of the rules of procedure and of evidence. I don't know where you have been practicing all these years that you would think for a minute that—" He broke off, choked by his anger.

"You want to know which courts?" Hawk asked mildly.

"I want to know how you possibly can consider this is a proper comment and you have thought that you could continue to persist in this kind of remark—this recommendation he not take up flying?"

Hawk insisted he was not doing anything different than he had ever done. The judge brushed it aside. "You know it is wrong, Mr. Hawk; and I don't intend to put up with it." He held Hawk to be in contempt, assessed him a two-day jail sentence, then took up the persistent questioning—over objections—of the undersheriff about the tire tracks.

Hawk was having difficulty restraining his anger. Patton might as well be sitting at the counsel table with them. "I have a right to protect my client, and I know as well as I know anything else that those tire tracks don't match, and that they made every effort in the world to match it; and I am going to implant that idea in the jury's mind just as soon as I can in this case."

"And you are doing it improperly and you know it." Hawk did, in fact, know he was pushing the bounds of courtroom etiquette; he only resented Judge Patton's protective rulings of the two prosecutors apparently unable to protect themselves.

This time the sentence was for three days.

Judge Patton's anger had waned, but he was no less firm. Now he went after the prosecution. The failure to turn over discoverable material "has caused delays in this proceeding and also raises a question as to whether this defendant has been substantially prejudiced or not. And it certainly gives the defendant a basis and argument on appeal. I feel you should both be held in contempt."

"As the department head, Your Honor," the district attorney volunteered, "I would assume the responsibility; it would be my responsibility, and not Mr. Williams'." Teja would join Hawk in the Solano County jail at the end of the trial for five days. By accepting full responsibility, he had saved his deputy a similar maximum sentence on the contempt citation.

Judge Patton turned back to Hawk, this time to review the defense attorney's opening statement. For referring to Judge Arnason as "an old friend of mine," three days and $200. For referring to his client as "Juan," five days; for asserting that the Sheriff's Department and the press had stripped Corona of the presumption of innocence, three days and $300. By the end of the day, Hawk had pending a total of thirty-two days in jail and fines of $2,700.

Judge Patton was a stern churchwarden. "We seem to have a very basic disagreement as to what the duties and responsibilities of an attorney are in a case. An attorney's professional responsibility is not to try to get away with everything that he can. An attorney's responsibility to his client and to the profession and to the law is to act within those matters of procedure and evidence which the attorney knows to be proper."

The lecture was over. "Now, I suggest that you all shape up and start to act like gentlemen, so that this case can proceed in a proper manner."

"I think it is," Hawk insisted as they stood up to return to the courtroom.

Captain John Purcell was a surprise. Soft-spoken, circumspect in his answers, he appeared to be a school principal or a pharmacist, perhaps, rather than a law enforcement officer, a man more familiar with Rotary and Elks' meetings than morgues and lockups.

Teja began by reviewing Cartoscelli's testimony concerning Whitacre's body. Judge Patton was curious about the necessity.

"We have a problem here, Your Honor," Teja explained. "It relates to the voir dire questions that Mr. Hawk has put to the prospective jurors in this matter; it relates to the extrajudicial comments that he made to various people; and it relates to comments he made in his opening remarks to the jury this week: namely, that these bodies are all confused."

Hawk smiled openly. He had forced them into a defensive posture even before the trial really got underway. In the interests of time, Judge Patton ordered Teja to "move forward and cover it by the least amount of testimony possible."

"The body was rigid when we removed it, and there was some bleeding after we got him out of the grave," Captain Purcell testified. In his capacity as deputy coroner, Purcell had followed the freshly killed Whitacre's body to the mortuary, and there had taken rolled impressions of the fingerprints.

"In some cases in order to take fingerprints are fingertips removed?"

"Yes, sir. When it's impossible to print someone because of the condition of the body—decomposed or drowning victims that have been in the river for some period of time, cases like that." Captain Purcell rebuttoned the jacket of his suit and sat back in the witness chair; in his nine years as a deputy sheriff, he had testified in court and at inquests repeatedly.

Hawk's cross-examination was centered on the tire tracks, what Cartoscelli had earlier called the most significant clue at the grave site. Why had Purcell, as the man in charge of the investigation, selected those to be cast in plaster?

"They looked pretty good. I have to say they looked fresh, to be honest, and they were close to the grave site."

Had the vehicle stopped? Purcell "honestly" couldn't say. Why make casts if the vehicle hadn't stopped? Purcell couldn't recall, but agreed Hawk's logic made sense. The likelihood was the vehicle had stopped there and "it was from this vehicle that the body was carried."

The captain made a good impression. He was straightforward; he was obviously telling the truth, even when it appeared to damage his case. Hawk was courteous; jurors resented lawyers browbeating fatherly figures.

"Now, you directed that those tire tracks be compared to Mr. Corona's vehicle, did you not?"

"Yes, sir, later on."

"Did you at any time from May 20 until today direct anyone to take those tire tracks and compare them against vehicles belonging to someone besides Juan Corona?"

"I don't believe I did, sir."

"Did you at any time have any information which would lead you to believe that you ought to check these tire tracks against someone else's vehicle?"

"No, sir."

"I take it then they matched Mr. Corona's tire tracks."

"I didn't say that." The captain was defensive.

"My question is besides Mr. Corona's vehicle how many other vehicles in Sutter County have you checked these tracks with, these treads against?"

"None, sir, unless someone else did and didn't tell me."

"You were in charge of the investigation?"

"Yes, sir."

"All right, my question is for $64. Why didn't you?"

"For $64, I can't answer that. I didn't." Purcell was unflustered. "I didn't have any other vehicle to check them against, sir."

"How about Ray Duron? Did you check his vehicle? Has he got a vehicle?"

"Yes, he drives a Ranchero or El Camino, I believe."

"Did you check the tread on his vehicle to see if he was connected?"

"No, sir."

"You are familiar with all of those men that work regularly at the ranch?"

"Yes, I have seen them all."

"Did you check their vehicles?"

"No, sir."

"How about Jack Sullivan?"

"No, sir."

"Just Mr. Corona and nobody else?"

"Yes, sir."

Deputy Sheriff Roger Mason was the next witness, called to identify a series of photographs he had taken of the grave site and the body; and, because of Hawk's questioning, to verify a sketch of the immediate area around the grave. The tire tracks had been drawn in on Mason's diagram.

The tracks were poor, and appeared to end at the grave site, he told the deputy district attorney. They were the only two tracks on the dirt access road. Like Purcell before him, the stocky Mason was composed, the only sign of nervousness his constant buttoning and unbuttoning of his sports jacket.

"Nobody talked to you about these tire tracks from time to time until today?" Hawk began.

"Mr. Williams asked me if I had knowledge of them."

"He asked you today?"

"Yes." Mason fingered a small moustache he had recently grown.

"Was that after Captain Purcell had testified?"

"Objection," the district attorney complained. "Counsel is making it appear there is something improper in an attorney asking questions." The judge permitted Hawk to continue.

"Was it after Captain Purcell testified?"

"Yes, sir." Mason, hopefully, could minimize the damage.

"Your statement that they are poor tire tracks has something to do with your eyeballing the thing and saying they don't look too good to you?"

"Yes, sir." Mason buttoned, then unbuttoned his jacket.

The deputy agreed that he hadn't "the faintest idea whether they are usable tracks at all."

Hawk asked the young deputy to estimate from his diagram the distance of the nearest track to the grave. "Between five and eight feet, sir."

"Just one vehicle had been in there?"

"It appeared, yes, sir."

"No other tire tracks on the road, just this one?"

"Just this particular set, yes, sir."

"Didn't that kind of indicate that if Mr. Whitacre came in there by vehicle that he came in the vehicle that left those tracks?"

Williams' objection could not eradicate the logic of Hawk's conclusion.

Hawk took a series of pictures his daughter had removed from a file in the catalogue cases. He selected one at random and handed it to the deputy. "Just looking at that, how do you know that's a photograph of Whitacre's grave?"

"I was there, sir."

"What if you died? Didn't anybody ever teach you you are supposed to write something down and take a picture of that label in the photograph too?"

"We do it now." But Mason had not done it during the Corona investigation, and he had made a serious error.

"You know that is Whitacre's grave because you were there?"

"Yes, sir."

"Then I take it you can tell me where this one came from?" Hawk asked, handing Mason an eight-by-ten enlargement, a photo of the bearded man.

"Yes, sir, I can."

"Where did it come from?"

"That's Donald Dale Smith, victim number six. It is indicated on the back as being W-2-4."

Mason had made another mistake. "W-2-4? Look at that." Hawk flipped the photograph over to the label on the back. Mason read it.

"Correction. E-2, sir, my mistake."

"And no figure four, right?"

"Yes, sir," Mason growled.

"That's all your handwriting?"

"Yes."

"Don't get hostile," Hawk warned.

"I am not." Mason fumbled for the button on his jacket.

"Why did you mark it E-2?"

"Because at the time it was my impression that was E-2." The report of the finding of that grave, like the photograph, placed a bearded man in E-2. The bearded man was Donald Smith, whom Mason now said was in E-4, some 300 yards down the riverbank.

Mason, too, had been at a departmental meeting in June that the deputy prosecutor called "a bull session," along with the undersheriff and other members of the department who had worked on the Corona case.

"Now, what was the purpose of that meeting?"

"To discuss the body hunt, go over it, and possibly bring up anything that anybody could remember."

"You are sure that the purpose of this meeting wasn't to straighten out the 'mistakes, errors and omissions' that Sutter County had made in handling the evidence in this case?"

Williams' objection that Hawk's question was beyond the scope of the direct examination was sustained. The deputy prosecutor would rue the cover letter he had written; Hawk would never tire of referring to the "mistakes, errors and omissions" of the investigation.

Goro Kagehiro, after waiting three full days, was the last prosecution witness of the day. He told of locating the open hole in the morning, then returning that evening to find it filled in. There was nothing in his testimony in dispute.

Hawk's cross-examination was calculated to elicit character evidence. The rancher had known Corona for ten years, first as a laborer, then as a contractor. He worked hard, he was peaceful, he didn't fight with other men. Kagehiro was satisfied with Corona's work as a labor contractor, and had used his crews six or seven years. It was all beyond the scope of the direct examination, and all asked without objection. Hawk was delighted.

"Between the time you were out there that day digging this hole up until Mr. Corona got arrested, did anybody from the sheriff's office ever come and ask you if you knew anything about Mr. Corona's activities on that day, where he was or anything?"

"No."

"They never did?"

"No."

Hawk was leading. "The next thing you knew, Mr. Corona got arrested?"

"Yes."

"Nobody ever asked you if you could account for any of his time, did they?"

"No, nobody asked me."

Goro Kagehiro went home to his peach and prune orchards, vaguely curious why he had had to wait three days to say nice things about the dark-haired man sitting at the table so quietly.

Chain Singh Khera had been called for one purpose, to testify that he had seen Corona in an orchard adjacent to the Kagehiro property shortly before the body was found—perhaps a day or two before, as Khera had told the Grand Jury.

District Attorney Teja, however, was having problems. The rancher testified he had been driving west on an access road in his orchard when he was approached by Corona in a white van driving east.

"Well, I stop him and ask him, 'What you doing here?' He told me he just come to look my tree, how much I going to pay for the tree, you know. And then we walk in the orchard and look, look at the tree. And then I told him, 'These are late Briardale peaches. Wait till the time come, you know. Hard to tell what I'm going to pay for the tree.'"

Corona leaned over to Hawk with a slight smile and whispered, "He cheap man. I don't like him." Hawk laughed.

"Do you recall the date of this incident?" Teja asked.

"Between first week of May, around first week of May," Khera replied.

"This conversation with the defendant was the first week of May?" Teja was dismayed; Khera had told the deputies and the Grand Jury it was the seventeenth or eighteenth.

"Maybe around tenth or eleventh or something. I don't remember the right date."

"Do you recall whether or not you told the Grand Jury precisely when you saw the defendant on your property?"

"Well, exact date, I don't remember what date I saw him. Just saw him, you know, on—between first, fifth—" Khera tried to remember. "I mean within fifth day of May and around, you know, fifteenth. I don't know what date."

The district attorney was forced to read into the record the Grand Jury testimony Khera had given. "Yes. Yes. I tell the Grand Jury, yes."

"Which is correct then?"

"I don't know. What date, exactly what date it was." Khera was confused.

"Was your testimony before the Grand Jury correct," Teja finally concluded.

"Yes," Khera assured him.

"Nothing further, Your Honor." Teja returned to his seat as Hawk looked up from his note pad.

"Is your testimony here today correct?"

"Yes."

Hawk, in his opening, had told the jury that if there were two equally reasonable interpretations of the same evidence, the jury was sworn to adopt the one pointing to innocence.

"Was there anything at all unusual about the way Mr. Corona acted that day?" Khera didn't understand. "I mean, did he talk funny?"

"No. He talk nice."

"Did he have any blood spattered all over his clothes, or anything like that?"

"No."

"Did he look like he was excited?"

"No."

The first week of testimony ended with a series of witnesses who said they had seen a man with buck teeth in a long overcoat walking on the highway. Thirteen-year-old Gina Cross Chapman, home in bed with the mumps, had seen him as late as one o'clock on the day he was killed.

Miss Chapman's testimony narrowed the time period for which Corona had to present an alibi; now only five hours were in question.

As Williams had feared, the prosecution was taking its lumps.

18

The Odyssey of the Bearded Man

October 10-12, 1972

It had been a long three days for Bart Williams, much of it spent pondering a dilemma he could not resolve. It was finally a question of ethics—his, both personal and professional. Bart Williams doubted Juan Corona's guilt.

After a three-day weekend of thinking, he had reached a decision—almost. After all, if he himself had a reasonable doubt, how could he go on in good conscience, asking a jury to believe what he didn't? Or wasn't certain about? It was a private matter, the sort of thing each man solved for himself.

Right now, Bart Williams wanted out of this case. At the same time he had a contract with Sutter County to prosecute.

If the evidence wasn't clear, at least the prosecution's situation was, Williams admitted ruefully. Its case was in a shambles after just one week's testimony. Williams had known things would be bad, but Hawk had found errors he and Teja had overlooked. And there were more to come. Here they were, entering the second week of testimony, already behind the schedule of witnesses he had drawn up, and still investigating the case. Even more embarrassing to him, he would have to go into chambers on Tuesday morning and confess they were still trying to organize themselves. He had located another witness' statement in the files never turned over to Hawk, and Mason had found a missing set of plaster tire tracks in the evidence locker. Those tracks had gone out air special for analysis at the ATF lab in Washington this morning, seventeen months late. As things stood now, it was clear enough that Judge Patton didn't think too highly of him, or of the case they had put together. This could only make it worse.

Williams was accustomed to more proficiency from law enforcement; the sheriff and police in Santa Clara County were sophisticated professionals. Maybe he had expected too much of Sutter County; he had spent a lot of time lately wondering if Roy Whiteaker's department was as good as it could be, or whether Sutter County might have done better. Certainly they could have brought in professional criminalists before Williams himself did.

At Williams' insistence, he and Teja had talked finally about the precariousness of their case and the tenuous evidence they had. Teja didn't agree—he couldn't, considering he was the district attorney, and thus responsible for bringing the action—but others, including Captain Purcell, did. They would meet tonight in Fairfield to discuss the case with Sheriff Whiteaker and Larry Cilley, the chief administrative officer of the county.

For Richard Elwyn Hawk, the three-day weekend had been a lark. From Friday evening's television news right through to the photographers taking his picture this morning, it had been fun. Reporters calling him at home all the time, lawyers at the restaurant complimenting him, the bartender saying he looked good on TV. He was on top, dominating the trial and the best was yet to come. Patton could take the thirty-two days and shove it, but Hawk wasn't going to let up.

Williams was forced to confront Hawk and the judge in chambers alone on Monday morning, first to turn over the witness' statement, then to report that the second set of tire tracks—Williams mistakenly thought they were from the north riverbottom orchard—had turned up in the evidence locker. They had laid there, unexamined, for the past sixteen months, the contrite Williams explained.

"You mean there were some other marks which were at one time believed to be significant and casts applied, and it was never pursued at all?" Judge Patton was incredulous.

"It was never pursued at all," Williams repeated.

"I just can't understand how anyone who claims to have prepared a case for trial and after some fifteen months have gone by that this sort of incident repeats itself." Judge Patton's anger sputtered in his throat. "This is outrageous, absolutely outrageous, and the significance of these tire tracks and the impressions of the vehicle . . ." Anger choked him.

"The thing that bothers me at this juncture, Your Honor," Williams confided, "is that there has been enough of this in the last two weeks that we have run across and that I have uncovered that my question is how much other stuff is laying back there in the files." He would have a secretary begin an immediate inventory.

Patton exploded. "This is ridiculous. This case has been in progress for investigation for, what?, fifteen or seventeen months, and now you say you have got to start cataloguing. You don't know what you have got or what you haven't got. It seems to me that this case is being handled by a bunch of amateurs. I have never heard of such a handling of a case of such substantial significance."

The judge held them in contempt for not turning over the statement earlier. On Hawk's request, he added that he would consider a pauper's oath on behalf of his client as a first step in ordering the county to pay for an investigator to look into all the evidence withheld. He would also consider permitting Hawk to make a second opening statement at the beginning of the defense case so as to incorporate the useful material he had obtained since the trial began.

Once started, Williams could not stop himself. "There is one other thing I wanted to bring out, Your Honor—and these are things that just more or less jelled in our office within the last thirty days—and I would like to indicate to the court that there will be some specific items that we are going to check out, because to be honest, it is almost a consensus of opinion now that there could very well have been somebody else involved in this thing."

There were two major inconsistencies, Williams confessed: the failure to match the machete to the striations on the bone fragment removed from Whitacre's skull, and "the fact that you have got a cigarette butt in Mr. Sample's grave that is group type O, and Mr. Corona's blood type is A, and Mr. Sample's was type A." Moreover, the blood found on Corona's gun did not match either Corona or the one victim shot, "so the blood evidence is extremely damaging," he admitted.

It was a long day for Williams sitting alone at the counsel table since Teja was in Yuba City asking the Board of Supervisors for an additional trial deputy in Yuba City. Hawk bided his time, allowing Williams to work his way through the finding of the second grave, barely paying attention since no evidence had been uncovered there linking his client to the murders. Corona sat beside him, as emotionless as he had during the first week, intently listening to the testimony. (He smiled only when the bailiff, Ed Hehr, escorted him in and out of the courtroom, when he could wave quickly at Gloria, and the four girls if they were not in school.)

Hawk waited until Deputy Sizelove was on the stand. Williams had led Sizelove through the digging of the first body on the riverbank and the receipts bearing Corona's name.

In the grave, Sizelove had also found a half-smoked cigarette above the victim's midsection. Sizelove had picked up the butt and turned it over to the recording officer, Detective Gregory. Resting on the victim's chest was a package of Pall Mall cigarettes, all but empty; Sizelove had passed that over to Gregory as well.

"On victim number three, do you recall whether the body was loose or rigid?" Williams asked.

Sizelove had been well briefed. "It was loose. When we picked him out of the grave he bent in the middle and his legs were free."

"Was this body relatively clean or bloody, or what was the condition, as far as dirt was concerned?"

"It was clean."

"There was no odor from this body?"

"No, sir; none whatsoever."

"Did somebody call your attention to something about the victim's hands?"

"Yes, sir. There was the little finger missing on one of his hands."

Hawk began his cross-examination. "Do I understand correctly that Frank Cartoscelli handled that receipt?"

"Yes, sir," Sizelove agreed. The undersheriff had been one of two people crouched at the edge of the grave sifting by hand the loose earth Sizelove shoveled out. Without gloves, Cartoscelli handled the paper, "just enough to unfold it and look at them, is all." Deputies with just four years' experience did not criticize their superiors.

"Well then, he separated them—"

"Yes, sir."

"—And pretty soon he handed them to Mr. Gregory?"

"Yes, sir."

"And Mr. Gregory handled them. Right?"

"Yes, sir."

"Sir, have you ever heard of taking fingerprints off of paper by the use of iodine crystals?"

"Yes, sir, I have."

"Well, why didn't you guys try to take some fingerprints off of that, rather than handle the evidence?"

"I didn't handle it, sir." Deputy Sizelove was calm.

"Well, why didn't you say, when you saw Mr. Cartoscelli do this, 'Frank, stop! You are destroying the evidence. There might be finger-prints on that.'?"

"No, sir, I didn't."

"Well, why didn't you? Weren't you aware at this time that you could lift fingerprints off paper with iodine crystals, or did you find out later?"

Sizelove agreed that he had also handled both the package of cigarettes and the cigarette butt. Any prints would have been destroyed. Hawk turned to a footprint found close to the grave, "close enough that some-body thought it was of significance." The cast taken of the footprint did not match Corona's, did Sizelove know that? Williams' objection was futile; the jury now knew.

At the noon recess, Williams asked the exuberant defense attorney if they could go into chambers. The prosecutor wanted to quit at four o'clock so he could attend a meeting about the case that evening. Over-whelmed by the tension, neither man could clearly remember what was said in the brief conversation; both agreed that the prosecutor told Hawk that he now had a reasonable doubt about Corona's guilt, doubt great enough to raise ethical and professional problems for him. The meeting, he explained, was to discuss the future of the prosecution, whether to fold up or continue. The judge insisted the trial continue to the end of the day.

The first witness after lunch was a deputy coroner from Sacramento County who had been assigned to process the bodies received in metal shipping containers from Yuba City. Jody Ulrey, a slight, dapper man, had been responsible for itemizing the clothing and property of each of the victims, then writing reports.

According to Ulrey's reports, Melford Sample, the nine-fingered man, was in E-2-4, not E-1-3 as the prosecution asserted.

"Mr. Ulrey, the body which you have marked as E-1-3, what is that man's name, according to your report?"

"It is unidentified."

"How many fingers did he have?"

"It is not noted on our report, sir."

Hawk handed Ulrey a second set of papers. "What grave site is that?"

"E-2-4, sir," the second grave dug along the river and the fourth victim overall.

"What is that man's name, according to your report?"

"Melford Sample, sir."

"How many fingers does he have."

Ulrey quickly skimmed the report. "Finger left hand missing."

"E-2 had missing finger on left hand," Hawk paraphrased for emphasis.

"Yes, sir."

"Not E-1?"

"E-2 number four, sir, had missing finger."

The shipping containers had come to Sacramento marked with the body number in large black letters in three places. The bodies inside were also tagged, Ulrey testified. Those were the numbers he had used in preparing his reports.

Without objection from the dispirited Williams, Hawk began a series of questions beyond the scope of the direct examination. An objection would be senseless because Hawk would get to it sooner or later anyway.

"We have been told that Donald Smith was the sixth body found." The defense attorney handed the witness another of his coroner's reports. "What body does that refer to?"

"Body number five, sir, E-3-5."

"Okay. What is that man's name?"

"Smith, sir."

Hawk whispered to his daughter Cristi who retrieved the photograph of the bearded Smith which Mason had marked E-2-4. He showed it to Ulrey who was unable to recognize the victim. "What are those marks on the back?"

"Number E-2."

"Well, E-2 wasn't Donald Smith, was it?"

"According to my report, no, sir."

"Donald Smith wasn't body number six either, was he?"

"Not according to my report."

Russell Parmer, the head of the latent fingerprint division of CII, was Williams' next witness, called to identify the victim in the second grave. A large man whose weight had settled in his midsection, Parmer was retiring after thirty-five years with the Department of Justice, bowing out with his last and biggest case.

Hawk was far more interested in the failure to secure fingerprints from the evidence than the identity of victim number 2. No, Palmer had not been asked to lift prints from a cigarette package.

"How should police officers handle it? Should they all pick it up and handle it and get their prints on it?"

"It wouldn't be a very good idea."

Yes, he might be able to lift prints from two receipts, even though they had been in the ground, the one on the inside would more likely yield a print than the one on the outside.

"Ever try to lift prints off anything that came out of those graves?"

"One bottle."

"What did you find on the one bottle?"

"A lot of mud." Hawk broke off his questioning until the laughter died, watching the jury. All but Mrs. Blazek, juror number 8, the schoolteacher, had laughed with the judge. The retired marine, Johnson, number 4, and Hicks, number 6, seemed to enjoy the humor the most; Hawk liked them, especially the young Vietnam veteran.

Parmer testified he had worked through all three of Corona's vehicles lifting fingerprints. None of the victim's fingerprints had matched the latent prints Parmer recovered.

Frank Cartoscelli returned to the stand, Hawk smiling as the under-sheriff sat down. Give him twenty-five chances at a witness and sooner or later he was going to get to him. It was an odd way to arrange the case. While a chronological exposition made it easier for the jury to understand, it meant keeping witnesses like Parmer and Ulrey and the sheriffs around day after day. It also gave Hawk unlimited opportunities to recapitulate previous testimony which was favorable, or try once again to diminish testimony that hurt his case.

Cartoscelli had been called to identify the receipts taken from the grave. The undersheriff told Williams that he and Detective Duncan had been sifting dirt at the side of the grave. The undersheriff had picked the re-ceipts up from the pile of dirt, Duncan on his right, Gregory on his left. "And they were folded, and I very carefully unfolded them and looked at them."

"What did you do with the receipts after you unfolded them and read them?"

"I immediately handed them to Detective Gregory."

Hawk began his third cross-examination of the undersheriff after the recess, off on another tangent. "Mr. Cartoscelli, sir, you were telling me the other day about how you reviewed the reports to make sure they were all correct. Right? Do you remember telling me about that?"

Cartoscelli was experienced enough now to be wary. "I said I reviewed them."

"You told us the head was to the south, is that correct?"

"To the southwest."

But Gregory's report indicated the victim's head was at the north end of the grave. "Explain that, would you?"

"It's just going to have to be explained by Officer Gregory. It's his report and I don't know what he was referring to there."

"Well, when you reviewed these reports, like you said the other day, for accuracy, didn't you run across that little mistake?" Hawk was smiling at the uncomfortable man in the witness box.

"These reports were reviewed by me many weeks after that particular incident and—" He broke off lamely.

"And what?" Hawk prompted.

They were Gregory's reports; Hawk would have to ask him, Cartoscelli insisted, once again passing the responsibility to someone else.

Hawk then quarter-folded two pieces of paper as the receipts had been. Handing the papers to the undersheriff, he demanded: "Show us how you unfolded them. Get them up there so everybody can see."

His little finger arched in an imitation of an overly mannered tea drinker, Cartoscelli gingerly held the folded papers between his thumb and forefinger, then shook them. The papers remained folded together. Again and again he rattled the papers, trying to open them.

Hawk looked at the jury, smiling. The entire back row, numbers 1 through 6, was openly amused. So was Phillips, number 7, and Mrs. Underwood. They no more believed Frank Cartoscelli had unfolded the receipts that way than he did. Hawk could just see Cartoscelli snatching the receipts up; fumbling them open; yelling, "Hey! lookee here what I found fellas," and everyone passing them around.

"No, no. You didn't have a table out there. Just do it like you did out there."

"I had this one opened. I looked at it and handed it to Gregory and I did the same with the other one."

"I see you were very, very careful there, weren't you?"

"I was trying to be."

"You held it just by the edge, right? You didn't want to destroy the evidence, right?"

"That is right," the undersheriff agreed.

"How did Gregory take hold of it?"

"I don't remember how Gregory took hold of them."

"Gregory took it directly out of your hands?"

"Yes."

"And you don't know how he took ahold of it?" Hawk was angry. Cartoscelli was interested only in protecting himself. "Well, now, and that was because you knew that you could get fingerprints off of it? Right?"

"It's a possibility, yes, sir."

"Did anybody ever try to get any fingerprints off of it?"

"Not to my knowledge."

"And for all you know, Jack Sullivan's prints could have been on that originally. Right?"

Williams interrupted with one of his infrequent objections of the day. "He's asking the witness to speculate."

Hawk ignored Williams. "Anyone, Mr. Williams, me, Ray Duron, anybody could have handled that. Right?"

"Probably true, yes."

"Okay. According to the report, where is the grave located?"

"He doesn't have a location on this particular report."

"Is that the correct way to write a report, without even locating the grave site?"

"Things were pretty hectic."

"Yes or no. Is that the correct way to do it?"

"It probably should have been noted on that report, yes."

"Okay. Along with having the feet and the head at the right end of the grave, right?"

"That is right."

By the end of the day, the regulars in the press section sensed something was afoot. For the first time, Teja had been absent the entire day. There were rumors, too, of a meeting arranged for that evening, unconfirmed but persistent. Hawk, always willing to talk before, seemed to know something about it, but would say only that Williams had told him two or three times that day that the deputy prosecutor now had a reasonable doubt.

That night Hawk's mood veered from uncontrollable giggling, to dejected fatigue, to shouting anger. "It makes me ill to think of them keeping that man in jail and that fucking, gutless judge, if he had any balls at all he would have thrown the God damn case out today."

Hawk took the coffee cup his daughter handed him. "God, that this man should be the victim of a backwoods D.A., a green sheriff, and this judge. Pitiful." His voice trailed off.

"You're pretty disheartened right now."

"Not in the sense that I think I'm going to lose it. I know I'm going to win it, but God damn it, jail for that man. It's six more months without a piece of tail, or seeing his kids. It's six more months living like a God damn animal, in a tiny room, in a fictitious kind of existence, when they know they haven't got it. They *know* they haven't got it."

Hawk set the coffee cup down heavily, and slowly rubbed his face with his open hands. "They don't fold tomorrow," he said looking up, "no holds barred. I don't give a shit how much time I get. I'm going to punch those bastards every chance I get." The more he talked, the more enthusiastic he became. "I'm going to get outrageous tomorrow, just tear those assholes up. 'Your Honor, how can you tolerate this God damn prosecution any longer when you know the People said there's a reasonable doubt?'" Hawk laughed, plotting his speech. "'How long we going to play this charade, protecting this sonofabitch politically? And that's what they're doing. Nothing else.'"

Hawk lapsed from his anticipation. "God, what a bunch of bad breaks in this trial. Bad break with the judge, bad break with the D.A., the sheriff just—" He croaked in disgust.

The coffee cooled in the cup, then turned cold. "I'm going to jump their ass immediately. Not say a word. No chamber session, nothing. Judge walks in, I'm going to say, 'Your Honor, I move to dismiss this on the basis that the district attorney yesterday three times said he had a reasonable doubt about Juan Corona's guilt or innocence. I move you throw this crummy case out of court, that you show some kind of manhood they can't show.' Which will be denied. Then I'll say, 'I want bail. My God, in the name of all that's right, if you call yourself a Christian, grant him bail.'"

Hawk twisted a fist into his eye, crushing a tear. "How the hell can they hold him?" he asked the walls of the kitchen.

"Good morning, ladies and gentlemen," Judge Patton said to the jury to open the sixth day of the trial. "Are you ready to call your next witness?" he asked Williams.

"Yes, Your Honor," the deputy district attorney said as Hawk rose.

"Your Honor, in view of Mr. Williams' statement yesterday that he has reasonable doubt as to Juan Corona's guilt—"

"Just a moment, Mr. Hawk," Judge Patton shrilled. "Please don't proceed with any such remarks in the presence of this panel. We will go in chambers." The reporters with deadlines broke for the door as the judge left the bench.

"Your Honor," a tense Williams began in chambers, "I am convinced that twelve or sixteen people on this jury heard that remark, and because of the prejudicial nature of that remark I think the Court should exercise its discretion and declare a mistrial."

"May I say," Hawk began the speech he had promised the night before, "that the fact that this trial is continuing this morning in view of the statements that Mr. Williams made is an absolute travesty and a mis-carriage of justice.

"I want to make a motion to dismiss. I think it is just outrageous that this man is held in custody all of this time on a case that the prosecutors say they have a reasonable doubt about. Your Honor, there has got to be some justice in the world for Juan Corona. There has just got to be," Hawk pleaded.

Williams was apologetic. He was merely a private attorney under con-tract to Sutter County. "The man empowered by law to make these decisions is the district attorney. Merely because I have made these ex-pressions doesn't mean that I am in the driver's seat and able to make the legal decisions on whether to proceed or not to proceed."

The decision made the night before had been to continue with the prosecution.

Judge Patton then held the defense attorney in contempt for his remark at the beginning of the session. "Five days and $500. It is absolutely out-rageous that you would stand up in front of the jury and make such a remark."

"Not as big an outrage as this case going on this morning, Your Honor," Hawk was bristling. "This man is being held in custody on a trial that this man [Williams] doesn't believe in. To me that is much more outrageous than anything I said."

"Mr. Hawk, I have been outraged a number of times in this case because of the prosecution's attitude and procedures in this belated furnish-ing of documents at least five times." Judge Patton was stabbing the desk top with his finger, his anger at the defense attorney turned upon the crest-fallen Williams. "Apparently there wasn't even an attempt that this case be investigated until this case got down here in Solano County after your client had been held in jail for sixteen months. It is an absolute out-rage and I say it is. But nevertheless, there are substantial matters as to guilt or innocence, and the trial should proceed on that basis."

As Hawk had predicted, Judge Patton denied his motion to dismiss and Williams' motion for a mistrial. "Just because Mr. Williams may express some reasonable doubt, that doesn't mean the case cannot be proven or otherwise. I don't know what the status of the evidence is. This is a very significant case involving twenty-five possible homicides."

"And probably the worst investigated case in the history of juris-prudence," Hawk added.

"I would say at this point," the judge agreed, "it appears that the investigation was inept, the preparation inefficient, and the prosecution inadequate.

"Let's proceed."

Detective Jerry Gregory, nine years a deputy sheriff and a recent transfer to the district attorney's staff to work on the Corona case, was Williams' first witness. He had been called to identify those items of evidence from the third grave: a set of false teeth, a tin which once held Prince Albert tobacco, clumps of bloodstained grass, the receipts, a blue baseball cap.

Gregory had prepared himself for the direct examination as well as he knew how. He had talked with those officers who had testified earlier, and had been warned about the cross-examination. Now it was his turn, and he was nervous.

Policemen wrote reports, Gregory replied to Hawk's questions, to keep a record of events, to serve in place of memory. Occasionally, yes, he left important things out. Gregory cleared his throat, suddenly clotted with a nerve-born frog. "No one is perfect."

If something were omitted, it would be an error on his part. Yes, he reviewed his reports to make certain they were accurate.

"And you did in this case, didn't you?"

"I don't believe I did. No."

Gregory had been the recording officer at the riverbank graveyard sixteen months before. "In the last sixteen months you have never had an opportunity to review your report, to see if it is accurate? Is that what you want to testify to under oath?"

"I wouldn't say I have not had the chance, but I didn't have occasion to review it, no." Gregory cleared his throat.

"Is that because you just assumed it was accurate?"

"That is possible. Yes."

"Well," Hawk snapped, "Did you assume that it was accurate?"

"Yes."

"And you reviewed it before you came in here today, didn't you?"

"Yes."

"And you found it to be accurate, right?"

"Basically so, yes. There is a couple of typing errors in there."

Hawk pointed out one of them, savage in his persistence, scornful of Gregory.

"What happened at 1904 hours?"

"That should have been 1940 hours."

"Now, what happened then? You can explain all day long your mistakes, but what happened on the report?"

"At this time the Prince Albert can and set of dentures was removed from the victim."

"All right. Now, is it possible to remove dentures from the victim when he wasn't even found until about thirty minutes later? Is it possible?"

"If the time was right." Gregory was feisty.

"Is it possible?" Hawk demanded. The more Gregory resisted, the harder Hawk would hit.

"As I said—"

"Is it possible?" the attorney insisted.

Judge Patton had heard enough. "That is argumentative. Mr. Williams, why don't you object? It is obviously argumentative."

Gregory, Williams, the judge too—Hawk would battle them all, the frustration-born anger choking him.

"Is that a mistake?"

"Typographical error." Gregory's creased neck was red with suppressed rage.

"Your mistake?"

"Not mine."

"Did you review this before you came in here today?"

"Today. Yes."

"Did you find that mistake today?"

"Yes, I did."

"Why didn't you tell us about it on direct?"

"I wasn't asked about it."

"You weren't asked about it." Hawk looked at the silent deputy prosecutor sitting at the counsel table intent on his hands. "Did you point that out to Mr. Williams?"

"Yes." Gregory answered, clearing his throat.

Five minutes on the witness stand under questioning by a hostile attorney can be an eternity. Gregory would be on more than an hour.

"Weren't you the recording officer out there that day?"

"Yes." Gregory had been given the choice assignment over the more experienced Purcell and the more intelligent Duncan.

"And weren't you designated by Undersheriff Cartoscelli to record the location of the graves and the items recovered?"

"Yes."

"And you didn't record the locations, did you?"

"No."

"On any one of these seven graves?"

"That is right."

"You have no record in Sutter County whatsoever as to what the distances were, or where these graves were, do you?"

"No. We had the graves." Gregory was pugnacious still.

Hawk began on victim number 4, E-2-4, the man with the beard. Yes, he was in the second grave. His report was accurate; this was the information "that I was given by Captain Purcell. Exactly what is in the report."

"You were never even there?"

"No."

"Did you record on the basis of hearsay information?"

"Yes."

"You don't know anything at all about E-2-4?"

"No."

"Never saw it?"

"No."

"You don't even know where the grave is then, do you?"

"Basically, no."

"Is Mr. Purcell's name written on that report?"

"No."

"Are you saying you observed it?"

"I didn't say I observed it."

"Does it state, 'Purcell observed it,' or 'Cartoscelli observed it'?" Gregory hawked loudly, his neck a wattle red. "And you wrote a police report indicating what your observations were, and they weren't yours at all?"

"That is right."

Gregory was weary of the hammering. Hawk then asked the detective to demonstrate how he had taken the receipts from Cartoscelli, Gregory fumbling clumsily as he said, "I accepted them by one corner of the paper itself."

Gregory conceded he had not told anyone to lift prints from the receipts or packages. Days later he attended a meeting, he testified, at which the district attorney decided not to attempt to secure fingerprints for fear of ruining the documents.

"Do you know of any expertise that Mr. Teja has in lifting finger-prints?"

"I am not aware of any."

On direct examination by Williams, Gregory had testified that the body in the first grave was "pliable, soft and cool," without the odor of de-composition. Where was that in Gregory's report, Hawk asked.

"It's not in the report," Gregory answered softly.

"That's from memory from seventeen months ago?"

"Yes."

"Is that an important fact?"

"I think so, yes."

"You left it out of your report. Right?"

"Yes."

"Another mistake, huh?"

"You might say so, yes."

During the noon recess, Hawk asked Judge Patton to fix bail for Corona, Williams declining to stipulate that bail might be set on the ground that the decision was Teja's to make. Patton was concerned with the effect Corona's release would have upon the prosecution's case. "Certainly it would appear to me if he is released on bail and the pub-licity connected necessarily with it would be practically a finding that the People's case is of such a nature that it might be expected that the jury would certainly be prejudiced by it—to the extent that they couldn't there-after determine the question of innocence or guilt." The judge was on un-familiar ground again, unsure of the law or his reasoning.

"I might point out that under the law that isn't the real test," Hawk replied, "and that what you are really confronted with is the evidence that you have heard so far taken together with the representation by the district attorney that the blood evidence that they have damages them, and that there is reasonable doubt as to the guilt or innocence. The question of Juan being released on bail shouldn't turn on what effect there might be on the jury."

Judge Patton agreed. They would set a date for a bail hearing in the morning.

The noon hour was only a furlough for Detective Gregory. Amused by the ease of it, Hawk resumed his questioning. What were the dimensions of the graves? They weren't on the report.

"You didn't take the dimensions of any of these graves, did you?"

"No."

"And you don't have the depths, do you?"

"No."

"You don't have the location, do you?"

"No." Gregory was docile, anything to get the ordeal over.

"You didn't take any soil samples out of the grave, did you?"

"No."

"And you don't know the temperatures in the grave, do you?"

"No."

"You didn't measure anything."

"No."

"And nobody else did."

"No."

"Nor did anyone at any time fix the locations in writing as to where those graves were?"

"Not to my knowledge."

"That's all, Officer. Thank you very much." Hawk was smiling as he sat down. Gregory walked heavily from the courtroom; he understood now Cartoscelli's warning.

Later that afternoon, Hawk questioned Russell Parmer, the state's fingerprint expert, about the process of lifting fingerprints from paper. Did it destroy the document as the district attorney claimed? Not as a rule. The documents were photographed first. Certain mixtures of the chemicals used would make the ink run, but CII did not use those. The originals might be slightly discolored for a period of time, the discoloration fading gradually, but the photograph taken before the examination was a control and precaution.

"Did Mr. Teja, the district attorney, ever consult with you about this problem?"

"No, sir."

"Anybody from Sutter County ever bother to ask you anything at all about trying to lift prints off that?" Hawk asked, pointing to the receipts.

"Not that I recall."

Called to identify photographs he had taken of the third grave site, Deputy Sheriff Roger Mason leaned forward into the microphone on the witness stand as Hawk began his cross-examination.

Designated the prosecution's evidence officer, Mason was the only witness permitted in the courtroom while others were testifying. "You were present in court today and you heard Mr. Gregory testify that his report showed that this bearded man was E-2-4. Do you remember that?" Hawk asked.

Mason nodded. "Yes, sir, I was present."

"And that was the only bearded man out there, wasn't it?" Hawk prowled the open area between the counsel table and the jury box.

"To my knowledge I only observed one bearded man. Yes, sir." Mason was calm, an effective witness, perhaps the prosecution's best to that point, Hawk realized.

"How did you mark him?" Hawk held up Mason's photograph of the bearded man.

"This is not the one that I observed."

"Would you answer my question?"

"I marked that photograph E-2, sir," Mason said, his voice falling in resignation.

"Which coincides with his report, doesn't it, that the bearded man was E-2?"

"Yes, sir."

"Okay, now, that photograph that I have shown you, you have told us that there was only one man that you recall that had a beard?"

Mason realized where Hawk was leading him. He shifted in his seat, trying to find a more comfortable position.

"Yes, sir."

"And this is a picture of that man?"

"Yes, sir."

"Is that your testimony here under oath, that this man, this bearded man, was not at E-2-4, as you testified yesterday?"

"No, sir."

"Where was he?"

Mason had to affirm his earlier testimony. "He should have been marked 4-6."

"And if his name is Donald Smith, Donald Smith should be E-4-6?"

"Yes, sir."

"Not E-2-4?"

"No, sir."

"As the photograph is marked?"

"Yes, sir." Mason's calm was shaken, his answers more terse.

"And not E-2-4, as Mr. Gregory's reports say?"

"Mr. Gregory's report relates to a bearded man. I observed a bearded man."

"In E-2-4?"

"Yes, sir." Trying to protect a fellow officer, Mason had erred.

"Are you sure you want to say that?"

"Yes, sir." Mason looked surprised.

"Well, then, when this is marked E-2, why did you say it was previously mismarked? Are you saying that photograph is correct?"

"That photograph is incorrect," Mason hewing to his earlier testimony.

"The marking should be what, then?"

"4-6."

"So any report written by the sheriff's office up there which says the bearded man was in E-2 would be inaccurate?"

Mason erred a second time, trying to protect Gregory. "There was a bearded man I observed in E-2."

"Are there two bearded men?" Hawk's voice was mild. Mason was either stupid or lying. Hawk didn't care which; the photograph and report contradicted the indictment.

"I have no knowledge there were two. I only observed one bearded man."

"Well, how do you wind up with two numbers for the same man?"

"I mistakenly numbered that photograph E-2. The subject I saw at E-2 had a beard. I did not see the subject removed from the grave at E-4, but it is my understanding that he has a beard."

"You are saying that there are two bearded men?"

"The information that I have at this time—Yes, sir." Mason had now contradicted himself.

Hawk showed Mason a second photograph which Cristi had pulled from the files, a photo Mason had marked E-4. "Show me the beard."

"I can't observe a beard in this photograph, sir."

"Is that because there isn't any beard? Isn't that right? Unless you shaved him down at the morgue?" Ten of the jurors were openly smiling at his joke, Hawk noted. Only Mrs. Blazek and the man next to her, Donald Rogers, were straightfaced. "In view of those two photographs, do you still want to sit there under oath and testify there were two bearded men?"

"To my knowledge."

"You haven't got any other photographs of bearded men except this one you marked E-2?"

"No."

"Do you still want to say under oath that there were two bearded men?" Hawk asked again.

Mason was caught. "Yes, to my knowledge."

"How do you account for the fact that the photograph shows that the man in the photograph has no beard?"

"I cannot, sir." Like Gregory before him, Mason had seen the elephant. Hawk resumed stalking across the room from Mason. "Now, you are telling us the bearded man was Smith?"

"Yes."

"And you testified today that Smith is down at E-4-6?"

"Yes, sir."

"Looking at this photograph, that is not correct, is it?"

"That is a mistake on the photograph also." Mason elected to shoulder further blame in order to avoid challenging the indictment.

"I see. The only bearded man you got a picture of is marked E-2, isn't that so?"

"Yes, sir."

"And that is consistent with Gregory's report, isn't it?"

"Yes, sir."

"And it is inconsistent with the rest of this case, isn't it?"

"I don't quite understand."

Hawk could not resist. "Well, tell me how it is that Smith wanders up and down that river?"

"That is argumentative," Judge Patton broke in. "It is ordered stricken."

To explain the obvious confusions surrounding the numbering of the bodies, and especially the "body switch" of Melford Sample from E-1 to E-2, Williams called four of the mortuary workers who had picked up the bodies from along the riverbank. Successively, the four men agreed they had loaded the bodies in two station wagons; then driven to the mortuary in Yuba City; and had unloaded the bodies, wrapped in canvas bags, on the floor of the mortuary garage in the order in which the bodies had been picked up. They contradicted one another, however, as to the procedure—whether the first body was loaded on the left- or right-hand side of the wagons, and laid out from the left to the right on the floor of the garage. Though ostensibly tagged on the Sullivan ranch, some bodies had come into the mortuary without identification; the morticians took the responsibility of labelling them prior to the autopsies. They had erred too.

That afternoon's news about the trial centered on the "collapse looming in the case, already wobbling from continued attacks by the defense," as the *Appeal-Democrat* put it.

On the following morning, District Attorney Teja appeared in chambers for the first time in two days to oppose the bail motion on the technical ground that his office had not received the notice required by law. Teja was frightened; even if the case were not dismissed, the granting of bail would be tantamount to a not-guilty verdict.

Hawk reviewed the evidence presented in court and summarized Williams' previous admissions that the physical evidence damaged their case. "So at this point it comes down to the additional thing which you have twice in chambers heard Mr. Williams express, not that he had a reasonable doubt whether he could convict Mr. Corona, but that he as a man has reasonable doubt as to Mr. Corona's guilt or innocence." Hawk was earnestly appealing to Judge Patton, pleading for his client, no longer the conqueror of the courtroom, but an advocate in chambers.

"The test is, as I understand the law, that Mr. Corona remains in jail so long as the presumption of his guilt is great—or how is it?—great or—"

"When the proof of his guilt is evident or the presumption thereof great," the judge amended.

"To hold Juan Corona in custody any further is just inhuman, and in the name of all that is real and human and right, that they have reached the stage where Juan is just entitled to bail, Your Honor."

Judge Patton needed time to talk with colleagues. "It is a very simple proposition. Does the court have either the power or the responsibility to reevaluate testimony or other matters presented during the course of the trial, to determine whether a defendant who has previously been held not to be entitled to bail should be admitted to bail."

The black robe seemed heavy that morning. "This is a most startling suggestion, that the court would have this responsibility or might have the power to do that during the course of trial. Because when is this particular point to be reached? What further consideration is to be given, if something else comes in which is very strong, for example? Are you going to revoke bail then?"

This case was distinguished from all others, Hawk argued, in that "the man who is chiefly responsible at this point for having carried the ball has twice told you that he has reasonable doubt as to the man's guilt or innocence."

"I agree that that is an astounding comment, Mr. Hawk," Judge Patton said with a faint smile.

"And I notice that Mr. Williams sits here very silently—and I don't think it is any secret, Your Honor, that this case is going on at this point not because Bartley Williams wants to proceed with it. I think Bartley Williams is an honest and ethical guy and does not wish to proceed to prosecute a man when he believes there is a reasonable doubt as to his guilt.

"I think the only reason this case is continuing today and will continue hereafter is that Dave Teja and Roy Whiteaker are fighting for their political lives and nothing else."

The bail hearing was set for the following Friday, ten days off.

19

The Duty of the Court

October 12-20, 1972

It was probably the oddest week in the history of American jurisprudence, Hawk said later, and he was enjoying every minute of it. Judge Patton had set Hawk's motion for bail for a hearing on the twentieth, a motion in midtrial without precedent anywhere in the country, if Hawk read the case books right.

Hawk had talked privately with enough reporters to be sure that the story would be out. The press section was full again. Half the reporters were still ferreting out the possibility of a deal that would end the case, dropping the civil suit against the county in exchange for dismissal of all charges against Corona. The other half took Williams' denials at face value and turned instead to the possibility of bail for the defendant. The headlines were big again, the Corona story near the top of the TV news programs, alternating with the McGovern–Nixon campaign and presidential advisor Henry Kissinger's worldwide efforts to end the Vietnamese war. There was no way the jury could miss hearing about these new turns even though the judge's instructions barred them from news reports of the trial. This jury didn't pay that much attention to the judge anyway; one juror even joked with Cristi Hawk in the hallway during recesses. If anything was prohibited, that was. Hawk could just see those jurors, running home as he did to see the evening's news. It was understandable; for the first time in their lives, they were part of a big news story.

On Thursday, the deputy prosecutor had called Wilbur Terry, one of the officers who had dug for bodies along the riverbank. Terry came into court with a manila file full of reports that neither Hawk nor Williams had ever seen. In chambers, Judge Patton had raged, "I am appalled. This is about the seventh time additional reports have come forward since we started this case." It was just insufferable, the judge pounded, "The district attorney's office certainly has a responsibility to inquire of its Sheriff's Department to see what reports they had, and to get all available reports, instead of just popping up in this manner. It is absolutely ridiculous. It is outrageous."

Williams conceded there were "occasions when there has been difficulty. We keep getting more things from the sheriff's office that we did not know were in existence." The discovery matter "is an obvious mess," Williams added, as frustrated as the judge was angry.

Judge Patton ordered the sheriff and district attorney to be in court the following morning. The sheriff was to commence an immediate search of his file on the case—by then bulking to a four-drawer filing cabinet.

In chambers on Friday morning, Hawk persuaded Judge Patton to order a chagrined Sheriff Whiteaker to bring the entire file into court. It was an unparalleled order, permitting the defense to comb through the law enforcement agency's files on a case. Hawk asked for a day to go through the material, urging, "Your Honor, I feel that if you don't give me the time, the defendant's rights are being prejudiced to go on. It is not my fault. I could respond to all this"—the district attorney's insistence that the defense had everything. "I was warned several times about Mr. Teja's practices. Your Honor has seen all of this late filing routine that he has when a hearing is coming up on Monday, he mails out points and authorities late Friday night. And in my opinion he's less than the most frank and honest attorney I have ever dealt with."

The one day stretched to three. On Monday, Hawk discovered eighty-three reports and a clutch of photos in the files which had not been turned over to him, the most important dealing with the investigation of Natividad Corona and the Guadalajara Café incident. By the end of the search through the records, Hawk had accumulated 1,656 pages of material. Much of it was of no value, including correspondence between the Sheriff's Department and people who had written in May and June 1971, seeking information about missing relatives, but Hawk could not know that until he had read it all. He needed a continuance of at least two weeks to read the reports and decide which ones needed investigation. On the other hand, a postponement of the trial would, in effect, punish his imprisoned client for the dereliction of the prosecution. But if he pushed ahead, he would be forced to cross-examine witnesses without having fully prepared himself, a technical but real violation of Corona's right to effective counsel. The obvious answer, Hawk reasoned, would be to grant bail and delay the trial.

The decision to grant bail lay entirely within the discretion of Judge Patton, upon his estimation of the weight of the evidence. On Monday, Hawk believed he had found the means to tip the balance in Corona's favor.

Jerry Cohen was an experienced reporter, assigned by the Los Angeles *Times* to a loosely defined "crime" or "police" beat. Skeptical, admittedly prosecution-minded, Cohen was both persistent and friendly. In July of

1971, he had been one of three reporters picked by Hawk to share the exclusive interview of Corona in jail. Because of that, Hawk considered him to be one of the first recruits to Corona's cause, even though Cohen repeatedly expressed his doubts—about Hawk's capacity in the courtroom, Corona's innocence, the prosecution's case.

Attracted by wire service accounts of the secret in-chambers sessions, of the rumors that the case would be dismissed, Cohen flew from Los Angeles to Fairfield in hope of getting another exclusive, or near-exclusive.

Jerry Cohen was to be the lever, along with his prestigious newspaper, and its Times-Post News Service, Hawk believed. Through the paper, Hawk could bring public pressure to bear on Judge Patton, a man who appeared to be sensitive to community sentiment. At the same time, Hawk would be able once and for all to convince the skeptical Cohen that Corona was a victim of an inept Sheriff's Department.

Risking another contempt citation, Hawk gave Cohen a copy of the transcript of the in-chambers session of the previous week. On Tuesday, October 17, the *Times'* front-page story headlined "Prosecution, Sheriff Bungling Corona Case, Judge Declares." Cohen's story hung on Judge Patton's remark, "I would say at this point it appears the investigation was inept, the preparation inefficient and the prosecution inadequate."

Cohen's story was on the streets with the Los Angeles *Times* bulldog edition on Monday evening. By Tuesday morning, every reporter covering the trial had it, either from Hawk or from the wire services. In a statement to the *Appeal-Democrat* that day, Sheriff Roy Whiteaker agreed that mistakes had been made, but that the investigation had been thorough.

For the next two days, the Corona story came from Yuba City, newsmen scouring the town for reactions to the judge's comment and the apparent weakness of the prosecution's case. "Hell, no way, are we interested in any deal with Hawk," the county's administrative officer, Larry Cilley, told Eric Davis of the *Appeal-Democrat*. Davis' story reported:

> The administrator said there is "no lack of confidence for those of us in the county family" for the way the case is being handled and he said that Teja is "smart like a fox" and he "works just like a football coach."

> Of the judge's comments on the case, Cilley said, ". . . I don't think they're in the best interest of the case for either side." Cilley said that the prosecution "fully anticipated that this segment of the case would be difficult" but that "apparently the judge has become somewhat impatient."

> Cilley said the "only thing" that bothers him about the way Williams is handling the case "is that he was too open" during in-chambers sessions.

> Williams "has indicated some dissatisfaction," Cilley said, adding that if the attorney is "really bothered . . . I think we should arrange for some gradual phase-out of his services."

Goaded by the adverse publicity, Sheriff Whiteaker took the risk of a contempt of court citation to tell Los Angeles *Times* reporter Ken Reich, "I've never been involved in a major criminal case where there were not mistakes." In this instance, Whiteaker acknowledged that "a couple of bodies were mislabeled," but declined further comment.

The gag order was ignored by everyone. A reporter asked Judge Patton during a recess on Tuesday if the Corona case were the "strangest" in his career. The usually distant judge surprised the reporter by answering, "Yes, it is."

On Friday afternoon, October 20, the courtroom was filled for the bail hearing, the second floor hallway crowded with spectators turned away when the seventy seats were taken. The Corona family sat in a row, Gloria twisting and untwisting a wrinkled handkerchief. In the holding cell across the narrow hall from the courtroom, her husband stood uncomfortably, shifting from one leg to another, a Bible gripped in his hands. He had prayed last night; he was silently praying now. God would provide, he assured his attorney. Hawk smiled with him; God and a good argument in court.

Hawk began, pointing to a blue suitcase he had placed on the counsel table. "This is the material which we received in the last few days. It consists of 1,656 pages. It weighs twenty-two pounds."

Standing behind the counsel table, Hawk spoke quietly for five minutes. "At this point, the legal checkmate that Mr. Teja has put the court in and myself in is do we proceed on Tuesday, and in so doing violate Mr. Corona's right to effective counsel or is the trial delayed and thus violate his right to a speedy trial?

"His right to due process, I think, has already been violated by Mr. Teja, and what I consider to be nothing short of the sheerest and rankest dishonesty I have ever seen on the part of the district attorney. That is the background; therein we stand."

Hawk then began a review of the evidence, arguing that the facts had changed considerably since July 1971, when "Mr. Teja put on what I would consider a dishonest representation" to the Grand Jury. "The situation as it stands now is such that the evidence is no longer great that Mr. Corona is guilty. There is no longer a presumption and I am pointing out to you the things that have happened, the hopeless confusion on this gigantic board here"—Hawk waved vaguely at People's Exhibit 1, the large map—"officers who can't put anything anyplace. Tire tracks that were never checked other than against Mr. Corona after he was arrested.

"You know, I think, from the representations of Mr. Williams on the day in which he said that he personally had reasonable doubt as to Mr. Corona's guilt or innocence—you know that the machete will not match. You will find when Mr. Stottlemyer testifies that nothing Mr. Corona had cut these branches in any way."

From the testimony, Judge Patton would now know, Hawk continued, that the "police officers most miserably mishandled the evidence at the site of grave E-1." The cigarette butt found in the grave was smoked by a man with Type O blood; Corona and the victim were both Type A. The blood on the end of the gun barrel was also Type O; the only man who was shot was Type A also.

"At this point Juan has been in jail seventeen months. Based upon what I believe to be the poorest investigation I have ever heard of or could consider—"

"Your Honor, I'm going to object to that characterization." The district attorney was angry.

"Very well," the judge noted. "Proceed, Mr. Hawk."

"And it seems to me that seventeen months is long enough. That Mr. Corona, by reason of the fact that I have in front of me almost seventeen-hundred pages of material approaching the seventh week of this trial, that the only way Mr. Corona's rights can be preserved at all is to grant him bail or to release him on his own recognizance. Otherwise, if we proceed on Tuesday, we violate his right to effective counsel and I think we would irreparably damage it.

"I think you are in a very difficult position, and I at least want to say publicly that I think it is no fault of yours and I think it is no fault of mine, nor is it any fault of Juan Corona's, and that just basic human decency just seems to demand that this man ought to be released after all this period of time being held on what is called an investigation.

"I have nothing further," Hawk said with a half sigh. Lacking a legal precedent, he had done the best he could to argue on behalf of his client.

The district attorney began his reply by defending the Grand Jury proceeding, adding that most of the material in the blue suitcase had long since been turned over to Hawk. Teja then picked up an argument he was to use again in his closing argument.

"We don't know from Mr. Stottlemyer's report, nor will we know until he testifies, whether or not it is indeed a fact that nothing the defendant had will match the striations, but what Mr. Hawk is pitting this portion of his argument on, Your Honor, is the fact that the evidence does not show that one particular weapon found in the defendant's possession killed one particular victim. There is no suggestion whatsoever on the basis of Mr. Stottlemyer's report, which the court has before it, or on Mr. Hawk's representation that this particular weapon was not used to kill one of the other twenty-four victims."

The blood on the two knives found in the mess hall, the splatters of blood in the van, the ledger with "several of the identified victims in this case," the cocked pistol found in Corona's desk—all spoke for themselves, Teja continued. At the very least, the cigarette butt suggested was that "somebody else was involved in the burial or the killing of that particular victim." That the blood on the pistol did not match "certainly does not exclude the practical consideration that the gun may have been used as a bludgeon" on another victim.

"Your Honor," Hawk asked, "is he going to be allowed to conjecture when the jury can't?"

"I am not conjecturing any more than Mr. Hawk was conjecturing today," Teja retorted.

"He talks utter nonsense. The court knows enough about the evidence to realize that," Hawk insisted.

"Very well. Leave the judgment to me then, Mr. Hawk," Judge Patton said equably.

There was not, Teja recognized, any controlling legal precedent for granting or withholding bail. Four prior bail motions had been made by the defendant, all unsuccessful; the fifth placed the court "in a very ticklish situation."

Hawk interrupted to point out that the judge had previously agreed "that whether or not Mr. Corona is entitled to bail does not turn upon what effect it might have upon a jury either way."

Hawk had upset the district attorney by breaking into the middle of his argument; now he refused to yield. "We are talking here, Your Honor, not just in the abstract, we are talking about a man. He lives and he breathes and he has had to do it for the past seventeen months under the most abnormal circumstances that could be known to any person. He has had to do it incarcerated; he has been away from his wife; he has been away from his children and he has been away from them on what has been described by me as an outrageous and very inept investigation."

He was wound up, the words coming easily, rebutting again rather than opening. "You are in a very difficult position, I know it, but it just seems to me that in view of all of this and in view of Mr. William's statement that he has reasonable doubt, how can the prosecution, any part of it, get up and tell you now that the presumption of his guilt is great?

"It is not great when one of the prosecutors expresses reasonable doubt," Hawk's voice rose with excitement. "And I ask you in the name of all that is right and human in this world to set bail for Juan." The passion was burned out. "I have nothing further to say."

Above all else, Judge Patton enjoyed this—a close legal question to be decided. "Both counsel have referred to a section of *Corpus Juris Secundum* on this subject, which I would like to take the credit for having pointed out to counsel in my previous research, and the quote from that article is: 'That once the trial begins, the right to be released on bail is circumscribed by pressing considerations and admittance to bail during trial has been held not to be of right.'

"I believe there are very obvious reasons as to why the court during the progress of a criminal proceeding should not be expected to and should not review a consideration of the possible right to bail based upon testimony from time to time during the course of the trial. That would place the court in a position of perhaps reevaluating additional testimony, and forming other tentative opinions."

The judge scanned the notes he had drafted in the past week. This was to be a ten-part case, the trial was only in the first part. Hawk's face fell; the district attorney smiled slightly. Patton was going to rule against the motion.

"Certainly there have been many inconsistencies developed in the testimony. It would appear to me, however, that not only is the case in a very preliminary stage, but also it might perhaps be more aptly stated that the evidence so far does not relate to certain of those items [by] which the court would be perhaps most influenced.

"The court believes that it should not endeavor to weigh the testimony at this stage—at least to determine whether or not the defendant may have a right to bail."

Hawk slumped in his chair, wilted, not even anger left. For the first time, Bartley Williams looked up from the table, a load lifted.

The judge cleared his throat. "However, the matter that really touches me strongly relates to the representation that has been made on several occasions by the special prosecutor in this matter, the man really employed to try this case, the man who is principally responsible for the preparation and presentation and the man who should be most knowledgeable as to the extent and character of this case, and that man has told the court on several occasions that he has a reasonable doubt as to the defendant's guilt."

Corona listened intently, sensing something in the judge's words. He fingered the rosary through the cloth of his pants. God would provide.

"What that statement really says to the court in a layman's language is, as we recognize, the jury's duty would be to return a verdict of not guilty." Judge Patton was speaking to the reporters and through them, to the public. "So the special prosecutor, Mr. Williams, has really told the court that under his analysis of this case it is his judgment that the proper verdict is that of not guilty. Is that not a matter which should weigh most heavily in the court's consideration and determination as to whether the court should set bail for Mr. Corona?"

Hawk had heard it now. Patton had found one of the "pressing considerations" his lawbook told him about.

"The court is an instrument to see that justice is done. Justice for the

People, justice for Mr. Corona. And here is a man who has been held in jail without bail for almost seventeen months. The People represent that this trial is going to take from six to eight months, and now they urge the court to refuse to set bail for this man when their chief agent has told the court that under his view of this case the proper verdict will be that of not guilty."

Staring at the deputy district attorney, Judge Patton demanded "some further explanation from the People as to how they can possibly urge that this court refuse to consider any bail."

Williams stood up slowly. "There were five or six evidentiary areas that were of concern to the prosecution and that these areas, unless clarified or straightened out or something, could very well constitute reasonable doubt in this case. And, of course, I indicated to the court that these investigations were continuing." Williams was shading his earlier statement, attempting to back off from it.

"Now, I would like to point out to the court that it is entirely possible that that tentative opinion expressing reasonable doubt could very well change back and forth a half-a-dozen times during the course of a trial, and I don't think this is unusual in a long and complicated trial based primarily on circumstantial evidence."

His right hand in his pants pocket, the change there rattling, Williams went on. "We had two sets of tire tracks in the case. And now we have found out that it was the tire track from the north riverbottom orchard that went to CII and not the tire tracks at Kenneth Whitacre's grave. We have investigated this and found out that there is an extreme likelihood that the actual tire tracks at Kenneth Whitacre's grave match up with Juan Corona's vehicles."

Because of the continuing investigation's results, "I can actually represent to the court as of this time I no longer have any reasonable doubt as to Mr. Corona's guilt." Hawk was disappointed, Corona quizzical. Hawk wondered if Williams had been pressured into changing his mind. "He's just not the man I thought he was," Hawk said later.

"In other words," Williams concluded, "my position has changed within ten days on this issue. So I just think that the court should not hang everything onto this very frank and honest admission made to the court ten days ago in chambers. I think the People's case would be extremely prejudiced by granting bail." Further, there were six other areas still under investigation which could solidify his new-found conviction. Reports would be forthcoming "throughout the trial. I feel it is wrong for the prosecution to get banged over the head every time we come forward with a new report, because this is the nature of the case."

Judge Patton shook his head slowly. "I can't accept the representation that you haven't gotten around to investigate these matters before. I think this representation that you've still got an investigation going on after almost a year and a half is almost incredulous.

"And I know, of course—and I am not accusing the prosecution of it in this case—the strategy might be that the investigation is not completed intentionally so that reports need not be turned over to the defense until a very late date. I know it has happened in others and this is a matter that concerns me." Judge Patton was scolding Williams.

"But then you represent also that, well, as these additional matters come in, you are not certain what they are going to be, it may be that your belief of reasonable doubt might change back, and so you really are equivocal as to what your attitude really is in this case.

"Again, I would remind the People that their duty is to see that justice is done and that conviction is not synonymous necessarily with justice."

Judge Patton wagged his finger at the two prosecutors. "I expect and the law demands that the State be fair with all defendants before the Bar and it is the duty of the court—and every sense of justice—demands that this be done."

Williams stared at the floor in front of the bench. "All we can do is merely be very frank in our disclosures to both the court and to counsel."

"Well, I am not satisfied with frankness. It almost approaches a dereliction of duty, in my view," Judge Patton snapped, borrowing an argument Hawk had made repeatedly in chambers. "The court instructed this jury panel at various times while they were being questioned and pointed out to them the fact that the defendant's being in custody is not evidence as to his guilt, and they are not permitted to infer or speculate from this that he is more likely to be guilty than innocent. The court could just as well tell the jury the fact that the defendant has been released on bail is no evidence whatsoever of his innocence and that the verdict must be based solely and entirely upon the evidence presented here during the course of the trial."

Reporters could sense the tension in the courtroom. Hawk inched forward to the edge of his seat, his right hand reaching for Corona's arm. Patton was going to give it to them, finally going to give him one of the "goodies."

Williams was struggling. "I know that the court can instruct the jury, but as a practical matter, do you think that rejoinder or admonition to the jury is really effective in light of the publicity attendant with this case?"

Judge Patton had had enough argument; he was ready to rule. "The matter before the court is of utmost significance involving twenty-five homicides and it is most imperative that the matter be fully and fairly presented, recognizing the rights of both sides and this matter of bail which has been presented to the court before and refused and, as I have stated, in reviewing arguments I would give no weight and would not grant or set bail merely upon an evaluation of partial evidence during the presentment and during the course of trial.

"And my concern has gone, as I stated, Mr. Williams, to your representation to the court as to your belief that you had reasonable doubt as to the defendant's guilt."

Judge Patton turned to the excited defense attorney. "Anything further, Mr. Hawk?"

The excitement churned in his stomach. "No, Your Honor."

"For the People?"

The district attorney stood up. "I might say two things, Your Honor, in connection with the case of this magnitude. It is my personal opinion, for whatever value this might have, that the Juan Corona case will never be completely investigated. For years and years matters are still going to be called to people's attention that would require some effort if the facts are ever indeed to be nailed down as finally they might be." Teja's voice was thin, barely audible. "But insofar as Mr. Williams' representation to the court of ten days ago is concerned, I might make the representation that I have never had any doubt in this area myself, Your Honor, not at the time the matter was presented to the Grand Jury, not ten days ago, and not now." The district attorney sat down woodenly.

"Very well. Submitted, gentlemen?" Judge Patton asked.

"Yes, Your Honor," Hawk answered, his heart pounding.

Judge Patton paused, conscious of the tension and the air conditioner's hum in the silence. "Denied."

Silence. Hawk shook his head, trying to clear the disbelief. "Bail is denied, Your Honor?"

"Yes, denied." Judge Patton half stood as a woman in the audience shrieked, "Oh"—despair, protest, lament in the cry.

"You're no judge," a man shouted, the restraint gone. "Justice, justice. There is no justice here. There is no justice for us," yelled another as the judge scuttled for the door to his chambers, the bailiff quickly following. The door closed as someone shouted, "What kind of judge are you anyway?"

Hawk had miscalculated. By releasing the transcript of the in-chambers session to the Los Angeles *Times* he had made it possible for Judge Patton publicly to excoriate the prosecution. Had his private scolding not been made public he would not have said anything in open court. His "ineptinefficient-inadequate" comment widely circulated, the judge could balance his denial of bail with a further scolding. Once again, he would appear to be fair, denying bail yet scorning the prosecution as he did so.

Judge Patton had a rigorous sense of even-handed justice.

20

Shannon's Confusions
October 24-November 3, 1972

For the next two weeks, Richard Hawk pecked away at prosecution witnesses, humiliating those whom he didn't like, ridiculing others. Williams and Teja were helpless to stop the defense attorney, all the more abrasive since Judge Patton had denied both bail and a continuance to review the reports culled from the sheriff's files. So Patton too was an opponent, but Hawk no longer cared. He would fight them all, including the new attorney Teja was hiring to work on the case. The trial of Juan Corona had become the passion of Richard Hawk. Juan Corona had become Richard Hawk's cause.

The strain was telling. Hawk was doing battle on behalf of Juan Corona, but he was doing it alone, against two attorneys, eight members of the district attorney's staff, and, sometime soon, a third trial deputy to help Williams. In the evenings, after the court session, Hawk would drink with newsmen at the Vista Club across the street while Cristi waited in the car—talking about the day's proceedings or, when that was talked out, telling and retelling anecdotes of other cases, other clients, other times.

The nights were restless hours of fitful sleep on the couch, late-late television movies; the mornings before court laced with temper-tossed demands for his jacket, his new glasses, his briefcase, or the tie he had left in the back seat of the car.

The case was too big for one man, Hawk complained. Only because he had lived with it so many months could he keep it manageable. Things sometimes slipped by him which he would have to pick up when the witness came back—thank God for their strange organization of the case. He was behind in his filing, and Cristi didn't know enough of the intricacies to do it for him.

Hawk and the reporters agreed he had the jury, though. The only hostile member was Mrs. Blazek, the retired schoolteacher who frowned disapprovingly when he cross-examined witnesses. Mrs. Blazek didn't smile at the prosecutors though; that was something. It suggested that her animosity was directed at Hawk personally, not at Corona. Juror Number 2, Owen, the fundamentalist who always wore a tie, was smiling now. If Owen found the prosecution's case humorous, that meant the whole back row of the jury shared that opinion, Hawk believed. The best by far was Hicks, the young Vietnam veteran; when Detective Gregory came into court to testify for the third time, Hicks had looked at the defense lawyer and frankly smiled. Hicks and Johnson, the retired marine, seemed to be the strongest personalities on the jury, the most likely to be foreman. It wouldn't be Phillips, the other ex-master sergeant; Hawk would bet against him. Hawk doubted he was even a very strong man. Johnson would be the most likely foreman. He was independent, strong-minded, the sort of person who could ramrod a jury. He had even started kidding Hawk about Cristi lugging the heavy catalogue cases into the courtroom, the banter in total disregard of the judge's orders against conversation between jurors and attorneys.

Lorenzo was with him, Hawk estimated; that gave him another strong personality. Right now only two or three in the front row were a puzzle: Rogers, Broksell, and Gallipeo, hard to figure, but followers. Mrs. Underwood, juror number 11, he couldn't count her as being especially good. She smiled at the Corona family sometimes, but she didn't seem to be particularly strong. Another follower.

"Phillips, Johnson, Hicks, Lorenzo, you give me those four and I'll give you the other eight." It was his jury, thanks in part to the actions of the prosecutors.

This jury was a laughing, happy group of people, and Hawk had never seen a smiling jury convict anyone. You could feel that cold wind come off the iceberg when a jury was going to convict. They started getting tense. They didn't say much, didn't show any emotion, wouldn't let you catch their eyes.

By day—in the courtroom—Hawk was confident; only at night did doubts set in. In contrast, Williams was woodenly going through the day in court, often alone at the prosecution's table; at night he was guardedly optimistic. Doctor Guy was checking her tests of the cigarette butt, the cup and spoon which Corona had used, and the gun. The ATF lab was working on the tire tracks sent three weeks before. The two handwriting experts concurred that most if not all of the writing in the ledger was Corona's; they were making up courtroom exhibits now. Best of all, they now had Ronald Fahey reading the transcript, catching up on the case.

Preparing witnesses out-of-court while Williams examined them on the stand, a tired Dave Teja knew he needed help. With Larry Cilley's approval, he had gone hunting for a skilled prosecutor, someone with the trial experience he and Bart Williams lacked to keep Hawk in check. Ronald Wayne Fahey, chief criminal prosecutor for neighboring Sonoma County, had not been Teja's first choice. A half-dozen others had turned Teja down, some with polite excuses, others with barely suppressed laughter. None of them were about to become involved in a case as screwed up as this one was.

Fahey sensed his nine years' of daily trial work were worth a great deal to the anxious district attorney. They finally settled upon $45 an hour, with a minimum guarantee of $10,000. Three hundred sixty dollars a day seemed a lot of money, Cilley agreed with Teja, "but I guess that's what it takes to get a man of good quality and extensive trial experience."

The forty-year-old Fahey took a five-month leave of absence to work on the Corona case, knowing he had everything to gain, and nothing to lose coming in at this point. If Corona were found guilty, he could take credit for having turned the trial around; if it went against them, he could claim that the case was lost before he ever got into it.

Now he was commuting, paid $45 an hour from the moment he said good-bye in the morning to his three children to the moment he got home at night to cold suppers and a sleepy wife.

Teja was delighted with his new associate counsel. Fahey had the quick wit and sharp tongue to match Hawk. If he merely kept a rein on Hawk, it would leave Teja and Williams free to prepare the case.

Teja and Cilley had discussed letting the reluctant Williams out of his contract, of phasing him out of the trial. They agreed that if Williams left now, it would undoubtedly have a bad effect on the jury. Moreover, Teja was unprepared—even afraid—to handle the remaining phases of the case alone. Much of it was highly technical, scientific evidence; Williams had talked to the experts; Williams understood about the blood tests, the neutron activator. Teja had his hands full with the handwriting phase alone. Williams would have to stay on, and do what he could to salvage the first part of the case.

There was little Williams could do. Grave by grave, Hawk had found mistakes. If the defense attorney could not find anything new, he rehashed the old, eliciting the same damning errors from new witnesses. Six sets of fingers from the first seven graves found along the riverbank had been sent to CII unlabeled; the two morticians contradicted each other as to who was responsible. Captain Purcell admitted that no one was in command at the morgue; the morticians—who would be paid for burying the unclaimed bodies—had gone about the grisly business of removing fingertips without supervision. Purcell, in charge of the investigation, was made to appear inadequate.

Grave 6. Detective Jerry Harrison had appeared no better than Purcell. On direct examination, he told Williams he had not handled any evidence, that Gregory had collected it as Harrison shoveled the dirt out of the grave. But the next witness, Deputy Sheriff Mason, identified a photo of Harrison reaching down to pick up an item of evidence from the grave. It was embarrassing; deputies were patently lying to avoid responsibility.

The state fingerprint expert, Russell Parmer, resplendent in flowered tie and deep red shirt, repeatedly insisted that his records showed the body in E-1-3 was ten-fingered; that the nine-fingered man was in E-2-4, where Mason's photographs had placed the bearded man. Parmer was also critical of the careless way evidence had been handled, destroying any opportunity to lift prints.

Grave 10. No measurements were taken of the grave. Rather than wait for the morticians, Reserve Deputy Mel Johnson had looped a chain around the body, "and helped pull him out of the hole." Why had Johnson used a chain, Williams asked. "Well, you got to get it out some way and I don't think I wanted to have carried him out by hand."

Grave 11. The evidence, snaked by a mortician from William Kamp's pockets, had not been itemized; some now was missing. Evidence tags were wrongly dated.

Grave 12. The location on the police report differed from that on "the bingo board" by 160 yards.

Grave 15. Evidence was added to an evidence bag after it had been sealed by the officer. Deputy Sizelove's field notes as recording officer differed from the typed police report.

Grave 16. The large map sited the grave in the wrong location. Evidence was handled at the grave site. In some cases no evidence bags were made up, in others the date was omitted. A Social Security card once in the sealed evidence bag was now missing. The red hard-hat attributed to number 16 was actually found at grave 18.

Grave 17. Deputy Rodemaker testified he found a wallet and personal papers while excavating the grave.

"And where was the wallet?" Hawk asked.

"Lying right on top of his stomach."

"Who handled that?"

"I don't recall. I picked it up and handed it to Deputy Sizelove."

"How did you handle it when you picked it up?"

"Just picked it up," Rodemaker said with a shrug.

"You picked it up when you saw it lying there. Do you think maybe the man dug his own hole, laid down and laid the wallet on his chest and chopped his head apart?"

"Objection, Your Honor. That is being facetious," Williams protested.

"No. It is not," Hawk insisted.

Grave 18. Evidence recovered from the grave was missing. The state's fingerprint examiner was not asked to lift prints from any of the items found in the grave. Could Parmer do it? "You never know until you try," he answered. He had done it before, lifting usable prints from cigarette butts, leather wallets, soiled papers.

Grave 21. Officer Sizelove's report did not detail the evidence found in the grave.

Grave 22. Sizelove's field notes were not complete. Evidence was now missing. So, too, was an evidence tag he had placed on a plastic bag at the grave site.

Grave 23. Evidence tags did not coincide with Sizelove's reports, nor did they indicate the chain of possession of the evidence.

Grave 24. Williams attempted to elicit from Russell Parmer a statement that wet or muddy documents would not yield fingerprints. Hawk put the ball back into Williams' court.

"You have looked at a great number of paper documents here during the course of the trial, have you not?"

"Some, yes," Parmer allowed.

"And most of the ones you have looked at, I believe you told us, it would be possible to process for fingerprints?"

"Yes."

"You also told us that Sutter County never asked you to do this?"

"That is correct."

"Did you ever attempt to lift latent prints from a ledger?"

"No, sir."

"They didn't ask you to lift latent prints from a ledger?" Hawk pretended incredulity.

"No, sir."

Grave 25. The trash dump, from which detectives recovered two deposit slips with Juan Corona's name printed on them, a child's knee-length stocking, a wristwatch, the folded shopping news, a shattered mirror, and a broken votary candle holder. One evidence tag was misdated by a month; another had the writing of two different officers on it.

The first attempt to secure fingerprint evidence occurred in December 1971, Captain Purcell testified, after Sacramento Police Sergeant Dave Perales suggested to Teja the two deposit slips be tested. "He wanted to take the documents to his office and test them for prints."

"And, of course, you didn't know at that time whether it was too late, did you?"

"No, sir."

"Nor do you know if it came out negative, that meant there were never any prints there or might have been there and left?"

"No, sir, I don't."

Hawk's next question to the composed Purcell was intended to raise doubts about evidence yet to be introduced. "As a policeman, are you aware of the relative scientific reliability of fingerprint evidence as opposed to handwriting evidence?" The expected objection deflected Hawk to ask, "Have you ever heard of Clifford Irving?"

"Objection. Hearsay. And what is the relevance?" Williams sputtered.

"I don't know whether this is some gentleman involved in this investigation," Judge Patton said with a straight face. "I don't know whether it is relevant or not."

"I should withdraw that," Hawk volunteered. "Clifford Irving, Your Honor, is the man who bilked McGraw-Hill for $750,000."

"Oh. Well, that is clearly irrelevant. Sustained. I don't expect he has had anything to do with the investigation of this case, has he?"

"No, but he sure fooled a lot of handwriting men." Hawk was having trouble hiding a grin.

The entire month of October was a succession of embarrassments for the prosecution. Beyond discrediting the prosecution's case, Hawk's abrasive cross-examinations were reiterating that the state of undress of the victims suggested that these were homosexually motivated murders. Later his expert witness would testify that Corona was totally heterosexual.

Virtually unchecked by the prosecution, Hawk converted even the most innocuous witnesses to his own purposes. District Attorney's investigator Leonard Brunelle had been called only as a foundational witness for the testimony of Byron Shannon, to identify a map of lower Marysville and a series of enlargements of pictures of the area.

"Mr. Teja told you what to take pictures of?"

"That is correct, sir."

"He didn't tell you to take a picture of the Guadalajara Café?"

"He did, yes, sir."

"What happened to that photograph?"

"I was told to remove them from the file." Brunelle's answer made it appear the prosecution was hiding something, as Hawk had broadly hinted all along.

"And when did Mr. Teja tell you to pull out the photographs of the Guadalajara Café?"

"Three days ago."

"Did he tell you why?" Hawk knew he was asking for hearsay testimony and the prosecution would object.

"Yes, sir."

"Why?"

Williams' objection was sustained, leaving the unanswered question hanging over the jury's decision.

Hawk reviewed the photographs Brunelle had taken. "Now, you have seen pictures of a number of hotels, right?"

"Yes, sir."

"And would it be fair to describe these hotels generally as kind of broken down places where a shower is twenty-five cents and a bed is a dollar?"

"That would be a fair description, yes."

"And as places rampant with bedbugs and lice and things like that, old broken down hotels. Is that right?"

"Old broken down hotels. That is right."

"You have to be pretty much at the bottom economically to stay there. Is that fair?"

"Yes, sir."

"Would you tell us the name of the well-known homosexual who registered in those hotels?"

Williams had sensed it was coming, Hawk leading Brunelle to the point of Williams' objection. "Beyond the scope of direct."

The next witness, Byron Shannon, the black recruiter for the labor contractor J. B. Johnson, was even more confused. Slowly, simple question by simple question, Williams pulled Shannon's testimony from him.

Shannon recruited in lower Marysville; he had seen Corona for five or six years in the area. Shannon recognized the photograph of the twenty-first victim, John Henry Jackson, as the man he knew as "Johnson." He had first met Johnson-Jackson at the Day Center in January 1971; they talked for twenty minutes over coffee, Jackson asking for work, Shannon without a job to offer.

He had next seen Jackson in May 1971, when they chanced to meet at the corner of Second and D Streets sometime around the third or fourth of the month. The two men had stood near a stop sign and had talked for five minutes. Shannon was unclear about which corner they had stood on, near which sign; the more the patient-of-necessity Williams attempted to clarify it, the more confused Shannon became. It took more than fifteen minutes of contradictions, confusions, misstatements, and corrections before Shannon could continue. Through it all, Hawk sat with his hand over his mouth, patently hiding his smile. The jury too was laughing.

According to Shannon, as he and Jackson-Johnson stood there talking, Corona drove up to the intersection in a blue-and-white Chevrolet pickup truck. Jackson had yelled at Corona, asking for a job.

"He stayed in the truck and they was talking. So he [Jackson] hollered back to me, 'Well, I ain't going with you. I'm going with this fellow.'" Jackson-Johnson had thrown his bedroll into the rear of the pickup and climbed into the cab with the two men. He had never seen Jackson again.

Williams then moved to have admitted photos of miscellaneous clothing; Hawk "banged him on the head" once more. "I would like the record to show that these exhibits have been in existence, apparently, for some several months. Now, today is the first time I have seen them." Williams admitted Hawk was correct, the jurors following the exchange, aware that they were sharing what had previously been privately argued in chambers. "I move he be cited for contempt and be given time in jail."

Williams picked up his interrupted examination of Shannon, reminding him that three months earlier he had identified clothing worn by Jackson. Slowly, enjoying the attention centered on him, Shannon identified the clothing and bedroll in the photographs as Jackson's. Williams moved the admission of the photographs, Hawk asking they be suppressed on the ground they had been "wantonly withheld." Findings of contempt were not enough after all the lapses, he argued.

The photographs were admitted; Judge Patton had no intention of prejudicing the People's case, already in shaky condition.

Hawk began his cross-examination late in the day with a ploy to circumvent the law stating that a misdemeanor conviction could not be used to impeach a witness. Where did Shannon live?

"419 Thirteenth Street," Shannon answered.

Hawk then moved to mark for identification two photographs of the Yuba County jail. Williams protested, "He is trying to bring out something obviously prejudicial, Your Honor."

"No," Hawk responded. "I am trying to point out the fact that he gave a phony address. He lives at the Yuba County jail."

"As an inmate?"

"Yes; he is a thief. He is doing time in jail. I am entitled to show that." Now the jury knew. "It is a misdemeanor," Williams broke in quickly. The judge ruled any further questions about Shannon's misdemeanor conviction out of bounds.

The following morning, November 1, Hawk, Williams, and the judge began the day in chambers, Williams to receive a five-day jail sentence for withholding the photos in contempt of court, Hawk an additional five days for bringing out Shannon's misdemeanor record.

Only after Shannon had testified did the prosecution furnish the defense attorney a copy of the labor recruiter's arrest record ordered by the court months before. The record indicated that on August 8, 1972, Shannon had been booked for receiving stolen goods, burglary, and conspiracy to sell stolen property; and for four traffic violations run up when he attempted to flee police: reckless driving, failure to yield to a red light and siren, hit and run, and unsafe lane change. Despite a confession to the receiving charge, Shannon was charged in court only with reckless driving and failure to stop for a police officer, both misdemeanors. The felony charges had been dropped by the Yuba County district attorney. In exchange, Shannon pled guilty to the reckless driving charge and received a twenty-day jail sentence; the court dismissed the remaining charge as part of the bargain struck between Shannon and the district attorney. Teja's witness had been salvaged.

Hawk began his cross-examination of Shannon by reviewing the placement of the stop signs at the intersection, deliberately confusing the situation even further and using that lapse to question the witness' reliability as an observer of anything.

"Incidentally, what kind of truck was Mr. Corona driving?"

"A Chevy truck. Blue and white."

Corona's pickup was red and white. Hawk looked through a copy of a statement Shannon had given to sheriff's deputies more than a year before. "Now, what part of the truck was blue?"

"Bottom part. And top was white. It had a canvas on it."

"What color was the canvas?"

"Kind of greenish color. The cab part was white."

"And I believe you also said it said on the side, 'Juan V. Corona, Labor Contractor'?"

"I believe it said it on the side," Shannon answered agreeably. "Wrote right on the side of the pickup, on the canvas." Corona had never owned such a vehicle.

At noon, an excited friend of the Corona family told Hawk that there was such a truck to be seen in lower Marysville. It was owned by Juan Reynosa, a labor contractor who recruited in the Skid Row area, and a brother-in-law of Ray Duron.

Hawk tested Shannon's color perception on William's suit and tie, on a blouse worn by a spectator, a man's pants, a stack of green paper. "You are not color-blind at all, are you?"

"No, I am not."

"And the truck that you saw Mr. Corona in had a blue bottom, white cab, and green top that went over the back of the truck, and the writing said 'Juan V. Corona, Labor Contractor'?"

"That is what it said on there."

What year was it Shannon had seen Jackson-Johnson climb into Corona's pickup?

"Have to be in '70, 1970." A full year before the mass murders.

"What year is this now?"

"1972." Shannon smiled. That was a silly question to ask a grown man.

"So that was about two and one-half years ago that you and Mr. Johnson were standing there. Is that right?"

"That's right." Shannon nodded vigorously. "Yes, about two years ago we were standing there."

On and on Hawk went, Shannon contradicting himself or simply not remembering accurately, insisting the sun rose in the west "the way the street is in Marysville." Yes, he had given two statements to investigators, once in 1970, again a year later. Hawk handed Shannon transcripts of the statements taken in 1971. Yes, these were the ones; Mr. Williams had given him a set to take home and study.

"Would you look at the transcripts, and would you point out to me where you told this big story you have got about Juan Corona in the blue-and-white truck with the green canvas top and how he picked Mr. Johnson up and the bedroll?"

"Objection to the characterization as 'a story.'"

"Sustained."

Hawk challenged Shannon again. His "story" was not there, Williams conceding the transcript impeached his witness.

For the balance of the morning Hawk crossexamined Shannon, who shifted his testimony from moment to moment. The first of the circumstantial evidence witnesses left the courtroom in a snarl of confusions.

21

The Suspect
November 3-10, 1972

Ronald Fahey disliked Richard Hawk, intensely, relentlessly. From the first morning in court on November 3, when Hawk had deliberately humiliated him, Fahey realized he would have to keep a close rein on his own temper.

Hawk had walked over to Fahey standing at the counsel table and introduced himself, the two of them shaking hands. Then Hawk had led Fahey by the elbow to Corona's side, saying, "Juan, I'd like you to meet Ronald Fahey." Corona had stood up and extended his hand. Reflexively Fahey had reached for it. "He's the man they hired to put you in jail for the rest of your life." Fahey snatched his hand back, his face darkening with embarrassment.

The judge, the jury, and the spectators watched the two attorneys closely. Whatever the publicly announced reason—that Williams and Teja needed additional help preparing the case—there was no doubt that Fahey had been hired to keep some check on Hawk; the only question was his capacity. A full day passed uneventfully.

Like fighting cocks circling warily, on the morning of the second day, Fahey and Hawk clashed. Hawk was cross-examining Captain Purcell about the deposit slips taken from the twenty-fifth grave, entered into evidence, and then transported to Sacramento without a proper evidence tag. Deputy Mason had the real responsibility for keeping track of the evidence, didn't he, Hawk asked solicitously.

"Yes."

"Okay. And I assume that you must have believed in good faith that a record was being kept and was somewhere?"

Before Purcell could answer, Fahey objected strenuously to the form of the question.

"Sustained," the judge ruled.

"Well, it is sort of preliminary, laying the groundwork, Your Honor.

I want to make a demand for that record, if it exists. I want to be able to inspect it." Hawk knew there was no master log to the evidence locker, a departure from accepted law enforcement practice. "I will argue it out of the presence of the jury if Mr. Fahey is going to get all excited; I don't want him to get upset and develop an ulcer." Hawk nodded to Fahey.

"Well, I wish, Your Honor," Fahey fired back, "counsel would not make personal comments. And if counsel wants to testify I would ask that he be sworn in, if he has any evidence that he feels should come before the jury." Fahey could hold his own.

Moments later, Fahey took the offensive. Hawk had objected to passing to the jury a partial exhibit—the deposit slips found in the twenty-fifth grave. "This matter went into evidence with a tag. It contains among other things, not only the box that Mr. Fahey is referring to, but it contains some kind of an oil-type paper, oilcloth—"

"We would be—" Fahey interposed.

"Just a minute, please," Hawk cut him off. "You don't really mind, do you?"

Judge Patton frowned. "Address your remarks to the court, not to each other," then admitted the entire exhibit. Fahey gathered up the items and walked to the jury box. "Thank you, Mr. Fahey," Hawk said, smiling unctuously.

The new prosecutor handed over the exhibit, adding, "And at Mr. Hawk's request we are giving you this Winchell's Doughnut box and also this plastic bag which he has described—"

Hawk was on his feet, stung in return. "Your Honor, is it really proper for Mr. Fahey to approach a juror like that and discuss things? I object to his fawning and smiling and telling them what he is doing."

Fahey asked to have the record marked by the court reporter, as if the exchange of tempers were legally significant.

Hawk cut him off. "We have the record typed up, Your Honor; it is not necessary to mark it."

Judge Patton had had enough. "Let's desist from this quibbling back and forth, gentlemen."

The confrontation came in the middle of the afternoon, while Hawk was cross-examining Sacramento County Deputy Coroner Jody Ulrey on the evidence found in grave 25.

"In one of those bags there was a watch?"

"Yes, sir, it appears to be a calendar-type watch."

"What date was showing on the watch when you recovered it?"

"I have no idea, sir."

"Did you make any record of it?"

"No, sir, we didn't."

"Was the watch running?"

"No, sir, it was not."

"You didn't consider that important to make a record of whether it was running or not?" Hawk asked, scanning the property report Ulrey had prepared.

"The condition of the watch was in, I saw no relevance to writing down that it . . . [showed a date numeral of] fourteen or fifteen. Anyway, I couldn't tell because it was . . . [in between]." Ulrey's excuse angered Hawk the more. The matter of the watch was crucial for Corona. It had stopped either at the time Joseph Maczak had been killed, or shortly thereafter, depending upon the tension of the main spring. Maczak then had been killed prior to the fifteenth—of May? Of April? Perhaps of March 1971?

The folded newspaper found in Maczak's grave was dated April 21; such throwaway newspapers were usually either opened immediately, or thrown away immediately upon receipt. The householder either found them of value in selecting Thursday's food bargains, or disposed of them promptly, for the market specials were gone by the weekend. If Maczak had been killed before April 15, a newspaper published on the twenty-first of the month could only have been placed in a reopened grave—with the other refuse—to point a finger at Corona.

"The watch was in bad condition?"

"It was in very bad condition when I got it out of the pocket," Ulrey answered, his nose wrinkling in distaste.

"Are you a watchmaker too?" Hawk demanded.

"Your Honor," Williams interposed, "I am going to object."

"Sustained."

Then Fahey joined, "Your Honor, I ask Mr. Hawk to get away from the witness."

Hawk spun round, appearing solicitous. "Oh, really? I am sorry. Is he running things now or—"

Judge Patton interrupted. "Pardon me, it is proper for counsel to approach a witness when he is asking a question. Mr. Fahey, are you fiinished?"

The new prosecutor nodded, then, half to himself said, "I think it served its purpose. Thank you."

"I am sorry," Hawk mocked, "if I offended the high-priced lawyer."

Judge Patton ordered the remark stricken and called the attorneys into chambers. "This remark about the 'high-priced lawyer,' how could you possibly feel that is any proper comment to make in front of this jury?"

Hawk was still angry. "It is just as proper as Mr. Fahey's comment that it served its purpose when he just lost an objection. That is just as improper as anything I said and I think it is unfair to select me and pick on me, Your Honor." Patton was hardly impartial, Hawk thought. "I didn't start this incident. He did. I was doing a proper thing. The only time I approach witnesses is when I have documents to show them."

Patton's anger matched that of Hawk. "I held in effect that Mr. Fahey's remarks in that regard were not justified, but he was gentlemanly. Five days and five hundred dollars for that contempt," he said firmly.

"I think you misunderstood the record," replied Hawk, "because after he lost the ruling is when he made the gratuitous remark, 'It served its purpose,' and that is just as contemptuous as anything I said and I think you are selecting me and picking on me and it seems to me that you are showing prejudice against me and against Mr. Corona, and siding with Mr. Fahey." Hawk was following the lawyer's maxim: "Make a record" for a possible appeal. A judge's bias could overturn a conviction.

Judge Patton now had been challenged. "I will let anybody read this record that wants to and let them see the contemptuous attitude and conduct that you have put forth in this trial and I will stand on the record, and I certainly feel very hurt that you feel that there is anything personal about my ruling in this case."

The first phase of the prosecution's case was completed, after 3,776 pages of trial transcript, five weeks of testimony, and twenty-three days in court. The contempt citations notwithstanding—Hawk had now lost count of the total jail time and fines he had been assessed—the defense attorney believed the prosecution's credibility had been thoroughly destroyed.

District Attorney Teja would attempt to recover some of the lost ground in presenting alone the second phase of the case dealing with the search warrants served on the night of Corona's arrest.

Teja began with Deputy Steve Sizelove, one of the members of the team that had searched the mess hall on the Sullivan ranch. The eight men and an interpreter had gone to the ranch at approximately three-thirty in the morning on May 26, 1971. They had gone first to the mess hall, found it locked, then awakened "several Mexican males" sleeping in the bunkhouse. None had a key. Sizelove had finally removed a screen from a mess hall window and, with Undersheriff Cartoscelli boosting him over the sill, had climbed in. The window was over the kitchen sink.

"I crawled through upon the drainboard and onto the floor and I observed what appeared to be something burning in the sink and I walked over to the sink and there was a glass candleholder sitting in the sink and it was burning," Deputy Sizelove testified.

"Have you ever seen anything like it since?" Teja asked.

"Similar? Yes, sir."

"And when and where was that?"

"This was where the pieces of glass were that came out of grave 25," Sizelove answered.

The search party had spread out through the mess hall, Deputy Rodemaker assigned to the desk. Rodemaker was unable to open the locked drawers and asked Mason to pick the lock, using a paper clip.

In the lower left-hand drawer of the desk, Rodemaker found a sheathed knife and a Browning automatic pistol in a holster. Mason photographed them in the drawer before "Undersheriff Cartoscelli took them out of the drawer and took them over to Detective Gregory, who was at a table tagging evidence." Cartoscelli unzipped the holster, saw the pistol in a cocked position, and handed it to Mason, asking him to unload the weapon. Forty-five minutes later, the team had left.

On cross-examination, Hawk elicited the testimony that Sizelove did not see any of the search party lift fingerprints from the desk, the gun, or the knife.

"When did you prepare a report on your activities of that night?" Hawk asked.

"Oh, it has been several months ago."

"And what did you do with that report after you prepared it."

"It was turned over to the D.A.'s office, I believe."

Hawk looked at the report in his hands, then passed it to the deputy. "That doesn't have any date on it as far as when it was typed. Why is that?"

"I don't know. It should have." Sizelove was sheepish.

"It doesn't even say who typed it?"

"No, sir." The chagrin turned to embarrassment.

"When was this report prepared, please?"

"First part of June this year, I believe."

"First part of June." The belatedly prepared report of the search at the ranch—drafted only after the officers attending the review of the body hunt realized no one had been designated recording officer—had been illegally withheld from the defense for four months.

The next witness, Deputy Bill Rodemaker, testified that he had climbed through a second window of the mess hall, and had also seen the votary candle left burning in the sink. "It was a glass vase that was a religious-candle-type deal, a tall candle inside burning."

The district attorney showed Rodemaker a photograph of the candleholder reconstructed from the fragments found in the twenty-fifth grave. Approximately ten inches high, silk-screened in three colors, the two candleholders appeared to be "the same type."

Hawk's cross-examination of Rodemaker underlined the points Sizelove had reluctantly made. Rodemaker had written no reports of the search. No instructions were given about preserving fingerprint evidence. Rodemaker had touched the desk top and the drawer handles.

Hawk changed subjects. "Now, sir, have you ever heard of a man named Emilio Rangel?"

"Never heard of him before," Rodemaker answered.

Hawk showed Rodemaker a photograph of an outbuilding behind the mess hall on the Sullivan property. "Did you get close to that building that night?"

"Yes."

"Was somebody sleeping there?"

"Yes. A short, heavy-set Mexican."

"Did he tell you what his name was?"

"Not to me."

"Emilio?"

"I never heard the name."

Rodemaker could recall no one searching the small building where Rangel slept; it was obviously not in Corona's possession. However, in December 1971, seven months later, Gregory and Perales discovered bloodstained pants in the quarters that Rangel had used.

The third witness, Deputy Wilbur Terry, had recovered several Del Pero Brothers receipts among a dozen charge slips and paid bills skewered to a nail on the wall of the mess hall. Corona's name was on each of them.

In cross-examination, Hank asked: "Receipt number 26008 from Del Pero Brothers. What is the date of that?"

"I am not sure about the month. I would say the date is the nineteenth. I am not sure about the year." Terry sensed Hawk had found something —another mistake?—and was wary.

"Okay. Do you see a Y in that?" hawk asked pointing to the month. Sometime on May 19, Hawk knew from Gore's early investigation, Corona had purchased meat at the market for the evening meal; the receipt, introduced inadvertently by the prosecution, was alibi evidence.

"Now, sir, you found these on a nail, right?"

"Correct."

"Out in plain, open sight, right?"

"Correct."

"Anyone who had any kind of access to that building would have had no trouble at all getting something with Juan Corona's name on it. Isn't that correct?"

Teja's objection was futile. Hawk's question had made the point to the jury.

Hawk was almost finished. Was anybody assigned the duty of determining how the building was locked?

"I don't recall."

"Okay. It is true, however, that there is a person who once associated with a well-known homosexual that had access to that building, isn't there?"

Teja objected, the judge ordering the question stricken.

"Let me put it this way," Hawk began again. "Do you know Ray Duron had access to that mess hall?"

"I have no knowledge of it, no."

"Thank you, sir." Hawk sat down as the district attorney rose to ask questions on redirect examination.

"Do you know whether Richard Hawk had access to that mess hall?"

"No, I don't."

"Do you know who had access to that mess hall?"

"No, I don't, outside of Mr. Corona."

Teja had recouped. "Nothing further."

Detective Gregory was Teja's next witness in the chain-of-possession of the gun, holster, knife, and sheath. Gregory had examined the holster, pulling out a box of cartridges from the zippered pouch. Inside the box, tucked beneath the styrofoam packing, Gregory had found an oil company credit card made out to Corona with an expiration date of April 1970; a GMAC time payment plan card made out to Corona; Corona's Social Security card; a business card from a local businessman; the stubs of seven checks made out to the defendant by the Sullivan ranch in July, August, and September of 1969; and Corona's farm labor contractor license. The cards established the gun as Corona's. They also suggested that he had not touched the weapon at least since 1970.

Hawk's cross-examination was quick. Gregory was not responsible for lifting fingerprints; no one had been designated as fingerprint officer that night. Mason had handled the gun extensively while uncocking and unloading it, and had handled the clip to remove three cartridges. Whatever fingerprint evidence there might have been—and, yes, one could often see the fingerprints with the naked eye on a blue-steel revolver—had been destroyed.

Having spotted Ray Duron sitting on a hall bench, Hawk surmised he would be called as a witness. He intended that a curious jury listen to Duron's testimony, whatever it might be. "Well," Hawk asked Gregory, "isn't it true that on the Sullivan ranch they have a number of [hasp] locks on which the tumblers are identical and it is marked 'twenty-twenty'?"

"I believe so, yes."

"Okay. And so there is one key and it opens a number of locks?"

"Right."

"And if that was a 'twenty-twenty' lock, of course, Ray Duron had access to Juan's building, didn't he?"

Teja's objection was ill-placed, making it appear as if he were protecting

Duron. Hawk merely rephrased it. "Isn't it true that Ray Duron is ranch foreman and has keys to all of those locks?"

"He is the ranch foreman, and I would presume that he does have keys."

"Where was Ray Duron on May nineteenth between noon and six o'clock?"

"Objection," Teja shouted. "That is totally irrelevant."

"Sustained." First Natividad Corona, then Rangel, now Duron. Judge Patton was perturbed.

"Was any investigation ever conducted of Ray Duron to find out what his whereabouts were on the critical dates?" Hawk persisted.

"Objection, Your Honor. That goes beyond the scope of direct examination."

"Sustained."

"It is not beyond the scope of common sense," Hawk replied.

The ranch foreman, Duron, was Teja's next witness, called to identify the buildings of which Corona had exclusive use: the mess hall, which was locked when Corona was not there, and the bunkhouse, which was for Corona's crews only.

"Do you know how he secured the mess hall?" the district attorney asked.

"Well, by putting a padlock on the front door. The back door was locked from the inside and I had given him a key to the side door, so therefore he was the only one that had keys to the mess hall."

"Do you know what sort of padlock was on the front door?"

"No, I don't."

Corona listened intently, occasionally whispering into Hawk's ear, the attorney nodding and writing notes on the pad in front of him.

"Can you tell whether or not it was a Sullivan ranch padlock or whether or not it belonged to the defendant?"

"I cannot swear that it was or wasn't a Sullivan ranch padlock. However," Duron volunteered, "I am inclined to believe that it was his own personal lock." Duron sat calmly in the witness box, a small man who fussed with the microphone in front of him, raising and lowering it. As Teja concluded his direct examination, Duron licked his lips anxiously, frowning as Hawk stood up to cross-examine.

Until Duron's volunteered comment, Hawk had had no personal animus toward the ranch foreman. Corona was not fond of him—none of the family seemed to be—but that was their problem, not his. Now he began to share their dislike.

"Mr. Duron, I take it that the same lock is on the front door of the mess hall as was there the night that Juan Corona was arrested?"

Duron was evasive. "I don't know."

"Has the lock ever been removed?"

"Several times. The one that is there now, it is a 'twenty-twenty' lock."

"If this was Juan Corona's own personal lock that was on the door, how did you get it off?"

"He had his crew boss, Emilio—I don't konw what his last name was—who I notified early in the morning of the twenty-sixth [the day of Corona's arrest] to feed the men at Mrs. Corona's suggestion. I presume that he had a key to it."

If that were true, then Rangel had access to the mess hall.

Hawk's cross-examination was as harsh as any he had conducted. "Why did you tell the police on December 22, 1971, that Mr. Corona had exclusive control of the small white house out behind?"

"Because he did," Duron answered confidently.

"And where was Emilio Rangel sleeping?"

"I don't know." Duron would be a tough witness, unbending, difficult to trip up.

Did Duron know Emilio Rangel. Yes, he was Corona's crewboss, a short man who weighed perhaps 145 pounds, dark-complected, a short, stocky man who spoke no English, only Spanish. Duron's description jibed with Rodemaker's of the man in the white shack, and Shannon's description of the man riding in the blue-and-white pickup with the green canvas top.

Where did Rangel stay on the ranch? Duron didn't know. "Well now, isn't it true that you told the police officers on December 22, 1971, that the small white building from which the bloody clothes were recovered was in the possession of Juan Corona alone?"

"I said it was part of Juan Corona's buildings. That he had the right to the use of that building."

"Did you tell them that the lock on that small building had not been removed since Juan Corona was arrested?"

"That is correct."

"Okay." Hawk nodded. "Now, sir, if there was a person sleeping in that building on the night that Juan was arrested, and Juan went into custody, do you know of any way that Juan could have come out and put the lock on the building?"

"Your Honor," Teja protested, "that is argumentative." Hawk had intended it to be.

"Sustained."

"Now sir, at this time I take it you don't really know what kind of a lock was on the front door of the mess hall." Corona had told him it was a "twenty-twenty" lock, for which Corona had a key.

"No, I don't."

"It might have been a 'twenty-twenty' lock, for all you know?"

"It might have."

"And that would mean that you and everybody else that had a key to the 'twenty-twenty' lock had access to that building, as far as going through the locked door. Is that correct?"

"Yes."

Hawk leaned against the bailiff's desk, his hands playing with a pencil as he questioned Duron. "Incidentally, weren't you at one time in business with a well-known homosexual?"

"Objection, Your Honor. That has nothing to do whatsoever with Mr. Duron's testimony."

"Sustained."

From Corona, Hawk had learned that Duron knew the contractor had an automatic pistol in the mess hall. "Did you on one occasion tell him if he wanted to target practice his nine-millimeter gun, to shoot it down on the river?"

"I don't recall telling him that."

"You don't?"

"No."

"Wasn't it common knowledge that Juan had a gun at the ranch?"

"Not to my knowledge."

With Corona providing the lead, Hawk asked Duron to identify two telephones that were hanging on the wall of the mess hall. Disconnected in the summer, Duron explained, they were used during the winter as direct lines to the local flood control district.

"Now, my question to you is: during these winter months, how do they have access to these phones?"

"Well, if there is any question of danger, then the lock is taken off of the front door and the levee district directors use that building as their headquarters." The only lock that might have been on the door if it was to be opened was the ranch's standard "twenty-twenty" lock. Twenty-five people who had worked on the ranch in the past few years might have had "twenty-twenty" keys and access to the building.

"And if the 'twenty-twenty' lock then was on it on May 26, any of those twenty-five people might have had a key to that lock? Right?"

"If there was a 'twenty-twenty' lock on there."

Teja's redirect examination of Duron was misguided. "After the defendant was arrested on the morning of May 26, did you see anybody in or about the mess hall other than the police officers, Mr. Duron?"

"I saw Emilio and instructed him to feed the men, as per Mrs. Corona's instructions."

Teja's next question was a mistake. "Were the men fed from the mess hall that morning?"

"Yes, they were," Duron answered.

Teja had accidently established that Rangel at least had access to the mess hall which had been locked when the deputies left earlier that morning. (In fact, as Hawk knew, Duron himself and Pedro Corona, among others, had been in the locked mess hall after Juan Corona was arrested.)

Teja sat down, leaving Hawk to cross-examine again. "Emilio is the one that drove Mr. Corona's red-and-white pickup during May, isn't he?"

"Yes."

Hawk returned to the morning of Corona's arrest. Did Emilio get into the mess hall?

"He did."

"Then he must have had some keys and had access to the building?"

"Yes."

"And this is the same man you saw driving the red-and-white pickup?"

"Yes."

"A short, stocky man?"

"Yes." Hawk sat down, leaving it to Teja.

"Did you see the defendant driving anything during that period of time?" Teja asked.

"Other than his van or his personal car or the pickup, I don't recall him driving anything else." No blue-and-white pickup.

"But you did see the defendant driving his own pickup during that time?"

"Yes."

"Did Emilio use either the defendant's personal car or the van which you have mentioned?"

"I never saw Emilio drive Mr. Corona's personal car." Bloodstains had been found on the latch, rubber molding, and floor mat of the trunk of the family car.

"Mr. Corona drove all three of them, however, during that particular spring and summer?"

"Yes."

Teja had recovered from his mistake, profiting in the exchange. Only Corona had driven all three vehicles, two of which had bloodstains in them.

Captain John Littlejohn was the first prosecution witness to describe the arrest of Juan Corona and the search of his home on Richland Road. "Mr. Corona gave me the impression that there was a language barrier," Littlejohn testified. "At that time we requested our interpreter to come, and he was summoned from the camp area on that part of the search. He did arrive and he, in turn, read the defendant's rights—read the search warrant to the defendant in Mexican."

Hawk's cross-examination centered on the reason Littlejohn and the interpreter read Corona his rights under the law yet never asked him a single question.

"Why didn't you ever talk to him?"

"Because it was my understanding that he declined to give a statement."

"Who told you that?"

"It came from Mr. Escovedo."

"Where is the report that says that?" There was none.

"I don't know."

"Who was the boss out there?"

"Then-Sergeant Purcell."

"Why did you read the search warrant to him?"

"Because Sheriff Whiteaker directed me to." Littlejohn shifted uncomfortably.

"You were aware that there is no legal requirement that you read him the search warrant at all? All you have to do is have it. Who do you read it to if there is nobody there?"

"I wouldn't read it to anyone."

"That is right. So there is no requirement that you read the search warrant to anyone, is there?"

"No." Littlejohn felt foolish.

Hawk respected Captain Purcell as an honest man who had been forced to shoulder the blame for the mistakes in the investigation. The cross-examination was low-key, the defense attorney deferential. Purcell agreed that he was in charge of the group at the Richland Road home, despite the fact that at the time he was outranked by Captain Littlejohn.

"Mr. Teja was there, wasn't he?"

"Yes, sir."

"Mr. Teja and Sheriff Whiteaker were there virtually all the time?"

"Yes, sir."

"Now, would you tell me, sir, whose decision was it to arrest Mr. Corona before you asked him any questions?"

"There was a discussion between Sheriff Whiteaker; Mr. Teja; Mr. Mathews, the deputy district attorney; and myself."

"And was it some kind of a joint decision?"

"Yes, sir."

"Now, as of that time had anyone attempted to talk to Mr. Corona and ask him such things as where he was on May the nineteenth of 1971?"

"Not to my knowledge, sir."

"And I take it then that no attempt was ever made to find out where Mr. Corona was during those hours" between one and six o'clock when Kenneth Whitacre had been killed and buried.

"No, sir. Not to my knowledge." Purcell's straightforward answers spoke well for him personally, if not for the department's failures.

"Why did you not give him the opportunity to explain where he had been on this critical day of May the nineteenth of 1971?"

"I don't know. I can't answer that."

"I see. Now, being in charge of the investigation, was it your decision not to attempt to lift fingerprints from this ledger?"

"It probably was a joint decision between myself and some superior officers."

"Can you tell us ultimately who was responsible? Was it you?"

"I guess so. Yes, sir."

"It sort of turned out that way, huh?" Hawk was sympathetic.

"Yes, sir."

"Did you realize that you were going to be responsible, not Sheriff Whiteaker, for what happened that night?"

"No, sir."

"You had a district attorney, a graduate lawyer, there, talking; and you had the elected sheriff of the county. Right?"

"Yes, sir."

"But now it turns out you are responsible. Right?"

"Yes, sir."

Was Purcell aware that Corona had two crews working on the nineteenth. No. Yes, he was aware Corona had men working for him that day. No, none of the laborers Corona used had been interviewed prior to Corona's arrest.

"Did you ever hear of a man by the name of Carlos Leon Sierra?"

"Possibly," Purcell said with a frown, trying to remember.

"He's the guy that fell out of the tree on May twelfth. You know about that, don't you?"

"Oh, yes," Purcell smiled. "Now I remember."

"Mr. Corona took him down to Doctor Vasquez?"

"Yes, sir."

"After you arrested—"

Teja finally objected to Hawk's questions on the grounds of irrelevance.

Judge Patton corrected him. "I don't know if it's irrelevant. It goes beyond the scope of direct."

"It goes beyond the scope of direct," Teja echoed.

"Sustained."

Hawk continued to use Purcell to discredit the prosecution's case. Purcell had never seen a blue-and-white pickup with a green top with the name Juan V. Corona on it. The investigation had turned up only one suspect, Corona. It wasn't until after Corona was arrested that Purcell learned the tire tracks at Kenneth Whitacre's grave did not match Corona's vehicles. Purcell was not aware at the time of the arrest, though he was now, that Corona had a leg infection in March and April of 1971.

Judge Patton was disturbed. What he deemed the orderly progress of the trial was being upset, first by Hawk deliberately asking questions beyond the scope of the direct examination—Patton could understand that as the defense's effort to plant doubts—but, worse still, by the failure of the prosecutor to make proper objections. Teja permitted matters to come into testimony which simply had no place in this trial. Perhaps Fahey would have curbed some of this, but he was preparing the medical phase of the case.

Denver Duncan was called to identify the ledger and an immigration slip he had found in the top drawer of the four-drawer filing cabinet in Corona's bedroom. On cross-examination, Hawk pointed out the immigration form was not on the report of the search at all. Duncan conceded the ledger had not been dusted for fingerprints. "It was found in Mr. Corona's file cabinet, so we assumed it was Mr. Corona's property."

"And do you know how long it had been there?"

"No idea, sir."

Duncan agreed that the ledger with its multicolored entries might have been out at the camp. (Corona had earlier told Hawk he had moved the ledger, but could not remember when.) No pen with multicolored inks had been recovered on Richland Road, the detective agreed.

"There was a pen recovered at the camp with multicolored ink?"

"That is correct."

"At one time, if that's the same ink, the ledger and the pen were together and they somehow got separated?"

"Yes."

Detective Jerry Harrison had been the recording officer, noting the evidence taken from Corona's home and who recovered it. On cross-examination, Hawk discovered a contradiction between the evidence tag on the machete and Harrison's report. Hawk was amused; the young sheriff was going to claim credit for the major link in the case.

"The evidence tag says that Sheriff Whiteaker found that, is that right?"

Confused, Harrison glanced toward the prosecutor.

"Don't look at him," Hawk ordered. "You can testify from what you saw, can't you?"

"I wasn't looking at him," Harrison protested.

"Which is correct? Did Sheriff Whiteaker find that like the tag says, or did you find it?"

"I wrote the tag."

"Is the tag correct?"

"No, sir."

"Who did recover it?"

"I did."

Hawk reviewed for the balance of the day the search of Corona's home. The family sedan was used as a work bench by the deputies searching the garage, without the car being processed for fingerprints. The posthole digger was caked with mud, a few strands of hair embedded in the soil; no one had taken a soil sample from Corona's back yard. No, Harrison did not know that Corona had recently installed a fence around the back yard. No, he had not seen the washing machine in the garage where the maid or Mrs. Corona did the family's laundry. The garage and the two vehicles parked there had not been vacuumed before they were sealed. Evidence was not tagged and was now missing from the courtroom.

The search warrant itself, Hawk summarized, "didn't it authorize you to look for items of personal property belonging to a number of the victims which you had dug up?"

"Yes, sir."

"Now, when you went out there, did you find anything, any personal property of any of the victims?"

"No, sir."

From the evidence taken at the ranch and turned over to Harrison were there any items of personal property of the victims? No. Any bloody clothing that you knew belonging to the victims? No.

Deputy Mason was the last witness in the second phase of the trial, called to identify photographs of the two vehicles impounded by the sheriff at Corona's home. As the department's technician, Mason had been given joint control with Captain Purcell of the evidence locker.

Hawk's cross-examination ranged far and wide. In July 1972 all the evidence had been removed from the locker, sorted, and new evidence tags written—all contrary to good police practice. No records had been kept of the rebagging of the evidence.

Hawk rummaged through the growing pile of evidence stacked against the clerk's desk, coming up with the machete. Did it appear the same now as it had in July, rusted and nicked.

"Ain't very sharp, is it?" Hawk asked, handing it to Mason.

"I wouldn't want to run my hand over it."

Hawk did so, firmly stroking the length of the blade against his palm, then held up his hand. "Do you see any cuts?"

"No, sir."

"Well, did anybody dull this knife after they took possession of it?"

"Not to my knowledge, no, sir."

"A knife that has been sharpened is shiny along the cutting edge, isn't it?"

"Yes, sir."

"This one isn't like that, is it?"

"No, sir."

"Pretty dull knife, isn't it?"

"I couldn't say, sir."

"See any heavy calluses on my hand?"

"No, sir."

"Didn't cut though, did it?"

"No, sir."

"Your Honor," Teja interrupted, "if Mr. Hawk wants to volunteer to courtroom experience, I will volunteer to hit him with it and we will see what happens."

Hawk's constant jibes and his success in cross-examination had finally provoked the district attorney. It had taken six weeks of testimony.

22

A Collection of Little Stories
November 10-December 4, 1972

Day after day the two court reporters, John Zandonella and Pat Kane shuttled in and out of the courtroom, spelling each other every twenty minutes, at 225 words a minute taking down 200 or more pages of transcript each day.

James Pervis was the first witness in what Williams had termed the circumstantial phase of the case, "a collection of little stories" that cumulatively would point to Corona's guilt.

Pervis testified that on April 10, 1971, Corona had offered him a few hours' work as a handyman around the camp. At the time, Pervis was on foot, Corona in "either a panel or pickup." Because he was color-blind, Pervis did not pay "too much attention" to the vehicle's color; he recognized it from the photograph of the yellow van because "it was such a new car."

Hawk concentrated on the discrepancies between Pervis' prior statements and his testimony in court. He read Pervis' statement to Detective Duncan on June 3, 1971; Pervis then had claimed Corona was driving a pickup, "a two-tone job, green-color." Before the Grand Jury in July 1971, Pervis had described the truck as a pickup, "painted two different colors." He couldn't remember the colors. Asked to explain the contradictions, Pervis could only offer lamely, "Well, a fellow can make a mistake, you know, in cars, all right."

Had Pervis seen Corona pick up other casual laborers in lower Marysville? "Maybe a guy or two. Some Spanish, some white." Before the Grand Jury, however, Pervis had testified that Corona picked up "mostly Americans." A month before that, he had told Detective Duncan he never saw Corona pick up anyone in lower Marysville, not in the eight or nine years he had seen the labor contractor around town.

The next witness, Byron Shannon, returned to testify that he was with three of the victims on the morning of May 12, 1971, in "Wino Park" when Corona "and another fellow" drove up in a pickup truck, "the same color pickup where he picked Johnson up in."

"That he picked Jackson up in?" Williams asked.

"Yeah," Shannon agreed.

"No, he said 'Johnson.' " Hawk corrected.

Allen and Riley had climbed into the back of the blue-and-white pickup with the green canvas top, Jonah Smallwood into the cab. "I didn't see them no more until my wife told me about the pictures in the paper."

"This Mexican fellow that was with Mr. Corona," Williams asked, "did you ever see him drive around and pick anybody up?"

"I seen him two or three times in the red-and-white pickup about January there."

Williams and Fahey struggled to protect their witness as Hawk tediously cross-examined Shannon, forcing the vague witness into contradictions, eliciting the prosecution's agreement that Shannon's testimony conflicted with earlier statements.

"Mr. Shannon, sir, you weren't drinking that day, were you?"

"I told you I don't drink." Shannon was indignant. "I find out I was a diabetic about twenty years ago, and I had to stop drinking."

Hawk deliberately studied Shannon's arrest record, belatedly turned over to him by the prosecution that morning. "Would you explain to me, sir, how it was you got thirty days in jail on March 7, 1968, for being drunk in public?"

"Well, I told them I wasn't drinking."

"Well, you got a $190 fine and thirty days in jail for being drunk on March 7, 1968, according to CII."

"Then I wasn't drunk, though."

"You weren't drunk, but you pled guilty to being drunk?"

"Yeah," Shannon conceded. "I pled guilty." Shannon's explanation, to an experienced criminal lawyer, was common enough; to a jury, it sounded far-fetched. "I hadn't had my pills and I was out of pills, and when I get out of pills, well, then I stagger, like I be drunk."

"Didn't you explain that to the policeman?"

"I told it to the policeman. But they don't pay you no attention."

Williams and Fahey were helpless. To rehabilitate Shannon's credibility, they would have to attack both the police and the municipal court in Marysville.

Two months later, Shannon was again arrested, and again pled guilty to being drunk in public. "I hadn't had no pills. We plead guilty over there. Nearly everybody pleads guilty. You don't find nobody hardly pleading not guilty, unless they just want to lay around in jail thirty days waiting for their trial."

Hawk reviewed Shannon's long rap sheet. There were two felony convictions, one in 1965 for forgery, the other in 1966 for illegally cashing two United States Treasury checks. His record included arrests dating back to 1945 for robbery, assault with a deadly weapon, a third forgery, grand theft, and, just four months before, for burglary.

Despite his confusions and poor memory, Shannon maintained he had seen Riley, Allen, and Smallwood drive off with Corona and the unidentified companion.

The first setback for the defense came in the eighth week of testimony. In the middle of the circumstantial evidence phase of the case, the defense lost Bill Hicks. The smiling juror number 6 suffered a severely broken arm in a motorcycle accident. Because Hicks was to be confined to hospital and home for two weeks, Judge Patton considered it an undue delay. Hawk was dismayed, the three prosecutors privately delighted to be quit of such a patently not-guilty vote. Drawn by lot from the four alternates, Richard Bremen was sworn in to replace the man Hawk considered his guarantee of a "hung jury, no matter what."

That afternoon, Hawk visited Hicks in his hospital room. Still smiling, despite the compound fracture of his arm and broken fingers, the Vietnam veteran told Hawk that at least eight jurors believed Corona not guilty. Hicks thought only the schoolteacher, Mrs. Blazek, was against Corona; she might, however, have one or two others on her side. The jury, Hicks added, was constantly discussing the case, despite the judge's daily instructions not to do so until all the evidence was in. That in itself, Hawk told an aide, could be ground for a mistrial were Corona convicted.

With eight votes—seven now that Hicks was gone—Hawk was elated. Even if he just held his own through the balance of the prosecution's case, he would begin the defense case decidedly ahead.

The former Sharon Ann Reeves, now Mrs. David Schmidl, retold the story that she had seen Corona come out of the bushes perhaps a hundred feet from where she was sitting in her boyfriend's pickup truck. He was carrying a long gun. Yes, she told Fahey, she was certain it was a gun and not a posthole digger.

Her husband's account remained virtually the same except that now he testified Corona had driven off in his red pickup truck "faster than the dusty conditions of the road permitted." Seventeen months earlier, he drove off "not too fast and not too slow."

Joseph Breceda was the first of the farm workers to testify. In January 1971, another farm worker, Ernesto Garcia, had seen Corona driving at night on a dirt access road near the freeway. Five months later, after

Corona's arrest, Breceda finally told his foreman, Ray Duron, of the night-time sighting. Why had they started searching for a body a quarter of a mile away then? asked Hawk.

"Because Raymond told us to start at the Rand block."

"Raymond Duron told you to start at the Rand block and, lo and behold, when you got there you found an indentation, but Mr. Garcia didn't tell you he saw Mr. Corona in the Rand block, did he?"

"No."

"Okay. Raymond told you, 'Go look in the Rand block,' right?"

"Right."

Ernesto Garcia, testifying through an interpreter, told the same story Breceda had, adding that when he and Corona met on the access road, Corona had told Garcia he was hunting for his strayed dog. Garcia later that evening had seen the dog in the camp area.

Quickly and confidently, Fahey led Garcia through a second of "the little stories." In April, Garcia had been operating a tractor-drawn earth borer called a chisel in the south riverbottom orchard. The holes the chisel drove into the earth were to permit irrigation water to seep deep into the orchard soil.

"Did Mr. Corona ask you anything about how deep the chisel would go?"

"Yes." The contractor had measured the height of the dirt clinging to the chisel against his leg.

On cross-examination, Hawk brought out the fact that the chisel had been used on the ranch only during the winter months, when Corona was not working regularly. Seeing it for the first time, and interested someday in owning his own ranch, Corona had asked about the tool.

The next witness, José Ramirez, had helped to locate victim number twenty-four after he remembered seeing Corona's pickup parked near the grave site in March. At another time, while putting out ladders in the north riverbottom orchard, he had seen Corona pull into the orchard in his pickup, park, and walk into the bushes.

Hawk's cross-examination again elicited the innocence of Corona's actions until after the discovery of the bodies.

"Now, sir, when Mr. Corona came down to the north riverbottom orchard that day, was he attempting to hide in any way what he was doing?"

"No. I didn't see him doing anything. I saw him walking, that is all."

Corona was evidently doing what Schmidl had been doing—urinating in the bushes.

"Did you consider anything that you saw that day to be suspicious?"

"No."

"It wasn't until after Mr. Corona was arrested that you even thought about that again."

The ranch carpenter, James Cummings, was the next witness. On May 17, 1971, Cummings had been detailed to repair the toilets in the concrete block washroom and shower used by Corona's crew. "Would you describe the general condition of the toilets in that concrete blockhouse, when you were there on May seventeenth?" District Attorney Teja had presumably discovered the slaughterhouse.

"It was immaculate. Just been cleaned out."

"Okay. How had it been cleaned out?"

"Been washed by a hose, completely, the walls, everything."

"What time of day did you go into the toilet there at the bunkhouse, do you recall?"

"Oh, it had to have been a morning, so I would say around, oh, six-thirty."

Just as promptly, District Attorney Teja undercut his own theory. "Were there any people living in the bunkhouse at that time?"

"Yes, there was. I guess the bunkhouse had the maximum amount of men it would hold." Had the toilet been used as a slaughterhouse the night before, the killer would have risked discovery by any of thirty-five men answering a nocturnal call of nature.

With the district attorney examining him, Cummings retold the story of seeing a blue Chevrolet van driving over the levee from the riverbank into the Sullivan camp at six-thirty in the morning of May 22, 1971. The van had turned in behind the barn to park beside the mess hall. Within fifteen minutes, Cummings had seen the van back to the edge of the orchard, and stop.

"Did you get a glimpse of the driver in the van?"

"I got a glimpse, but I can't—I don't know. It was just a glimpse, so I couldn't say, definitely state whether it was him in the van." Cummings nodded in Corona's direction. Not until after Corona's arrest did Cummings think anything of the early morning incident. Six hundred feet from the spot at the edge of the trees another grave was located.

Hawk began his cross-examination by reading to Cummings his testimony before the Grand Jury, when he had described the truck as a yellow van or tannish van. Cummings discounted his testimony there, asserting the district attorney's question in July 1971 was "misleading." He had told detectives, he had told Hawk earlier, he had told the prosecutors "a dozen times" that the truck was blue, bluish-green.

"And you didn't see Mr. Corona in that truck?"

"I can't state that I saw him, no, in the truck." Cummings had just assumed Corona had bought a new truck.

"When you saw this blue panel later backing up against this orchard, you didn't see Mr. Corona then either?"

"No."

In chambers at his own request, the defense attorney complained to the judge. "What they have done is apparently gone out and got a picture of Pedro Corona's blue panel van, they brought that in and had this man look at it; and he says it is similar. He winds up not even being able to say it is the same make of van. The whole thing is really very prejudicial. I would like some kind of offer of proof of what he thinks he is doing."

Judge Patton too was confused. "It seems to me, insofar as the blue van is concerned, actually the testimony favors Mr. Hawk's client. Certainly, there is no showing that Juan Corona ever had a blue van."

"But his brother does have a blue van," Hawk interrupted.

"But he is not charged with anything," Judge Patton answered.

"They are going to try to suggest that Juan had access to his brother's van, maybe. They are going to try apparently some sort of a conspiracy theory with conspirators that aren't charged, and a conspiracy charge that doesn't exist."

Judge Patton reserved his ruling, indicating he was inclined to agree with the defense.

In turn, Teja renewed his long-standing motion for a list of the witnesses the defense intended to call, still seeking the names of the experts who would testify on the question of homosexuality.

Hawk's only answer was evasive. "I am not sure I will be calling any witnesses."

Before the jury once again, Hawk asked Cummings, "It was Mr. Corona's responsibility to clean the bunkhouse and the toilets, right?"

"Yes."

"And as I understand it, it was all nice and clean?"

"Yes, it was." The other toilets on the ranch were "not washed down like that one is. Maybe he is a good housekeeper, I don't know." Cummings shrugged.

Hawk changed subjects. In December 1971, Cummings had broken the lock from the small cabin in which Emilio Rangel had been sleeping; inside, Gregory and Perales discovered clothes with small bloodstains.

"There was a bed in that little cabin, wasn't there?"

"Yes, there was."

"And how would you describe that little cabin when you broke into it?"

"It looked like a sloppy housekeeper is about all."

"Did it look like the way Mr. Corona kept his things?"

"No."

Hawk passed the carpenter back to Teja, pleased with the unexpected testimony on behalf of his client.

Teja asked Cummings how often he had seen Corona on the ranch at five-thirty in the morning.

"Oh, I'd say on a couple of times. He'd be at the mess hall or be coming from the levee side there."

Hawk was enjoying himself. Without Fahey in the courtroom to protect him, Teja was easy prey.

"Now, you say Mr. Corona was up early," Hawk asked on recross-examination.

"Yes," Cummings nodded.

"You wouldn't fault a man for getting up early to go to work?"

"No, because I always have."

"Of course, you understand he had people working there that he had to feed, right?"

"Yes."

"And what time do these men go to work in the fields?"

"About six or six-thirty."

"So if you're going to feed them you have to get up pretty early to get the food ready and have them fed so they can be out in the fields by six or six-thirty, right?"

Teja objected, Judge Patton ruling, "I think that is obvious."

"Well, there wouldn't be anything particularly unusual about Mr. Corona or his wife being up early to prepare food for the men?"

"I guess not, no."

Teja picked up where Hawk left off. "You saw the defendant coming over the levee here in early morning; was there a grocery store anywhere down there in the riverbottom?"

"No."

"Is there any storage area where the defendant might store foodstuffs that would be used to prepare breakfast for a crew of hungry men?"

"No."

"Nothing further." Teja sat down with a faint smile.

"But there was a place to take trash where a neat person would take his trash, right?" Hawk asked from his seat at the counsel table.

"There is a trash pit over there, yes."

"Mr. Corona took good care of his buildings. He was neat, right?"

"Well, cleaned up, yes."

"Do you know of any other way to get to the trash dump other than go over the levee at this spot where you saw Mr. Corona?"

"Not unless they fly over there, no."

Hawk was laughing as he closed his notebook for the day.

There were few moments like that now. Many of the witnesses called by the prosecution were prefatory to the experts to come later: directors of rescue missions to testify when victims were last seen alive; custodians of records from blood banks up and down the Pacific Coast, brought to Fairfield to put into the transcript the blood types of the victims; another group of witnesses—storekeepers and clerks and bank officers—to testify that checks used by the handwriting examiners were, in fact, given to them by Corona. There was nothing incriminating, nothing to challenge. Hawk used his cross-examination of the storekeepers to bring out the fact, obvious enough, that the firms took Corona's checks because they were good, because his credit was good. Character evidence never hurt.

Only a handful of witnesses during the month of November stirred Hawk's interest. One was Yuba County Undersheriff Robert Day, called to identify the letter that Corona had written to his family to explain visiting procedures at the Marysville jail. The letter, Day testified, was written in Corona's cell with the undersheriff present, Day having brought along a ballpoint pen and paper.

"And for what purpose did you contact Mr. Corona on June eleventh, about midday in the cell?"

"I contacted Mr. Corona for the purpose of obtaining this handwriting sample."

Casually, a furious Hawk began his cross-examination "Undersheriff Day, you are a liar, aren't you?"

"Objection, Your Honor," Williams shouted.

"I'll definitely say he is a liar," Hawk said over Williams' voice.

"I will ask he be cited for contempt."

"Yes, cite—" Judge Patton was yelling too. "Mark the record and we will step into chambers, gentlemen."

"Into chambers for what?" Hawk demanded.

"Into chambers." Judge Patton's voice was shrill. "Because I ordered you into chambers, that's why. Into chambers."

Once alone with the judge and Bart Williams, Hawk explained mildly, "He lied to Mr. Corona when he got that note. He is a liar."

"That is a grossly abusive way to question a witness pertaining to any matter."

"I don't think so," Hawk answered. "You know what they did to him? They went down and told him they were having some trouble with visiting with his family and they asked him to write a note to his family. It is dishonest. It was a critical stage of the criminal proceedings. He had an attorney; he had a right to an attorney being present. That guy is a sneak and he is a liar, and I don't like him."

Judge Patton held that Hawk's question was contemptuous and sentenced him to five days in jail and a fine of $500.

Hawk's questions to Undersheriff Day in the courtroom were pointed.

"What was your purpose in going down and asking Mr. Corona to write this note: to get a handwriting exemplar or to straighten out visiting?"

"Well, my purpose was for the handwriting exemplar."

"Did you tell Mr. Corona it was your purpose to take a handwriting exemplar."

"No, sir, I did not."

"Did you tell him he ought to call his attorney?"

"No, sir. I did not."

"And you lied to Mr. Corona. You didn't tell him your purpose."

"I didn't tell him that I was not getting a handwriting exemplar so I did not lie to him."

"Sir, you took the oath today to tell the truth and the whole truth; that's what an oath is, isn't it?"

"That is correct."

"You didn't tell Mr. Corona the whole truth, did you?"

"I wasn't under oath when I talked to Mr. Corona."

Williams asked that the note, in Spanish, be read by an interpreter into the record, inadvertently providing more character evidence on Corona's behalf:

> Mrs. Gloria Corona. My esteemed wife, give greetings to my mother and to the children and to all those there. The tenth of June I was waiting, but we did not understand, but the officer told me to let you know that you had to make the visit at the window by the microphone. Give my regards to the children and to all. I am well. Juan V. Corona.

Mrs. Sarah Vallejo came to the witness stand to verify that the rent receipt she had furnished the Sheriff's Department was in Corona's handwriting.

Speaking through an interpreter, Mrs. Vallejo testified she paid her rent on the house Corona owned in Live Oak in cash, and the defendant gave her receipts, including this one written in brown ink.

Hawk could not quarrel with the receipt. Instead, he showed Mrs. Vallejo a series of photographs. Did she notice the screen door?

"Yes. This is the door where he put the screen."

"Mrs. Vallejo, isn't it true that on May 19, 1971, after lunch, Juan Corona spent several hours working on that house?"

Williams objected, protesting Hawk's cross was well beyond the direct. Because of the difficulty in arranging for a translator, Judge Patton permitted Hawk to make Mrs. Vallejo a defense witness while she was here, without recalling her later. Now Hawk would not be bound by Williams' direct.

"What day did Mr. Corona do that work?"

"I don't remember very well. It was a little after he picked up the rent, he fixed the door."

"How much time did Mr. Corona spend working on your home?"

"He worked in the morning on something that was difficult to tighten up; and then he went home, or I don't know where. Both he and his wife went to come back to tighten it up. And then they came back after, and then they finished kind of late."

Corona now had an alibi, more or less, for the time period in which Kenneth Whitacre was killed. It needed to be firmed.

"Was it nearing dinnertime when they left?"

"I believe, yes. They were waiting for their children to come out of school, and the lady was quite worried to get the children."

"Do you know when they generally eat, up there?"

"Well, in the fields, five or six o'clock."

"What would be your best estimate of what time it was when Mr. Corona left with his wife?"

"It wasn't late." Mrs. Vallejo contradicted herself. "It was early. About three-thirty or something like that, because I heard Mrs. Corona say that she was in a hurry to go pick up her children."

"Mrs. Vallejo, was there ever any time when Mr. Corona left the Live Oak address by himself that day?"

"No. Gloria was always with him."

"Do you recall any occasions that Mr. Corona came to the house alone?"

"No. Gloria always went." Hawk intended to call Gloria Corona to reinforce Mrs. Vallejo's testimony that husband and wife were together the entire afternoon.

Williams suddenly realized he was fighting to save the case of the People versus Juan Corona. "Mrs. Vallejo, how do you recall that it was May the nineteenth that Mr. and Mrs. Corona were at your house?"

"Because they came to fix the door."

"Mrs. Vallejo, how do you recall at this time that it happened to be on May 19, 1971?"

"Because I said I am not very sure whether it was the nineteenth as I said, or the twentieth. If I only would have a better memory," the interpreter translated without expression. Mrs. Vallejo appeared worried about her uncertainty; she wanted to do better.

The close of the court's day gave Williams time he needed to attempt to organize a rebuttal. The following morning, he was better prepared.

What time had the Coronas left in the afternoon, he asked Mrs. Vallejo.

"It was at the time the children were coming out of school."

"Was it 3:30 or 4:00?"

"My daughters get out of school at 3:15."

"Were your daughters home, Mrs. Vallejo, when the Coronas left your house?"

"It was a little bit after. About fifteen minutes."

"How long does it take your daughters to get from the school back to your home in the afternoon?"

"About five minutes."

"Mrs. Vallejo, how do you recall that Mr. and Mrs. Corona left your house around lunchtime that day?"

"They left around twelve o'clock or so and that is around lunchtime and—may I speak?" She paused, waiting for the judge's permission. "They said to me, 'We have to go and pick something up that we need in order to either fasten or finish the door and to eat.' "

"Mrs. Vallejo, isn't it true that you told the police that you did not want to come to court?"

"Yes, I told them that I didn't want to come."

"And is it also true, Mrs. Vallejo, that you indicated that if the Coronas had asked you to come to court you would have been more than willing to do so?"

"I didn't say the Coronas," she corrected him. "I told them that if the Coronas' attorney would say that I should come, I would come." Hawk smiled at the indirect praise. The lady was doing quite well.

Hawk's redirect of his unexpected witness was short. "You indicated when you were cross-examined by Mr. Williams that you liked the Corona family."

"I appreciate them because they had never done anything wrong to me. He is a courteous person, very respectful."

"Do you like Juan?"

"I esteem him."

Williams had an impeachment witness in Sutter County Sheriff's Matron Theresa Arechar.

On November 2, 1972, Mrs. Arechar and Lieutenant Fred Smith had talked to Mrs. Vallejo for an hour, Mrs. Arechar acting as interpreter. Mrs. Vallejo at that time had told them essentially the same story—with one significant difference.

"She stated Mr. and Mrs. Corona had come over early that morning. She said they returned that afternoon. She said 3:30 or 4:00 in the afternoon. And that they hadn't taken very long, and repaired the door, and left again."

Mrs. Arechar was obviously nervous, a newly hired deputy unfamiliar with the courtroom, warned about the defense attorney.

"Where is the tape recording you made of this conversation?" Hawk asked.

"We didn't tape that conversation."

Mrs. Arechar had merely interpreted Mrs. Vallejo's answers, Smith writing down answers to the questions he posed. Mrs. Arechar herself had not written a report, but had typed Smith's longhand version.

"Now, did you ask her what she meant when she said 'early in the morning?' "

"No, sir."

"Were those her exact words: 'Early in the morning?' "

"She said they came in the morning."

"She did say both?"

"Yes, sir."

"Well, which did she say first?"

"First she said, 'In the morning.' "

"So when she said to you 'early in the morning,' you don't really know what time she was talking about, in terms of hours. Is that correct?"

"No, sir. I don't."

Question by question, Hawk reviewed the entire conversation. At the end of the review, he pointed out it had taken just two or three minutes to recapitulate the interview. What was said during the balance of the hour?

"Mrs. Vallejo takes a long time in explaining different things."

"Will you give us the exact things she said in the explanations, or exact wording, from beginning to end?"

"I don't know the exact wording," Mrs. Arechar confessed.

"Now do you see the value of tape recorders?" Hawk pointedly asked. Judge Patton ordered the remark stricken.

"You can't give us even any idea of the subject matter when she was making explanations?"

"No, sir."

"Did you translate this for Mr. Smith, these explanations?"

"Yes, sir."

"And is that all in the report?"

"No, sir."

The groundwork for an alibi had been laid.

The medical evidence took five days, four doctors in turn reviewing their autopsy protocols. Little of the testimony was of any concern to Hawk; the defense agreed that there were twenty-five homicides in the case. The details in most instances were unimportant.

Hawk did, however, take an obvious dislike to Doctor Thomas P. Connolly, Jr., the first of the two Yuba City doctors called to testify.

"I take it you are a diplomate of the Board of Internal Medicine," Hawk asked, knowing Doctor Connolly was not.

"I am board-eligible, not board-certified."

Hawk was clearly amused by Connolly's unique status. "How many times have you taken the exam to become certified as a diplomate?"

"I have taken the written examination on two occasions and I have passed the written examination on two occasions. I have taken an oral examination on six separate other occasions. All of the oral examinations I have been unsuccessful in."

"You have failed the oral examination six times?"

"That is correct."

"You are not a pathologist?"

"That is correct."

"Generally, basically, what you are is a general practitioner, isn't that correct?"

"That is not correct. One does not have to have *per se* a board certification in this particular specialty. I am certified by the type of practice I have, by the fact that I have a large amount of referral type of practice, consultation practice, my colleagues, the community, the people that I work with." Connolly was sputtering in his anger.

"In other words, Doctor, what you are really saying is that you are sort of self-certified?"

"That is not correct."

"Okay, all right. Thank you, Doctor."

Fahey began with the first victim, Kenneth Whitacre, killed by a stab wound that penetrated from eight to ten inches through the chest, the blade severing Whitacre's aorta.

On cross-examination, Hawk showed the doctor the machete, asking if it could have inflicted the death wound. No, the blade was too wide. The hunting knife had a blade four inches long. Could that have made the wound?

It could have. "I think one of the things that we have to remember is that the chest wall is compressible."

"But this blade being four inches long, for this to have cut the aorta, all the man would have to do is put this knife in and depress the chest four to six inches?"

Connolly agreed. Hawk looked at the jurors. They appeared dubious.

The last weapon was the eight-inch Tennessee Toothpick, long enough to have reached the aorta. But the last inch of the cutting edge of the knife had a pair of sharp hooks projecting, the hooks designed to tear the bottom of the wound.

"My question to you, sir is: Do you see any evidence that one side of the wound was ripped?"

"I did not, and I did not look for it."

Connolly's next autopsy was on a body from the riverbank graveyard, the victim labeled John Doe, number 1. He had been killed by a massive blow to the skull.

"Where did you get the number 'one'?"

"I think they were just picked as we went along doing them."

"You mean, you just picked some guy out of a casket and said, 'Well, we will call him number one, and we will call him number four?' Is that what you did?"

"I think we tried to do it in more or less chronological order."

"Where did you get the 'John Doe number one?' Did you just make that up?"

"That is correct."

Connolly estimated the victim could not have been dead less than four days, "and could be anything beyond that."

"How many fingers did he have?"

"I don't know how many fingers he had, counsellor. I was looking for causes of death."

Sample, the victim the prosecution now claimed was in the first of the riverbank graves, had nine fingers and had been stabbed in the chest.

Connolly's third autopsy had been labeled "John Doe number three. Someone from the sheriff's office that was there identified the remains as Donald Smith."

"Was this person, Donald Smith, a bearded person?"

"I noted no significant beard or mentioned it. I presume in the absence of mentioning it he wasn't."

Donald Smith had a full beard.

Doctor Connolly had talked to Fahey before testifying; his testimony reflected it. "John Doe, number six. The body is that of an apparent white male. In the left parietal area, a horseshoe-shaped laceration is present with an underlying skull fracture. Cause of death: skull fracture, multiple; stab wound of the chest."

"As to the wounds that you observed on this man's skull," Fahey asked, "do you have an opinion as to the instrument or instruments used to cause these wounds?"

"The first wound that I described, the horseshoe-shaped wound, was such that it immediately called to my mind, as I was doing this, something like a posthole digger."

"Like a what?" Fahey asked to be certain the jury had it clearly.

"A posthole digger."

Fahey ostentatiously showed the tool found in Corona's garage to the doctor. "You mean something like this, Doctor Connolly?"

"Yes, that is something like that," the doctor agreed.

It was too clumsy for Hawk; his cross-examination was contemptuous.

"Have you got your report there about this body?"

"Yes, I do."

"Would you read it over to yourself and then show me where it talks about a posthole digger?"

"It says nothing in the report of a posthole digger."

"All right. Sir, now, you have reviewed your testimony before you came to court here at one time, didn't you?"

"Yes, I did."

Fahey realized his witness was in trouble. "Your Honor, I note it is almost twelve o'clock and—"

"Well, let me finish the one question," Hawk cut in.

"We have about five minutes to go," Judge Patton ruled, placing his pocket watch on the bench.

"Well, counsel appears to be somewhat upset, and he wanted time. I have no objection to giving him some time," Fahey was the model of courtesy.

"That is correct, Your Honor. That kind of nonsense always upsets me." Hawk turned back to the doctor.

"Do you want to look at page 210 of the grand jury transcript, and after you find the spot where you talk about the posthole digger, would you show me where it is?"

Doctor Connolly conceded he had not mentioned a "posthole digger type of wound" in either his Grand Jury testimony or his autopsy report.

"Now, sir, you say that this wound could have been caused by a posthole digger?"

"That is correct."

"I assume it also could be caused by a thousand-year-old metal vase from the Ming Dynasty in China. Right?"

"If it had a similar shape, I would think so."

"You are not suggesting that you think that a posthole digger caused that wound, are you?"

"I have no idea what caused the wound." Doctor Connolly had reversed his position.

The second local doctor, Charles Clement, was a board-certified internist. Doctor Leavenworth had described him to Hawk as a competent doctor.

Clement had autopsied the nine-fingered man in whose grave the meat receipts were found. He could estimate that the victim had been dead "a few days to a few weeks." It was a critical point; if the jury believed the body had been in the first grave with the receipts—that sheriffs and morticians had simply made a numbering mistake and had not switched bodies deliberately—then Hawk had to reinforce the notion that the receipts had been deliberately planted after the nine-fingered man was killed.

"First of all, I'd like to know what you mean when you say 'a few,'" Hawk began.

"Two, three, four, five days."

"Pardon?"

"A few, three—"

"Three, four, five, along in there, something like that."

"Yes."

"And that is one reasonable medical conclusion?"

"Right."

"You said the other limit is a few weeks. Does that mean three, four or five weeks old?"

"Correct, sir."

"And that is also a reasonable medical opinion on your part, is it not?"

"Yes, sir."

Doctor Clement's necessarily imprecise estimate of the time of death had given the defense attorney an important argument. If there were two reasonable interpretations of the evidence, the law mandated the jury adopt the interpretation pointing to innocence. It was an argument Hawk had hammered at repeatedly while picking the jury, it was an argument he would repeat at trial's end.

Later in the first of the five days of medical testimony, Hawk established that the victims would have bled profusely because of the "great number" of blood vessels severed in the attack. The victims in these cases would lose between two and four pints.

"Now, how would you expect this to appear? Would there just be a few little, fine drops here and there?"

"It would spread out over an area possibly of several feet."

"There would be a lot of blood on the floor?"

"There would be a lot of blood on the floor," Doctor Clement agreed.

Joseph Masters was one of the two Sacramento pathologists who had reexamined the bodies of the first victims, then autopsied the later bodies. Doctor Masters too had seen the nine-fingered man.

Fahey pointed to the head wound on the protocol drawings. "Do you have any opinion as to the type of instrument that might have inflicted that wound?"

"This is a chop-type blow, a fairly heavy cutting instrument with a cutting blade almost certainly four-and-one-half inches or longer."

"Would this type of wound you have described be consistent with, say, a bolo machete?"

"Yes, it would."

On cross-examination, Hawk asked, "When you say some of these wounds were consistent with a bolo machete, were those wounds consistent with any other types of weapons that you can think of?"

"I think they represent a cutting instrument with a sharp edge which has a fairly heavy blade. I am sure that there are other cutting instruments that would fit my qualification. I am not saying that a bolo machete is the only instrument that could have caused all of these chop-type wounds."

"Have you ever in your experience as a pathologist gone out to a crime scene where a victim was lying there cut up and dead?"

"I have."

"Now, what do you usually find? A little drop of blood here, a little drop there?"

"Not in cases where the wounds are as extensive as we are describing in the case at hand."

"If you put this man in a van, would you find a little drop of blood here and there?"

"I would not expect to find a little drop of blood here and there, if blood was still flowing from these wounds."

Doctor Masters agreed that, when considering exhumed bodies dead more than two days, fixing a time of death "is at best kind of an educated guess." The nine-fingered man had been dead, he estimated, "a few days to a couple of weeks," perhaps longer.

The medical testimony was a sparring match between Hawk and Fahey, the prosecutor repeatedly asking if the wounds were "consistent with a machete," Hawk countering by establishing that they were also consistent with meat cleavers, broad-blade axes, swords, even a scimitar.

Some of the wounds on the victims appeared to be postmortem blows, inflicted as a coup de grâce. The doctors had not taken rectal swabs or checked for semen or feces after the first body; decomposition militated against it. The stab wounds indicated that whoever had used the knife was an expert. The victims who struggled apparently were more severely hacked about the head than those whose bodies lacked defense wounds. Only one of the bodies appeared to have laid in the open air for any period of time before being buried. Stab wounds in the chests of the victims "were consistent with" both knives found in the mess hall on the Sullivan ranch.

Doctor Pierce Rooney was the most qualified of the four doctors, and the most impartial. He agreed that the prior autopsies in Yuba City had placed him at a disadvantage; he didn't know what else he might have found had the bodies not been opened, then handled by the morticians, washed, and prepared for burial. The bearded man Doctor Rooney had marked as the fifth victim; the photograph of the bearded man labeled E-2, the fourth, appeared to be the same man. Yes, Doctor Rooney knew Sutter County now wanted to label the bearded man as the sixth victim. Rather than hastily unearth victims, the best practice would have been to call for an experienced pathologist; had he been on the riverbank that night, he would have been in a better position to estimate the time of death of the nine-fingered man.

Late in the fourth day of the medical phase of the prosecution's case, Fahey asked Doctor Rooney, "If this person were, or these other bodies that had these head wounds of this nature, if they had survived would they have been horribly disfigured?"

"What is the relevance of that?" Hawk interrupted.

Judge Patton too was puzzled. "I don't understand it. How would it be relevant?"

"If they would have survived would they be disfigured? I will stipulate that they'd be disfigured," Hawk agreed.

"All right," Fahey smiled.

"What has that got to do with anything?" Hawk asked him.

"It may," Fahey said enigmatically.

The following afternoon, Hawk understood. José Romero Raya had changed his story and now claimed it was Juan, not Natividad, who had hacked him in the rest room of the Guadalajara Café in February 1970.

23

The Evidence

November 13, 14, 15, 1971
December 12, 13, 14, 15, 1972

"If this came in and you are wrong on it," warned a troubled judge Patton, "you have lost your case. You have got a reversal there without any question at all. It is just that significant and you are risking everything on this point."

Williams and Teja had worked for two months on the Guadalajara incident, first to get Raya to change his story, then to research the labyrinthine legal issues involved in introducing it in the trial. Not until mid-November did Williams succeed—"by taking a different tack," he explained in chambers to Judge Patton on the afternoon of November 22.

"The different tack involved more or less ingratiating ourselves to the responsible members of the Mexican community and through them approaching José Raya. Mrs. Paula Reynosa heard Raya say when he got out of the hospital that 'Juan assaulted me.'" Mrs. Reynosa, the sister-in-law of Ray Duron, finally had convinced Raya. "And that's when José finally comes around and says, 'Well, the initial story that I told was the correct one, that I wanted to seek my own vengeance against Mr. Corona and that is why I have been giving law enforcement the runaround for the last year and a half.'"

Judge Patton was confronted with the biggest decision he would have to make in the Corona trial. When Hawk had earlier sought to use the attack to implicate Natividad Corona, the judge had temporarily barred testimony about the Guadalajara incident on the grounds of remoteness.

Now the prosecution—which had opposed introduction of the Guadalajara incident when it cast some doubt on Juan Corona's guilt—was claiming it had new evidence, and wanted to use it. Under the law's theory of common scheme or plan, the prosecution could not use testimony about a crime for which the defendant was *not* on trial unless two conditions were met: first, the crime for which he was not on trial was closely similar to the offense for which he was in court; and, second, the prosecution could establish by a preponderance of the evidence that the defendant had, indeed, committed the crime for which he was *not* charged.

There was no more certain way to a reversal of conviction, Judge Patton realized, than wrongly to permit the jury to hear testimony about the Guadalajara incident. The rules of admissibility were vague, but the appellate courts were harsh with judges who violated them.

Williams outlined the prosecution's theory: "The primary relevance of this prior criminal act that we are seeking to introduce is that it goes to the identity of the perpetrator of the twenty-five homicides involved." The syllogism was simple: if Corona cut Raya, and Raya's wounds were similar to those on the twenty-five victims, then Corona murdered the twenty-five.

"Let me ask a couple of questions," Judge Patton interrupted. "José Raya, he brought a suit, didn't he?"

"He sued Natividad Corona and Juan Corona—"

"He was *named,* they didn't serve Juan," Hawk cut Williams off.

"I recall the People telling me a short time ago that they had no case, they couldn't tie Mr. Juan Corona into it," Judge Patton remarked.

"They got Raya to change his story, that is all," Hawk said with a shrug, interpreting the effort to raise the Guadalajara matter as a sign of the prosecution's desperation. The three prosecutors had spent hours discussing pros and cons, finally deciding to proceed only because they had no alternative. Their case was in bad shape anyway.

Patton needed time to research the admissibility problem. Time pressed; the controversy would extend the trial another two months at least, as each side staged a trial within a trial. In effect, the Guadalajara incident could be aired twice, once before the judge alone to determine its admissibility; then, possibly, a second time before the jury. And each airing would require weeks.

To expedite matters, the judge decided to handle the limited issue of the similarity between the assault on Raya and the murders of the twenty-five; he asked both sides to prepare briefs on that narrow issue only. The briefs in, he would then schedule a hearing in midtrial to hear prosecution witnesses on this issue.

If the prosecution established the similarity of assaults to his satisfaction —and Judge Patton was frank in his doubts—then he would hold a hearing on the larger question of the preponderance of the evidence pointing to Corona's involvement in the Guadalajara incident. Only if he were satisfied there too would he permit Raya to testify before the jury that Juan Corona was his assailant.

The hearing on the similarity of the assaults was set for the conclusion of the prosecution's case. Meanwhile, there was still the remainder of the Peoples' case-in-chief to be heard.

As a criminalist for the state, Don Stottlemyer had examined most of

the physical evidence gathered in the case. Essentially a specialized laboratory technician, Stottlemyer had attempted to group and type dried blood,
had conducted ballistics tests, and examined striation marks. He would
become a familiar witness.

It took the entire morning for the district attorney to work through the
evidence that Stottlemyer had studied in Sacramento. There were small
drops of blood on the Levi's jacket thrown into the garage rafters. There
were small drops of human blood on mats found in the trunk of Corona's
Impala, on what appeared to be a buckle-less child's belt recovered from
the car trunk, on the latch, and molding. There were specks of human
blood on both rubber boots found in the van, and one on the fly of a pair
of men's shorts stuffed under a seat in the van. Stottlemyer had recovered
eight small stains, seven from the interior of Corona's van, one from
the exterior, behind the rear bumper. It appeared that the stain on the
rear of the van "originated from the bed portion, ran down the outside
rear end of the van, and onto the gas tank immediately under it. All of
the stains—those from the interior were "quite small, like splatters"—were
of human blood.

"Would water wash away a bloodstain in every event so that it would
no longer be present for testing?" Teja asked.

"No, I couldn't say it would in every event."

"Which tends to wash away faster, an older bloodstain or a newer
bloodstain?"

"A fresh bloodstain."

"Now, insofar as the eight stains that you found in and outside the van
itself, did any of them appear to show signs of having been washed?"

"The ones in the interior of the van did not. The one on the outside
of the van appeared to. This would be an opinion."

Stottlemyer had also analyzed the bullet taken from the skull of the
thirteenth victim. "After cleaning it I examined it microscopically to determine certain class characteristics of the bullet. The barrel imparts the
characteristic striations or engravings along the bullet's land and groove,
striations which are characteristic to that particular weapon and that
weapon only."

"Did you form any opinion as to the type of weapon which fired the
bullet into Mr. Kamp?" Teja asked.

"The opinion was that the bullet could have been fired in this Browning
weapon, but I would like to explain to the jury that the basic class
characteristics were similar, or the same. But this doesn't mean that the
bullet was fired in that particular weapon for this reason: the striations on
a bullet are the only way you can make an identification as to a bullet
being fired from a particular weapon, and in this particular case the
striations on the bullet were gone. In my opinion, they were gone because
of the decomposition products within the body. They just did not have
the fine line striations."

Stottlemyer had cut a crucial link in the prosecution's case. Hawk smiled to himself. Stottlemyer had voluntarily testified to a fact that Hawk had intended to ask on cross-examination. It was more effective here, and still gave him an opportunity to reinforce it on cross-examination.

There was "a small amount of human blood on the pistol," near the muzzle. Stottlemyer had looked at the gun but was unable to determine when it had last been fired. The weapon was dirty, with a "little bit of rust in the barrel," uncleaned since it had last been fired.

It was not until after lunch that Teja broached the problem of the machete found in Corona's van. "Did you do any other striation testing in this case?"

Stottlemyer had. "A portion of a skull from one of the victims was submitted to me. This portion of skull had beautiful striation marks on the skull. I made attempts over probably a five-month period with numerous instruments submitted to the laboratory to see if I could identify the striations as having been made by any particular instrument."

"Were you ever able to identify an instrument as having made those marks?"

"No."

Handing Stottlemyer the bolo machete, Teja asked, "What in particular on that blade would leave these striations, or these marks?"

"Well, any defects on the cutting edge attributed to usage, hitting other sharp objects, sharpening."

"Now, there are some rather obvious defects to the cutting edge of that particular exhibit, are there not?" Teja was attempting to minimize the damage Hawk could cause by exploring the failure to match the machete to the skull.

"Yes, there are nicks and gouges on the cutting surface."

"As a result of your examination could you testify that that blade never did have human blood on it?"

"No, I couldn't say that."

"This is rank speculation, Your Honor," Hawk protested. "If it doesn't have blood, it doesn't have blood."

"Sustained," Judge Patton ruled, but Teja too could plant suspicions in the jury's mind.

Now it was Hawk's turn. Carrying the machete with him by the blade, occasionally flipping it into the air to catch it once again by the blade, he began his cross-examination. "Now, you spent six months trying to match that machete against that skull, didn't you?"

"I would say approximately five months."

"Would it be fair to say that of all the items of evidence that you examined, that they seemed most interested in this and the skull?"

"They were interested in it. I don't know whether they were more interested in that than, say, the bloodstains. I myself thought this [machete] would be a better piece of evidence if I could identify it."

"Right. In other words, if you had matched this, it would be a pretty good circumstantial evidence that Juan Corona killed somebody with it?" The blade flipped in front of Hawk's face.

"Objection, Your Honor." Teja was struggling now with the evidence. "That's conclusionary."

"Overruled."

"Yes, I would say that," Stottlemyer agreed.

"But you didn't match it, did you?"

"No, I didn't."

"Does that mean that machete didn't cut the skull?"

"Yes, that's right. Either that machete didn't produce these marks, or if it did, the machete had to be altered subsequently."

"How?" Hawk whacked the machete into his open palm.

"By hitting another hard-surfaced object. Filing. Sharpening. Anything that would change that cutting edge."

"Would it be fair to say that that machete is just ridiculously dull?" Hawk offered the blade to Stottlemyer. "You run your hand up and down it."

"That's right. It's not like a razor."

"Well, now, you wouldn't suggest to us that since May 26, 1971, all by itself it got dull?" Flip. Flip.

"No."

"If this had been ground along, say, a piece of rock, that would make the metal shiny, wouldn't it?" Flip.

"Right."

"Would it be fair to say that you have no evidence whatsoever that this blade was altered or had been altered in any recent time when you first looked at it on May 26?"

"I would say that's a fair statement. There would be no way I could prove that it had been altered." Once again Stottlemyer's volunteered comment helped the defense.

Hawk turned to the blood found in the van. Stottlemyer did not know whether the floor had been cleaned or not. "It was dirty at the time I saw it. It didn't appear to be freshly washed, in other words."

Did it appear anyone had "got in there, hosed it out, steamed it, anything to clean it up?"

"It didn't appear that way to me, no." Blood on the exterior could have been rain washed.

"And you found a few little drops of blood in the back of the van?"

"Splatters. Splatters of blood. Yes."

"And you understand that at that time you looked at that van, it was used to transport farm workers?"

"I don't know."

"Now, did you find a whole bunch of blood, indicating that a man with his skull split had been transported in that van?"

"No, I didn't find any evidence of this."

Stottlemyer was confident, sure of the work he had done on the case, firm in his conclusions. His doubts about the handling of the evidence, upon the priorities given the machete rather than the blood he kept to himself.

"Now, sir, would you tell me if the blood you found was connected with any of the twenty-five men who died in the Marysville-Yuba City area?"

"No."

"Is it possible to do this?"

"No. By grouping blood you could determine maybe an individual had the same type blood, but this doesn't individualize that individual where you could say the blood came from a particular individual."

"Okay."

"Not possible," added Stottlemyer.

"So you conclude it did or you conclude it didn't, and either interpretation would be reasonable, wouldn't it."

"Right." Even before Doctor Ruth Guy, the prosecution's blood expert, testified, she had, in effect, been challenged. Given two equally reasonable interpretations of the evidence, the jury was sworn to adopt that which pointed to innocence.

Through the afternoon, Hawk continued his cross-examination of Stottlemyer, enjoying himself hugely. At one point he picked at a cut on his finger, squeezed a drop of blood onto a Kleenex and asked, "How big is that cut."

"It's very small."

"That drop of blood there," Hawk pointed to the Kleenex. "How does that drop of blood compare with the drops of blood you found in the truck?"

"I would say similar; this is a little bit larger even."

The Kleenex entered into evidence, Hawk picked up the pistol. "Now, sir, do you know from any test that you ran whether anyone other than Juan Corona ever handled that gun, or even if Juan had handled the gun?"

"No."

"How would one find out?"

"Check it for fingerprints."

"Were you ever asked by Sutter County to perform a test on this gun to see if anyone besides Mr. Corona had ever handled it?"

"No, I was not asked."

"Were you asked by Sutter County on any of the things given to you to perform a test to see who might have been handling them?"

"No, I was not."

"Okay. And you told us, earlier, that fingerprint evidence is pretty reliable, isn't it?"

"Yes."

The hairs on the posthole digger: No, it was not unusual to find hair in a garage, especially if the lady of the house did her washing there. If there were children playing, the hair could well be theirs. Hair blew around a great deal.

"Anything about that posthole digger to indicate that anyone ever bashed someone in the head with it?"

"No, I didn't see any bloodstains or anything." So much for Fahey's theory.

The pistol. There were hundreds of thousands like it manufactured by Browning since World War II. The bullet in Kamp's head could have been fired by any of them. Fifteen different manufacturers now made some seventy-one different nine-millimeter automatics; any one of them might have fired the bullet.

The blood on the child's belt, "What kind of blood was it?" asked Hawk.

"Just human blood is all I can determine." The test for the blood's grouping was inconclusive.

"Could the blood on there be consistent with a little girl that had a nosebleed?"

"This could be, yes."

"Okay. Incidentally, a person with a nosebleed produces an awful lot of blood, don't they?"

"It could, yes," Stottlemyer agreed pleasantly. It was not often that defense attorneys treated him so kindly on cross-examination.

"Now, is the amount of blood that was on that floor mat, would that be inconsistent with a child that had a nosebleed?"

"That wouldn't, no. There was a very small amount on that, as I recall."

"Would you be prepared to say, sir, that in your expert opinion as a criminalist, that one or more of the twenty-five men who died in Marysville or wherever they died, that one or more of those twenty-five men were transported in the trunk of that car?"

"No." Stottlemyer shook his head. "It might be possible, but I—I don't feel that I should say that."

Hawk handled Stottlemyer roughly on only one point during his recross-examination the following morning. In his final report, Stottlemyer had written:

> It was not possible to identify the machete as having made the striations on the portion of skull labeled as having been taken from victim W-I-I. This finding indicates that either this tool did not make the striations on the skull or that it did make the striations and the cutting edge was subsequently altered.

Hawk intended to close the loophole.

"You found no evidence whatsoever that the machete had been altered in recent time?"

"That is correct."

"So would it be fair to summarize that, in your opinion, there is no doubt in your mind that that is not the machete that cut the skull?"

"I can't eliminate it, counsel. But I can't identify it, either. I can't say that was the weapon." Stottlemyer was not going to give in easily.

"Then would you tell us, sir, in what way that weapon could have been altered so it was the weapon that did it?" Hawk was closing doors.

"Well, if in fact it were," Stottlemyer began.

"Yes," Hawk interrupted. But 'if.' Okay? How could this 'if' come about? You didn't find any evidence of it?"

"That's right. I didn't."

"You are an expert, aren't you? In this field?"

"Yes."

"You are trained to look for these things, aren't you?"

"Correct." Stottlemyer realized he was boxed. "I didn't see any signs of its being altered."

"Well, sir, I am not talking about absolute certainties, like absolute zero or stopping molecular action, but as a criminalist would it be your opinion that this blade did not cut that skull?"

Stottlemyer finally walked through the door Hawk held open for him.

"Yes, I would tend to believe that this weapon did not create those striations."

Ronald Fahey had been given the confusing problem of the tire tracks. His first witness was Jacob Compton, the engineer for the state Department of Water Resources who had been surveying in the north riverbottom orchard during the spring of 1971. On May 18 of that year, he had worked in the vicinity of graves 19 and 20, driving in a pickup truck equipped for better traction with distinctive mud-grip tires on the rear wheels. It was Compton's tire track of which Deputy Rodemaker had made a cast, and which Stottlemyer had summarily eliminated as not having been made by Corona's vehicles. Compton's earlier testimony before the Grand Jury—of seeing a light-colored van in the orchard twice on the same day—was ignored. Compton could not identify Corona as the driver. Furthermore, crews had been working in the orchard thinning; Corona would have every reason to be there.

Don Stottlemyer was recalled by Fahey, his task now to testify that a week before he had compared the casts Rodemaker had poured in the orchard with a mud-grip tire similar to that on Compton's truck. The tread patterns of cast and tire were similar. Stottlemyer added that in June 1971 he had compared the two casts from the riverbottom orchard with the tires on Corona's three vehicles and had found them totally different.

Stottlemyer had never been shown the plaster cast of the tire track taken by Detective Harold Cochran beside Kenneth Whitacre's grave on May 20, 1971. The cast had been lost in the evidence locker for seventeen months.

Detective Cochran identified the casts he had made, misplaced for the past seventeen months and not examined until the previous week. Cochran had picked the clearest spot in the track "just north of the grave site, at the northwest point of the tire track."

"Could you tell from where the tire tracks had come?"

"They came from the east."

"Did they continue indefinitely in a westerly direction?"

"No. They ended at that point." The vehicle which had stopped by the grave left by backing up. Except by the most unlikely of coincidences, the tire tracks at the grave had been made by the person who buried Kenneth Whitacre.

Roland Wilder had compared the casts with the inked impressions of the tires on Corona's vehicles on October 18, the day he received the material in Washington, D.C.

A firearm and tool-mark examiner for the ATF laboratory, Wilder had selected one of the four inked impressions of the Goodyear polyglass tires which came as standard equipment when Corona bought his new van. Wilder photographed it, photographed the cast, and prepared overlays. "I compared the shape of the impressions and the cast, the spacing of the grooves and the treads and the size of the grooves and tracks."

"And would you tell us what your opinion is?" Fahey asked.

"In my opinion, there is a strong similarity between the tread shape, spacing and the size of the tread."

"And based on that opinion, do you have an opinion as to whether or not the tires that made those inked impressions could have made that impression that is contained in this tire cast?"

"Yes, they very definitely could have made those."

Hawk was at a severe disadvantage. Wilder's report of work done almost a month before had been withheld until that day. While Judge Patton might have permitted him to defer his cross-examination, ordering Wilder to return to court after a suitable interval, Hawk did not want to leave the unchallenged testimony resting before the jury. Instead, he elected to cross-examine the federal criminalist.

"Sir, would you show me on your report where it says there is a strong similarity—that's a good word, strong, very emotional. Show me—"

"Your Honor, I am going to object to counsel's comments."

"Okay, I withdraw that," Hawk shrugged. "Show me the word 'strong.'"

"It's not in the report," Wilder conceded.

"Oh," Hawk crooned in mock understanding. "And show me in your report that expression, 'very definitely.' That's another good word."

"It's not in the report either."

"Oh, I see. Now, sir, isn't it a fact that Montgomery Wards sells tires?"

"Yes, sir, they do."

Hawk then read a long list of companies, Wilder agreeing each sold tires: Sears, Uni-Royal, General, Dayton, Goodrich, Goodyear, Gates— "a lot of tire manufacturers, aren't there?"

"Yes, sir."

"Now, sir, would you tell us of your own knowledge that Sears does not manufacture a tire like that?"

"I can't say of my own knowledge."

"Now, would you tell us, sir, of your own knowledge, that General does not make a tire similar in size, shape and space?"

"I can't say."

Hawk reviewed the entire list. "You only checked with one company, didn't you?"

"That's correct, yes."

"Goodyear, correct."

"Goodyear."

"And you checked Goodyear because there was some information given to you from somebody from the Sutter County sheriff's office, is that right?"

"That's correct."

"Now sir, are you prepared to say which one of those four inked impressions is the closest?"

"I couldn't say which one is closer than the other."

"Well, did you actually compare the four inked impressions against each other?"

"Not by means of overlay. Just visually compared the four."

"Now, sir, are you prepared to say that the tire which made one of those four inked impressions, that *that* tire and no other tire in the world could have made that cast?"

"No, sir, I am not."

Hawk had done all he could to minimize the damage.

The next witness, Charles Michael Hoffman, was another of the criminalists from the ATF laboratory who had worked on the Corona case. A forensic chemist, Hoffman's specialty was neutron activation analysis, an exotic and expensive method of weighing the elements present in samples. Hawk had prepared for Hoffman's testimony by long discussions with his own criminalist, John Thornton, and by digesting a long, highly complex article on the machine and its shortcomings.

Hoffman had compared the elements present in the bullet removed from Kamp's skull, two bullets from the clip of the nine-millimeter automatic discovered in Corona's desk, and two bullets picked at random from the partial box of ammunition Gregory had found in the holster.

"There was no significant difference," he answered Fahey, "in the composition of the bullet taken from the victim as opposed to the other bullets removed from the cartridges examined."

"Are you able to give an opinion as to whether or not that bullet from the victim came from the same batch of Remington ammunition?"

"I have an opinion concerning that," Hoffman answered formally. "It is I could not exclude the bullet from the victim as having come from the same batch. In other words, there was no significant difference between the bullet from the victim and the other bullets examined. I cannot conclusively state, however, that it came from the same batch."

Almost a year after Juan Corona's arrest, Bart Williams had asked Richard Brunelle (no relation to Teja's investigator, Leonard Brunelle), acting chief of the ATF laboratory's forensic staff, to compare ink samples. He was to match ink from the unusual multicolored pen found on Corona's desk in the mess hall with the three critical pages in the ledger recovered from the file cabinet, and with the pocket-sized notebook in which William Kamp had written biblical quotations and religious homilies.

"If through the analysis of ink color," Williams had advised Brunelle, "we can match the pen up with the notebook of the victim then we have established a direct link between property found in Juan Corona's possession and one of the victims in the case."

Brunelle was unable to establish the link Williams wanted.

The multicolored ballpoint pen was of Italian manufacture; only two gross had been shipped to the Sacramento Valley, by mistake. Its ink formulas were virtually unique, whereas the ink in almost all American-made ballpoint pens is furnished by a single manufacturer.

The many-colored entries in Kamp's notebook were not written by the pen found on Corona's desk, Brunelle testified. Two of the nine entries on the back of the immigration slip, one in blue and one in black, had been written with the multicolored pen; seven of the entries in the ledger—in five different colors—matched ink from the pen. None of these entries were of identified victims.

Hoffman had also done extensive work analyzing hair taken from each of the victims, then comparing it to that found in Corona's vehicles and on the posthole digger. All of the hair was compared to samples of Corona's hair belatedly obtained on December 2.

Hair found on the victims' clothing did not match Corona's. "I found there was some microscopic similarity between certain hairs taken from an automobile found on Mr. Corona's premises and hairs from victim number 23, his clothing; and to head hairs from victims number 1, 2, 3, 8, 20, and 21. In view of this similarity, I again examined these further by neutron activation analysis, and with inconclusive results."

Hair from the van did not match any of the victims. The two strands of hair on the posthole digger were similar to head hair from six of the victims. Again the neutron activation analysis was inconclusive.

"In the examination of the hair from the posthole digger, using the microscope, I was able to determine that it was human hair and that it had an actively growing hair follicle, indicationg that it had been forcibly removed."

"Would this indicate to you that the person was living at the time the hair was removed?" Fahey asked.

"Well, either living, or it was removed before the tissue had decomposed to any extent. It could be a dead person, as well."

"Freshly killed?"

"Yes."

Hoffman's hair analysis had been badly hindered. "The hair specimens that were taken from the victims were attached to a portion of the scalp. Whoever had selected these had taken a portion of the scalp and put this in a vial, and as a preservative had apparently added formaldehyde, or formalin solution, to prevent decomposition of the tissue.

"As it turned out, this contaminated the hair samples, either adding contamination to the hairs or extracting some of the trace elements upon which the test is based, preventing an effective comparison."

Hawk's cross-examination was confident. "The fact that you found an active follicle, you said, indicates that it was forcibly removed?"

"Yes, as opposed to the type of hair when you comb your hair that falls out, the dead hair."

"If a woman brushed her hair and there is a little snag, there might be a whole bunch of hairs right there on that brush now that got active follicles on the bottom. Right?"

"Yes, sir, that this true."

"And that is forcible removal. Right?"

"Yes, sir."

"Now, the fact that you find a hair that has an active follicle, that doesn't mean that the hair came from a person who was being murdered, does it?"

"No, sir."

"What does it mean when an expert says that hairs are similar, two hairs are similar to hair off of six different people's heads?"

"It means that they were microscopically similar and could have come from any one of those individuals."

"What does the phrase 'microscopically similar' in this case mean and how does it advance anyone in terms of identification?"

"Identification also encompasses exclusion," Hoffman answered smoothly. "The purpose of the microscopic examination in this case was to see if there was a possibility that it could have come from any of these sources."

"You understand in California, at least in criminal cases, they don't deal in possibilities?"

Fahey's objection was sustained.

"Well, beyond saying that two hairs on the posthole digger are similar to six people, did you find anything similar about those two hairs and the twenty-five victims that is significant?"

"No, sir."

Hawk then established through Hoffman that the average person had some 100,000 hairs on his head, that an individual's hair varied from strand to strand at any given time. "Isn't it true that hair as a means of identifying in any type criminal case is a very treacherous business?"

"Yes, it is," Hoffman agreed, still the scientist.

Hoffman's neutron activation analysis of the hair had been inconclusive because of the preservative in which the samples had been sent from the Sacramento County Coroner's Office to the ATF laboratory.

"You said to us that formalin messed up the tests?"

"Basically, yes, sir."

"And in so doing eliminated the possibility of your showing that these hairs did not come from these victims, and in so doing jeopardized Juan Corona?"

Fahey's objection was multiple. "It is argumentative, compound, complex, and misstating the evidence."

"Sustained."

For another ten minutes Hawk systematically minimized the hair analysis, concluding, "Would it be a fair summary to say that you examined a lot of hair in this case and that after all of this examination you found absolutely no connection between Mr. Corona and these victims?"

"Yes, sir, that would be a fair statement." *

Fahey's redirect was short. The hair on the posthole digger had a follicle, indicating that it had been forcibly removed. That hair was microscopically similar to that of six of the victims, including number one, Kenneth Whitacre. "Would the fact that victim one was buried and dead less than twenty-four hours give any greater weight to your opinion?"

Hawk cut off any answer. "Your Honor, that is improper unless they intend to introduce evidence that a hole was dug with a posthole digger, and to my knowledge at this point in the case I don't think there is any evidence whatsoever that anybody went out and dug a bunch of graves with a posthole digger."

"There isn't any evidence in the case that the graves weren't dug with a posthole digger, Your Honor," Fahey retorted.

It was the kind of argument that the prosecution would use again.

The burden of proof was to be Juan Corona's.

---

* But that evening, United Press International sent out a story headed in the *Los Angeles Times* "Seven Victims' Hair Linked to Corona": "A government chemist testified at the trial of Juan Corona Friday that human hair found on a posthole digger belonging to the defendant matched the hair of some of the mass murder victims." Juan Corona was not yet free of inaccurate reporting.

24

The Secretor
December 6-12, 1972

Except to curse the constant rain, Richard Hawk had paid no attention to the change of seasons. The heat of September had melded into December's cold fogs, the orchards flanking the highway between Concord and Fairfield barren now, often flooded.

Juan Corona had watched the seasons change from the back of the barred van which carried him each day between Vacaville and the county courthouse at West Texas and Union Streets. He saw little of the world beyond his cell and the courtroom, but a man who had worked on farms all his life watched the weather out of habit.

For Corona it was not so bad now. The trial would be over soon and he had promised Gloria, as Hawk had promised him, that he would be home soon. She talked about moving permanently to Fairfield; the neighbors were nice to her and the children liked the schoolteachers. He would find a job, maybe contracting, maybe in a factory, and begin again.

If the jury let him out of jail. That schoolteacher was bad, and he did not like the man with the beard, the Marine sergeant. Corona had his doubts about Johnson. He even offered to take a "lie detective" test if Mr. Hawk wanted him to, if that would help.

Hawk had thought about it for a while, then had dropped the idea; the state Supreme Court had held lie detector testimony inadmissible. Patton was not the sort of judge who struck off on his own, who made unprecedented rulings. They didn't need the lie detector really. All you had to do was look around to see that. Ronald Fahey had come into the case all steamed up; he had long since given up. "He's just going to earn his $45-per-hour and go home," Hawk told newsmen over drinks. Fahey was even laughing now when Hawk teased him about the posthole digger.

Williams and Teja knew it, too; they never bothered to look at the jury anymore; apparently the jurors' reactions to witnesses didn't matter any longer.

Hawk had picked up a number of signals. "It's got to help that we've got the clerk and the bailiff shaking their heads." More than half of the fifteen jurors and alternates had asked a friend of the Corona family for the "Justicia para Juan Corona" buttons the defense committee had printed up. "There may be two or three sadistic sonovabitches in there who want a button of someone they're going to convict, but I can't imagine that many of them," Hawk explained. Best of all, one of the buttons went to Mrs. Blazek, the schoolteacher. Apparently she shared the dominant view, no matter how much she personally disliked him. As far as Hawk could tell, "the attitude of the jurors was the prosecution was really fucked up." A number of them were openly perturbed with Fahey's salary; the new prosecutor made as much in two hours as the entire jury did in a day.

The reporters covering the trial sensed it, too. Jerry Cohen, of the Los Angeles *Times,* still unconvinced, had come up for a few days, then gone home to write an article stating "the best the prosecution could hope for would be a hung jury. As opinions stand now regarding testimony to date, it is believed that at least eight jurors would go along with a verdict of innocent."

The prosecution had two phases of its case left, the blood evidence and the handwriting. Hawk was not concerned with either. He had spent hours with his criminalist whose specialty was typing dried blood, and he had never lost a case in which the prosecution had used handwriting analysis against his man.

Doctor Ruth Guy had done the blood analysis for the prosecution. A professor at the University of Texas' Southwestern Medical School in Dallas, she was also associate director of the blood bank at Parkland Memorial Hospital. Her credentials were impressive: a doctor of philosophy degree in bacteriology and immunology from Stanford, teaching medical students, professional societies and honors, published research and guest lectureships.

The voir dire of an expert witness is normally a perfunctory matter, a listing of credentials which ostensibly establish the witness' competence in a given area. Two factors in Doctor Guy's case, however, prompted Hawk to undertake a detailed voir dire of the woman: Thornton had never heard of her, and by limiting her work to only the familiar ABO systems, she had done only a small portion of the work she might have.

Hawk did not consider the woman's testimony to be crucial. That she had found A-type blood in the van or on a garment did not mean she had found a victim's blood; some 90 million people in the United States had O-type blood, 80 million, type A, 20 million, B, and 10 million, AB. Had she further refined her work, conceivably she might have found enough classification factors to match victims and bloodstains. The prosecution, though, had only the gross ABO and Rh factors of the victims, culled from blood bank records.

Having read Hawk's cross-examination of another medical expert in a prior case—the transcript furnished to her by Williams—the once-brunet Doctor Guy was defensive. "Doctor, I understand you are not a medical doctor."

"That is correct."

"Your doctorate is a Ph.D., like somebody having a doctorate in political science?"

"Yes, but they would know about political science. They would not know about immunohematology, nor would I know about political science."

"Are you through?"

"Through," she agreed.

"What is the study of bacteriology?"

"Well, bacteriology is the study of microorganisms and I was specifically interested in disease-producing organisms." The woman smiled; lecturing was a familiar business.

"And what does that have to do with typing dry bloodstains?"

"Actually that has very little to do with it, but the immunological principles are the same. This is basic immunology."

Hawk leaned calmly against the rail that separated the bar from the spectators, nodding as Doctor Guy spoke. "I take it the answer to my question, Doctor, is the study of bacteriology has nothing to do with the testing of dry bloodstains."

"No, it doesn't," she replied.

The woman was associate director of the hospital blood bank; Hawk could not challenge her ability to type fresh or whole blood.

"There is a difference, a distinct difference between testing whole blood and testing dried bloodstains?"

"Yes."

"And the techniques are much more delicate when you test dry—"

"Yes, they are," Doctor Guy interrupted.

Question by question, qualification by qualification, Hawk established that Doctor Guy's accomplishments related to her work with whole blood. She had had little experience typing dry blood, or bloodstains, even less testifying in court. Her expertise was in another field, explaining why the criminalist Thornton had never heard of the immunohematolgist Guy.

Typing blood into A, B, and O groups is not difficult; high school students do it in chemistry classes daily. A blood sample is merely divided into thirds, each part placed in a separate test tube, and to each sample a specific antiserum added: anti-A, anti-B, and a plant extract known as anti-H which agglutinated with O-type blood. If the A antiserum adhered to the blood cell, the blood was type A; if both A and B antiserum agglutinated, the blood was AB. Similarly, the B and O antiserums indicated the blood type.

Doctor Guy used a little-known technique in typing dried blood—only six others in the country had mastered it—which could also be applied to other body fluids and cells, all of which carry the A-, B-, and H-antigens. (H is actually the antigen in the O-blood cell.) She herself had used it on amniotic fluid extracted from the placentas of mothers whose children needed blood transfusions *in utero*. From secretions on a glass eye, a cigarette, false teeth, a cup, she had been able to type the blood of the person who had used or worn the object in this case.

Working from notes he had taken during conversations with Thornton, Hawk asked, "First of all, you work in the ABO system?"

"Yes. In fact, actually I work in all of the systems in other contexts. But for our purpose here, we must confine ourselves to the ABO system because of the nature of the samples."

"Are you saying that your capability with a dry bloodstain is limited to the ABO system?"

"Yes, it is. Unless you get one that is clean-dried, or some clean material, uncontaminated, and you get it within, oh, within a few months."

In fact, though Doctor Guy was not aware of it, Thornton had told Hawk it was possible to further type dried blood.

There are at least eleven classification systems for human blood, each of them inherited: the ABO; the MN, and that divided into S, s, and U; the Rh, with six subclassifications. In those three systems alone, all of which could be identified in dried blood, there were 350 possible combinations of blood types: AMS and the Rh factor C, ANS and the Rh factor C, etc. Additionally, there are four hemoglobin types and eight haptoglobin types, the doctor agreed with Hawk. Conservatively, she also agreed that there were now close to 4,000 possible blood types. There were five iso-enzymes which had been identified by criminalists in dried blood cells. "If you multiply five by four thousand, we are up to twenty thousand different blood types, aren't we?"

"That is what you are saying," Doctor Guy was irritated. She sensed Hawk was minimizing the work she had done on the samples submitted to her.

"No, ma'am, I am asking you: Isn't that true?"

"Yes, it probably is, if you multiply it out, it probably would be that many."

"All right. You did not try in hemoglobins or haptoglobins and you did not isoenzyme-type this blood?"

"These samples were not adequate for that kind of test."

"The answer is 'No, I did not?' "

"I did not," Doctor Guy agreed.

"Let me ask you this, now, ma'am: In mathematics you understand that when I say two to the fortieth power that means two times two times two forty times?"

"Yes."

"And like this two to the fortieth power is approximately the number of grains of sand in the world, isn't it?"

Bart Williams objected. "What relevance does that have?"

Judge Patton was impressed with Hawk's knowledge of blood typing. Like some of the members of the jury, the judge was irritated by Doctor Guy's condescending explanations. More familiar with courtroom techniques than she, the judge had realized before Doctor Guy how Hawk was working to diminish her testimony. Williams' objection had interrupted the humbling of Ruth Guy; Judge Patton now inadvertently helped the defense attorney.

"How does this relate to the voir dire as to this witness' qualifications, the number of grains of sand in the world?"

"This way, Your Honor, because two to the eight-thousandth power is the chances against two people having the same blood type if you go through all of these tests." In fact, Hawk knew from Thornton's late-night instruction, there were those who believed that blood types were as unique as fingerprints.

The prosecution had missed an opportunity either to definitely establish the blood in Corona's van and car as that of the victim, or to clear him.

"What was your purpose in examining dried blood stains?" Hawk continued.

"Somebody submitted a sample to me and says, 'Can you tell me what the ABO group is?' "

"That's all they asked of you?"

"They said, 'Type this,' and they wanted it for the ABO group and that is what I was asked to do."

"Oh, oh," Hawk's mock understanding. Another Sutter County mistake. "You were never asked to test in the MN system?"

"I was not."

"Or the Rh?" Hawk was permitting the chastened Ruth Guy to escape responsibility.

She took the opportunity. "No."

"Or the hemoglobin, haptoglobin or isoenzyme?"

"No."

"Or any of the other known tests?"

"No."

"Oh, I see." Hawk smiled at the lady. "That is all I have on voir dire. Thank you, Doctor."

As Williams began his direct examination, Hawk immediately asked to see Doctor Guy's notes. "I have found from experience that it is best to check," he apologized as he took them from her. Doctor Guy's laboratory notes too, furnished to the prosecution the day before, had been withheld from the defense.

Doctor Guy's first finding was troublesome to Hawk. Four days before, she had gone to Vacaville and typed a sample of Corona's blood extracted by court order in August. His blood type was O, she testified.

Typing Corona's blood as O was a surprise to Hawk; he had assumed Corona was Type A, based on the test of saliva deposited on the cup and spoon that Corona had used in the jail. If Corona were an O, it once again opened the possibility that he had smoked the cigarette found in the crucial third grave.

Furthermore, if Corona were an O, it might well be his blood on the muzzle of the pistol, blood which did not match that of the single victim found shot.

A second finding by the doctor was also at odds with an earlier report. The victim in the third grave had been typed as an A; bloodstains on two samples of grass and on weeds taken from near the grave were also A. But Doctor Guy's tests in Dallas indicated that the false teeth found in the pocket of the victim were worn by a man with AB blood.

It would be a wedge for Hawk. Until that moment, he had only intended to demonstrate how little had been done with the blood; he was planning on calling John Thornton as a defense witness to establish that. The blame for the inadequate testing could be laid on the district attorney. With the new blood test, he would have to challenge Doctor Guy's techniques directly.

The doctor offered an explanation for the conflict between Corona's blood type and the type obtained from the cup. "There is not an error in the test. There was a problem in the sample that was sent to me because this was a cup out of inventory that had been used by many, many people and this cup material is not impervious, and what I probably got there were samples of A substance left behind from the saliva of many people who had used the cup before. It should have been a brand new cup never used before."

Hawk would have to check with Thornton about the solubility of saliva; that cup had been steam-cleaned and washed in detergent between meals at Vacaville.

Williams' most important evidence came at the end of Doctor Guy's first full day on the stand.

The woman had tested the cigarette paper twice, the first time before the cup, the second time after the cup turned up type A. Both times, she determined, the saliva on the cigarette butt was secreted by a person with type O blood. Only then had the prosecution filed its discovery order asking for a sample of Corona's blood.

"Doctor Guy, the testing of the cigarette paper," Williams asked, "depends upon the ability of the person who is using the paper to be a secretor; is that correct?"

"That is correct." Doctor Guy was lecturing again. "As I have mentioned before, A-, B-, and H-antigens are found not only on red blood cells but on all the cells of the body.

"In addition, seventy-eight percent of the people have inherited the ability to secret these substances into body fluids—saliva, tears, semen—all these different body fluids."

"So if a person is a secretor and smokes a cigarette, you can get a blood group off of that cigarette. Is that correct?"

"If he is a secretor."

"Okay. And, Doctor Guy, in relation to these samples labelled E-1-3, the dirt, the glass, the weed fibers, the cigarette butts, you made four blood group testings. Is that correct?"

"That is correct."

"And with the exception of the cigarette butt, they tested group A?"

"That is correct."

"And the cigarette butt tested group O?"

"That is correct."

Doctor Guy had offered Hawk another opportunity. If Corona were part of the twenty-two percent of the population which did not secrete the antigens, then he could not have smoked a cigarette with an H-antigen on it. That would explain why his blood type had not turned up on the cup he had used. Hawk planned to have Thorton or Doctor Loquvam check to see if Corona were a secretor.

Hawk's opportunity to challenge Doctor Guy's methods came sooner than he had anticipated. Don Stottlemyer returned to the courtroom on Friday, the day after Doctor Guy's direct testimony. He was merely to be one of seven chain-of-possession witnesses for the prosecution filling in a court day while the doctor fulfilled a prior speaking engagement over a three-day weekend. She was to return on Monday for Hawk's cross-examination.

Stottlemyer might have expected Hawk's questions, having told John Thornton at a seminar the month before that he had some doubts about Doctor Guy's techniques with dried blood.

Hawk posed a hypothetical question to Stottlemyer. "Supposing you have a victim that is type A, and you find a spot of blood and it is type A. Now, would you, as a criminalist, conclude from that that victim left the blood there?"

"No. Just from the fact that there is A blood doesn't mean that it had to come from a particular individual."

"Now, sir, the way that a criminalist has at least attempted to resolve this over the past few years is by dealing in other blood type systems. Right?"

"Correct, Rh and other systems."

"Now, as you commence to test blood in different systems, you then get to the point where blood begins to take on identification, doesn't it?"

"Yes. In other words, the percentage would be narrowed."

Hawk probed here and there in Doctor Guy's testimony, using the state's criminalist to challenge the state's blood expert. Bloodstains could be typed, even if they were a year old. Some of the systems could be typed only if the stain were recovered within two months, "but in a lot of systems, as you say," Stottlemyer agreed, "up to a period of one year you can still get accurate results."

"Now, sir, you made some observations about Doctor Guy's technique, didn't you?"

"Yes, I observed her put a demonstration on, yes."

With Williams and Fahey objecting constantly and Williams forced to challenge his own witness' credentials with a belittling voir dire examination, Hawk elicited the criminalist's description of the test. In Stottlemyer's opinion, she had improperly washed the anti-sera from the bloodstain; she could not have removed the rejected anti-sera, that which did not agglutinate to the blood cells. In his fifteen years of experience, Stottlemyer not seen anyone process blood samples as casually as Doctor Guy had done. Doctor Guy had given a hasty demonstration of her skills on a bloodstain from William Kamp's overcoat, little realizing that one of the people watching had a considerable amount of experience typing dried blood.

"Were you aware that she washed all of these samples four time before finishing her mixed agglutination?" Williams asked.

"Not in Yuba City, she didn't." Stottlemyer was sure of what he had seen.

"Is it your understanding that you observed the complete test in Yuba City performed by Doctor Guy?"

"Yes. She said it was group A."

The washing was inadequate, "but I was going to say her criteria for determining what the group was is what my question was," Stottlemyer volunteered when Hawk resumed his cross-examination. "After she conducted her test and gave her opinion it was group A, she wanted me to look at the agglutination of the various A, B, and O cells. I saw agglutination on all of them, which I would expect to with this type of washing because antiserum hadn't been removed. I asked her what she based her test on, or her opinion, that it was group A, and she told me that it was the ability to cling to the fibers. That was her criteria. This is totally new to me."

"Do you have an opinion about that result?"

"My opinion is, I think it would lead to inadequate results. The mere fact that you are relying on it to cling to fibers—this is just my opinion—It is not good technique."

Through the balance of the day Stottlemyer testified, Judge Patton impatiently checking his pocket watch. (In chambers later, the judge would complain, "I continue to be sort of amazed in a way as to how these things develop. Mr. Stottlemyer was called here to identify certain pieces of evidence in the chain of title, and now he is impeaching Doctor Guy's testimony. I don't understand how the People let this case get in such a position.")

Having scored one point, Hawk sought a second. Stottlemyer too had experience typing saliva; washing the cup in soap and water between usings would have washed off any traces of a previous user's saliva.

Then a third point: At the orders of the district attorney, Stottlemyer had waited six months before undertaking to type the blood. "I believe the district attorney was interested in whether or not the material on the various items was actually blood or not, and if it was human blood, and that was important to him at the time. I asked him how about grouping of the stains and I got the indication that that wasn't important at that time."

The following Monday, the prosecution again brought in a chain of evidence witness, and again encountered trouble. Lieutenant Fred Smith had been in the jury room on January 20, and had watched Doctor Guy conduct her test. A report which he had—and which Hawk had been denied until Smith appeared in court—confirmed she had announced the result as type A. Subsequently, she had retested the stain from William Kamp's overcoat, reclassifying it as type O, the same as that on the gun. When Hawk attempted to bring out that five other test results announced in Yuba City had been revised as well, Judge Patton ruled that impeachment testimony could only be brought forward during the defense case, with Hawk calling Smith to testify.

Doctor Guy was to have returned to the stand that morning, Hawk anxious to begin his cross-examination. But when the defense attorney complained the lady wasn't there, Fahey explained in chambers, "Now, Doctor Guy has traveled to Texas. She traveled back here and is dead tired. The plane was delayed two hours last night. She came in after midnight, and Mr. Hawk appreciates that and he would like to have us put on a dead tired witness. We are not in a position to put Doctor Guy on right now."

Hawk was suspicious. "I suspect that in view of what Mr. Stottlemyer said, that maybe they want a little more time to talk to Doctor Guy. What is the problem of putting her on? So, she got in a little after midnight."

"Your Honor," Fahey said, fighting for time, "I would like to put in the record that in terms of Mr. Stottlemyer and his testimony on cross, that I am sure the court was aware that was a complete surprise. Mr. Stottlemyer never at any time indicated to any counsel in this case that he was going to testify in such a manner, and I think it was quite clear by the way it came out in court." Fahey's anger reddened his face. "It leaves a bad taste in my mouth, I hope it is the first and last time I ever see a criminalist who is supposed to be testifying for law enforcement walk into court apparently prepared to testify for the defense, and how that was arranged I don't know, but I have my own opinions."

"May I say in defense of Mr. Sottlemyer—" Hawk began, Judge Patton shaking his head, "No defense is necessary."

"—Or the accusation made against me apparently," Hawk continued, "that I never talked to Mr. Stottlemyer about what he testified to at all, and for Mr. Fahey's information, the difficulty that they have with CII is the fact that Mr. Teja has a habit of going up there and accusing people of being security risks." Teja had not forgotten the leaking of the Roche Report. "He alienates almost everybody in CII. Mr. Fahey didn't do that. It was his co-counsel, Mr. Teja."

Doctor Guy was finally recalled to the stand after the luncheon recess.

Hawk began his cross-examination by asking, "Since you were here last week, you have talked to the district attorney or some of the D.A.s in this case, haven't you?"

"Yes."

"Okay. Did you read Mr. Stottlemyer's testimony?"

"Yes, sir. I did." Doctor Guy was no longer ebullient.

"They gave you his testimony to read?"

"Yes."

Hawk immediately requested an in-chambers conference. "Your Honor, I guess now I am the one that is caught a little off-guard. It rather surprises me that in view of the fact that Your Honor has made an order excluding witnesses, the purpose of which is to prevent one witness from hearing another one testify, that the district attorney would violate this order by delivering a transcript from Mr. Stottlemyer's testimony to a person who has not yet been cross-examined." He asked that Doctor Guy's testimony be stricken and the district attorney's office be held in contempt.

Teja explained his position. Hers was technical testimony, difficult for laymen, including attorneys, to understand. "Insofar as her being able to prepare herself to defend her reputation which extends nationally, we certainly felt that she had every right and that we had every right to make available Mr. Stottlemyer's testimony to her so that she could understand exactly how she had been challenged in court during Mr. Stottlemyer's cross-examination, and so that she could assist us in preparing her redirect examination on those particular points."

"Well, I submit, Your Honor," Hawk replied, "that if your order means anything at all, it means that one witness is not to hear the other testify and there is no difference between hearing—she certainly couldn't have sat here in the courtroom and listened to Mr. Stottlemyer testify—and showing her a transcript of the testimony. Whatever excuse they try to dream up, it is a clear-cut violation of your court order."

Judge Patton was no longer to be surprised by the Corona case. First the defense had willfully violated the gag order, now the prosecution was ignoring another court order. "We are faced with the situation where it was certainly the court's intention that one witness would not have the opportunity or benefit of someone else's testimony, whether by speaking to the witness personally or through an examination of the testimony of the witness by way of transcript." The problem now was the judge's.

"Now you argue that there should be a different rule involved with the expert witnesses. That may be. There appears to me to be some logic to the argument and I am just perplexed as to how I ought to approach this."

"I submit, Your Honor, that that is what this whole business is about when they wanted to put other witnesses on first—to give her an opportunity to read that and go over it with her and that is what the big stall was this morning."

"When did you give it to her?" Judge Patton asked the prosecution.

"I think it was this morning," Williams aswered vaguely.

"This morning you represented that she was tired out from her trip and then I think, Mr. Hawk is probably right, that that was the stall and that was misrepresentation for that purpose."

"Well, I think we have to advise the court," Teja interposed, "that we did give this matter some thought."

"Why didn't you bring this up with the court then before proceeding?"

"Well, it probably never occurred to us that we were violating any kind of order," Williams answered.

"Why did you discuss it then?" Patton snapped. "Mr. Teja just stated, I thought, that you did and now you say you didn't, so I don't understand."

"We concluded, Your Honor, that we were not violating any court order or the spirit of the order."

Judge Patton took Hawk's motion to strike Doctor Guy's testimony under submission, ordering him to proceed with his cross-examination. Eventually, he would allow her testimony to remain in the record, on the ground that his original exclusionary order had not specifically stated that witnesses could not read transcripts of others' testimony.

Hawk began his cross-examination by asking if Doctor Guy had talked about Stottlemyer's testimony with the three prosecutors. She had, both the night before and earlier that day.

"Now, did they ask you questions about why Mr. Stottlemyer was wrong and you were right?"

"I don't think it was a question of right or wrong." Doctor Guy was subdued. "Mr. Stottlemyer saw a demonstration under adverse conditions with bad equipment all the way around and none of the results from that demonstration that he saw entered into this at all."

"Did you say that the blood sample which you took from the Army overcoat was type A?"

"No, I said it appeared it might be, but it would have to be repeated under better conditions with better equipment."

"Are you aware of what Lieutenant Smith had to say about your announcement concerning the blood group A on the Army overcoat?"

"Yes, I am. That is not my official report at all because I was not satisfied with the test." Doctor Guy agreed Smith's notes did not indicate provisional results. Despite the blood groupings announced in Smith's report, "anything in his report is purely unofficial." Doctor Guy was plainly on the defensive.

Could not saliva on a cup be washed off? It might be and might not, she answered.

"Might and might not? Suppose it went through a washing system of cleaning dishes with some detergent?"

"It would all depend on how porous the material was; how many times it had been used. A clean fresh cup and spoon would have been a far better test to use than one that had been used many times before and washed many times before."

"Now, you tested the cup and spoon, and your finding was that it was type A?"

"I said there was group A substance on the cup."

"Yet Mr. Corona's blood type is O, isn't it?"

"Yes."

Hawk paced the rear of the bar. "If we are interested in identifying blood as coming from a particular person, we have to go beyond a simple typing of A, B, AB, or O, don't we?"

"That is correct."

"Isn't it also true, ma'am, that type A blood, for instance, has two sub-groups. It has A-1 and A-2?"

"Yes, this is true."

"Did you attempt to classify the A blood?"

"No, I did not. I could find nothing in the literature regarding dividing stains into A-1's and A-2's, so I elected not to do it."

Thornton had told Hawk that such subgrouping was routine work for a criminalist. "Well, doctor, if you had and you were capable of breaking down the A blood into A-1 and A-2, wouldn't that be another helpful piece of information?"

"It might; it might not be."

"Supposing the A bloodstains were all A-2, and none of the twenty-five victims were A-2, wouldn't that eliminate all of the victims?"

"It would."

Doctor Guy agreed that had she been called upon in the first week of the investigation, she could have done more refined analyses of the blood. She had not examined any blood until eight months had passed. The passage of time had limited her usefulness.

Others of Doctor Guy's tests were at variance, but Hawk was primarily concerned about the blood type of Melford Sample, the nine-fingered man in the third grave. Sample ostensibly had had A-type blood.

"Now, you ran some washing on some false teeth that were given to you?"

"Yes."

"And you found what in respect to that as far as saliva?"

"I found both A and B substance, so you would think that either came from an AB or possibly two different people had had the false teeth in their mouths."

"And you never are able then with saliva to determine if it was a type AB person who used the teeth?"

"No."

"Is that true also of blood?"

"No, it is not true of blood."

Well briefed, Doctor Guy had salvaged something from the cross-examination.

Hawk concentrated on the variance between Corona's blood type and the saliva type on the cup. "Now, Mr. Corona's blood type being O and saliva on the cup being A, we have a problem, don't we?"

"Yes, there is a problem with that cup."

If Corona were a secretor, Doctor Guy would have hoped to have found the H-antigen. Instead she had found the A, possibly left by a previous user.

"Well, now, Doctor, one reasonable explanation for your different finding between the blood test and the saliva test is that Mr. Corona is not a secretor, is that correct?"

"He might not be."

"Well, yes. Of course, Doctor, if Mr. Corona is not a secretor, that creates a problem on the cigarette butt too, doesn't it? He couldn't have left any O on the cigarette butt if he doesn't secrete."

"That is correct, if the person is indeed not a secretor."

25

The Death List

December 4, 5, 6, 11, 13, 27, 1972

Teja and Williams had saved what they considered their best evidence for last. Three handwriting examiners would testify in the tenth phase of the prosecution's case.

Terrence Pascoe was an examiner of questioned documents for the state's CII, a veteran of some 200 court appearances over the past twelve years.

"I examine documents in the light of about three basic areas: line quality, the ability to produce a line on a page; letter formations, the ability to produce the letter, whether or not it is free flowing; and then, thirdly, the proportions and the formations of this letter in relationship to those other letters which accompany either the word or the particular position of this letter."

Within these categories, Pascoe looked at the beginning and ending strokes of letters, connecting lines, the formation of the loops of each character, and word breaks or pen-lifts.

Pascoe had been provided a copy of the three critical pages in the ledger on July 1, 1971, along with a photograph of the back side of Corona's immigration document. He had not reached a conclusion for fourteen months.

"Let's concern ourselves specifically with pages 50, 51 and 52 of the ledger. Were you able to form any conclusions about the authorship of these pages?" Teja asked.

Pascoe's was a conservative opinion. He had found isolated letters or groups of letters from the various authenticated exemplars which appeared similar to entries in the ledger. "A lot of this material I was not able to resolve. I felt there were some areas which I had extreme difficulty with." Pascoe pointed to seven specific entries on enlargements of the ledger prepared for the courtroom.

"These are some of the areas in which, in my opinion, I never did find a writing in the specimen material which approximated those. I could not identify them. I could not even come to a good guess in regards to those. They were far superior, I thought, to that which was in the specimen material, and could easily be by another writer."

Pascoe, however, had an escape clause. "There are some other areas which I could not resolve. I don't know whether this author produced them. I think that they are well within the range of this writer; he could produce them. But I was unable to locate areas which would conclusively resolve these difficulties in my mind."

Hawk began his cross-examination by asking if Pascoe was familiar "with what Clifford Irving did to McGraw-Hill?"

"Yes." Hawk would return to the fact that a noted handwriting examiner had been duped by author Clifford Irving's forgery of Howard Hughes' name.

Preliminarily, Hawk intended to build up Pascoe's integrity in comparison to two other examiners who would offer more sweeping conclusions.

"You were telling them up until December 1971, that you didn't make Mr. Corona's writing this ledger, is that right?"

"Yes."

"And then they went to Los Angeles and hired Mr. Harris for money, didn't they?"

"Objection, Your Honor, as irrelevant insofar as Mr. Pascoe's testimony," Teja objected.

"It's not, Your Honor. They hired a mercenary, that's what they did."

"Objection," Teja repeated. "Mr. Harris is not a mercenary."

Judge Patton ordered Hawk's description stricken.

Hawk asked Pascoe to read the conclusion contained in his first report of April 1972. "It does appear that the names listed two through nine on page 50 are by one individual. However, from the entry marked ten through page 51, the writing becomes very erratic and does not necessarily reflect the same type as previous entries. The writing appearing on page 52 does exhibit stability and a general conformity which is different than either of the first two groups of writings."

Pascoe had summarized his report: "In any event, it was not possible to identify all the questioned writing to be by one person."

Tipped off by one of Pascoe's coworkers, Hawk asked the bespectacled handwriting examiner, "Do you recall after initial examination telling the people from Sutter County that if they thought this was Juan Corona's handwriting they were in trouble?"

"I don't know that I used those exact words. I could have alluded to this, however."

Hawk rephrased the question. This time the episode "escaped" Pascoe.

"You're saying you didn't say it or—"

"No, I'm not." Pascoe might have a lapse of memory, but he would not perjure himself. "No, I'm not saying that I didn't say that. I don't remember the episode." The co-worker could be called to impeach Pascoe thoroughly were he to deny making the statement.

Hawk considered Pascoe the most creditable of the handwriting examiners, but he intended to undercut all the handwriting testimony through the state examiner's testimony. "This business of examining questioned documents, would you describe it as a science or an art?"

"I would describe it as a science." Whichever answer he gave, he would be in trouble, Pascoe knew. He had once before been cross-examined by Hawk, and faced the same question, familiar to most criminal lawyers.

"And would you tell us the mathematical equation on which your science is based?"

"No, I can't." There was none.

"Would you tell us the statistical basis of your science?"

"No, I could not do that either."

"Would you say that mathematics is a science?"

"Yes."

"Would you agree that it might be more properly referred to as an exact science?"

The questions were uncomfortable. "Yes."

"Mathematicians can demonstrate that two plus two is four, can't they?"

"Yes."

"But you can't do the same thing in what you do, can you?"

Pascoe was prepared. "I think that is what we are doing. Of course, I am not dealing in an exact science. I am dealing with forensic science."

"Isn't there a great deal of subjective judgment in questioned document examination?"

"Yes."

"If you had 100 document examiners examining one questioned document, would you expect to find 100 percent agreement among those people as to their findings?"

"You should, if they are qualified people and all elements being the same. You should."

"But would they all have the same reasons for their opinion?"

"No, they may not."

Pascoe was calm, secure in his opinion, as Hawk's cross-examination continued.

"Do you know of any case that you have ever had where you had a more complete handwriting exemplar?"

"No."

Hawk began a detailed review of the three pages of the ledger, starting with one of the victims' names, Paul B. Allen. Despite all of the exemplars of Corona's writing, "you didn't make it?"

"No." Pascoe shook his head.

"Not even close?"

"No."

At times picking at single characters, comparing one "e" to another, questioned document to authenticated exemplar, Hawk's cross-examination continued. The "o-r" combination was different. "What do you think about that?"

"I think it's well within the range of this writer."

" 'Well within the range.' Now, what does that mean?"

"Well, it means that if we were to conclude on the basis of only that "o," then we'd have some difficulties."

"Gerome," the misspelled middle name of one of the victims. Pascoe believed the "—erome" portion was written by Corona, but the hand-printed "G" troubled him. "I did not find any of that nature in the specimen material."

"So you're saying to us that Mr. Corona wrote '-erome.' Are you suggesting that somebody else wrote 'Warren G-' and then skipped a space and wrote 'Kelley'?"

"No, I'm not." Despite Corona's copying the name in the exemplar, Pascoe had not been able to convince himself that Corona had written the name in the ledger.

Pascoe had identified the "S" of Smallwood as being in Corona's hand. "Would you be prepared to say on the basis of one capital letter that Mr. Corona wrote 'Jona R. Smalwood?' "

"No."

"You must think he wrote the 'S?' "

"Yes."

"What's different about Mr. Corona's 'S' that makes him the only person out of two billion people in the world who makes an 'S' like that?"

"I think that it would be a misstatement for me to say that that's the only person in the world who makes 'S's' like this. And I hope that I have not indicated it to the jury."

"Is Mr. Corona the only person in the state of California who has that range, as far as quality, formation and the other factors you talked about?"

"I don't know."

"Well, if you don't know how can you sit here and tell us that he wrote it?"

"By applying the science that we just described, and coming to that conclusion."

Hawk asked Pascoe to look at a series of checks signed "Natividad S. Corona." There was some similarity between the letter in the signature and the "S" of "Smalwood," Pascoe decided.

"Well, if you were continually fed handwriting of this person signing as Natividad S. Corona until something came in and looked like that, then it would fall within the range of that person's capability. Right?"

"Yes."

"And once it falls within the range of capability as to quality and formation and so forth, then you would be prepared to say that Natividad Corona wrote that 'S,' right?"

"Yes."

"Well, now then," Hawk smiled, the teacher leading the none-too-bright student to the correct answer, "we'd have two people writing that same 'S,' wouldn't we?"

"Yes."

"Juan and Natividad both?"

"Yes."

"Now, that's not possible, is it?"

"No."

"What kind of science is that?" Hawk looked over the courtroom exhibit. "Did you pick out an 'f' of Mr. Corona's in the middle of the word 'Bonafide' and say therefore Mr. Corona wrote that one letter in the middle of the word?"

"I felt that this was the case."

"And that's because his 'f' is a unique 'f?' He's the only person who makes an 'f' like that in the world?"

"No. Not that I know of. I didn't examine everybody in the world's writing." Pascoe was tiring.

"It's unique, like a fingerprint, to Mr. Corona?"

"I don't know about Mr. Corona's fingerprints, either. But I—I concluded, again applying the rules of the science, that that 'f' was prepared by Mr. Corona, on the basis of what I was submitted for examination."

"All right, I understand about your science. What I'm saying is, if your science is worthwhile at all, for you to be able to pick out a single letter in the middle of a word, don't you have to be able to say that Mr. Corona and Mr. Corona alone is the only person in the world that writes an 'f' like that? It's unique to Mr. Corona?"

"I could not say that Mr. Corona was the only person in the world who writes 'f's like that."

"Well, sir, would you tell us then, if Mr. Corona is not the only person in the world, or until you can say that, how can you pick out one letter in one word and one letter in another, and say this is Mr. Corona's handwriting?" Hawk was angry.

And Pascoe stubborn. "Applying the set of rules which, on the basis of identification of handwriting, letter formation, proportions, all of this, plus my background and experience, I suppose, in this area, I was able to conclude in my opinion that he prepared that 'S' in that 'Sam' and 'f' in 'Bonafide.'"

Out of a possible 312 letters—upper and lower case, script and printed, initial, middle, or terminal—Pascoe had found forty-four he believed were within Corona's "range."

At the conclusion of Pascoe's testimony, eight-by-ten enlargements of the courtroom exhibits he had prepared were passed through the jury box. The bearded Marine Corps sergeant handed them on without a glance, muttering, "If they can't figure them out, how do they expect me to?"

John Harris and Sidney Goldblatt would be more difficult. If Pascoe had reservations, these two were handwriting examiners untroubled by doubt. As Pascoe had suggested, they were able to reach the same conclusion—all, or substantially all, of the writing in the ledger was Corona's —but they did so without sharing common findings. Hawk would later argue, what was the jury supposed to do: Add them up and divide by three?

Harris had a considerable reputation in southern California. Like Pascoe, he was trained by older men, in Harris' case, his father; since 1948, he worked for the federal attorney in Los Angeles, the public defender's office, district attorneys in a half-dozen counties, and a variety of private companies.

Hawk was undecided about his cross-examination, whether to delve deeply into Harris' analysis or to skip lightly over it, relying instead on the contrast between Harris and Pascoe and the conflict in their testimony. His decision would depend, in part, upon how well Harris withstood questioning. Hawk expected him to be cool under the cross-examination; a man like that could hurt you. Knowledgeable in the ways of defense attorneys, he would be quick to exploit every opportunity to buttress the prosecution's contention. Unlike the civil servant Pascoe, Harris the private practitioner appeared anxious to please his employer.

"How many hours do you have involved in this case as of the present time?" Hawk asked on voir dire.

"I have billed Sutter County $1,400," the fee for forty hours' work on the case.

"And you are getting $35 for every hour you sit here. Is that right?"

"Yes."

"Okay. You were first contacted in this case about six months after Mr. Corona was arrested?" And six months after Pascoe had told the prosecution, "If you think this is Corona's handwriting, you guys are in trouble."

"I opened the file, I think it was, January 13, 1972."

"Do handwriting men ever get fooled, Mr. Harris?"

"Yes. Sometimes a clever forger, like Mr. Irving in New York, will fool a handwriting expert. But he didn't fool three others. He fooled one." Harris, like questioned document examiners everywhere, was sensitive about the McGraw-Hill affair. Irving, as casual a forger as ever faked a document, was now "clever."

"What you mean is he didn't fool Howard Hughes?"

"He didn't fool three other handwriting experts. Call it for what it was."

"After Mr. Hughes disavowed the contract," Hawk concluded his voir dire.

Although he had not written a final report, Harris' conclusion was "that substantially all of the writing on pages 50, 51 and 52 of the ledger book and the dated entries on the immigration document were written by one person; and these exhibits are in the same hand as found on the exemplar documents."

"What do you mean by the use of that word 'substantially'?"

"There are instances in the ledger book where the writing is very abbreviated or just a squiggle, which isn't really handwriting at all. And in those instances I can't specifically identify the squiggles."

"Did you find any indication that any other person's handwriting appeared on any of the questioned documents?"

"I found absolutely no indication that anybody else did any of the writing or any other person's handwriting on these documents." Harris was in direct conflict with Pascoe.

Hawk struggled to contain his contempt for Harris. "Sir, on your report of January 26, you indicated that you had looked at basically two things; is that correct?"

"Yes."

"And at that time you said you were not able to reach a definitive conclusion. Is that correct?" Harris agreed. "Now, then, later on, on June the thirteenth of 1972, you wrote another letter concerning Juan Corona, right?"

"Concerning the handwriting."

At that time, Harris had an additional eleven checks and two loan notes from a bank which Corona had signed. Harris had concluded, "As a result of these examinations and comparisons it is my opinion, with reasonable scientific certainty, that substantially all of the writing on pages 50, 51 and 52 of the ledger, as well as the names and dates occurring on the immigration document, were all done by one person. Further, it is my opinion that the person who has written the Juan Corona exemplars [a highway patrol report of an accident filled in by Corona, the eleven checks and the two bank notes] filled in these lists in the ledger book, and on the immigration form."

"At the time that you made up your opinion," Hawk asked, "in June of 1972, you didn't have any specimens that were written in the courtroom, did you?"

"No, I didn't."

Hawk began a line-by-line review of the photographic enlargements of sample words which Harris had prepared for his courtroom testimony. Of the seven on the first exhibit, Harris had had none when he reached his conclusion in June; all had come from documents and the courtroom exemplar received later. Similarly, on his next series there were no examples of Corona's writing received when he formed his opinion. Only one of three were in hand from the third exhibit. Four, five, and six were almost exclusively based upon material received after Harris had written his June report.

Hawk then challenged Harris to pick from the exemplars he had in June the letter combinations which would have permitted Harris to conclude Corona had written the name of one of the victims, Paul B. Allen, in the ledger.

"I found there was a certain combination of characteristics that went through this writing. That it was all, in my judgment, written by one person." Harris had lacked certain of the letters in Allen in the exemplar material of June. "I did it by process of interpolation, finding certain characteristics such as in the 'e's'."

"Excuse me," Hawk interrupted. "Are you saying that you didn't find any 'l's' in the exemplars?"

"No."

"So I take it what you did, then, was—what was that word? 'Interpolation?' You found some other letters that looked similar, and therefore you reasoned that he wrote the two 'l's' in 'Allen.' Is that your reasoning?"

"That is a step of it. Yes."

"Have you ever heard of the expression 'bootstrapping?' "

"Yes, I have heard of that."

"Isn't that basically what you are doing, pulling yourself up by your bootstraps?"

"No."

Tediously, Hawk pecked here and there at Harris' exemplars. The top part of a letter was similar; the bottom differed. The odd punctuation differed between ledger and exemplars. Another character was "about the same." The descenders of the letter "g" in the exemplars differed from those in the ledger, but the descender on the "y" was similar and would do. Harris was able to find similarities everywhere.

Corona's court-ordered exemplars were virtually vertical; the entries in the ledger had a marked diagonal. Harris attempted to explain away the difference. "Perhaps it could be because they are requested exemplars and he was trying to copy the names."

"I see. Well, then would this be an illustration of when slant is not important?"

"I believe it is, yes."

"I see. Now, supposing the slant was the same; would it be important then?"

"It might be, yes."

"I see. It is never important if it distinguishes the defendant's handwriting; it is only important if it helps you, correct?"

"No," Harris denied, but Hawk had made his point.

Sidney Goldblatt was the prosecution's last witness, the most prestigious of the handwriting examiners, the man whom Howard Hughes had wanted to hire during the McGraw-Hill controversy. Goldblatt too came into court without preparing a final report. Hawk objected to Goldblatt's testifying until he had had an opportunity to review the expert's notes. To study the notes and follow the direct examination was impossible.

"Your Honor," Teja explained, "we got these late last night from Mr. Goldblatt ourselves. We have dealt with Mr. Goldblatt verbally in this particular matter and we are at the same disadvantage."

"Well, Your Honor, the fact that the prosecution doesn't want to be prepared doesn't mean the defense doesn't have to be." Hawk was tense, aware that Goldblatt was to be the prosecution's major witness, angry that yet another report had been withheld. "There was a discovery order made months ago for notes of all these people and they come—they don't even write a report—in the last minute with a bunch of notes that are Greek to me. This is the only expert I have ever had who didn't write some kind of report in six or eight months."

In chambers, Judge Patton was critical of the prosecution. "I am concerned whether this is really a subterfuge, an attempt to avoid compliance with the court's order. There is no reason otherwise, if this man is retained months ago, that now at the last minute he comes to the court, for the first time somebody has seen some writing that this man has presented. This is a ridiculous situation and just causes further delays during the progress of this trial." The judge permitted Teja to continue with the direct examination, "but I will order this witness returned for proper cross-examination."

Goldblatt was an anomaly—a barrel-chested man wearing a blue double-breasted suit, a pocket handkerchief, and pencil moustache whose accent and occasional grammatical lapses gave away a boyhood on the streets of New York. A documents examiner for the Treasury Department's New York office for the past twenty-one years, Goldblatt had been trained on the job.

On voir dire, Hawk attempted to discredit Goldblatt's testimony immediately. "Did you tell Jerry Gregory on May the sixteenth of 1972 that you did not want to become involved in conflict with an examiner from another agency?"

"Yes, I did."

"Before you went ahead and examined, you wanted to know what the other experts for the prosecution said. Is that right?"

"No, it's not that at all. We have set down a policy previously, intergovernment policy. For example, the FBI conducts an analysis of documents within the government function, and they occasionally would call on us to re-examine the documents. And my policy in my laboratory is that we will not take the case."

Goldblatt's policy had peremptorily been changed by superiors in Washington despite the fact that he would be in conflict with an examiner for another government agency, the more conservative Terrence Pascoe. The district attorney never explained just how he had convinced the Treasury Department to change the policy, what political pressure he had applied or had asked the attorney general of the state of California to apply for him; nonetheless, the federal policy had been changed, and Goldblatt was to testify for the prosecution against Juan Corona.

Goldblatt, using different standards of judgment, had reached the same conclusion as did Harris before him. "I found cumulatively significant and repeated controlling, identifiable characteristics in both the handwriting and hand-printing with the exception of an entry on page 51 where there was a pen failure and no registration." Goldblatt had even made the squiggles beyond Harris' ability.

Teja asked him to explain. "By significant, controlling, repeated habits I mean those habits which are individualized and peculiar to one person. In order to establish an identification it is necessary to interpret and develop the controlling individual repeated habits."

Goldblatt too was a lecturer, speaking directly to the jury, his body turned away from Teja to face the jury box.

"Do your findings in connection with the handwriting and the handprinting independently of each other have any bearing on your total opinion?" Teja asked.

"Yes, it does."

"And how would you describe the effect of your findings in each of these areas separately upon your opinion?"

"Well, I have explained to the jury the basis and how we went about developing these. However, it is a cumulative effect. In other words, it is one identification built on top of another. When they coexist in that nature it certainly, in my opinion and my experience, is a more pronounced and firmer basis for a conclusion."

Goldblatt too had selected a handful of letters, at times agreeing with his predecessors, at times varying. Goldblatt had found fewer than fifty characters he judged to be similar, sometimes comparing a "p" to a "d" if no "p" in the exemplar matched the ledger.

Hawk attempted to pin Goldblatt on a cross-examination he had reluctantly decided to take up rather than leave the direct testimony unchallenged.

"You find no similarities other than the ones you've testified to in terms of capital 'F's' or capital 'J's' or things like that?"

"There may be one or two. But I'm not certain of these. What I pointed out was the repeated controlling and significant characteristics of this individual's handwriting."

"I understand that. But I am asking you at what point, at what number do you find that there is this sufficient amount for you to reach—"

"Well, handwriting is not like we would consider fingerprinting. Handwriting is the significance of the individual habit."

"So then I take it there is no formula as such, a mathematical basis on which you are able to work, is there?"

"No, there isn't."

"It is a lot of judgment?"

"There isn't," Goldblatt denied. "But sometimes you could apply the law of probability."

"Oh, you have got a statistical basis for your science?"

"No. But the law of probability is referred to in some of our textbooks. I'm not saying it necessarily applied in this case."

"I see. Do you deal in an art or a science, sir?"

"Well, I would say that the identification of handwriting is part art, as far as the forms are concerned. As far as science, it is not a science *per se*. The only application of some area of scientific application would be the fact that a statistical approach based on previous examination of other problems and other documents over the years might furnish and does sometimes furnish a statistical basis. But it is not considered a complete science."

Hawk turned to the courtroom exhibits, pointing out that like Pascoe, Goldblatt did not find a "G" for the misspelled "Gerome."

"I find 'C's' but the only difference is that this particular 'G' or 'C,' which I will agree it was intended to be a 'G,' comes up from the base line a bit but it has no cross stroke."

If letters varied, Goldblatt selected that aspect of the character closest to Corona's handwriting and ignored the balance. The variation between the lower case "g's" in the exemplar furnished by Corona differed from those in the ledger. "I think this is an individual habit of this author." Lacking a good match for the upper case "R," Goldblatt had dismissed it. "That one particular peculiarity is not sufficient to be concerned about [in] the overall evaluation of the writings." Inconsistencies in character formation between exemplar and ledger did not trouble the examiner. Having made up his mind, he had dismissed all contrary evidence.

Hawk continued his cross-examination through the day, finally deciding not to ask for more time, not to have Goldblatt called back. He had not forced Goldblatt to back down—he hadn't expected to—but he had managed to raise a clutter of questions. Those questions constituted reasonable doubt.

26

The Cutting

December 18, 19, 21, 27, 1972

"They don't give a rat's ass about a reversal at this point," Hawk laughed as he played with his new bifocals. "They couldn't or they wouldn't be trying to get this Guadalajara thing in. At this point, they're desperate men —at least Teja is."

God, it felt good, to be on top, to be in control, to know the prosecution believed its case lost. What was even more satisfying for Hawk was that he had done it with cross-examination alone, without putting on a single witness except Mrs. Vallejo. Just using his wits—and the incredible number of mistakes the sheriff's office had made.

The prosecution had tried everything, and now Teja was down to this far-fetched common scheme-and-plan business. They had gotten José Romero Raya to change his story and now they wanted him in front of the jury. There was no telling the effect his scars alone would have.

Judge Patton had recessed the trial, sending the jury home for a day, in order to hear arguments about the admissibility of the Guadalajara incident, and to hear Raya testify about a job offer Corona had extended on the night Raya was assaulted. Since Raya's very presence in the courtroom was crucial to the prosecution, Hawk had challenged Raya's competence to testify. A hospital report, he told Judge Patton in chambers, said the young man had suffered from epileptic-like convulsions since his assault. Furthermore, Hawk had argued, if Raya were to testify that it was Juan Corona who attacked him in the rest room of the Guadalajara, Raya could be committing perjury. He had won a $250,000 civil judgment against Natividad Corona as a result of the cutting. Later, he had repeatedly insisted when questioned by deputies that Natividad had assaulted him. If he now was going to change his story, it might well be that he did not understand what perjury was, or had been misled by the prosecution.

Hawk doubted that Judge Patton wanted to admit the Guadalajara incident. It would be time-consuming. Equally important, it would embarrass Judge Richard A. Schoenig who had awarded Raya the judgment. Though there was no transcript taken of the suit, Schoenig's opinion had concluded, "Natividad Corona did, in fact, assault the plaintiff, Raya, and inflict massive face and head injuries with a sharp weapon."

If Raya testified, Hawk would have to revise the defense case. At the moment, he was certain of calling only Gloria Corona and the man from the lumber company to verify the receipt for the screen door. Gloria didn't remember the exact day Juan and she had hung the door on Mrs. Vallejo's house, but was certain it was the day after Juan bought the screen. She wouldn't have to remember, actually; it would be remembered for her. The receipt was dated May 18, 1971. He could also call Stottlemyer to testify that he had found small pieces of screen wire when he vacuumed the van.

He would have to review the record to see which of the prosecution witnesses he wanted recalled for cross-examination. In view of all the material withheld from him, Judge Patton had given him that option, but he wasn't certain he would bother. If there was anything he really had to clarify, he could call witnesses in his own case. A few maybe. If only he had time to read the record; he was at least 5,000 pages behind now, long since having given up reading the daily transcripts in the evening.

And maybe, just maybe, he would not put Juan on. The possibility had occurred to him before, but now it seemed a good idea. Why subject him to cross-examination? There was no doubt that Fahey, their most experienced trial lawyer, the sharpest of the three, would handle the cross for them. What really could Corona do on his own behalf? He could say he didn't write in the ledger; three handwriting people said he did some or all of the three questioned pages.

If he did put Juan on, Doctor Evelyn Hooker would follow so the prosecution couldn't ask him a lot of questions about her testimony, about what he had talked to her. Never before had Hawk put on a defendant other than last, but in this case he might. Doctor Hooker could handle the tough ones about Corona's mental health; Corona couldn't, or wouldn't even know what they were talking about.

Doctor Hooker would be a great witness. Hawk could use her to point out the omissions of the investigation—not taking penile as well as rectal swabs, not checking the sex offenders' registration lists for possible suspects, not doing a damn thing to investigate the homosexual aspect of the murders. He could ask the doctor, "In your opinion are these homosexual murders?" Good scientist that she is, she would have to answer, "I can't say, but I would certainly suspect it." The jury was entitled to draw the inference—if it were offered to them—that these are homosexual killings.

He could do it all with two questions: "Is Corona a homosexual?" and "Is he capable of committing these crimes?"

Hawk sighed. "She's very important, and because she's so very important she needs a lot of time." Time he didn't have. He had talked to none of his witnesses. Carlos Leon Sierra was off following the crops; Hawk wouldn't be able to subpoena Sierra to testify that Corona had transported him in the van, bleeding, to Doctor Vasquez. The doctor could at least say Corona had brought in a bleeding worker on such-and-such a date. They had the state workmen's compensation forms to support the doctor's testimony.

Time. He had not gotten the children's blood typed, especially Yolanda who suffered from chronic nosebleeds. Time to locate someone to testify that Juan Reynosa, Ray Duron's brother-in-law, owned a blue-and-white pickup with a green canvas top and recruited in lower Marysville. Time to talk to some of the ranch workers and pin down Emilio Rangel's whereabouts and activities during May. Even earlier.

He had put off doing so much in order to concentrate on the prosecution's case. He wished he had some of the manpower Teja had—trial deputies, investigators, secretaries, sheriff's deputies, a sergeant on loan from another department, the attorney general's office to write his briefs.

Hawk could have used help the week before in writing his brief on the admissibility of the Guadalajara incident. Hawk's argument centered on the differences in the Raya assault and the deaths of the twenty-five. Raya was assaulted in a public place and was left there; the twenty-five victims were murdered in a secretive place and then buried. Raya was neither stabbed nor shot; eighteen of the victims were stabbed, one was shot. Raya had suffered severe facial wounds; seventeen of the twenty-five had no face wounds. Those on Raya were vertical; the eight had horizontal face wounds. Raya was twenty at the time of the assault and attractive, a permanent resident of the area; the twenty-five found in the orchards were between forty and sixty-five, were dissipated and "weathered." All but one were transients. In all, Hawk and an aide had found fifteen differences.

Hawk, who wrote briefs begrudgingly, was proud of the last paragraph of this one: "The defense respectfully suggests that the offer by the People [to admit the Guadalajara incident] is an act of desperation by a decisively defeated party. It would appear that the People have a reckless disregard for the state of the record and are clutching for a conviction at any cost. What they are doing is attempting to lure the trial court into making a reversible error to secure a conviction which would never withstand an attack on appeal. The trial court has a right to expect more of its officers, even in an adversary system."

If Hawk was confident, his client was not. Juan Corona was worried. "The trial, you know, it goes both ways sometimes. Some days are good. Some days are very bad." He wasn't complaining, "But the only thing, sometimes I don't have enough time to talk to Mr. Hawk, to explain some things, some questions. Sometimes I think that if I waste his time, you know—" His voice feathered off into perplexity.

José Romero Raya was a nervous young man. Despite the prosecution's attempt to prevent Hawk from talking to him, Judge Patton had ruled Hawk had that right. Raya did not have to answer Hawk's questions, but "in the interest of fairness," Judge Patton hoped he would.

Five minutes later, Hawk and the court reporter, John Zandonella, returned. Raya had refused to talk to him. "He's panicked, man, they scared hell out of him," Hawk whispered to an aide. "Bull-shitted him too."

As the attorneys walked from the judge's chambers into the courtroom, Hawk smiled at a grim Williams, "I compliment you, Bart. You did a good job on the kid."

Williams had done a far better job than Hawk imagined. With little difficulty, Williams brought out Raya's testimony about an offer of a job extended by Corona, an interpreter translating questions and answers, English to Spanish, Spanish to English.

About seven o'clock on the evening of February 24, 1970, Raya testified, he and a friend, Nick Ramirez, met Juan Corona by a phone booth near the Tower Theater in lower Marysville. According to Raya, Corona had asked them "if they were going to work." When they agreed, Corona had ostensibly said that the work was in the Sullivan ranch.

Raya did not know where the ranch was, so Corona had offered to take the two men in his "blue pickup." They had refused, preferring instead to follow him in a separate car, and then when Corona insisted, refused to go altogether.

Williams then showed Raya a photographic enlargement of page 50 of the ledger. Did his name appear on that list the way he used his name?

Raya pointed to the first entry: "Fev 24 1970 Jose Romero R."

At best, Raya was telling only part of the story, Corona explained to Hawk. When Sam Nevis had finally scraped up the money at the very end of the season to have his peaches pruned, he had asked Corona to get a crew together. Ramirez had already asked if Corona had a job for him and a friend. Fidel Lopez and two cousins in the country illegally had also asked for work, their jobs with Pedro Corona ending with the last pruning. Those five, plus Juan himself, would be enough to prune Nevis' small orchard.

The two Lopez cousins were staying at Pedro Corona's camp, not far from the Sullivan ranch, north of Yuba City. The Nevis orchard was nearby. To avoid driving into town in the morning to show Ramirez and Raya the way, Corona had offered to take them out the night before. Then the next morning, they could meet him at the Sullivan ranch, and they could all drive over to pick up Lopez' cousins before going on to the nearby Nevis orchard.

Corona complained to Hawk that it never happened, perplexed that Raya would say such a thing. Richard Hawk understood though.

"All right, Mr. Raya, I wonder if you can give me your present address."

"Objection, Your Honor. He is trying to bring out the fact that he is in protective custody, Your Honor." Williams would do everything he could to protect his witness.

"I don't know that he is," Hawk answered. "I don't believe anything they said, they have lied to me so many times." Hawk turned to Raya: "How many times have you discussed this with the police?"

"About this that we have been talking about, I have not talked to any policeman about it, no." In fact, Raya had given a prior statement about the job offer at the same time he had repeated his accusation that Natividad Corona was his assailant.

"How many times have you talked to this man here?" Hawk asked, pointing to Williams.

"I don't remember." It would be Raya's most frequent answer. Any question that differed from what Williams had earlier asked called for "I don't remember." Had he talked to Fahey? "I don't remember." Had he talked to Mrs. Reynosa, Ray Duron's sister-in-law? "I don't remember."

Hawk attempted to challenge Raya's new account. He could rely only upon his patience; the interpreter served as a buffer to Hawk's usual abrasive questioning of hostile witnesses.

"Now, you told us here this morning that the conversation between you and Mr. Corona and Nick Ramirez was around seven or eight o'clock?"

"Yes."

Hawk then read Raya's statement of June 2, 1971. Then Raya told the officers that he could not remember the time. Now he could not remember even giving the statement; Williams had prepared him well.

How tall was Ramirez? Raya suggested he was about Fahey's height, perhaps five-foot five-inches or six. Corona whispered in Hawk's ear. "Ramirez is big, like me. Six-foot tall. One hundred and eighty, ninety pounds." They could call Ramirez as a witness for the defense.

Hawk laboriously questioned the uncooperative witness. In his first statement he had said the conversation with Corona took place in a small café, not on the street. He had not mentioned a blue pickup at all. He had stated that Corona "wanted me to go at night so he could show me the ranch. Because I told him that we didn't know where the ranch was. And he said he would take us. I told him no, that in the morning at six o'clock to wait for us at the [movie theater]." Reluctantly, Raya conceded he had not told Gregory and Escovedo about the blue pickup, about the conversation in the bar.

Moments before the luncheon recess, Judge Patton ruled "as it now appears the court would declare that Mr. Raya is competent to testify [about the job offer]. Certainly, the court by permitting the testimony would not be passing upon the credibility of the witness, but would merely determine that the jury is entitled to hear it."

Doctor John R. Clark was the first of four doctors to testify for the prosecution on the admissibility of the Guadalajara incident. A neurosurgeon at Enloe Hospital in Chico, California, approximately fifty miles from Yuba City, Doctor Clark had been called in at four in the morning of February 25 to treat an emergency case brought by ambulance from Marysville.

Raya had seven head wounds and twelve on the face, Clark testified, "long lacerations that laid open the skin, but fairly clean-cut."

"Is this the first time that you have seen numerous chop wounds to the scalp?" Williams asked, beginning his effort to establish the uniqueness of the wounds.

"Yes."

"All of the injuries were to the left side of the head?"

"Practically speaking."

"These seven cuts on Mr. Raya's head, did they appear to all have been made by the same weapon?"

"Yes." The long facial wounds, too, could have been inflicted by the same weapon.

Williams drew the parallel. "And is it your opinion, doctor, or do you have an opinion as to whether or not the number of head injuries with these heavy chop-type instruments is usual or unusual?"

"It is very unusual in my experience, and pretty unusual in most other neurosurgeons' experience as far as I could gather."

At Williams' behest, Doctor Clark had called three other neurosurgeons around the country—including one in Puerto Rico, "where there are a lot of machetes used and a lot of machete injuries. The opinion is that this is an extremely rare type of injury, insofar as the number of slashes is concerned and the sparing of the other parts of the body is concerned."

Hawk believed he needed to make very few points with the doctor to buttress his contention that Raya's injuries and those on the twenty-five were dissimilar. Doctor Clark agreed there were no horizontal wounds on Raya's skull; the most nearly horizontal was one on a forty-five-degree angle. There were eleven or twelve facial wounds, all on the left side, all vertical.

"In medical history, say, in the last twenty or thirty years, is Mr. Raya the only person who had multiple head and face wounds with no wounds anywhere else on his body?"

"I doubt it."

"Can you give us some idea of how many people have been hurt in that manner?"

"No, I cannot."

"Then I take it there may be thousands of people who had just head wounds and face wounds?"

"There might be."

"And that is what you meant by 'unusual?' "

"Yes."

On Tuesday morning, Hawk made another demand for any recorded statements given to sheriff's deputies by Raya. Raya had been in protective custody—unexplained—for about a month, and in that time had surely talked with either law enforcement officers or the district attorney.

Joseph H. Masters, the forensic pathologist from the Sacramento coroner's office who had autopsied eleven of the bodies, was the second doctor to testify. Well-prepared for Fahey's examination, Doctor Masters felt "that there are definite similarities between the wounds suffered by Mr. Raya and the wounds in the Sutter County cases that I autopsied." A similar weapon was used, resulting in similar wounds. The distribution of the wounds too was significant. There were no chop-type wounds on the torsos of the victims. Raya's chop-type wounds too were "present only in the region of the face, head and neck."

"Do you have an opinion as to whether or not, medically speaking, in view of the type of wounds that the same person inflicted the wounds on these twenty-five is the same person that inflicted the head wounds on Mr. Raya?" Fahey asked.

"This opinion could change, but I would strongly suspect that these wounds might be inflicted by the same individual."

Hawk began his cross-examination. Using the large diagrams of the wounds to each of the victims, he led Masters through a description of the injuries. Nine of Masters' eleven victims were stabbed; Raya was not. The face wounds on the victims were horizontal; Raya's vertical. Raya had many more face wounds than any of the victims.

Pierce Rooney, Sacramento County's chief forensic pathologist, followed. In response to Fahey, he testified, "Mr. Raya and the victims both suffered chop-type injuries of similar type and the reason I believe that is because the wounds are similar." They were "roughly similar" in size, depth, and "therefore, probably the degree of force." Doctor Rooney was concise and professional, the most respected of the prosecution's medical experts.

"My opinion is that if you took each of Mr. Raya's individual chop wounds, especially those that cut the skull, and compared them to the chop wounds that cut the skull on the rest of the gentlemen, that they would be practically indistinguishable—well, they would be indistinguishable."

Under Hawk's cross-examination, Rooney agreed there were dissimilarities: the facial wounds to the victims were fewer than Raya's, they ran on a different plane. The most head wounds any of the mass murder victims had was five; Raya had nineteen, "many more than anyone else."

At the end of the noon recess, the attorneys met with Judge Patton in chambers. Williams turned over transcriptions of two interviews Sergeant Perales had conducted with Raya, and, "to show our good faith," the two tapes, in Spanish, which the sergeant had made. The transcriptions were inaccurate—Geneva Hawk would spend hours reinterpreting the tapes—but they further impeached Raya's courtroom testimony.

Doctor Russell McFall was the last witness, called to compare X rays of Raya's injuries and the twenty-five victims. Using a borrowed X ray viewer, the doctor pointed out fractures here and there. Hawk whispered to an aide, "I can't read X rays."

Like the others, Doctor McFall "was struck by the number of chopping fractures to the bony calvarium, incised fractures, fractures made by something with presumably a sharp metal edge. In my opinion, a sharp metal object, such as a bolo or machete or possibly a thin cleaver struck Mr. Raya on the front calvarium.

"It would be my opinion that it would be impossible to go to large institutions around the country that have a lot of homicide or even accidental death injuries and twenty-five or twenty-six cases that are so similar."

On cross-examination, Hawk asked, "Why do you use that word 'machete'?"

"Because I think I have some evidence that suggests that it is a striking object, with sharp metal and fairly thin."

"Right, but is that the only instrument in the world that fits that description?"

"Short sword, machete, thin or lightweight cleaver," Doctor McFall elaborated.

Hawk continued his cross-examination, the doctor answering in a splatter of Latin names of bones. Judge Patton leaned further and further back in his swivel chair, his attention slipping from the witness, lunch heavy on his stomach.

"You found a chop-type fracture in Mr. Raya's head?" Hawk asked.

"Correct."

"And of the nineteen you examined, you did not find such a thing in eighteen?"

"Correct."

Fahey began his redirect examination, the doctor answering short questions with short lectures. Williams tapped Fahey's arm. "The judge is asleep."

In the midst of a McFall lecture, Fahey called out, "Patton, are you able to see from that angle there?"

There was a second's pause before the judge answered, "Yes."

Both Fahey and Williams realized they were going to lose the plea for admissibility.

Prior to arguments from both sides, Judge Patton reviewed the scope of the hearing for the benefit of the listening reporters. "Ordinarily, a separate offense or incident is not admissible during the trial of another case if it merely purports to show criminal propensity or violence or that sort of a feature. The People here assert that there are two reasons, however, why the Raya incident is admissible during the course of this trial, exceptions to the general rule. The People contend, first of all, that the common features show a *modus operandi,* and also that the common features show identity that the assailant of Raya was also the assailant of the twenty-five victims here.

"It is not only a question of the physical injuries, but all of the other circumstances which it is argued caused the two incidents to be either similar or dissimilar and the Court, before the other incident may be admitted, must be of the view that the totality of the common marks and circumstances are such as to cause the court logically to conclude or infer that the assailant of one committed the assaults involved in this matter."

Williams' argument for the People was short. "We put on overwhelming evidence of medical similarity in the testimony. There has been no evidence put on by way of defense to indicate any contrary opinion. And I think that just on the basis of the medical testimony that we put on here today, Your Honor, it is overwhelming in terms of the similarity that they find."

"Are you resting your argument solely on the similarity of the wounds?" Judge Patton asked.

"From a medical standpoint," Fahey answered.

Hawk's argument was broader. The injuries might or might not be unique. "How many ways can you cut somebody with something?" But more important—and Hawk reviewed the dissimilarities he had pointed out in his brief—the prosecution had ignored all the other factors. There were "pretty serious questions in terms of letting this in."

Fahey's was a desperate last argument. The wounds were similar, Raya's name was "on this list of the known victims." Raya was solicited to work on the Sullivan ranch, at night.

"In reference to the alleged dissimilarity about Mexicans, again referring to the ledger that has been identified by two experts as a death list in Juan Corona's handwriting—"

"Excuse me, Your Honor," Hawk broke in. "That was not referred to by the experts as a death list."

"I am referring to it as a death list," Fahey maintained. "We have, I believe, thirty-three names on that list. We have twenty-five bodies pulled out of the ground. We have the inescapable conclusion that there are other bodies still out there, either at the Sullivan ranch or close by."

"Is your argument to the court," Judge Patton asked, frowning, "because they are on that list, the names of certain of the victims in this case, that, therefore, every other name on there is a victim?"

"We take that position." Fahey was now claiming, in effect, that Corona had murdered fifty-one people. There were Mexican names on that list; the bodies of the Mexican victims had either not been recovered or not identified, Fahey argued. Hence, the fact that Raya was a Mexican was not a dissimilarity.

"The only thing that is dissimilar is that Raya did not die. We submit to the court that if he had died, Raya would have traveled in that van out to the Sullivan ranch also, but that the fact that he did not arrive out at the burial ground is because he is virtually a medical miracle."

Hawk's rebuttal was terse. "I only point out to you, fourteen of the twenty-one identified victims are not on that list, if he [Fahey] seems to think it is very important. The only other thing I would like to point out is something that the court, I am sure, probably knows. I have never met anybody named Guadalajara Jalisco [an entry on page 50 of the ledger]. However, there is in Mexico a large, beautiful city called Guadalajara, Jalisco."

As Fahey and Williams had feared, Judge Patton ruled the Guadalajara incident inadmissible: each of the doctors had been forced to qualify his opinions, Raya had suffered many more wounds than any of the victims in this case, and "in reviewing the entire matter, I fail to find a single item of substantial similarity whch would allow the people to present this testimony."

Denied on the narrow ground of dissimilarity, Fahey informed the judge the prosecution intended to appeal his decision in order to open the larger matter of the preponderance of the evidence.

The last three prosecution witnesses were scheduled for Thursday, December 21: José Romero Raya, Ray Duron, and a former neighbor of the Corona family on Richland Road, Beatrice Valdez.

Raya was no more cooperative to Hawk in front of the jury on Thursday than he had been before the judge on Monday. Williams had little trouble eliciting the same account of the job offer from Corona, and the offer to take Raya to the Sullivan ranch that night. He even added some details.

Hawk's cross-examination was even more difficult than Monday's, Raya's memory more faulty. On Monday he had testified to meeting Corona in front of the theater around seven o'clock. Today, "I don't remember it any more the hour."

Yes, the pickup was blue. No, there was no other color, no green canvas top. It was parked in front of the Guadalajara Café. What other cars were parked there? Raya shrugged.

"Were they pickups?"

"No. They were automobiles."

"There were no other pickups there?"

Raya realized he had made a mistake. "I don't remember."

Hawk then read Raya's testimony on Monday: " 'There were two pickups and the other ones I didn't notice whether they were more than that.' Do you remember that answer, Mr. Raya?"

"Well, right now that you show it to me, yes."

"On Monday of this week you told us there were two pickups. Today you only remember one?"

"Well, it is possible that I would say one thing now and then if you asked me the same thing tomorrow, I don't know."

"Mr. Raya, isn't it true that when you talked to Detective Jerry Gregory in June of 1971 you did not mention a blue pickup?"

"I don't remember."

"How many police officers have talked to you about the blue pickup?"

"How many?"

"That's the question."

"That talked to me about that?"

"The blue pickup."

"That they asked me or that I told them?"

"Are you having some trouble understanding my question, Mr. Raya?"

"I think that's a responsive answer, Your Honor," Fahey put in.

"He doesn't seem to understand," Hawk complained to the judge. "He just keeps asking questions."

"I'll object to that," Fahey reiterated. "I think it's responsive."

"He doesn't seem to have any trouble understanding Mr. Williams," replied Hawk, frustrated. Fahey and Williams were amused. Their witness was doing much better than they had hoped.

"Do you understand what I'm asking, Mr. Raya?" continued Hawk.

"If I understand whom?"

The problem was not with the translator, Corona assured Hawk; she was doing well.

"The question is: how many officers have talked to you about the blue pickup?"

"I tell you, I don't understand you. The way you are asking me, I don't understand."

"You have testified in court about a blue pickup."

"Yes."

"First of all, did you tell some policeman about the blue pickup?"

"I don't remember."

"Did you talk to a police officer named Dave Perales who spoke to you in Spanish?"

"I spoke to one or two, maybe that spoke Spanish."

"Isn't it true that when you spoke to these two police officers who spoke Spanish that you didn't mention anything at all about a blue pickup?"

"I don't remember."

"Isn't it true, Mr. Raya, that you told Mr. Gregory in June of 1971 that the conversation you had with Mr. Corona about employment took place in the Mi Oficina Bar?"

"I don't remember."

"Do you remember testifying under oath in this courtroom on Monday that the only conversation you had with Mr. Corona was outside by the telephone booth?"

"I don't remember."

It took the balance of the morning and a portion of the afternoon for Hawk to work his way through the conflicting statement, Raya remembering little for him and virtually everything for Williams on redirect. If the prosecution expected Raya's appearance in court to turn the case around, Hawk believed, they had to be disappointed. Raya had not seemed to be that impressive to the jurors.

Detective Jerry Gregory followed, called by Williams to verify he had taken a prior statement from Raya in June of 1971. Gregory was on the stand under direct examination less than a minute, Williams deliberately bringing out that Raya had told Gregory the job offer was extended in the Mi Oficina.

Hawk was even more surprised when Williams called Sergeant Perales of the Sacramento Police to the stand. Perales had talked with Raya, on tape, once in January of 1972, a second time four or five months later.

"Do you recall what Mr. Raya told you concerning this conversation of employment?"

"Yes. The conversation took place in front of the theater."

Later, Raya had told Perales the conversation took place on the street, but not near the theater. At no time had Raya indicated the conversation took place in the Mi Oficina.

Hawk would never understand why they had called Perales as a witness at all. His testimony on cross, Hawk believed, "just shot Raya right out of the saddle."

Perales agreed that he knew about and had read Jerry Gregory's earlier interview with Raya at the time he conducted his own in January 1972. Yes, Perales was aware Raya had told Gregory that the job offer was extended in the bar.

"Okay. Now, being an intelligent police officer, of course, you would be aware that if the conversation took place in the bar, Mr. Raya couldn't see Mr. Corona walk up to the blue pickup, could he?"

"There was no mention made of any blue pickup."

"Right. So in order for Mr. Raya to see a blue pickup, that conversation has to be moved from the Mi Oficina Bar out to the street?"

Both Williams and Fahey objected, but Hawk had made his point. The prosecutors wanted to tie Juan Corona to a blue pickup such as that owned first by Natividad, then sold to Pedro Corona, and one that the jury might infer was the same as that identified by Byron Shannon.

Ray Duron followed Sergeant Perales to the stand. "Did Mr. Corona ever contract for pruning on the Jack Sullivan ranch?"

"Yes, but not in 1970." Corona had worked at the ranch that winter as a laborer, leaving on February 19 for at least a month's time.

Hawk needed answers to two questions. "Isn't it true, Mr. Duron, that Sullivan liked Juan Corona and let him use the facilities at the ranch when he was contracting with other farmers?"

"That's right."

"And I take it you have no knowledge as to whether or not Mr. Corona may have had some pruning contracts with other people in February of 1970, do you?"

"No. I do not. No."

Mrs. Beatrice Valdez was the prosecution's last witness of the day. A cook at Rideout Hospital in Marysville, Mrs. Valdez lived on Richland Road about a block from the Corona home.

Because she did not go to work until ten o'clock, she frequently spent the morning hours in her garden in front of her home. In the mornings Mrs. Valdez usually saw Corona leave between six-forty-five and seven o'clock. He usually drove the Impala, a red pickup truck, but most frequently the van.

"And did you ever see him doing anything in the way of washing this van?" Fahey asked.

"Yes, I saw him several times—well, I wouldn't say washing like you normally would your car like soaping it down or something. I would say I saw him several times with the hose and he was just washing the inside, this was all."

"Let me see if I get you right. He wasn't washing the outside of the van?" Mrs. Valdez was innocently disagreeing with Stottlemyer's earlier judgment that the bloodstains in the van showed no signs of washing.

"No, not like you normally would soap down your car on the outside and continue in the interior. He would just be squirting the car on the inside with the hose."

Fahey nodded, "Hmmmm," pointedly, for the jury's benefit.

"Have you got that 'hmmm' on the record, Your Honor?" Hawk asked.

"I am sorry," Fahey replied. "I guess it is a bad habit I picked up from you."

Mrs. Valdez, a widow, had also seen Corona washing out the interior of a blue van and the red pickup. "I wouldn't know how many times he did it, but he generally, when he would come back, he would wash his car down. I noticed it because I thought he was an unusually clean man."

"At least as to the inside of his vehicles?"

"Right."

"And about what time would this be when you would see him when he'd come back and wash the inside of these vehicles out?"

"He would never stay long. He would return in about, I would say, in about two hours, two and a half hours. That would be it."

There was little Hawk could do to shake Mrs. Valdez' testimony. She had gossiped about Corona washing his vehicles. Eventually word had reached the Sheriff's Department, and two weeks before testifying a deputy had first talked to her.

"I take it you must have seen a lot of blood coming out of the back with the water, a lot of red blood and stuff?"

"As a woman, we are all nosey but I never was that nosey. I just saw that he was washing his car is all."

"Did you ever see any pieces of scalp or flesh or anything floating down the street in the gutters?"

"No."

"Now, on these occasions when you saw Mr. Corona going by your home in the pickup or the van, was his wife generally with him?"

"Not very often."

"How many times a month did Mr. Corona wash his vehicles?"

"I wouldn't know, but he did it quite often, at least three times a week. Everytime I'd see him he would be out there cleaning them. Whichever car he was driving, he would come home and wash that. That's the way it was."

The court day ended with Judge Patton recessing the trial for six days, to reconvene on December 27 when he expected the prosecution to rest its case. "I certainly wish each of you a very merry Christmas with your families."

It was Juan Corona's second Christmas spent in jail.

27

The Final Arguments
January 8-11, 1973

It was raining again as the attorneys picked their way through the scurry of television cameramen outside the white courthouse, up the back eleva- tor to the second floor filled with spectators, and through the metal detector at the sheriff's checkpoint. Teja and Fahey were somber, Williams vexed by the crutches that supported an ankle broken in a skiing accident over the holidays. After fifty-nine days of testimony, Teja was to begin the prosecution's closing argument that morning.

They had been caught short five days before when Hawk had suddenly announced he would rest without calling witnesses. Only Teja's plea that they were unprepared had saved them from presenting a disorganized, *ad libitum* summary of the case, as Hawk had hoped for.

The end had come suddenly. On December 27, Teja filed a petition in the District Court of Appeal seeking an order that would have compelled Judge Patton to hold a hearing on the preponderance of the evidence in the Guadalajara cutting. At the noon recess, the judge had scolded them, his anger tightly checked. "I thought that I had been clear, but there ap- parently is a very obvious misunderstanding as to what the situation is. The petition [to the District Court of Appeal] represents that the court ruled on the *modus operandi* offer but refused to consider this question of identity. Actually, that wasn't the court's attitude at all, and I think the record is perfectly clear in that regard. The court's position was that there was no substantial similarity of any of the common items as to permit the matter to be introduced. I just mention to you that I question there the premise of the whole petition."

At three-thirty that afternoon, a reporter told Hawk the prosecution's appeal had been summarily denied. "They died with a whimper," the defense attorney crowed to an aide, Hawk as pleased as the prosecution was downcast. The Guadalajara incident was closed.

Hawk had made two tactical decisions in the last two weeks of the year. First, as soon as the prosecution rested, he would make a motion to dismiss the case against Juan. Such motions were not granted in very many cases, but "I've got as good a chance of getting it granted now as in any case I'll ever have," he explained. The judge could grant the motion if he thought there is not enough evidence to support a conviction on appeal. The prosecution could have something against Corona, but if it wasn't enough to affirm the conviction on appeal, Judge Patton could grant the motion.

Hawk wasn't optimistic. For one thing, Judge Patton had been solicitious of the jury throughout the entire trial; it was not likely that he would grant the motion and, in effect, say, "Thank you very much, ladies and gentlemen, for sitting here four months but your services weren't needed."

It was worth the effort though, Hawk decided. If nothing else, the prosecution's argument against the motion would be a preview of the closing arguments they would make. Knowing something of what they were going to say would be helpful.

The second decision was harder to reach. He had decided to rest the defense case, without warning, without putting on any evidence. A surprise move that would certainly be a big story. Hawk savored the idea; in effect, he would be telling the jury that the case against his client was so poor there was no need to bother with a defense. They had proved nothing.

With the exception of one member, he was certain the jury was his. "The schoolteacher just hates my guts; I can't do or say anything to please her. Nothing at all." Most of them, though, were like Vic Lorenzo, juror number 3. When the prosecution had rested, after presenting 116 witnesses and introducing over 900 pieces of evidence, Lorenzo had caught Hawk's eye, half-shrugged, and smiled, as if to ask, "That's it? That's their case?"

The decision had come slowly, the idea weighed, put aside, then reexamined. By Christmas, Hawk had firmly decided to limit the defense case to just three people: someone from the lumber company to verify the receipt for the screen door; Gloria Corona, to testify they had hung Mrs. Vallejo's door the day after they bought it; and Doctor Hooker. Motive, or lack of it, and alibi, as if he were telling the jury, "Look, they could have gotten this evidence too and saved us all a lot of trouble."

Four days later, he had reconsidered. The jury was likely to conclude that Gloria would lie for her husband anyway. He could put Doctor Hooker on, but that would undoubtedly open it up for the prosecution to call as rebuttal witnesses Doctor Andres from the staff of Sutter County General and the psychiatrist Sheriff Whiteaker had slipped into Corona's cell.

Hawk was certain he could discredit them on cross-examination. "Did you conduct any tests?" "How long did you spend with Mr. Corona?" "Do you always make snap judgments?" "If your judgment is sound, would you care to give us your opinion of Mr. Teja?"

But the whole thing would muddy the waters, Hawk decided, raising the all-but-forgotten business of Corona's previous hospitalization. That was seventeen years before, but he couldn't expect the jury to totally disregard the DeWitt commitment. Released as cured, certainly, but who knew about these crazies?

There was a rational excuse for not putting Corona himself on: his heart condition. That's all he needed, to come this far, to be so close to winning it, and have his guy die of a heart attack.

The prosecution would undoubtedly try to impress the jury by pointing out he had not fulfilled promises made in the opening statement, especially his pledge to produce Doctor Hooker with her explanation that provided a motive. He could handle that well enough with the logical argument that at the time he had made the promise, he had not known just how weak the prosecution's case was. Had he seen all the documents withheld illegally from him, he would have made a different opening statement.

Hawk had made his final decision on December 31, after flying to Los Angeles for a long midday discussion with Doctor Hooker. He owed the woman that much. She had not only interviewed Juan in his cell at Vacaville, but she had insisted on paying her own expenses. Then she had recruited colleagues to interpret her tests so as to be certain no subjective bias crept into her analysis.

Doctor Hooker's tests, Hawk learned for the first time, confirmed that Corona had no homosexual leanings, conscious or unconscious. The test profiles did not place him in the category of a person capable of multiple murders. Anyone, she explained, was capable of murdering once, but those who repeatedly killed scored differently on the tests she had administered.

Doctor Hooker understood Hawk's tactic, the implied contempt for the prosecution case. It would catch the prosecution off-guard—right to the end Hawk was showing them he could out-think them—and leave them holding whatever testimony and evidence they had planned to bring in during their rebuttal case. They would also be stuck with whatever evidence they had expected to use to refute Doctor Hooker's suggestion that these murders were homosexually motivated. Meanwhile, he had still gotten enough hints into the trial to have, at least, planted some question about the motivation.

For Hawk, the decisive factor was the impact of the ploy, the jolt to the district attorney, the judge, the jury, the press. In view of the judge's consuming anxiety about time, always pushing the case forward, Hawk had reasoned that Judge Patton would grant only a minimum delay, an early recess when he rested, and no more. He was wrong; once more the judge had helped to keep the balance "equal," giving the prosecution one last opportunity. By delaying the closing arguments for five days, Judge Patton gave them back the time Hawk had taken away so suddenly. The tactical advantage evaporated in that five days, the three prosecutors preparing a coherent final argument.

The time was now up. The district attorney rose to make his final argument.

G. Dave Teja opened the two-inch-thick notebook on the lectern. "It is my particular job at this point in the case to summarize the important features of the evidence which has been introduced by the people in the case, to outline the evidence for you so as to assist you in evaluating the evidence in drawing reasonable conclusions and deductions from it."

Teja's voice was expressionless, a monotone of argument. Like Williams' opening statement, the closing argument would have half of the jury asleep or bored before the day was out, Hawk estimated.

As the defense attorney had predicted, Teja began with an attack on Hawk. "We have all heard references to the fact that lawyers should be honest and you should be able to believe what a lawyer promises you when he tells you something. In his opening statement, the defense lawyer promised you he would prove a number of things, none of which he proved." Teja itemized the promises: Carlos Leon Sierra, Corona's leg infection, Emilio Rangel. "It is interesting to note that none of the witnesses who were called to testify here before you, associated this man Rangel with any of the grave sites.

"The defense apologized in his opening statement to the ladies of the jury for having to bring experts here to talk about *machismo, activo* homosexuals, *passivo* homosexuals—" Teja coughed. "None of this which was promised you was provided by the defense. The defense promised you experts, but produced none. The defense also promised you character evidence; none of these people testified.

"It is easy for an attorney to talk a great deal; it is easy for an attorney to promise a great deal; producing cold, hard evidence of fact is sometimes a great deal more difficult. Where are the medical records he referred to? Do they exist? Where is the evidence regarding this Emilio Rangel? Where is this expert testimony about homosexuality and heterosexuality? Where is the character evidence that was promised here?

"Finally," Teja asked, his voice rising in rhetorical excitement, "ladies and gentlemen, where is any evidence whatsoever that the defendant didn't kill these twenty-five people and bury their bodies in and about the vicinity of the Sullivan ranch?"

Hawk was on his feet. "Your Honor, I will object to that statement on the basis that he has been standing here for half an hour trying to shift off the burden of proof onto me, and I don't have it, and that last statement is just rank."

Judge Patton sat up. "Well, the jury will be instructed at the proper time as to the law to be applied to the case, and the last reference is ordered stricken."

Teja continued from notes, "There is, ladies and gentlemen, a mass of circumstantial evidence here which, when viewed cumulatively and altogether, establishes the guilt of this man, Juan Vallejo Corona."

Teja shifted from the written outline upon which he embroidered commentary to a prepared speech which he read. "What you will find here, when you critically examine the total evidence before you, is a series of little chains composed of circumstantial links of items of evidence or links in circumstantial chains which demonstrate and prove the defendant did in fact kill all of these twenty-five people."

Corona stared at the now-empty witness stand, occasionally toying with the copy of *Robinson Crusoe* he had brought with him to read when the court was in recess, a Christmas gift from his lawyer.

Teja began a long review of each phase of the prosecution's case. "Everything started on May 19, 1971." Hawk listened, his attention entangled in his own thoughts. May 19, 1971, an eternity ago. It was hard to remember clearly everything that had happened since then. His taking over the case; the long summer when he, Geneva, and Archie Gore were almost Corona's only supporters; the bail motions; the change-of-venue hearing; the capital punishment decision and the disappointment following Patton's denial of bail; Williams' reasonable doubt statement and the disappointment there. They had been so close, so often.

Teja was talking about the tire tracks at the first grave. Eighteen months, Hawk thought. His car, new in June 1971, now had 64,000 miles on it—all of it attributable to the Corona case. Add to that the 100 hours in the Bonanza, logged flying to and from Marysville. The plane was going to have to go; he couldn't maintain it. Eighteen months. In all that time, he hadn't taken a half-dozen other cases; no matter how much he loved that plane, he had to put food on the table, he thought ruefully.

In debt, behind in his house payments, he would now have to rebuild his practice. The publicity here would certainly help, but it would take time to recover.

Hawk rubbed his eyes, the fatigue he had pushed aside for months bearing down. It would all be over, finally, in a few days. He would feel lost for a while, he knew. No court session to attend, no sheriff's reports to read, no evidence to talk over with John Thornton. And no reporters to drink with after court. The end of the Corona case would mean he would have to readjust, and go back to being just another good defense attorney in northern California.

"It is a very, very serious question here, and one which you will have to ask yourselves about in view of the defense representation that the defendant was with his wife during this particular period of time, making purchases at stores, helping her prepare dinner, et cetera.

"She has not been called as a witness to testify to that fact, nor has anybody testified to the defendant's exact whereabouts at the time in question.

"No, if this evidence existed, why didn't the defense offer it to you? If, in fact, the defendant's wife was with him, she—"

"That is improper argument in view of the burden of proof in this case," Hawk interjected calmly.

"Well, the jury will certainly be instructed as to the burden of proof and all other proper rules of law," Judge Patton repeated.

Teja read on through the morning, summarizing the evidence, stopping only for the noon recess. It was not an impassioned argument; Teja was not a passionate man. Instead it was slow, methodically cumulative, excessive in its details. It would begin to take its toll in the afternoon.

The district attorney returned to the lectern after the noon recess to spend a half-hour "talking about the confusion of numbering between the body of Melford Sample and the body of the victim that we have yet unidentified who is labeled E-2-4."

By two o'clock juror number 1 was nodding, his eyelids heavy; alternate juror A, assuming none of this would concern him, had given up and was sleeping. Fifteen minutes later, juror number 5 was dozing; the ninth and twelfth were yawning, fighting drowsiness. Judge Patton missed it all; he was leaning back in his chair, his eyes closed.

Steadily Teja reviewed the prosecution's case: the trash found in the twenty-fifth grave all pointed to Corona; even the grass clippings could have come from the lawn in front of his Richland Road home; then three of the witnesses, Byron Shannon—"no evidence was developed here to show that Mr. Shannon had a motive to perjure himself"—James Pervis, José Romero Raya, whose name was in the green ledger.

"There are a host of miscellaneous circumstances here, ladies and gentlemen, which when taken together are significant things which the defense might have chosen to explain away but which—"

Again Hawk objected "to that kind of an argument. That is improper under the law; and I ask him to be admonished, to stop doing this." The defense attorney was becoming angry.

Judge Patton too was less accepting. "It is ordered stricken. The jury is admonished to disregard the last statement."

Teja droned on. Doctor Masters had looked at the machete found in Corona's van, and "he said that: 'This type of weapon is consistent with the weapon that could be the weapon that inflicted most of the wounds or all of the wounds.'

"Now, we know that at least in the case of Kenneth Edward Whitacre, or we have good reason to believe that, that particular bolo machete, ladies and gentlemen, did not cause the wounds to Whitacre's head, those massive wounds which undoubtedly contributed to his death.

"There is no evidence whatsoever other than the absence of any blood on that particular weapon that it was not used as a weapon to murder, as an instrument to murder any of the other victims other than Kenneth Edward Whitacre."

Wincing at Teja's attempt to shift the burden of proof to Corona, Hawk whispered to an aide, "I'm ashamed of the sonovabitch."

Juror number 1 was sleeping now. Number 6 had found something interesting to stare at between his feet. The schoolteacher had stopped taking notes. Number 9 had crossed his arms, rested his chin on his chest, and closed his eyes.

Teja had been reading for four hours when Judge Patton recessed for the day. Hawk teased Fahey as they waited for the spectators to clear the hallway. "Didn't you preview all that?"

"He's the D.A.," Fahey shrugged, laughing. "You should see his rebuttal file," referring to material which would never be used. "It's this big." Fahey spread his hands apart.

The following morning Teja picked up where he had left off the night before, ad-libbing a brief introduction. "Ladies and gentlemen, as we entered this particular trial, as the court instructed you, and as we all know, the defendent was cloaked with the presumption of his innocence.

"In the course of presenting the testimony of over a hundred witnesses here in the course of presenting the physical evidence and actual facts at this particular time in the case, with the evidence in the particular state that it is in at the time both sides rested here in this particular trial, the defendant has been stripped of that particular presumption—"

"That is a misstatement of law," Hawk was on his feet. "That presumption lasts clear into the jury room. And he knows that. That is a complete misstatement of the law."

"The remark is ordered stricken. The court will instruct the jury as to the proper law. The jury will disregard the comments."

Back to his loose-leaf notebook, Teja continued his summary of the prosecution's case: the blood evidence, the posthole digger, the ledger.

The ledger contained the names of seven, possibly eight victims, in chronological order roughly corresponding to the date when the victims were last seen alive or from the evidence in their pockets known to be living.

"Well, we don't find the name Whitacre on this anyplace, but if we look down here at the next to the last entry we see May 19 and the word 'S-o-r-t-o-r' or 'S-a-r-t-o-r.' I don't know what that word means; nobody has been able to explain that particular word. Certainly the defense has not explained what it means. But that is incriminating, that date of death—"

"Could he be admonished about trying to rewrite the United States Constitution and shift the burden of proof?" Hawk asked Judge Patton.

"I'm not attempting to shift the burden of proof," Teja responded.

"The last reference to the alleged failure of the defendant to explain is ordered stricken and the jury is admonished to disregard it," Judge Patton ruled. The judge was growing upset. Four times now he had ordered stricken Teja's references to the defense failure to produce evidence. It was unheard of, having to do such a thing, especially when the law permitted almost unlimited freedom in closing argument.

"At any rate, that side of the table hasn't bothered to explain that entry."

"Your Honor, can he be admonished? He just turned around and did the same thing," a disgusted Hawk protested.

"I can comment on their failure to introduce evidence, Your Honor," Teja argued.

The judge led the attorneys into chambers, Corona following, *Robinson Crusoe* clenched tightly in his hand. "Let's hear argument then," Judge Patton ordered.

"Well," Hawk began. "The law simply is that *they* have the burden of proof. It is improper for him to comment that we haven't explained something or that Mr. Corona hasn't testified on something."

"It is perfectly permissible argument on behalf of the prosecution," Williams countered, "to comment on the other party's failure to produce evidence in a particular area as long as it is very carefully noted that no reference is made to the fact that the defendant hasn't testified to that." The United States Supreme Court had held, in *Griffin v. California*, in 1965, that the prosecution's comments in closing argument that the defendant had not testified was reversible error.

Judge Patton was skeptical. "Apparently you are casting a burden of some kind on the defense to explain these things."

"He has made several interesting—" Hawk began.

"Well, Your Honor," Williams interrupted.

"May I finish? He is picking up some bad habits from Mr. Fahey," Hawk snapped. "He did virtually the same thing when he said that he conceded that the machete didn't cut the skulls but we didn't establish that it didn't cut the other twenty-four.

"Now if he wants to hang himself with the jury," Hawk continued, "he has lost, I believe, the only vote he had going in here."

Judge Patton waved Hawk quiet. "Let's not discuss that. Let's get to the legal argument."

"When he starts down to the problem of the ledger, it is obvious that the only one who could make an explanation as to the entries on that ledger would be Mr. Corona, as they view the case, and in effect what he really is saying is that Mr. Corona didn't testify and tell you about this, and that violates the *Griffin* ruling.

Judge Patton agreed. "You are really emphasizing and by inference trying to bring out that he, the defendant, has not testified. That is what you are really saying to this jury in this matter by inference." His voice rising in anger, Judge Patton insisted, "I don't care how you put it to me here in chambers, but that is what the thrust of the argument is, and that part is improper."

"I suggest that I think he already has committed a reversible error by violating the *Griffin* rule," Hawk put in.

"All right. The People should be very careful about any matters which infer that the defendant has failed to explain anything," Judge Patton ordered. The *Griffin* problem having been raised, Judge Patton brought up an earlier comment. "As I understood Mr. Teja to say to this jury, the defendant had been stripped of his presumption of innocence, and that to me is such a startling remark for the prosecution to make to a jury that I'm going to have a few more remarks about that comment."

Fahey sensed an opportunity. "Is there a motion?" he asked Hawk, who failed to hear him. "Are you making a motion?" Fahey repeated. "For the record, has any motion been made by the defense?"

Hawk realized finally that Fahey was asking him for a motion for mistrial, a motion which, if granted, would require an entire new trial. Not now, not when he was winning. "Well, I objected immediately to it."

"Well, what I am asking is has any motion been made to the court now at this time?" Fahey pressed.

"To strike." Hawk answered.

"This is a motion to strike?" Fahey could not hide the disappointment in his voice.

"And to admonish the jury that the comment was improper," Hawk added. The opportunity had passed.

On the bench once again, Judge Patton reminded the jury "that a defendant in a criminal action is presumed to be innocent until the contrary is proved; and that the entire burden of proof in this case rests entirely upon the People."

Teja turned back to his loose-leaf notebook. The ledger was the "most damning piece of evidence. It clearly demonstrates Juan Corona's connection with a number of the victims, and it clearly demonstrates his connection with something on the dates on which a number of these people obviously were buried.

"We know that the defendant had a crew boss, Emilio Rangel. He wasn't called to explain, ladies and gentlemen, what this list represented."

"Excuse me, Your Honor." Hawk had been waiting for another slip.

"He is at it again. May he be admonished not to try to change the Constitution and shift the burden of proof?"

"This relates to some other witness?" Judge Patton asked. "Overruled." Judge Patton would later reverse himself.

Teja was nearing the end. "We have shown by uncontradicted evidence that the ledger is Juan Corona's. It is also an uncontradicted fact that the ink formula and pen used by the defendant to write some of his checks and the rent receipt matched the ink and entries in the ledger. And, finally, the opinions of three qualified experts in the field of questioned document examination go uncontradicted in this particular case." The district attorney spent ten minutes reviewing in detail the analyses of the three handwriting examiners.

"Ladies and gentlemen, the only conclusion that you can make about this particular list containing the names of at least seven of the victims here, is that the list is in its entirety and completely that of the defendant, Juan Vallejo Corona."

Teja closed the notebook after taking six hours to present his interpretation of the case. His voice was strained with fatigue, dejection, and disappointment. "I submit after you perform your jobs in the jury room dispassionately and thoroughly that you will return to this courtroom, ladies and gentlemen, with a verdict of guilty as charged against the defendant, Juan Vallejo Corona."

Before Hawk began his closing argument, the attorneys met again in chambers at the judge's request. "I believe, under the circumstances in which the defendant has not taken the stand, that it is improper for the People to make reference or argue to the fact that a witness, if the defense had called him, might have testified to certain matters or might have clarified certain matters."

The judge was upset by his research during the luncheon break. "I think the People's argument addressed to me in chambers this morning in regards to this is clearly wrong. What, in effect, it amounts to then [is that] the defendant has not testified. You are in effect arguing the change in the burden of proof. I feel now as a matter of precaution any reference to this Emilio Rangel should be stricken from this record and the jury should be admonished to disregard it."

His anger rising, the judge continued. "You come in talking as if, you know, something is well settled in the law and when I look at it, it's not that at all and this is the type of matter which could have some consequence and the court is trying to protect the record in this matter to see that errors are not committed, and I expect both sides to help me in that endeavor."

In response to the judge's request for their comments, Teja conceded he could cite no case law supporting his position. Hawk was confronted again with a tactical decision. "The reason I am not moving for a mistrial is that Juan Corona has a year and a half of his life in custody at this time. I do not want and I am not making a motion for a mistrial because it is my considered judgment at this point that it would be a major victory for the prosecutor if he got one vote and could hang the jury, but at the same time, I think it is reprehensible of them and puts me in a difficult position to press on into any errors here such as the *Griffin* error merely hoping that I will somehow pull them out of the bag by moving for a mistrial."

Before Hawk began his closing argument, Judge Patton instructed the jury. "The burden of proof in this matter is upon the People and the reference to his possible witness and to what he may or might not have testified to had he been called is not a proper subject of argument, not a proper matter to be considered by the jury and you are ordered to completely put that comment and argument out of mind."

For the first time since the opening statements, Hawk was nervous. Corona sat beside him, gripping *Robinson Crusoe* in his knuckle-white hands. He had left uneaten his sandwich in the brown paper bag packed for him at Vacaville, and he had spent the noon hour on his knees in the holding cell, praying. There was nothing else he could do to help the man he still called Mr. Hawk.

The defense attorney had prepared his closing argument on Sunday evening, two days before, outlining the points he wanted to make while an aide marked specific points in the transcript which Hawk intended to read. The rest was in his head—the contradictions, the mistakes, the errors, the omissions.

Standing at the lectern, he looked at the jury. They called themselves the "Fairfield Fifteen" now. That was his jury, Juan's; he had picked it. In a few minutes, a couple of hours, he would be through talking to them, and there would be nothing more he could do for Juan Corona. Hawk was frightened, terribly frightened.

"May it please the court"—always the formal introduction "—Your Honor, Judge Patton; ladies and gentlemen of the jury; and the three counsels for the prosecutor there behind me; and last, but not least, my esteemed client, Juan Corona.

"This has been a very long trial for all of you. I know that it has taken a lot out of your lives. The Juan Corona case has taken an awful lot out of my life. I was just noticing last night that my boy, who the last time I looked seemed like a little boy, all at once seems like a teenage boy, and I noticed that the girls are calling him now.

"It has taken a lot out of Judge Patton's life, a lot out of other people's lives, but probably the person who has or the group of people that it

Sitting in the press section of the full courtroom, Los Angeles *Times* reporter Jerry Cohen watched the district attorney. Teja's eyes were shifting rapidly from juror to juror, "in a panic," Cohen thought.

After a ten-minute recess, Hawk explained the lack of a defense case. "No witness by the defense does not mean that there was no defense. As you recall, Sarah Vallejo, I called her as my witness.

"The doctor who examines you and finds that there is nothing wrong with you doesn't prescribe open-heart surgery or give you a lot of antibiotics. Lawyers are in much the same position. Had I known all of the things I know now, at the conclusion of this investigation, which was still going on in mid-December of this year, I would have made an entirely different opening statement to you than I did. I ask you to bear in mind that the material which I received quadrupled at the end of this trial, a good deal of which was from the investigation continuing some eighteen months after Mr. Corona was arrested."

Furthermore, Hawk argued, cross-examination "has always been deemed the surest test of truth and better security that the oath," quoting a lawyer's maxim coined in 1903 by Francis Wellman. Cross-examination brought out the full story; the prosecution's own witnesses could be made to raise a reasonable doubt.

Reasonable doubt, it was hard to define. "The only thing I have ever really been able to suggest to juries is that reasonable doubt is like love. If you are in love with someone, you know it. If you are not, you ought to know that too. If you consider the case, and in your heart and your soul you've got the same kind of feeling you have when you are in love, then that's reasonable doubt; and you don't have to apologize to anybody for it.

"And that's the genius of the law. That is what makes the jury system work. Because in the long haul, juries do the right thing. Occasionally there is a freaky jury, as lawyers use that term, for some reason. They do something that nobody can understand. But that is very rare."

Hawk then began a review of the case. Phase I "took somewhere between forty and forty-five percent of the trial time here to try to prove something that I never denied, that Juan never denied, that I don't know anybody that denied, that they had twenty-five bodies and they were first-degree murders." The mistakes, errors, and omissions. Jack Purcell, Hawk was not sure that he was responsible for all the mistakes committed. Cartoscelli, who did not know east from south. Detective Gregory, and the confusion at the riverbank graveyard. "The odyssey of Donald Smith moving up and down the Feather River and we have the elusive tire tracks that got lost in the evidence locker that at one point I facetiously referred to as the 'Goodwill Store,' but it really wasn't quite as facetious as I might have thought.

The tire tracks. All Wilder, the ATF expert," could say about that was 'could have been.' It doesn't mean it is Juan's at all. And if you apply the law of circumstantial evidence, you are bound to—and it is your duty to—accept the conclusion that says it is not his—and therein lies reasonable doubt."

The three prosecutors jotted notes on legal pads as Hawk talked on.

"You know, if you just read *Dick Tracy* and looked at 'Crime Stoppers,' you ought to know more about how to investigate a crime than Sutter County did. If you just watch television, your common sense would tell you that you don't handle evidence, or if it doesn't match one person you just don't ignore it and throw it away, lock it up somewhere and forget about it."

The meat receipts, according to the prosecution, dropped from Corona's shirt pocket into the first grave on the riverbank. "Well, Mr. Corona couldn't have dropped out of his shirt pocket a candlestick holder and all those other items from the last grave. So Mr. Teja has got a new theory: it was used as a dump, and Juan just threw the family trash in there. And I ask you to consider, isn't it a bit much that ten days after Juan is arrested and Ray Duron sends a man out to a specific orchard where the police have been in and out for days that they locate a grave—not with the help of the police—and they find all these goodies with Juan Corona's name on them?

"It wouldn't surprise me if there are more bodies up there and you will find some more things with Juan Corona's name on them. It's a bit much, that twenty-fifth grave, I suggest to you."

At four-fifteen, after one hour and forty-five minutes of argument, Hawk asked to recess for the day. He spent the early evening in the bar across the street, talking to newsmen until one by one they left to file stories or argue with angry wives, leaving Hawk looking around for someone to talk to, to drink with, finally finishing his last drink, the audience gone.

In the morning, the three prosecutors sought once again a ruling from Judge Patton which would allow them in Fahey's rebuttal argument to comment on the failure of Gloria Corona to testify. Confronted with a legal precedent, Judge Patton reluctantly agreed to permit the comment, adding, "It seems to me what the People are doing, they want to open up the whole case to argue these matters and really, as Mr. Hawk suggests, to infer to the jury that because the defense did not produce testimony in these areas that somehow or other the burden has shifted to them to prove this case."

Pinching the bridge of his nose, showing his fatigue for the first time since the first weeks of the trial, Judge Patton continued, "I think the people are on delicate and very dangerous ground and it really almost suggests to me that the People are inclined to just risk anything to get a conviction in this case.

Hawk, using a chart prepared overnight, picked up his argument in the morning with the confusions of numbering the first four bodies from the riverbank; Gregory's report listed the first four bodies from the riverbank as: Sample, Smith, Unidentified, Haluka. The autopsies, in order, were of the unidentified man, Sample, Smith, and Haluka. In court, the prosecution had identified the first four victims as Sample, the unidentified man, Haluka, and Smith. "Mr. Teja talked about the consistency of the inconsistency." The chart instead pointed out the inconsistency of the inconsistency.

Mishandling of the evidence. "I can just imagine the congregation myself, 'Hey, look what we've got here, guys!' " Gregory's manifold mistakes. The receipts themselves. "If this body was buried before May 21, and these receipts didn't exist before May 21, then we have to consider the possibility that these receipts were planted after the body was in the ground." Pierce Rooney gave an estimate that the body had been buried anywhere from four days to two weeks. In a circumstantial evidence case, the facts had to be inconsistent with innocence. Where the evidence was susceptible to two reasonable conclusions, the jury was obligated to accept that which pointed to innocence. In Doctor Rooney's opinion, two weeks was as reasonable as four days, and a two-week span pointed to innocence.

The lack of fingerprint evidence. "One of the graves you recall, and I asked the question that you might have thought facetious at the time, was, 'Well, what did that guy do, get in there and put the wallet on his chest and chop his own head?' Now they can talk all they want about mud on one side, but one side of that wallet was lying on his chest and it is protected by lying there. If there is a fingerprint there, who put it on there? The killer or one of the killers did. And you can get fingerprints off leather. Mr. Parmer told you so, didn't he? And nobody tried."

"Why do you think they really quit looking for bodies? The big problem is that Mr. Corona is in custody, and if it gets up to eight, nine, ten days, and they dig up a body that is only twenty-four hours old, school is out."

And there was "the elusive, helpful Ray Duron," one of a number of witnesses who found nothing suspicious about Corona's behavior until after he was arrested. Duron had access to the ranch, if access was important, as the district attorney had argued. In fact, there were any number of ways to get on the ranch, even driving along the top of the levee. Sheriff's deputies drove a patrol there routinely.

Teja's calm had returned. He listened impassively, elbows on the counsel table, staring at a spot on the wall above the jury box, as Hawk ridiculed his case.

"What they did in this case is they picked their man and arrested him and then they set out to prove he was guilty. And what happened to them was, it just backfired. Everything they touched turned wrong. His blood is O; the cup is A. And we got that explanation about, 'Well, it got all sunk into the porcelain cup.' If you believe that, throw your watch on the floor."

Hawk talked until the noon recess, rambling, interjecting asides. Doctor Guy's testimony. The blood on the gun not matching that of the one victim found shot. The ledger. "There are fourteen identified victims in this case whose names do not appear on that list. From that he wants you to guess and speculate that it's a death list.

"I don't know what to say about handwriting experts. I don't know whether it is a science or an art, or whether it is just science fiction. They never get down to any scientific principle. They have always got a range of things that it can be. And what the range is, or is not, you know, is never too clearly defined to any jury or anybody else. Any little problem there is, they ignore.

"If three handwriting experts can't agree on their reasons and what they find in this thing, how can they expect you to agree?" That was for the marine sergeant. "And therein lies reasonable doubt. And if you give them the ledger, so what? So there are six or seven names there. Does that mean that Corona killed twenty-five people? Where are the other identified names? Ask yourself that."

Hawk was near the end. "The last person who gets a chance to say anything in this courtroom about this case is going to be Ronald Fahey, the special prosecutor hired mid-trial to shore up or beef up, or however you want to consider it, the prosecutor's case.

"All I can really do is ask those of you here on this jury that are going to be deliberating, those of you who believe that Juan is innocent, I will have to rely on you, or, more importantly, Juan will have to rely upon those of you who believe he is innocent, to answer what arguments you think need to be answered.

"The final sentence, I guess, of the chapter in Juan Corona's case, will be written by you with your verdict. And I know that, and I believe in my heart, that you will treat Juan fairly. And I know that we wound up in the right place with the right twelve jurors."

Hawk folded his glasses, four hours and forty-minutes after beginning his argument. "That is all I have, Your Honor." He had let go his grip on Juan Corona.

28

The Verdict
January 18, 1973

Ronald Fahey's rebuttal was adroit. Working only from hasty notes scrawled as Hawk was making his closing argument, Fahey extemporized for the balance of the afternoon.

Speaking slowly, the associate counsel began with an attack on Hawk's argument. "Now, I believe in argument reference was made to the fact that Mr. Teja, Mr. Williams and myself represent some vague body known as the People of the State of California. Well, maybe you can characterize it as that, but in essence, we represent society.

"And while we talk about Mr. Corona being away from his family, let's keep in mind the fact that these twenty-five men that were systematically chopped and stabbed to death, one man being shot, they were part of this same society that we belong to.

"They walked the streets of Marysville and the surrounding area and there is no evidence to indicate that they were bothering anybody. Maybe they lived in an element that is not the same as yours or mine; maybe they worked when they could; maybe they slept outside some of the time, but the fact of the matter is there was no justification or excuse for their deaths.

"They are a long time dead; they are not coming back. They are not walking around any more, and that's what this case is all about. That's why society has a stake in the prosecution of a criminal case.

"Now, if you want to get back to this reference that has been made about $500,000, this trial in excess of $500,000, and I hate to dignify that type of a reference by a response, but I feel that it has to be done.

"Let's just do a little simple arithmetic and divide twenty-five dead men into an arbitrary figure like $500,000. What does that amount to? Something like $20,000 a body for the prosecution of what we consider the murderer of those men."

Speaking slowly, stalling, trying to stretch his comments until the evening recess so as to gain time to further organize his rebuttal, Fahey continued, "The technique used by the defense is not a new one nor an unusual one, and I think you can appreciate that by the tenor of the remarks that have been made, and that is talk about everything that wasn't done: try the Sutter County sheriff's office, try Dave Teja, the district attorney, but don't look at the cold, hard evidence in his case.

"The cold, hard evidence in this case is that once they started to unearth bodies out at the Sullivan ranch, when they got to the third body they found evidence of identification, the identification of a person who conceivably killed and buried that body. There is only evidence that is susceptible to one reasonable interpretation, the man whose name is on the meat receipts that came out of the ground with the nine-fingered man is the man that killed these men."

Fahey ranged about the courtroom, discussing specific items of evidence left unmentioned by Hawk, adding from the pile behind the clerk's desk exhibits to the stack in front of the counsel table. Floor mats from the trunk of the car, the child's belt with blood on it, a brace of photographs, a bloodstained overcoat, one by one heaped on the floor or the table.

"Now the defense has indicated that this ledger should have been checked for fingerprints and that would have been even better evidence that it belonged to Juan Corona. What better evidence can you have than that the ledger came out of his house in the early morning hours of the twenty-sixth as a result of a search warrant?"

Fahey turned to the twenty-fifth grave, the trash dump. "There aren't two reasonable interpretations or explanations for those bank deposit slips; there is only one. The man who they belong to dropped them in there. The man who put Mr. Maczak in the ground, the man who owned the van and the car with human blood throughout the interior of the van, throughout the trunk with the mats, with the human blood, the knives with the human blood, with the gun with human blood, clothing with human blood."

Though Judge Patton ordered Fahey to continue his argument until five o'clock, a half-hour past the usual closing, Fahey was able to secure the respite. Overnight, the three prosecutors fashioned an outline from which Fahey worked when court reconvened in the morning.

The jurors came into the courtroom smiling, laughing among themselves; warned by Judge Patton the night before to bring extra clothes because they would be sequestered during the deliberations, they realized it was now truly over. Or almost over.

Far quicker in his arguments, no longer stalling until the end of the day, Fahey scored Hawk's closing remarks. "Counsel quoted Wellman, saying, 'The surest test of truth is cross-examination.'" Hawk could sense what was coming. "And I would indicate to you that both defense and the People have the right to cross-examine any witness that is produced by the opposing party and that the People believe in what Francis Wellman said. But it was clear that there was an absence of cross-examination on the part of the People."

"Your Honor, that is an improper argument," Hawk broke in. "He is still attempting to rewrite the Constitution and shift the burden of proof on Mr. Corona."

"I am only responding to the comment on the surest test of truth, Your Honor: cross-examination."

"Very well, proceed to a different subject."

"All the People are looking for in this case, we are just looking for twelve jurors to exercise their common sense and the good judgment that they exercise in their everyday affairs, and look at the evidence and not deliberate on attorney's opinions, particularly opinions that are advanced by adversaries that have produced no evidence to rebut the evidence that the People have put on in this case."

Despite the judge's warning, the prosecution was going to continue to comment on the failure of the defense to put on witnesses. Hawk objected again, Judge Patton again reminding the jury "that the defendant is presumed to be innocent until the contrary is proved and the entire burden of proof is on the People in this case."

Walking about the courtroom, one hand in his pocket jingling the coins there, Fahey dealt with the vexing lack of motive: "Doctor Rooney said that in his opinion the person who inflicted these injuries was a very angry person, yet these bodies were systematically buried and concealed.

"I defy you or anyone to know what is going through the mind of a man who systematically chops and stabs twenty-five men to death and then buries them in a remote area in an orchard over a period of time.

"I submit to you that a team of ten psychiatrists could work years on a man that had done something like this and still not come up with the answer.

"And then in commenting on the testimony of the witnesses in this area, he fails to even mention José Romero Raya. Think about it. He wasn't even discussed by the defense. He wasn't mentioned to you. Why? Why wasn't he even commented upon?

"You saw and heard José Romero Raya. You saw him testify here. You saw him point to his name at the top of the ledger. You saw him testify he was solicited for work at the Sullivan ranch by Juan Corona, and the evidence is clear and uncontroverted there was no work on the Sullivan ranch.

"Why didn't they want to talk about José Romero Raya?" Fahey was excited by his own argument.

"Reference has been made to Sarah Vallejo's testimony and the fact that she provides some sort of an alibi. She couldn't even put Mr. Corona out at her place in Live Oak on the nineteenth; it was either the eighteenth or the nineteenth, and I think the evidence is clear that she gave a statement at one time that Mr. Corona was out there for a short time in the morning and then returned for a short time in the afternoon. In no way can her testimony account for Mr. Corona's time during the time Mr. Whitacre was killed and buried."

Fahey was at the end. "Look at this evidence, examine it. Examine the fact that there has been no evidence that contradicts it or rebuts it, and you will arrive at one inescapable conclusion, the only man living in the area of Marysville having access to the Sullivan ranch, having access to the lower end of Marysville, being seen with the people down there, having a virtual conglomerate of weapons consistent with the way these men met their death, having vans, vehicles, clothing, all stained with blood, being in areas all over the ranch where bodies were found, leaving evidence of his identity there, and you arrive at one inescapable conclusion:

"That there is only one explanation that this evidence gives you. And that explanation is that only one man in that area could have committed those crimes, and that man is Juan Vallejo Corona."

At five minutes after eleven o'clock Judge Patton began reading in a carefully unaccented voice the forty instructions to the jury which the prosecution and defense had suggested he deliver: legal definitions of murder, probable cause, reasonable doubt, alibi, the credibility of witnesses, weighing conflicting testimony, motive or its lack, circumstantial evidence. The jurors were no longer smiling as they had been when they took their seats; the responsibility was now theirs.

A half-hour later, Judge Patton formally ordered six bailiffs, in the cant of an archaic charge, "to take custody of this jury and conduct them to some secret and private place."

On the 590th day of his imprisonment, the case of Juan Vallejo Corona went to the jury.

Dave Teja was elated with Fahey's rebuttal argument. Boarding the elevator with newsmen, he spotted Mrs. Corona walking past, and murmured to those around him, "Too bad, Gloria. Maybe they'll have conjugal visits."

Gloria Corona and Geneva Hawk were trying to make their way through the crowded rotunda to where Richard Hawk stood by himself, suddenly alone. Geneva translating, the three talked softly. "She is crying, because you told her not to cry, not to be sad. And she said she wasn't crying because she thought they would find Juan guilty, but because she had been holding it back and knew in her heart that the jury would find Juan not guilty and would bring her husband back home to her,"

Mrs. Hawk translated. "She wants you to know you have done everything to help. The whole family understands, whatever would happen. It would not be your fault if there was a guilty verdict. You have done everything in your power. They can never repay you for everything."

Hawk rubbed at the tears on his cheeks. "Tell him not to be sad," Geneva translated.

Juan Corona sat stiffly on the wooden bench bolted to the wall of the holding cell across the hall from Courtroom Number 4 where the jury was deliberating. He stared at the walls painted the inevitable jail house green, confused by the inscriptions scratched there, permanent until the next coat of spackle and paint: "Robert Hardcastle, flagged out."; "Stanley, Marilyn, Dixon, California, agents for narcs"; "Dillon, Thanks and take it easy. G.B."; and the ultimate condemnation, "Fuck 'Em If They Can't Take a Joke."

"They take too much time to adjust everything?" He asked his attorney.

"I don't know," Hawk admitted. "You never can tell about a jury. There may be one stubborn guy who wants to hold out for a while. No way they can convict you, Juan. The only thing that worries me is a hung jury. Some person gets stubborn and hangs it. The only person who worries me is that schoolteacher. If she gets stubborn and wants to convict you, she's gonna hold out, but she won't hold out for a long time."

Hawk patted Corona's arm. "The best they can hope for is ten to two" [in favor of Corona].

Corona nodded. "I feel sad, you know. I can never get to the point where I were, before I mean, when I had my car, my house. And all the people, they have bad impression of me. But I be pretty happy to get out."

Hawk laughed. "You're in a lot better shape than in June of 1971 when I first met you."

"Oh, yeah," Corona chuckled.

At one o'clock, the jury asked to speak to the judge. In the reassembled courtroom, juror number 7, retired Air Force master sergeant Ernest Phillips stood up. As the elected foreman, the first member picked for the jury asked, "If we find him innocent or guilty on one count, do we have to find him innocent of all?"

Hawk squinted. The alibi for the time Kenneth Whitacre was killed obviously had influenced them; they might even have taken a vote on that first count. Not guilty on that meant not guilty on the other twenty-four; the prosecution had argued that one man, and one man alone, was responsible for the mass murder.

Driven into the basement cafeteria by the continuing rain, the newsmen settled down to wait for the verdict. Television crews and reporters for national news magazines, long absent, joined with the reporters who had staffed the trial. The experienced hands had brought cards, books to read, games to play. The CBS correspondent was the Washington Redskins, NBC's cameraman the Dallas Cowboys. An artist sketched Geneva Hawk where she sat in the midst of the Corona family, while her husband alternately talked to reporters or stalked the three-floor courthouse.

Judge Patton wandered downstairs from his office, to be met by a friend of the Corona family soliciting money for their lunch. The judge contributed ten dollars, answering in Spanish when the woman said, *"Gracias."*

At five-forty-five, the jury ended its deliberations for the day, to be transported by an ex-Greyhound bus belonging to the Vaca Valley Bus Line to a local motel. They would sleep there for the next seven days.

The four Corona girls scampered about the courthouse basement on Friday, January 12, the second day of the jury's deliberations. A few blocks away, in the rented apartments they had converted to temporary offices, the three prosecutors desultorily cleaned up paperwork. By agreement, the judge and the four attorneys were to be within a half-hour of the courtroom in the event the jury returned; no one could go far.

Corona spent a good part of the day in the vacant Courtroom Number 3, near where his jury was meeting, talking with his family while a relaxed deputy read a newspaper. Lieutenant Robert Stanton, the sheriff in charge of courthouse security, had decided Corona looked tense; the visit with his family might ease the waiting, he decided.

Hawk wandered about the courthouse, unable to keep still, speculating that there was one stubborn juror holding out for conviction, one mule who could not be coaxed into a not-guilty verdict so they could all go home.

The van transporting Corona from Vacaville to the courthouse was late on Saturday morning. At nine-twenty, the judge told the attorneys in chambers that he had received a call from Vacaville. "Mr. Corona has suffered a heart attack." Court clerk Jane Caley was near tears. A half-hour later, Judge Patton went downstairs to the basement to answer questions from reporters. Doctor Ralph Prout, in charge of the medical facility at the state hospital, had told the judge that Corona had been having chest pains for the past two days, but had complained of them only the night before. Doctor Prout diagnosed the pains as either another cardiac deficiency or a full-fledged myocardial infarction. The electro-cardiographs he was taking would help him make a surer diagnosis later that day. Corona would be bedridden a month if it were a heart attack, perhaps a week if it were the less traumatic deficiency.

Pedro Corona took Gloria and Rosario Corona and his mother to the community hospital for sedatives while Hawk talked to newsmen. Corona's new heart episode proved he had made the right decision in not putting his client on the stand.

The jury deliberated for eight and one-half hours that day, oblivious of the tumult outside the courtroom doors.

Judge Patton permitted the jury to stay in recess on Sunday, January 14, most of the men to watch the Super Bowl football game in their rooms at the Holiday Inn.

Hawk called Doctor Prout at the medical facility and learned that Corona had only suffered a coronary insufficiency. Prout had given Corona medication for high blood pressure and a mild tranquilizer. On a modified bed-rest program, Corona would not be able to travel to the courtroom for a few days. If it were necessary, they could use a wheelchair to bring him down from the hospital ward to the auditorium at the prison.

On Monday, January 15, after more than twenty-seven hours of deliberations, the jury asked to speak to the judge once again. Hawk was delighted; they would hold court at Vacaville. One more ploy, one little argument more for Corona: the jury would suspect that something was wrong with Corona if they had to travel to the prison.

The prosecution was just as anxious that Corona not appear as a patient, not elicit a sympathy vote. Judge Patton ordered Corona dressed in his street clothes; he was to be seated before the jury so that the wheelchair could be kept hidden.

A makeshift courtroom was rigged in the visitors' room, cafeteria tables converted to a judge's bench and counsel table. The judge, attorneys, the Corona family, and reporters filed through the electrically controlled gates, the jury traveling by bus into the prison, a group apart.

The jurors looked tired: Mrs. Underwood drained, Mrs. Blazek nervously picking at lint on her dress. The men were strained, a contrast to the three relaxed alternates who had taken no part in the deliberations but waited in a separate room should they be needed.

Phillips stood up. "Your Honor, we have reached an impasse. If we can't decide on guilt or innocence, does this constitute a hung jury?"

"Without telling us in which direction, can you tell us how you stand?"

"Eight to four."

In an access area to the visitors' room, the judge discussed the impasse with the attorneys. The three prosecutors were pleased, Hawk disturbed; the prosecution had more votes than either side had imagined possible.

Judge Patton proposed sending the jury back to deliberate further. This was, after all, only their fourth day, after a trial that had lasted more than four months. The district attorney discreetly reminded the judge of a series of state and federal decisions that barred judges from coercing verdicts by prolonging deliberations until holdouts gave in so as to go home. (Ironically, all the cases cited were based on appeals by convicted defendants.) Teja was willing to accept a hung jury and a mistrial.

As the court attachés and spectators walked out through the security gate, the rain started again. Inmates on the "Main Line" shouted through barred windows, *"Viva Corona!"* The shouts echoed off the concrete walls in the drizzle.

On Tuesday, January 16, the jury deliberated the full day; the judge, by agreement, polling them at four o'clock. Phillips announced they were eleven-to-one.

The sun was shining for the first time in two weeks, the skies clear on Wednesday morning. Hawk was whistling in the car as he drove into Fairfield; they would have a verdict that day. Judge Patton suggested it would come before eleven o'clock. The three prosecutors waited in the office-apartment for the clerk's telephone call, somber, resting their hope for a hung jury on the one holdout.

The number of newsmen waiting at the courthouse had grown; the longer the jury was out, the bigger the story seemed to become, Hawk noted. Four or five reporters asked about exclusive interviews with Corona when he was freed. Anticipating a verdict that day, the television and radio newsmen set up a microphone stand in front of the courthouse steps; fourteen microphones were taped to it.

They were wrong. By two o'clock Hawk realized they would not reach a verdict that day. "What we need is a diplomat on that jury now," he muttered, someone to convince the one holdout.

It was raining again on Thursday, January 18. At ten fifty-four A.M., after forty-five hours of deliberation, the foreman notified the bailiff that the jury wished to see the judge.

It took more than an hour to reassemble in the courtroom, reporters filing through security checks grown more stringent, filling the entire spectator section with the exception of the two rows of seats deputies had saved for the Corona family and close friends. Teja, Williams, and Fahey were grim.

Corona sat stiffly in his padded swivel chair, nodding when Doctor Prout asked him how he felt. Hawk patter Corona's knee.

The jurors walked through the door from the jury room quietly, in ones and twos, unsmiling. Mrs. Blazek stared at the floor between her feet, exhausted; Mrs. Underwood was no longer smiling. The rest stared across the courtroom to the large map on the opposite wall. Hawk could feel the cold wind.

Phillips was carrying a rolled sheaf of papers. "Do you have a communication, Mr. Phillips?" Judge Patton asked.

"Yes, I have, Your Honor." He handed the verdict forms to the bailiff who carried them to the bench.

Judge Patton looked at the top form, the left corner of his mouth turning up in a faint smile, then scanned the balance of the twenty-five forms.

"The People of the State of California versus Juan Vallejo Corona," the judge read. "Verdict, First Count. As to Count I of the indictment herein, which said count accuses the defendant, Juan Vallejo Corona, of the murder of Kenneth Whitacre, an alleged violation of Section 187 of the Penal Code of the State of California, we, the jury, find as follows:

"Guilty."

Afterword

When you beat them on the facts, beat them on the law, you are supposed to beat them in the jury.

I didn't.

The trial of Juan Corona has to be the most bizarre in American legal history, just as the mass murder was the most terrible in the annals of the American crime. So too was the jury's decision the strangest imaginable.

Within two hours after the jury's verdict was read, Mrs. Naomi Underwood was telling reporters, "I have doubts yet. I do feel Juan Corona deserves another trial." For two days Mrs. Underwood had been the lone vote for acquittal, a brave woman finally worn down by the arguments of the other eleven. Had she held out, perhaps another day, Judge Patton might have ruled it a mistrial.

Mrs. Underwood, like some others on the jury, was troubled by the fact that I had not put on a defense. "It bothered me very, very much; it bothered everybody," she told another reporter.

But only Mrs. Underwood seemed reluctant to place the burden of proof upon Corona. The failure of Corona to testify, the foreman told a Sacramento *Bee* reporter, bothered him, "as I'm sure it did all of you." At other times, Matthew Johnson, the retired marine sergeant, and James Owen, the conscientious fundamentalist, said similar things.

All this might not have mattered had not the prosecution consistently attempted to rewrite the Constitution of the United States. The jurors apparently were swayed by Teja's effort to shift the burden of proof to the defense. Foreman Ernest Phillips told another reporter that the jurors agreed there was no evidence to show that Corona's machete *had not* been used to kill the other twenty-four.

I might now be preparing for a new trial rather than writing this afterword had Judge Patton showed even the least courage. On Wednesday night, before Mrs. Underwood finally voted "guilty," Sheriff's Matron Mrs. Georgia Wallis told Mrs. Underwood, "If you have any worries about your decision"—Mrs. Underwood had already made up her mind to change her vote—"I will tell you things about Juan Corona that will ease your conscience after you vote. . . . If you have any qualms about the way you voted." In a statement Mrs. Underwood gave Edward McCollian, chief investigator for the Solano County public defender, and John Zandonella on the evening of January 18, Mrs. Underwood claimed the matron had explained the lack of blood on Corona's clothes by saying, "Well, his wife took them home and washed them."

In 1966, in reversing a conviction for second-degree murder, the United States Supreme Court held that jury tampering was inherently in violation of due process and ordered a new trial. With this decision, Judge Patton had one of his dearly treasured precedents.

Yet on February 5, 1973, after listening to both women's testimony, Judge Patton turned down my motion for a new trial. "The court," he said, "is not persuaded Mrs. Underwood is telling the truth"—though for what reason she would lie escapes me—"or that the matron was lying." At the same time he said Mrs. Wallis' testimony under oath was "in a sense contradictory, evasive and uncertain." He simply was unable to tell "whether her intent was not to tell the truth or a desire to tell the whole truth."

As I said, it was a strange verdict.

Once again Judge Patton, given an opportunity to prove himself a distinguished jurist, an independent man, had failed. The Corona case was too great for him. Basically, I believe, he's a little man from Colusa with a walnut farm, who aspires to greatness but rose only to mediocrity in this case. I don't believe he understands the adversary system of justice at all. The moment he interjected himself into the proceedings, attempting to right what he considered an imbalance between the opposing attorneys, it was no longer an adversary proceeding.

If I took advantage of Teja's and Williams' inadequacies, it is because I like to think of myself as an aggressive lawyer protecting my client. Going to jail for contempt is one of the risks I might run, but if I am held in contempt, for example, I believe it should be on the prosecution's objection, not the judge's motion.

I misjudged Patton on one crucial point, and had I not, perhaps the outcome would have been different. The one thing I thought he was consistent about was his hangup about time. When he finally ordered the sheriff's files brought into court, he gave me just two days to digest all that material—some of which still is not integrated into my files. I just reasoned if he gave me two days, and as anxious as he appeared to be to get out of the trial, that he would force the prosecutors to argue immediately.

If I had to do it over again, I would put a defense on, probably just the alibi testimony, since that really should be enough. But at the time I rested, I reasoned that the maximum Patton would give the prosecution would be until the following morning. I never thought he would give them five full days; after all, Teja had been doing nothing but the Corona case for almost nineteen months. He should have had it all in his head.

You give three guys—I don't give a damn how incompetent they might be—five days to sit around and think about what they are going to do, and they can get ready pretty good. I lost every benefit of waiving my defense and arguing.

At the time I did it, it seemed the right thing to do. It seemed like I was riding on a crest there; everything and everybody was going with me.

Damn it, I started off with seven votes on that first ballot. And at one point I got to eight.

I made other mistakes, to be sure. In retrospect, I should never have bothered with the Field Poll at the change of venue. It was costly and it apparently had no effect upon the appellate court whatsoever.

The money might have been better spent running down Emilio Rangel, or finding Carlos Leon Sierra and getting a blood test. Archie Gore, a resourceful guy, might have been able to stay on longer had I been able to pay him.

Perhaps the biggest mistake I made, however, was disqualifying Judge Hauck. The single reason I disqualified him was because I thought Corona had a shot at bail after the capital punishment decision, and I believed Hauck would screw me, while an outside judge, someone from some other county, unaccountable to the voters of Sutter County, would do as others were doing all over the state.

Judge Hauck understands the adversary system as Judge Patton does not. He would have been a hell of a lot better during the trial, and it wouldn't have mattered in terms of prejudice against Juan at the sentencing because if Juan were guilty, he would spend the rest of his life behind bars no matter who the judge was.

The prosecutors. I think Bart Williams, basically an honest man, compromised himself when he told the judge that he no longer had a reasonable doubt about Corona's guilt but that his opinion could change again. He just was not very strong, and capitulated under whatever pressure Teja applied.

Ron Fahey is a pretty competent guy, more competent than most prosecutors. He was an opportunist, but he held up his end of the bargain.

Dave Teja is different: it showed at the beginning of the case with his trick of mailing stuff out on Friday night. It showed by the eighteen separate times I discovered reports to which I was entitled in the course of the trial. It showed by the fact that crucial witnesses—Goldblatt and Guy especially—failed to write reports.

I have those reports now, and I will be even better prepared for cross-examination at the retrial.

There will be a new trial. The jury tampering, I believe, is the most obvious ground for reversal. I think that gives the appellate courts a ground for reversal that I don't think they can ignore when they read that entire 3,200,000-word record. They can reverse without hurting the judge, or the district attorney either, ignoring errors on the admissibility of evidence Patton made, ignoring his bias, ignoring the failure to honor the discovery rules by the district attorney, ignoring Teja's incredible final argument. They don't have to touch the Establishment, except to pick on one part-time sheriff's matron.

Juan Corona will have a new trial. Somewhere there must be some justice, somewhere there must be some mercy for that man.

Concord, California
April 6, 1973

On a bitter cold January morning in 1973, Mrs. Judy Freeman, three clergymen, and three newsmen gathered on the west side of Sutter Cemetery.

It took five minutes for the internment service in front of the five graves in Potter's Field.

On the fourteen sheet metal casket liners in which the unclaimed bodies would be buried, the black felt-pen numbers assigned by the sheriff's office were still visible.

Author's Note

This is, I believe, the first book written by an author who was privy to the inner workings of an American jury trial, yet was not himself a direct participant. It is, hopefully, objective—though it is not dispassionate, nor impartial for that matter.

The reader may have guessed that Hawk's aide—who turns up now and again in these pages—is the author. My role was first as a writer, later as a reader of sheriff's reports, pointing out "the mistakes, errors and omissions" (I found over 100 in Gregory's two-and-one-quarter-page report of the dredging of the riverbank graveyard); finally, as a sometime advisor when I was in court.

Whatever my role as an advisor to the defense, this book is mine alone. The conclusions, the judgments, the very tenor of this work are the author's. Richard Hawk agreed to our arrangement: I would not tell him how to try the case, though I sometimes disagreed strongly wtih him, and told him so; he would not tell me how to write the book nor attempt to censor what I wrote.

I believe Juan Corona innocent. I believe the jurors—good people all —violated their oath, and in some "secret and private place" demanded an explanation, some rationale for the slaying of twenty-five human beings. Consciously or unconsciously, they needed to solve the terrible mass murder and felt deprived by the defense. Despite the failure of the prosecution to prove its case against Corona, Corona did not prove he was innocent. Needing a solution, the jurors resolved their reasonable doubt in favor of the state. If this violates the Fifth Amendment's guarantee that no man shall be compelled to be a witness against himself, it rationalizes the jury's verdict.

A number of people were notably kind to the author over the year spent in research and writing: Geneva Hawk; Evelyn Hooker, generous and authoritative both; Fred Montez, Dennis Pallarazzo and Louis Ortega, friends of the Corona family and, now, of mine; court clerk Jane Caley and bailiff Maurice "Ed" Hehr; court reporters John Zandonella, Patrick Kane, and Peggy Grover; newsmen Earl Caldwell, Jerry Cohen, Eric Davis, Wayne Kint, Walt Stegmeir, Don Wegers and Tom Woods; Judge Richard Patton, unfailingly courteous; and Cristiann Hawk, who became a young woman in that cauldron of Courtroom 4.

This book is for Diane, who endured so much.

Los Angeles
October 1972–April 1973

Index